NATIONAL GEOGRAPHIC
TRAVELER

sydney

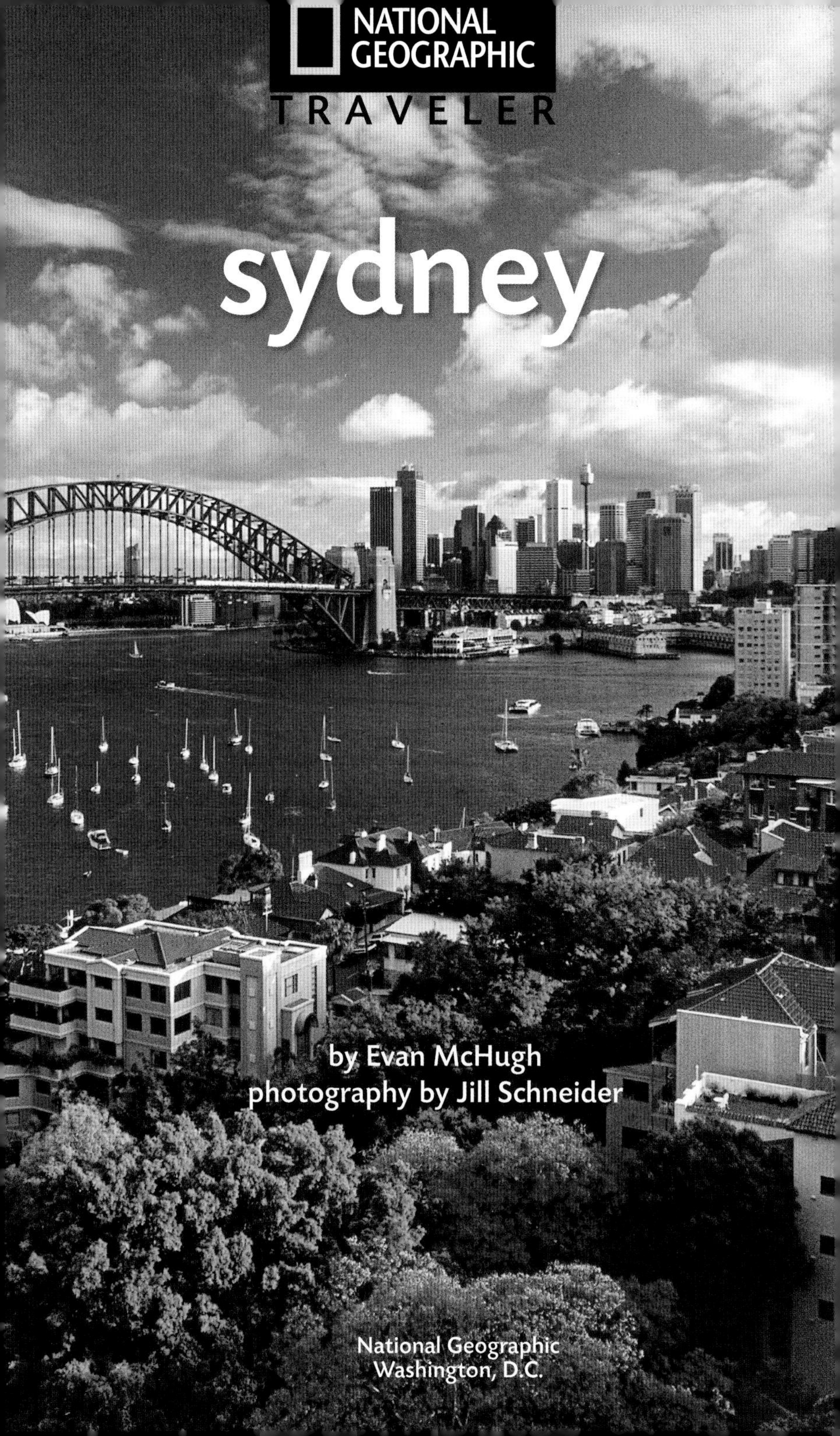

NATIONAL GEOGRAPHIC

TRAVELER

sydney

by Evan McHugh

photography by Jill Schneider

National Geographic

Washington, D.C.

LUNA PARK

CONTENTS

TRAVELING WITH EYES OPEN 6

CHARTING YOUR TRIP 8

History & Culture 13
Sydney Today 14
Feature: Food & Drink 22
History of Sydney 26
The Arts 36

Circular Quay & East 43
Introduction & Map 44
A Walk From Hyde Park to Circular Quay 58
Feature: Artists' Views of Sydney Harbour 64

The Rocks 71
Introduction & Map 72
The Rocks Walk 76
Feature: Architectural Sydney 82

Sydney Harbour 85
Introduction & Map 86
Harbour Bridge Walk 94
Feature: Shipwrecks 100
A Walk From The Spit to Manly 102

City Center & South 107
Introduction & Map 108
A Walk to the Chinese Garden of Friendship 118

Darling Harbour 121
Introduction & Map 122
A Walk to Sydney Fish Market 128
Feature: Indigenous Sydney 134

Eastern Suburbs 141
Introduction & Map 142
Feature: Mardi Gras 148
A Walk Around South Head 152
Feature: Eighteen-Foot Sailing Skiffs 156

Western Suburbs 159
Introduction & Map 160

Day Trips 171
North 172
Introduction & Map 172
West & South 184
Introduction & Map 184
A Walk in Cronulla 190
Feature: Wildlife of the Sydney Region 196

Excursions 203
Introduction & Map 204
A Drive to the Hunter Valley Wineries 208
Feature: Australian Wine 210

TRAVELWISE 229
Hotels & Restaurants 238
Shopping 258
Entertainment & Activities 262

INDEX 266 **CREDITS** 270

Pages 2–3: Sydney Harbour Bridge and the city's skyline, viewed from Lavender Bay
Opposite: The iconic smiling face of Sydney's Luna Park, an amusement park on Milsons Point

TRAVELING WITH EYES OPEN

Alert travelers go with a purpose and leave with a benefit. If you travel responsibly, you can help support wildlife conservation, historic preservation, and cultural enrichment in the places you visit. You can enrich your own travel experience as well.

To be a geo-savvy traveler:

- Recognize that your presence has an impact on the places you visit.
- Spend your time and money in ways that sustain local character. (Besides, it's more interesting that way.)
- Value the destination's natural and cultural heritage.
- Respect the local customs and traditions.
- Express appreciation to local people about things you find interesting and unique to the place: its nature and scenery, music and food, historic villages and buildings.
- Vote with your wallet: Support the people who support the place, patronizing businesses that make an effort to celebrate and protect what's special there. Seek out shops, local restaurants, inns, and tour operators who love their home—who love taking care of it and showing it off. Avoid businesses that detract from the character of the place.
- Enrich yourself, taking home memories and stories to tell, knowing that you have contributed to the preservation and enhancement of the destination.

That is the type of travel now called geotourism, defined as "tourism that sustains or enhances the geographical character of a place—its environment, culture, aesthetics, heritage, and the well-being of its residents." To learn more, visit National Geographic's Center for Sustainable Destinations at *www.nationalgeographic.com/travel/sustainable.*

NATIONAL GEOGRAPHIC
TRAVELER

sydney

ABOUT THE AUTHORS & THE PHOTOGRAPHER

Evan McHugh is a native of Sydney and has traveled throughout Australia, Europe, and the United States. He has worked as a journalist on a range of subjects, including technology, travel, and literature, with the national newspaper, the *Australian,* and for the television program *Beyond 2000.* He has written several books, including *The Dry Rot, Pint-sized Ireland,* and *Shipwrecks: Australia's Greatest Maritime Disasters,* and assisted Aboriginal designer John Moriarty, whose designs are featured on two Qantas 747s, in the writing of his biography.

Peter Turner wrote the updates and sidebars for this edition. Australian by birth, journalist by trade, and wanderer by nature, he has worked as an editor, publisher, and journalist in Australia and for newspapers in Indonesia, Thailand, and Brunei. As a travel writer and photographer specializing in Southeast Asia and the South Pacific, he has contributed to newspapers and magazines worldwide and to more than 20 guidebooks.

Photographer **Jill Schneider** received her MFA from the Academy of Art University in San Francisco. For her master's thesis she spent nine months documenting Himalayan life in Nepal, northern India, Kashmir, Bhutan, and Tibet. She later returned to Asia, taking travel photos for marketing campaigns. Now a freelance photographer working out of San Francisco, Schneider is represented by the National Geographic Image Collection and also has led the photography portion of a National Geographic Student Expedition to Ecuador and the Galápagos.

Charting Your Trip

Sydney is a huge city with a vast suburban sprawl, but fortunately for visitors, most of its delights are central and easily reached. Circular Quay, the site of Australia's first colony, it still the heart of downtown Sydney and the gateway to expansive Sydney Harbour. Historic districts such as The Rocks are an easy walk away, the tourist hub of Darling Harbour lies nearby, and the only serious diversions beyond the harbor are the famed Pacific beaches, such as Bondi and Manly.

Getting Around

Sydney Harbour is the focus for many visitors, and what better way to get around than on the Sydney Ferries *(www.sydneyferries.info)*. From Circular Quay, ferries go to Manly, Taronga Zoo, the harbor islands, east as far as Watsons Bay, and west all the way to Parramatta. Riding the ferries is as much an attraction as the destinations.

Rail is the next best way to travel. Sydney's efficient CityRail network *(www.sydneyrail.info)* will get you west to Newtown, the Olympic site at Homebush, Parramatta, and as far as the Blue Mountains. To the south, trains go to the airport and Coogee, but services east are limited to Kings Cross and Bondi Junction, which is still a couple miles from the beach; the City Circle underground loop is handy for getting around the city center.

Light Rail trams *(www.metrotransport.com.au)* from Central Station take in Chinatown, Darling Harbour, the fish market, and some inner western suburbs such as Glebe.

For everywhere else, buses *(www.sydneybuses.info)* are the main form of transport. Take them to the eastern suburbs and beaches (Bondi to Coogee).

Only rent a car (see Travelwise p. 233) if you intend to visit the national parks or beyond the city.

If You Have Only a Week

Many visitors to Australia, desperate to tick off the big attractions of Reef (Great Barrier Reef), Rock (Uluru), and Bridge (Sydney Harbour Bridge), travel across the continent in barely a couple weeks, leaving just two or three days for Sydney. A week will give you a much more considered and leisurely appreciation of the city.

Except for the famed surf beaches, the city's main attractions fit in a grid less than 1.5 by 2 miles (2 by 3 km) on a map of central Sydney, but they could easily take four or five days to explore. That leaves a couple of days for the beaches, or you could day trip to the Blue Mountains (see Day 12) or add a harbor island trip (see Day 8).

Australia has several species of kangaroo; the eastern gray can be spotted in some of the national parks near Sydney.

Devote **Day 1** to the two great icons of Sydney—the Harbour Bridge and Opera House, lying either side of Circular Quay in downtown Sydney. As you wander the city streets, the soaring arch of the Sydney Harbour Bridge provides a regular backdrop. Walk across the bridge to the north shore for wonderful vistas back toward the city skyline. Like ants to honey, thousands of tourists swarm around the Sydney Opera House every day, taking in the marvel of its curves. To fully appreciate its grandeur, guided tours of the interior go every hour during the day, or take in one of the many performances.

Start **Day 2** under the shadow of the Harbour Bridge on the northern edge of the city center, where The Rocks is a sandstone-hewn trip through time to Old Sydney Town. Once a rough port district, its renovated buildings include Sydney's oldest house, oldest pub, and many of the original bond stores, now home to fashionable hotels, restaurants, bars, and shops. The Rocks is worth at least half a day—more on weekends to browse The Rocks Markets that sets up on George Street. That still leaves time for a daytime harbor cruise or a nighttime dinner cruise, departing from Circular Quay or Darling Harbour.

NOT TO BE MISSED:

The Sydney Opera House, a World Heritage masterpiece 46–49

The Rocks, the Old Sydney Town historic precinct 71–84

Climbing the iconic Sydney Harbour Bridge 91

Taking the ferry to Manly 101

Darling Harbour, the attraction-packed waterfront 121–140

People-watching at famous Bondi Beach 149–150

The cool air and panoramas of the Blue Mountains 215–220

On **Day 3,** head to Darling Harbour, on the western edge of central Sydney. An old port area, Darling Harbour was completely redeveloped in the 1980s. It is now a major tourist area with hotels, waterside restaurants, entertainment centers, museums, and tourist attractions—such as the very popular Sydney Aquarium and the nearby Powerhouse Museum and Maritime Museum—to occupy you all day long. At the southern edge of Darling Harbour lies Chinatown, the perfect spot for a lunch of *yum cha.* Here you'll also find labyrinthine Paddy's Markets, the city's biggest general market, selling everything from clothes and cell phone accessories to fish, fruit, and luggage.

Wander around the city center itself on **Day 4.** Here, between Chinatown and Circular Quay, skyscrapers soar, but a number of historic buildings tie the city's history together. One distinctive high-rise is Sydney Tower, perched on a spike above the city. Elevators rush you to the top for the best views in town. Imposing heritage buildings include the Town Hall, State Theatre, and ornate Queen Victoria Building, filled

Visitor Information

Tourism Australia has a good website for trip planning *(www.australia.com),* while the state government has detailed information on Sydney *(www.sydney.com),* New South Wales *(www.visitnsw.com.au),* and area national parks *(www.environment.nsw.gov.au/NationalParks).* On the ground, the Sydney Visitor Centre *(www.shfa.nsw.gov.au)* has offices at The Rocks and Darling Harbour, while the City of Sydney *(www.cityofsydney.nsw.gov.au)* has information kiosks at the Town Hall *(George St.)* and Circular Quay *(Pitt & Alfred Sts.).*

Tipping

It used to be that only Americans tipped in Australia, but tipping is becoming more common. Tipping is by no means mandatory, but a tip of up to 10 percent for good service in fancier restaurants is appreciated. Tip taxi drivers for good service by rounding up the fare, up to 10 percent, and in top hotels, you can give porters A$2 for toting your bags.

with upscale shops. Nearby Pitt Street Mall is the epicenter of Sydney consumerism.

On **Day 5,** wander around the parks, museums, and art galleries that dominate the eastern edge of central Sydney. Just behind the Opera House, the Royal Botanic Gardens is one of the world's great gardens, with sweeping lawns down to Sydney Harbour. Nearby, the Art Gallery of New South Wales holds an imposing collection of international and Australian art. On Macquarie Street are some of Sydney's oldest and most significant buildings, including Hyde Park Barracks, now a must-see museum for its evocation of convict Sydney.

Wrap up your week by spending **Days 6** and **7** relaxing at the beach. Bondi Beach is a mere 5 miles (8 km) by bus or taxi east of the city. Laze on the beach, learn to surf, browse the shopping strip, or walk south along the cliff top to more great beaches. Manly is the other iconic beach, easily reached by ferry from Circular Quay, one of the best trips you can do in Sydney. From Manly Wharf it is a short walk to the long surf beach, and you can also explore North Head or walk to The Spit.

If You Have More Time

More time allows you to get a real feel for the character of the city, exploring interesting suburbs, fashionable shopping precincts, and historical areas. Or head out of the city to more distant beaches, mountains, and national parks.

Take a ferry or cruise around Sydney Harbour on **Day 8.** Visit one of the islands—the most interesting are Fort Denison, with its historic fort, and Cockatoo Island, the former convict prison and shipyards—or Taronga Zoo, a short ferry ride across the harbor from the city and the best place to see native animals. A ferry ride to Watsons Bay makes a great day trip for seafood dining and a walk around South Head at the harbor entrance.

On **Day 9,** venture over to the diverse and interesting eastern suburbs. Within walking distance of the botanic gardens, chic renovated Finger Wharf in Woolloomooloo is far removed from its working-class history, while lively Kings Cross still clings to its seedy

When to Go

Any time is a good time to visit Sydney, though it is not eternally balmy and subtropical. In summer (Dec.–Feb.), the days are long and ideal for outdoor activities. The beaches beckon as temperatures soar, particularly in late summer. The main holiday break for Australians is from Christmas to the end of January, when accommodation becomes tight and prices climb. In Sydney, the peak is around New Year's Eve, when the whole city is booked for the fireworks, while February is Mardi Gras. Autumn (March–May) is pleasantly cooler but wetter, while winter (June–Aug.) is too cold for the beaches but not freezing, with plenty of crisp sunny days; this is the main football season, and the arts also come alive with myriad festivals. The city starts warming up again in spring (Sept.–Nov.), one of the best times to visit.

Among its many attractions, the Darling Harbour quarter boasts a popular outdoor dining scene.

roots. Nearby, exclusive Elizabeth Bay is home to Elizabeth Bay House, one of Sydney's finest historic homes. Strung out along (and just off) Oxford Street, other interesting inner suburbs include Darlinghurst, the spiritual home of gay and lesbian Sydney, Paddington, Woollahra, and Surry Hills with interesting shopping strips emphasizing fashion, food, and nightlife. Farther east are the exclusive harborside suburbs of Double Bay, Rose Bay, and Vaucluse, where historic Vaucluse House is a highlight. You can reach them by ferry and bus, but a car would come in handy here, and you could drive on south to the eastern beaches of Bondi, Bronte, and Coogee.

Explore the western suburbs on **Day 10.** A short train ride from the center, funky King Street in Newtown is an eclectic stretch of shops, restaurants, and pubs. Balmain has lots of heritage character, as does Glebe, while Leichhardt is a Little Italy. Farther west, reached by ferry or train, historically important Parramatta has the oldest buildings in Australia and makes an interesting day trip.

Spend **Day 11** north of Sydney. Close to the city, Balmoral Beach is one of the most attractive harbor beaches with safe swimming, but Sydney's best surf beaches are along the Pacific coastline north from Manly all the way to upscale Palm Beach. From here, water taxis go to Ku-ring-gai Chase National Park for walks, water views, and Aboriginal rock art, but a car provides better access to the park.

Save **Day 12** for the number one excursion outside the city: the Blue Mountains. Reached by train (2 hours) to Katoomba or by one of the many one-day bus tours, the panoramas and fine walks of this spectacular area could easily merit a couple days.

For **Days 13** and **14,** rent a car to explore a host of other sights beyond Sydney. To the north, the Hawkesbury River offers beautiful valleys and houseboat rentals, but the main destination is the wine region of the Hunter Valley, with good hotels and restaurants catering to weekenders from Sydney, 2.5 hours away by car. South of Sydney, the sandstone outcrops, beautiful beaches, and good walks of Royal National Park, an hour away by car, beckon. From here, a good coastal drive south will take you past Wollongong to the beaches of the South Coast with a detour into the lush Southern Highlands. Farther south still and inland is Canberra, the country's planned capital. ■

History & Culture

Sydney Today 14–21

Feature: Food & Drink 22–25

Experience: Savoring Vegemite 24

History of Sydney 26–35

The Arts 36–42

Aboriginal art frequently features Australia's many unique animals. Opposite: The Sydney Aquarium brings the wonders of the South Pacific Ocean up close and personal.

Sydney Today

Stand on the busy promenade of Circular Quay, with the city of Sydney behind you, the Opera House on the right, and the harbor sparkling between the ferries edging to the wharves in front, and you get a sense of standing at the birthplace of a nation.

More than 200 years ago, on January 26, 1788, the flag that marked the beginning of European settlement in Australia was planted on this very spot. The First Fleet—11 sailing vessels battered by eight months at sea during their voyage from England—dropped anchor in the cove right in front of you. All around, the ships' crews, convicts, guards, and soldiers pitched their tents.

Sydneysiders celebrate Christmas with sun and surf on Bondi Beach.

Today, most people enter Australia by air, yet the place where one has a true sense of arrival remains Circular Quay. On the left is the Overseas Passenger Terminal, where visitors from around the world have been arriving for two centuries. On the right, its white curves etched against the blue of sky and water, the Sydney Opera House is one of the jewels of 20th-century architecture. Yet it also speaks of the city's maritime history. Its "sails," unfurled against the waves that lap around them on three sides, whisper of voyages in square-rigged tall ships, convict transport vessels, and flying clippers. On weekends, when pleasure craft skim past its feet, the Opera House could be voyaging still.

Greater Sydney covers more than 4,700 square miles (12,200 sq km). Physically, its boundaries have expanded to engulf other towns and cities around it.

Discovering the City

Circular Quay is the ideal starting point to discover the city: ferries in front of you; buses, trains, and taxis behind; and a lot of sights within easy walking distance. But pause a moment, take time to orient yourself before venturing into this vibrant city. Then be ready to explore the history, the indigenous culture, the waterways, the natural environment, or the modern global city that Sydney has become.

You might think that you can see Sydney's major sights—the Opera House, the harbor, Bondi Beach—in less than a day and not miss a thing. Actually, no. You can't get a real taste of the city without visiting Lion Island and Pittwater, or seeing the bizarre and beautiful flora and fauna. Then there are some of the best wines and food in the world to taste and diamonds, opals, or indigenous art and artifacts to buy.

For entertainment, choose from a performance in the Opera House or the outdoor events of the Sydney Festival, or watch half a million people line the streets for the spectacular Gay and Lesbian Mardi Gras parade. Discover how friendly and full of life the people are in the cafés, pubs, restaurants, and streets; walk, swim, sail, dance, have a picnic, or just sit and watch life in all its richness pass by.

See it all in a day? Ideally, you should allow a year. That way, you can experience the full range of the seasons, the full calendar of annual events, and have just enough time to really embrace the lifestyle and amenities that make this city such a fun and stimulating place to be. Beyond the obvious attractions, the internationally known sights, there are literally dozens of things to visit and do.

Greater Sydney covers more than 4,700 square miles (12,200 sq km). Physically, its boundaries have expanded

Talkin' Aussie

Australian English—called Strine, from the clipped local pronunciation of Australian—is one of the more colorful variants of the English language.

A broad Australian accent is more noticeable in the bush (countryside) than the cities, but it can be characterized by nasalized vowels spoken through clenched teeth (to keep out flies), abbreviated words, and the addition of suffixes such as "ie" or "o"—thus utility becomes ute, Australian becomes Aussie, tin becomes tinnie, and David becomes Davo.

In addition, Australians use many words of unique meaning, ranging from the humorous to the baffling. Common Strine words include the following:

agro – aggressive
arvo – afternoon
barbie – BBQ
billabong – waterhole or cut-off branch of a river
blowie – blowfly
bludger – work-shy person
boomer – large male kangaroo; anything large or successful
chook – chicken
cobber – see *mate*
crikey – exclamation of surprise
crook – sick, unwell, bad, inferior
digger – see *mate;* also World War I soldier (in the trenches)
drongo – fool, simpleton
dunny – toilet
fair dinkum – true, genuine
galah – fool; pink and gray parrot
g'day – universal greeting, often accompanied by "mate"
grog – alcohol
hoon – lout, show-off, reckless driver
mate – buddy; general term of familiarity
milk bar – convenience store
no worries – no problem, good, fine
ocker – stereotypical uncultured Australian, redneck
piker – someone who chickens out or shirks their duty
ratbag – rascal, eccentric
ripper – great, fantastic, as in "you little ripper"
roo – kangaroo
sheila – woman
snag – sausage
swag – bedroll used for camping
thongs – flip-flops
troppo – mad, as in "gone troppo" (too long in the tropics)
tucker – food
two-up – traditional coin gambling game
walkabout – nomadic wandering, as in "gone walkabout" (disappeared)
Woop Woop – remote imaginary place, back of beyond
yobbo – see *ocker*
yonks – a long time

to engulf other towns and cities around it. Parramatta, 12 miles (19 km) to the west, is now an inner suburb. Newcastle and Wollongong, around 100 miles (160 km)to the north and 50 miles (80 km) to the south, respectively, are now considered commuter suburbs—part of what has been called the New-Syd-Gong urban conglomeration. The population within commuting distance of the Central Business District (CBD) is over five million. And it is a diverse assortment of people, with more than 140 different nationalities represented.

Lifestyle: The people of Sydney enjoy a lifestyle that is the envy of many other cities. Sydney is circled by national parks and no fewer than six major waterways (some far larger than Sydney Harbour) within 60 miles (96 km) of the city center. As for the climate, it varies from hot to cool; compared to most cities, there is no winter—just a season where you'll need a coat in the evening and maybe a sweater during the day. Consequently, most of the recreational activities tend to be outdoors—barbecues, picnics, trips to the beach, boating, sports, or simply walking.

This outdoor lifestyle encourages the informality and friendliness so noticeable in Australians in general and Sydneysiders in particular. It's hard to be insular when little time is spent behind closed doors. An example: If you happen to be in the city on a balmy summer evening, take a taxi down to Mrs Macquaries Point, at the eastern head of Farm Cove across from the Sydney Opera House. On the lawns facing the cove, people are having picnics, fishing, or just strolling up and down. It's nighttime and no one is worrying about being attacked or robbed.

City Areas: Unknown to much of the population, the sections of the city are not so different from those chosen by the Aboriginal people who first inhabited the area. There is also a certain amount of "tribalism" to the different sectors of the city. For example, an expression you may hear is "OTB." It means "over the bridge" and refers to the reluctance people from the south side have to going anywhere on the north side of the city—even those who were born there and have moved into the inner city. There are people who live in the affluent eastern suburbs who don't believe anyone of consequence lives west of Rushcutters Bay; those who live between Rushcutters Bay and Kings Cross believe you can't get a good cup of coffee west of Darlinghurst. The people of the northern beaches are considered to be rather like New Age Californians—tanned, healthy, keen on dolphins and crystals—while those on the southern beaches are thought to identify with the less sophisticated 1950s and '60s.

This outdoor lifestyle encourages the informality and friendliness so noticeable in Australians in general and Sydneysiders in particular.

The Westies are divided into two: the Westies proper—the vast swath of bedroom communities stretching to the Blue Mountains, and the inner west—the suburbs close to the city on its western side. In these inner suburbs, the radicals, the grunge elements, and the agitators gather in their cafés near the University of Sydney to discuss issues and make plans.

In the Blue Mountains, where it gets cold enough to convince you there are four seasons in a year (sometimes it even snows), the property prices are cheaper and artists can afford a drafty garret in which to shiver and create.

These are incredibly broad generalizations (just try them on a local and see), but they're a good start. If you overlay all this with the multicultural elements of the city, the picture becomes a little more detailed: There are Greek, Italian, Chinese, Vietnamese, and Indian neighborhoods. There are communities of Pacific Islanders, Aborigines, Balkans, Spanish, Africans, Japanese, and Lebanese, as well as Christian, Jewish, Muslim, and Buddhist places of worship. It goes on and on.

The remarkable thing about this diversity is the peaceful manner in which everyone lives side by side: no walls, soldiers, riots, or tensions. Even the sizable gay community goes largely unmolested. Certainly there are isolated unpleasant incidents, but the prevailing attitude can best be described in ten words—respect, tolerance, and understanding for every race, religion, and creed.

Within this kaleidoscope of cultures and cuisines is an easygoing, outgoing population that can hardly believe its luck. It is not uncommon to dine at an upscale restaurant and find on its menu influences from nearly every inhabited continent. Asian visitors have looked on in amazement at noodle bars full of Australians hungrily and expertly wielding chopsticks. In some of the city's restaurant strips, you can choose from up to a dozen different national cuisines. Sydneysiders love food.

The people of Sydney are inordinately proud of their city, with good reason, and they never tire of hearing visitors praise it.

Leisure Time

Not surprisingly, a great deal of Sydney's leisure activity is outdoors, with sports such as cricket, rugby league and rugby union, Aussie rules, and soccer in the lead. Basketball and baseball are becoming increasingly popular, too. On any weekend, you'll find thousands of people out on Sydney Harbour in powerboats, sailboats, and kayaks. And then there's the beach. Walking is also extremely popular, whether on the various coastal walks, the harbor walks, or longer options in the national parks that surround the city.

Sydneysiders love to unwind after work. Friday nights in the city's pubs and bars are a boisterous affair as office workers and laborers alike relax and socialize over a few beers. In summer particularly, you'll find people spilling into the streets, noisily discussing the week's events, the weekend's plans. Many pubs have beer gardens that take advantage of the balmy climate and the desire locals have to get out into the warm night air. There will often be barbecue and bistro facilities, and you'll see children running around in the garden while mom and dad line up for dinner.

The people of Sydney are inordinately proud of their city, with good reason, and they never tire of hearing visitors praise it. "Sydney is the best address on Earth," they will tell you. One of the city's best known contemporary artists, Ken Done (1940–), who specializes in brightly colored, simplistic images of the city's landmarks, even went so far as to put the slogan on a T-shirt.

As journalist and writer Miriam Cosic, who moved to Sydney from Australia's other major city, Melbourne, put it: "When Melbourne people talk about Australia, they mean Australia. When Sydney people talk about Australia, they mean Sydney." Not only that,

Special Interests

Sydneysiders have a diverse range of interests and are generally very willing to share them with like-minded visitors. So, whether you are keen on aviation, trains, or quilting, there is sure to be a club or company that can cater to your needs.

To find a particular organization, Sydney phone numbers are available on the Internet. The white pages *(www.whitepages.com.au)* list all business and home numbers alphabetically; the yellow pages *(www.yellowpages.com.au)* list businesses by activity. The phone numbers are also linked to a street directory.

Destination NSW *(www.visitnsw.com and www.sydney.com)* and the Sydney Visitor Centre *(The Rocks & Darling Harbour, tel 9240 8788)* have extensive databases that may be useful to you, as well as full calendars of events.

Rugby is an all-consuming passion of many Sydneysiders.

Sydney now considers itself so cosmopolitan that it identifies more closely with New York, Paris, or London than it does with Melbourne, Brisbane, or Canberra.

Visitors' Sydney

Sydney is as relaxing a place to visit as it is to live in. The level of personal security is on a par with or better than other major cities. This is not to say that there is no crime, nor that pickpockets don't congregate around tourist areas.

It is also a relatively easy city to navigate. Most sights are within walking distance of each other; if not, there is plenty of public transportation. Everyone speaks English and most people are friendly and helpful. Sydneysiders are not quickly offended, and it is almost impossible to commit a cultural faux pas.

Bear in mind that there is an egalitarianism in Australia not found in many other countries. The flip side of this, though, is that Australians have a healthy dislike for anyone in authority or who behaves with a superior attitude. Talk down to someone, for example, even if they are providing a service, and you may be surprised at the consequences. On the positive side, most people you meet will assist you out of a genuine desire to be helpful. This means you only need tip when you are in a restaurant, and you don't have to do that if you don't like the service. And a word of advice: "g'day" is an informal greeting, not a farewell. Say "g'day" to an Australian at the end of a conversation and he or she will probably look bemused.

As much a part of Sydney as its museums, theaters, and galleries are its beaches, waterways, and nature reserves. The city also invites you to participate in its lifestyle. So when visiting Bondi, don't just take a photo—kick off your shoes and wiggle your toes in the sand. Go for a swim or follow the spectacular headland walk that winds away to the south. In the harbor, pick one of the numerous venues that offers a view of the water and a sumptuous meal to boot. Rent a yacht. Perhaps arrange to spend a night on the water and awake to the gentle rocking of your boat and the sight of the harbor in all its glory. Above all else, remember that this city is meant to be enjoyed.

A Few Precautions

One of the most attractive features of the city is its proximity to the countryside and its wildlife. In the national parks that surround Sydney, kangaroos jump and kookaburras laugh. In the seas, whales spout and dolphins leap. However, there are some hazards to watch out for.

Sharks probably loom largest in most people's imagination. There are sharks in Sydney Harbour, and swimming in open water is not recommended. However, most of the popular harbor beaches are netted, as are the popular ocean beaches, which are closely patrolled by both aircraft and lifeguards.

The headlands of the northern beaches tempt hikers.

Bluebottles—small marine stingers with an inflated "sail" and long blue tendrils—usually blow in toward land when there is an onshore wind, and you'll see them washed up on the beach if they are about. Although painful, their sting is not fatal; the best remedy is to pour vinegar over the affected area, or buy a cream called Stingoes from the drugstore.

Small, pretty, blue-ringed octopuses are found in rock pools. They are fairly timid, but if you do come across one, under no circumstances attempt to pick it up as its bite is fatal.

There are two venomous spiders you should be wary of: funnel-webs, which have a fatal bite, and red-backs, whose bite can be fatal to a small child. Both are found under rocks or wood in damp areas. If you are bitten, immobilize the affected area, apply a pressure bandage, and seek medical treatment immediately. If someone else is bitten, be prepared to administer cardiopulmonary resuscitation as long as necessary.

Not all snakes are venomous, but assume they are and give any snake a wide berth. Treat a snakebite in the same way as a spider bite.

Sydney's mosquitoes do not carry any nasty diseases, although there are concerns about the debilitating Ross River fever. However, mosquitoes can be annoying when you are outdoors, and insect repellent is recommended, especially when you are out and about in the evening.

Visitors from cooler climates may find it takes some time to adjust to the heat and sun of a Sydney summer. Always wear a hat, put on sunscreen, drink plenty of fluids, and if it is very hot, slow down. Heat stress can lay low even the fittest people.

Safe Hiking: In the spring, keep a look out for magpies, as they can be territorial at this time and may swoop, clack their beaks, and sometimes actually strike. Wear a hat.

A number of precautions should be taken with regard to bush fires during the summer (Nov.–Feb.). On entering a national park, check the level of fire danger on the indicator boards or with a ranger. If the danger level is extreme and there is a high wind, seriously consider curtailing any extended bush walking. At any hint of smoke, immediately move to safe ground. In the event of a total fire ban, open fires of any description, including barbecues, are forbidden anywhere in the Sydney area. If you are caught by advancing fire, do not try to outrun the flames; find an open area if you can, or find any depression in the ground that can afford some shelter, cover yourself as much as possible, and let the fire pass over you. If you are in a vehicle, stop in an open area, get down on the floor, and cover yourselves with clothing until the fire has passed. If you are in a house, stay there. And if you are given instructions by emergency services personnel, do what they tell you.

Another danger of walking in the national parks is that gum trees sometimes shed their dead branches, known as "widow-makers," without warning. If you go camping, always check the branches above the tent.

In the national parks that surround Sydney, kangaroos jump and kookaburras laugh. In the seas, whales spout and dolphins leap.

Safe Swimming: Most of Sydney's ocean beaches are patrolled by lifeguards, and if the beach is unpatrolled, take great care. Safe swimming areas are designated by pairs of flags. Always swim between the flags. The main danger is a rip, an area where water carried in by waves flows back out to sea. Rips are typically channels of deeper water with few if any breaking waves. This makes them inviting to swimmers lacking confidence to face the surf, which is why they claim so many lives. If you get caught in a rip, the most important thing is not to panic. By trying to fight the current, you can rapidly become exhausted. If possible, swim across the current until you are out of the rip, then make your way back to shore through the surf. Otherwise, relax and float, raising an arm or shouting to signal for help.

To get a tan, 15 minutes a day is plenty. Half an hour of hot sun on sensitive skin can leave you very uncomfortable for days afterward.

Depending on what your day will involve, it is a good idea to put together a small survival kit to carry with you. This should include a hat, sunscreen, sunglasses, a bottle of water, and mosquito repellent. ■

Food & Drink

Nearly every ethnic group to arrive in Sydney has brought its own cuisine, and many of the foods are ideal for the Sydney climate—crisp and tangy, perfect for freshening your palate on a warm sunny day. Salads have always been popular, but the addition of chili, lemongrass, or coriander has added another dimension to the experience.

Friends meet for drinks at one of the many outdoor bars at Circular Quay.

Restaurants in Sydney tend to emphasize good-quality, local ingredients rather than heavy sauces and layers of flavor, though plenty of fine-dining establishments exhibit all the culinary pirouettes of contemporaries in London or New York. Add in strong influences from Asia and the Mediterranean and you have the "Modern Australian" interpretation of international cuisine. Don't be surprised if you find Japanese sushi or Thai beef salad on the same menu as risotto and pasta. Keep an eye out, too, for Australian bush foods, which add variety to any menu. In some restaurants, you will be able to tuck into the national specialties kangaroo and emu, as well as crocodile, buffalo, and even camel. All delicious. Then there are such items as loquat (a small, plumlike fruit) ice cream and lilli pilli jam, made from an Australian fruit resembling a bunch of grapes.

Ethnic Diversity

To get an idea of the range of cuisines found in Sydney, visit Cleveland Street with its Middle Eastern and Indian restaurants, or Darlinghurst's Italian restaurants. Leichhardt (named after Ludwig Leichhardt, an explorer who disappeared in 1848) is a long way west of Darlinghurst, but the Italian cafés here are great—even if you don't like the coffee, watching the people on parade is worth the price of a cup. Alternatively, try the Spanish restaurants on Liverpool Street south of the city center, Chinatown just around the corner, the Japanese restaurants in North Sydney and Crows Nest, or the Thai restaurants on King Street, Newtown. There are also Vietnamese restaurants in Cabramatta and Korean ones in Campsie.

A range of eating experiences can be had on or near the water in The Rocks, Darling Harbour, and the eastern suburbs, as well as at Sydney Fish Market. Don't forget the idea of packing a picnic and heading for one of the waterside parks. If you're on a budget, you can have a pleasant time at the tables set outside at the northern end of the Opera House complex.

In some restaurants, you will be able to tuck into the national specialties kangaroo and emu, as well as crocodile, buffalo, and even camel. All delicious.

Top Choices for Fine Dining

All of the following restaurants are discussed in detail in the Hotels and Restaurants section of Travelwise (see pp. 238–257), but some names to remember are Tetsuya's (a regular top-restaurants-of-the-world inclusion, book well in advance), Guillaume at Bennelong (the restaurant at the Sydney Opera House), Sailor's Thai (sumptuous Thai food in historic surrounds), and the Bathers Pavilion (breakfast or a long lunch watching the boats drift by).

From Chinese to Thai, Asian cuisine is very popular in Australia.

Other fine-dining options to note are the restaurants Marque, Rockpool, Est., Bécasse, Bilson's, and Quay. And there are some fantastic places missing from this list. Choose any of these, however, and be assured of a vacation memory.

Alfresco Dining

Sydney's climate makes it ideal for dining outdoors, day or night. Many restaurants, from the most upscale to the humble suburban eatery, have outside seating somewhere on their premises. Some, such as the Sydney Cove Oyster Bar, have almost all of their tables outside where the views and the balmy evenings can be enjoyed. Other restaurants are so open in design that you might as well be outside.

When making a reservation, you will probably be asked if you would like to sit inside or out. And if you walk into a restaurant that doesn't appear to have outside seating, it's always worth asking, because you'll often find that there's a spot tucked down a side passage somewhere.

Nearly every pub in the city has a beer garden; even those in the heart of the Central Business District will try to squeeze a couple of tables onto the sidewalk. Others have space on their roof where you can enjoy your refreshment under the sun and stars.

One of the city's most impressive pubs is the Newport Arms, up in Newport, in the northern beaches. In The Rocks, you'll find several beer gardens in the pubs along George Street, as well as the rooftop garden at the Glenmore Hotel on Cumberland Street; the Fortune of War Hotel in The Rocks claims to be the oldest pub in Sydney. Don't be surprised to see customers spilling out onto the street where there is no other option.

Native Fare

Perhaps the most recognizable contribution that Australia has made to world cuisine is the sharply flavored, vile-looking black paste known as Vegemite (see sidebar this page). Try it if you want, perhaps on toast, or console yourself with the knowledge that there are more palatable items you can seek out. Seafood is the obvious place to start. If you can find it, abalone from South Australia is in great demand. Most of it is exported, particularly to Japan.

More readily available is a fish called barramundi, native of the estuaries of northern Australia. It is a great game fish and, more importantly, excellent to eat. Barramundis are now farmed, and while those caught in the wild are said to taste better, these come a very good second. The fish farms in the waters surrounding Tasmania are also producing delicious Atlantic salmon.

Closer to home, rock oysters from along the New South Wales coast are highly prized and readily available. Usually termed Sydney Rock oysters, they are likely to be found on almost every restaurant menu. However, you can save a lot of money if you buy them from one of the many retailers at the Sydney Fish Market in Pyrmont, west of Darling Harbour.

You won't be disappointed by the produce from King Island, which is situated in the storm-swept Bass Strait between the Australian mainland and Tasmania. The "must tries" are King Island beef, cheese (such as brie and camembert), and cream. If you don't see these items on menus, they can be found in delicatessens and the David Jones Food Hall in the city.

B.Y.O.

Outside many restaurants are the letters "B.Y.O." or "B.Y.O. Only," which indicate that the restaurant permits you to bring your own beverages. Once very popular, B.Y.O. restaurants are on the wane after restaurants realized they could make almost as much from the markup on alcohol as on food. Many restaurants charge a corkage fee per person or per bottle for B.Y.O., which can be prohibitive, but it is usually only a few dollars, or nil, at cheaper restaurants.

EXPERIENCE: Savoring Vegemite

Resembling axle grease and tasting like salty malt, this bitter yeast extract is widely regarded as the national food. An Australian icon, although now manufactured by U.S. company Kraft, Vegemite is a very popular spread on toast for breakfast. Invented in Australia in 1922, it closely resembles Marmite, the British spread that inspired its creation. Immortalized in the Men at Work song "Down Under," the Vegemite sandwich remains a classic, despite attempts to update the formula to make it less bitter and salty. In 2009, Kraft added cheese and launched an offspring, iSnack, to widespread derision and commercial failure. You can find jars of Vegemite in just about any grocery store. Try it at your peril.

Offering a large selection of local produce, Paddy's Markets has operated for more than a century.

Wine & Beer

The wine lists of most restaurants in Sydney are almost exclusively comprised of Australian wines. And why not? In Europe, the United States, and Japan, the wines from nearly every state of Australia are recognized as among the best and most consistent found anywhere.

You may see wine from other countries in the best restaurants, of course, or in those that specialize in a regional cuisine.

If homesick for your local brew, you'll probably find it in one of the larger liquor stores around the city, especially if it's a premium beer. Guinness is widespread in pubs, while the likes of Lowenbrau, Heineken, Miller Genuine Draft, Carlsberg, Corona, and Stella Artois can be found at most supermarkets. For a greater range, seek out liquor specialists such as Kemeny's on Bondi Road and Camperdown Cellars (several stores across the city).

As for the local beers, the big names in the premium market include Boag's and Cascade, while light beers such as Hahn Premium Light and Cascade Premium Light make pleasant drinking if you are watching your alcohol intake.

The major brewers are adding to their range at an impressive rate, but keep an eye out for some of the microbrewery beers. In The Rocks, there are some nice lagers and ales to be tried at the Lord Nelson Brewery Hotel pub, while the Redoak Boutique Beer Cafe in Clarence Street in the city and the 4 Pines in Manly are also worth a visit. In pubs, order beer by the brand and glass size: A "middy" glass holds 10 fluid ounces (284 ml), while a "schooner" contains 15 fluid ounces (426 ml).

If you're looking for something marginally healthier and nonalcoholic, there's a huge range of exotic fruit drinks to choose from: fruit pulp with ice, fruit with milk, et cetera.

History of Sydney

It is still being debated exactly how long Australia has been inhabited by Aboriginal people, who are believed to have arrived from Southeast Asia. Conservative estimates by archaeologists, based on carbon dating of charcoal from fires and food remains at known sites, put it at 40,000 to 50,000 years.

Whatever the time scale, scholars estimate that before the arrival of the First Fleet in 1788, there were about 3,000 people living in the Sydney region. They were split into three main language groups: the Dharawal in the south, the Dharug to the west, and the Ku-ring-gai to the north. The region between Botany Bay and Sydney

Captain Cook's 1770 landing at Botany Bay, depicted in a 1902 oil by E. Phillips Fox

Harbour was populated by a dialect group of the Dharug who called themselves the Eora.

People from the different areas–the coast, the wooded plains, the mountains–used different tools and weapons as appropriate to the terrain: clubs, spears, axes, throwing sticks (a hunting tool, heavier than but similar to a boomerang), baskets, canoes, or fishhooks.

Within these regions, small groups of about 50 people, representing different families, had their own areas where they hunted and gathered food. Each of these groups also displayed slight language differences, although they had little difficulty understanding each other. Despite their attachment to particular areas for finding food, groups traveled widely throughout the region and moved around for ceremonies. This suggests there was considerable social, if not economic, interaction.

Aboriginal life was governed by tribal law that was enforced by the elders (both men and women) of each group. Punishment could be severe, with wrongdoers often being repeatedly speared by the offended parties. Initiation ceremonies marking the transition to adulthood were also brutal. One ceremony witnessed in Sydney in 1795 involved the removal of a front tooth from each initiate. Scarification of the face and body was also widely practiced.

Aboriginal life was governed by tribal law that was enforced by the elders (both men and women) of each group.

First Europeans

For the Aboriginal people living in the Sydney region, the first contact with Europeans came in 1770, when the English navigator James Cook, captain of the bark *Endeavour*, dropped anchor at Botany Bay and took on water and botanical specimens. Cook's exploration of the entire east coast is marked by some as the "discovery" of Australia, even though the Dutch had known of the north and west of the country for centuries. They named it New Holland. Searching for the Great South Land, Magellan suspected he had passed it on his voyage of 1519–1522, and Makassar seafarers from the Indonesian archipelago had been trading with the Aborigines of the north for hundreds of years.

Cook's arrival at Botany Bay, however, proved to be the vanguard for the permanent European settlement of the country. Cook and his botanists, Joseph Banks and Daniel Solander, said that the coastal district was sparsely inhabited by Aborigines, having met no more than "30 or 40 together" (although the true number was in the thousands). As a result, the country was considered (wrongly) *terra nullius*–no-man's-land. Banks suggested that a penal colony should be established there to alleviate the problem of overcrowded prisons in England.

Not until more than 200 years later was this error of ownership rectified when what has become known as the Mabo Case was conducted before the Australian High Court and the legal existence of native title finally recognized. The case involved an Aboriginal man named Eddie Mabo (and others) who had enjoyed the use of parts of an island off the Queensland coast but never held native title. It was established that, because they and their progenitors had inhabited the island in an unbroken line since before white settlement, they had a right to claim ownership. The implications for the rest of the country were momentous, not just because it meant other Aborigines could claim similar titles, but because it meant that a lot of assumed ownership by the Crown and the total control of the various Land Titles acts were thrown into question. But by then, of course, the Europeans were well and truly established.

Bennelong

An elder of the Eora people, Bennelong (1754–1813) played a pivotal role in the relationship between Aborigines and early colonists. He quickly learned English and developed a lasting rapport with Gov. Arthur Phillip, who initially had him kidnapped to learn Aboriginal customs and language. Bennelong played a vital role as a translator and intermediary, and Governor Phillip built him a brick house at Tubowgule (Bennelong Point), now the site of the Sydney Opera House. When Phillip retired, the two sailed together to England in 1792. Two years later, Bennelong returned and led a semi-traditional life as a respected elder until his death in 1813.

First Settlement

By any fair assessment, the first 20 years of settlement in Sydney were not a success. The First Fleeters nearly starved, the convicts were horribly mistreated, the marines were there against their will, and the first free settlers resented the dictatorial military governors. In addition, the Aborigines, who were more numerous than the first governor had been led to believe, were driven from their lands and faced death either from introduced disease or at the hands of the new arrivals. If storms didn't destroy the colonists' meager crops, fire did. Several food stores also burned down and floods destroyed boats and property. At one point, all the colony's cows escaped (they were found years later in a fertile area now called "Cowpastures"). Eventually, though, the catalog of disaster and misery ended in outright rebellion.

The story of Sydney's European settlement starts with the First Fleet. Eleven ships were assembled in Portsmouth, England, to transport more than 1,350 convicts and marines on an eight-month, 13,900-mile (23,500 km) voyage to the other side of the world. Under the command of Capt. Arthur Phillip, they arrived in Botany Bay in January 1788. Shortly behind them, two French vessels under the Comte de la Pérouse—after whom a suburb in the city is named—entered the same bay.

Not finding the bay to his liking, however, Phillip ventured northward along the coast to a bay (Sydney Harbour) that Captain Cook had sighted in 1770 and named Port Jackson after the judge advocate of the fleet at the time. Phillip described it as "the finest harbour in the world" and immediately decided to move the colony there. The English Union Jack was hoisted in Sydney Cove on January 26, 1788, the date celebrated ever since as the anniversary of Australia's foundation.

Not one ship visited the fledgling colony in its first year, and as each of the original vessels departed on other missions, the settlers' sense of isolation deepened. The prospects for farming around Sydney Cove were not good either, with poor, sandy soils thinly covering the yellow sandstone of the rugged headlands.

With no roads through the inhospitable country, it was natural to use the waterways to explore the area. Within the first year, the harbor waters had been navigated inland to the present-day Parramatta (Aboriginal for "head of the river," or "place where eels lie down"). Here the settlers found more fertile soils and were able to plant wheat, corn, and other crops.

By this time, however, stocks had shrunk considerably. The fleet's flagship, *Sirius,* had been sent in October 1788 to obtain supplies from Cape Town and did not return until May of the following year.

Capt. Arthur Phillip, commanding officer of the First Fleet

By now the Aboriginal people had been exposed to smallpox. Lacking any resistance to this and other European diseases, the death toll was appalling. Throughout the Sydney region, the population is believed to have fallen to one-third, with social structures and the traditional way of life devastated.

Meanwhile, the settlers had their own problems. In January 1790, an expected supply ship failed to arrive, and rations were reduced to half. On April 5, Phillip estimated that the colony—more than a thousand people—had enough food to last just six weeks, and further reduced the rations. The following week, two convicts were sentenced to 1,000 lashes each. Their crime? Stealing food. Early in May, the first convict died of hunger. Starvation and disease were to remain a threat to the new settlement for almost two decades.

It wasn't until June 1790 that the long-awaited *Lady Juliana* arrived, carrying much needed supplies, as well as more convicts. But she also brought bad news, reporting the loss of another supply ship that had struck an iceberg east of the Cape of Good Hope and had to return to port. The crew also reported the imminent arrival of the Second Fleet, carrying several hundred more hungry convicts.

Nevertheless, despite further difficulties in the early years—disastrous floods, fires in the granaries, attacks by the natives—the colony gradually built up its resources, and as its population grew, it became clear that there was no going back.

On November 1, 1792, the brig *Philadelphia* from the United States became the first foreign ship to arrive in Sydney with goods to trade—cured beef, wine, gin, rum, tobacco, and tar. Then in January 1793, the first free settlers arrived aboard the *Bellona;* she also carried official permission from the English government for commissioned officers to receive grants of land. Among these officers was Lt. John Macarthur, who immediately claimed 100 acres (40 ha) near Parramatta, which he called Elizabeth Farm after his wife.

No longer merely a penal colony, Sydney was on its way to becoming one of the most prosperous of Britain's dominions. However, this put the new settlers on a collision course with the colony's military governors.

Early 19th Century

During the colony's early years, the military and a handful of unscrupulous traders (including Macarthur) managed to gain monopolies in a number of desperately needed commodities. One of these, rum, had virtually become the currency of the colony, especially among the convicts. The governors, meanwhile, were so autocratic that the free settlers began to complain about the lack of even the most basic freedoms that they enjoyed in England.

Macarthur, who had become a captain in the New South Wales Corps, was sent back to England in 1801 to answer charges of causing trouble for Gov. Phillip Gidley King (1758–1808), former second lieutenant on the flagship *Sirius*. King became lieutenant governor of the colony and finally governor from 1800 to 1806.

The charges were dismissed in 1804, but Macarthur took the opportunity to purchase a number of prime Spanish merino rams and ewes, and these founded the flocks that were to fuel much of the prosperity of Australia during the 19th century.

In Macarthur's absence, the Vinegar Hill Rebellion took place near Parramatta on March 4–5, 1804. It involved 260 Irish convicts rebelling against their harsh treatment. Although quickly put down and the ringleaders hanged, the uprising heralded the storm that was to envelop the entire colony.

Macquarie was a man whose vision was matched only by his ego. However, no other governor has left such an indelible mark on the city of Sydney.

In 1805, amid growing tensions in the Sydney colony, English naval officer Capt. William Bligh (1754–1817) was appointed governor as successor to King. When he arrived in 1806, he set about breaking the power of the monopolists and stopping the barter in rum. In 1807, he outlawed the barter in goods of any description. This brought him into open conflict with Macarthur who, on January 26, 1808 (coincidentally the 20th anniversary of the founding of the colony), led the Rum Rebellion. It took until October for news of the rebellion to reach England, and another year for Bligh's successor to be appointed and make the journey to Sydney.

When the new governor, Lachlan Macquarie (1761–1824), arrived in the colony, he was appalled at what he found. Sydney was in a state of foment, the few buildings were ramshackle or derelict, and exploration reached only 30 miles (50 km) inland—thwarted by the seemingly impenetrable barrier of the Blue Mountains.

Macquarie was a man whose vision was matched only by his ego. However, no other governor has left such an indelible mark on the city of Sydney. In the decade of

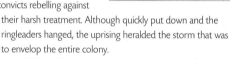

An 1888 lithograph of Sydney by M. S. Hill shows the growth of the settlement in the 19th century.

his government (1810–1821), Macquarie constructed more than 200 major public buildings and established the Royal Botanic Gardens. He was assisted in his endeavors by English-born architect Francis Howard Greenway, who was transported to Australia in 1812 for forgery.

No less important was the roadbuilding that linked towns such as Parramatta and Windsor and the farmlands to the southwest and northwest. Perhaps Macquarie's greatest achievement, however, was the construction of a road through the Blue Mountains in 1813, opening up vast areas of rich farmland that lay on the other side.

Meanwhile, in the colonial office of London there were concerns about the cost of Macquarie's increasingly extravagant projects. He found himself under growing pressure to curb his expenditure, and in 1820 his resignation was accepted. The following year, hundreds of people turned out to bid the governor and his wife farewell.

Although Macquarie's successors spent money more carefully, by now the colony was generating enough wealth to fund its own development and to demand services and facilities to support its endeavors. Thus Gov. Ralph Darling, who was in office from 1825 to 1831, found himself embarked on the major engineering feat of the 1820s: the convict-built Great Northern Road leading north to the Hunter Valley that enabled produce from the farms to be transported back to Sydney.

The 1830s saw rich landowners constructing magnificent harborside estates, some of which survive to this day. In 1840, transportation of convicts to Sydney ceased, though felons continued to be sent to Australian settlements in Tasmania and on Norfolk Island. In 1842, a partially elected legislative council was instituted and Sydney was incorporated as a city.

So, less than 60 years after it had been established, Sydney had become a prosperous trading port and the center of a rich agricultural economy. As good as life was, however, it was nothing compared to what was to follow after the discovery of gold became known. In 1823, gold had been found in the Bathurst region west of the Blue Mountains. It was kept a secret, however, as landowners with agricultural interests were fearful they would lose laborers in the face of more lucrative competition. When word finally got out, though, in 1851, the rush was on.

The *Dunbar* Goes Down

The colony's worst shipping disaster occurred in 1857. Approaching the harbor one night in bad weather, the crew of the passenger vessel *Dunbar* mistook a gap in the line of cliffs facing the sea (called The Gap, just east of today's Watsons Bay) for the entrance and the ship was driven onto the rocks. Many of the passengers were returning to Sydney from England, where they had been spending their newly acquired wealth. James Johnson, the only crew member who survived (121 people died), was washed onto the rocks and clung to a ledge for 36 hours until he was rescued.

Late 19th Century

From the 1850s until the early 1900s, new fields of gold were discovered all over New South Wales. In the 1880s, the richest lead, silver, and zinc deposits in the world at that time were found at Broken Hill in the far west of the state. With these discoveries came a period of growth and prosperity, and the fruits of that prosperity are everywhere to be seen around the city of Sydney.

The substantial buildings in Martin Place, including the former General Post Office (G.P.O.), date from these years, as does the University of Sydney (1853) with its Great Hall designed by Edmund Blacket (1817–1883). Many of the city's major buildings—the Australian Museum, the Town Hall, the Queen Victoria Building, and the Art Gallery of New South Wales—are also from this period. The handsome houses of inner suburbs such as Woollahra, Paddington, and Stanmore, with their elaborate Italianate facades and wrought-iron and leaded windows, reflect the desire of well-to-do Sydneysiders to display their wealth.

The city's newfound wealth also saw the need for improved security for the colony, and over a period of several decades, steps were taken to fortify parts of the harbor. The striking Fort Denison, rising in the middle of the harbor, was completed in 1857. Prior to that, the island on which the fort was built had been called (somewhat unimaginatively) Rock Island. During the first year of the colony, wrongdoers were abandoned there for a week or two to contemplate their misdeeds.

Despite such setbacks, the years leading up to the turn of the 20th century marked Sydney's coming of age. The population was growing rapidly as new settlers, attracted by gold, arrived. Numerous municipal councils were constituted, and the first railway opened in 1855. The Royal National Park was dedicated in 1879, making it the second oldest national park in the world after Yellowstone in the United States.

In 1888, the thriving city of Sydney marked its centenary with the laying out of Centennial Park. This area, originally swampland and the colony's first major water source, has since been developed into one of the city's best recreational assets. A century earlier, a member of the First Fleet, Capt. Watkin Tench (circa 1758–1833) of the Royal Marines, had expressed the hope that the expedition would lead to the establishment of a new empire. He would have been impressed at what had been achieved in the space of just one tumultuous century.

Perhaps even more extraordinary, just 13 years after the centenary, on January 1, 1901, Sydney and the rest of the country celebrated the formation of the Commonwealth of Australia. Appropriately, the federation documents were signed in a ceremony at Centennial Park. And as part of the celebrations of the nation's bicentennial, in 1988, the Federation Pavilion was built on the exact spot of the 1901 signing.

Federation to World War II

Just as the increasing wealth of Sydneysiders was expressed in the opulence of their houses during the second half of the 19th century, in the wake of nationhood the architecture of many Australian homes reflected national pride. The style that dominated in Sydney at the turn of the century actually came to be called Federation. It was characterized by large houses standing on sizable blocks of land (the extension of the railway system made it possible to live farther from the city) with gardens full of Australian native plants.

The houses themselves typically featured wide verandas, carved detail, and Australian motifs. Look for kangaroos, kookaburras, and gum leaves in leaded windows in suburbs such as Mosman, Haberfield, and Strathfield.

Yet, despite enjoying its status as a new nation, Australia still retained close ties with the country that established it—its highest court of appeal was the Privy Council in England. And when England was threatened by war, the Australian people stood ready to support it. Thousands of young men from Sydney and every other city and town across the country answered the call to World War I. Many never returned.

In 1914, the cruiser H.M.A.S. *Sydney* took part in Australia's first major naval victory during an engagement with the German cruiser *Emden*. *Sydney*'s mast is now located on Bradleys Head in the harbor. In 1915, Australian troops suffered severe losses while attacking Turkish positions on the cliffs of Gallipoli. The incident has become Australia's defining moment in war. During the campaign, 7,594 people were killed and 19,500 wounded. The remembrance day for Australians killed in all wars is held on the anniversary of the first Gallipoli landing—April 25. It is called Anzac Day, after the Australian and New Zealand Army Corps. All over Australia, parades, dawn services, and wreath-layings are held at memorials in towns and cities.

After the war, not even Sydney's wealth could protect it from the financial storm that swept the world during the Great Depression.

After the war, not even Sydney's wealth could protect it from the financial storm that swept the world during the Great Depression. From 1929, the worsening crisis saw more than a third of the Australian workforce unemployed. In Sydney, cliff caves around the harbor formerly used by Aborigines now sheltered many of the homeless.

Parades are held annually on Anzac Day—April 25—to recall Australians' sacrifices in war.

Amid the atmosphere of crisis, the Sydney Harbour Bridge was opened in 1932. It was one of the largest construction projects undertaken to that date and finally linked the north and south shores of the harbor, giving a considerable boost to the development of the city's northern suburbs.

When World War II broke out in 1939, Australian men and women found themselves fighting at much closer quarters than they had during World War I. The Japanese push south through the Pacific and Southeast Asia was halted in the waters and jungles adjacent to the country's north coast—the Coral Sea and Papua New Guinea, respectively.

The arrival of U.S. trading vessels in Sydney's early days had assisted the fledgling settlement's chances of survival. In 1942, it was America that once again came to Australia's aid as the country was threatened by the advancing Japanese. The decisive Battle of the Coral Sea in early May 1942 halted the Japanese advance. Nevertheless, Sydney was attacked by three midget submarines later in the month. Part of one of the submarines can be seen at the Naval Museum on Garden Island, and most of another is at the Australian War Memorial in Canberra. The third submarine disappeared without a trace. In June 1942, Japanese submarines also fired on the eastern suburbs. No one was injured, but property values fell—a rare occurrence in this affluent area.

Postwar Era

The United States' support during World War II marked the beginning of closer relations between the two countries, and greater recognition of Australia's position in the Asia-Pacific region. The end of World War II also heralded an era of mass immigration from Europe as people left the shortages and devastation there in search of a better life. The spread of communism in Europe in the late 1940s and early 1950s added to the flow.

For Sydney, this meant a rapid growth in population and a building boom in the 1950s. Vast outer suburbs of cheaply built "fibro" houses (fibrous cement sheets nailed to wooden framing) were constructed to accommodate the thousands of people arriving every day. In the 1960s, sturdier dwellings of red brick and red tile were mass produced. The Australian dream came to be a quarter-acre block with a three-bedroom house–a dream most of the population was able to achieve, as by now unemployment was virtually nonexistent.

The downside to the dream, however, was the monotony of the suburbs; while life was generally good, it was not particularly stimulating. New arrivals from Europe may have felt they had landed in a city that at first glance resembled paradise, only to find it was a cultural wasteland. Fortunately, many brought their culture with them. A new word entered the vocabulary: multiculturalism.

During World War II, the Korean and Vietnam Wars, and peacetime, through to the present day, U.S. warships have been visiting Sydney in quantity, their crews contributing greatly to the "worldliness" of the colorful suburbs in the vicinity of the naval base on Garden Island, just east of the Central Business District. In a sense, they have maintained the regular contact between the two countries that goes back to the first trading vessel in 1792, the whaling ships of the 19th century, and the clippers bringing gold-hungry prospectors.

The end of World War II . . . heralded an era of mass immigration from Europe as people left the shortages and devastation there in search of a better life.

The end of the Vietnam War in 1975 brought another wave of immigration. Boatloads of Vietnamese refugees made their way to Australia to escape the hardships of their homeland.

Symbols of the 20th Century

On October 20, 1973, the Sydney Opera House was officially opened on Bennelong Point. The setting is appropriate. Bennelong was one of the first Aboriginal people befriended by the settlers (see sidebar p. 28), so the site provides links both to Sydney's European beginnings and its indigenous culture. With the opening of the Opera House, the arts in Sydney gained a focus and a profile. Ever since, the artistic community has grown in size and confidence, to the benefit of the entire city. At the same time, the Opera House has given Sydney a unique identity, showcased to the world in 2000 when Sydney held a spectacularly successful Olympics.

Over the past few decades, Sydney has grown as a financial powerhouse for the Asia-Pacific region. Along with the rest of country, it is reaping the benefits of a new mining boom, supplying the growth economies of Asia, which is helping to drive this multicultural metropolis pulsating with youthful energy. It is given to bursts of extravagance that can be overwhelming at times (witness the frequency and scale of its fireworks displays and the unbridled hedonism of the Mardi Gras parades), but its enthusiasm and vibrancy are undeniable. ■

The Arts

You could be forgiven for thinking that, given its geographical distance from the major world centers of performing arts, Sydney might be rather light on live drama, opera, music, and dance. The reality, however, is very different.

For a start, Sydney is the headquarters of the National Institute of Dramatic Art, whose alumni include Judy Davis and Academy Award winners Mel Gibson, Geoffrey Rush, and Cate Blanchett. It is not uncommon to catch the likes of Rush in productions by Sydney's two main theater companies—the Sydney Theatre Company (venues at the Wharf Theatre in The Rocks and the Opera House Theatre), now under the artistic direction of Blanchett and her playwright husband Andrew Upton, and Company B (at its theater in Belvoir Street, Surry Hills, just south of the city).

Names visitors may not be familiar with include Richard Roxburgh (who has played in everything from *Hamlet* to *Moulin Rouge*), Hugo Weaving (with a long string of movie and theater credits), Max Cullen, and Miranda Otto. These and many others are on a par with the big names and cover a repertoire that ranges from William Shakespeare to Tennessee Williams and Henrik Ibsen, from Anton Chekhov to contemporary Australian drama by names such as Michael Gow, Tim Winton, and David Williamson. Directors Neil Armfield and Barrie Kosky in particular enjoy pushing theater to its limits.

The standard of performance in the city is helped by the focus of the Australian film industry in Sydney.

In the summer, keep an eye out for Shakespeare's *A Midsummer Night's Dream* performed outdoors in the Royal Botanic Gardens. Look, too, for the Bell Shakespeare Company, a touring company that stages productions at the Playhouse in the Sydney Opera House, the Royal Botanic Gardens, the Wharf Theatre, and the Opera House steps.

The standard of performance in the city is helped by the focus of the Australian film industry in Sydney. The National Film Television and Radio School is based here, and Rupert Murdoch's Fox Studios operates in the former Showground near Centennial Park.

Of course, no visit to Sydney is complete without a night at the opera, or at least the Sydney Opera House. The concert halls on Bennelong Point host performances by the Sydney-based Opera Australia that range from the light works of Gilbert and Sullivan to the heavy artillery of Richard Wagner. While the opera company handles the big performances, its smaller division, Oz Opera, mounts smaller-scale productions that are easier to take on tour. Also based at the Opera House is the Sydney Symphony Orchestra, an accomplished group of musicians under the baton of Russian conductor Vladimir Ashkenazy. The youthful exuberance of the Australian Chamber Orchestra, under the young but immensely talented conductor Richard Tognetti, throws caution to the wind and excites concertgoers with its varied and innovative repertoire. Musica

Posing atop the Opera House, Amber Scott of Australian Ballet and Patrick Thaiday of Bangarra Dance hint at an upcoming collaboration of the two companies.

Viva Australia, meanwhile, is the world's largest chamber music presenter; it has an extensive touring program and stages performances in Sydney year-round.

As for dance, classic ballet is well served by the Australian Ballet, which also performs at the Sydney Opera House. The innovative and provocative Sydney Dance Company and the Bangarra Dance Company, combining indigenous and contemporary dance influences, are both based at the Wharf Theatre in The Rocks.

A number of smaller organizations ensure there is a never-ending supply of stimulating performances going on around the city. Throw in blockbuster musicals and numerous appearances by visiting performers and groups, and hardly a night passes when there isn't something worth going out for.

The busiest time of the year, however, is January, when the Sydney Festival is in full swing. Free outdoor performances of opera, classical music, jazz, and country and western draw thousands of people to the Domain. Major touring companies visit, and there is a packed schedule of events.

Art

There are two distinct art traditions in Australia—Aboriginal and European—as Australian art goes back further than the arrival of the First Fleet in Sydney. The Aborigines have inhabited Australia for more than 40,000 years, and for them, artistic expression is, and was, a way of life. They painted and engraved all kinds of surfaces and used their art to convey knowledge of sacred sites and tell complex stories.

Dot painting is but one of many Aboriginal art traditions.

Today, Aboriginal art has become an essential element in the field of contemporary Australian art as modern artists adapt traditional painting techniques to new media, tools, and technology.

Aboriginal Art: Traditionally, Aboriginal art adorned a wide variety of surfaces—the human body, rock, and bark, for example. Designs were also drawn on the ground and on everyday items. Some designs and images had great ceremonial significance, others were simply decoration for spears, boomerangs, clap sticks, didgeridoos, and domestic objects. Clays, dyes from certain roots, charcoal, and animal blood were used. In the northern areas, figures were carved in wood; some were quite large and planted in the ground like totems.

A great deal of Aboriginal art is closely linked with ritual and mythology. It also expresses the way the world is formed and how it functions. The landscape, together with water and food sources, is a common theme. In some areas, rock art was used to warn of danger. For example, a dangerous looking spirit figure painted on rocks indicated barren land ahead.

The northern areas of Australia, where resources were more plentiful, tend to have more developed painting styles: x-ray painting, in which the anatomical features of animals are shown, often giving the art a three-dimensional effect; an "elegant" style, with elongated figures and crosshatching; and contact art (reflecting encounters with Makassar traders and Europeans). On Bathurst and Melville, islands just north of Darwin, huge slabs of bark are painted. Since the availability of metal axes and the lure of big art prizes, the scale of these works has increased dramatically.

Central Australia is another major center for painting, with the dot style predominating. Until recently, there were few examples of this painting in existence because of the nondurable nature of the surfaces that were used. However, with the increasing demand for Aboriginal art and the ready availability of more lasting modern materials, the style is being revived.

The first Aboriginal artists to paint in the European tradition came from this area. Members of the Hermannsburg school, based in a settlement 150 miles (240 km) west of Alice Springs and led by Albert Namatjira (1902–1959), mainly painted landscapes in oils and watercolors. And yet they retained the principal concerns of Aboriginal people. If you look closely, most of their paintings are full of Dreamtime (see sidebar this page)

Dreamtime

One of the most frequently used expressions you'll encounter in association with Aboriginal culture is "Dreamtime." But what does it mean? In essence, it is a simple term used to describe a remarkably complex set of stories and beliefs. These provide a detailed description of the creation of the world and many of its features, plus the Aborigines' relationship to the land, their responsibilities to it, and the code of conduct by which they live. For example, a particular feature of the landscape will mark where someone was punished, perhaps for breaking the tribal law. Other Dreamtime stories relate to journeys made by mythical creatures across the bare landscape and the features they made along the way. In other words, a Dreamtime story can also be a "map." So what happens if a new feature is made? Easy. A Dreamtime story is created to include it.

Artist Sydney Nolan gained fame and acclaim for his series of highly stylized paintings of the bushranger Ned Kelly. This one was painted circa 1955.

images: Faces and figures can be found everywhere—in the rocks, the trees, the hills.

Most pieces of Aboriginal art either represent the land to which the artist is attached or tell a story relating to it; sometimes a painting will do both. A work may show how the land was formed or indicate when to expect certain food sources to become available. In central Australia, because water holes are vitally important, it is common to represent the trails between them with dotted lines. A creature's tracks are frequently presented, too, particularly if it can be eaten.

Paintings may also be "layered," with representations of the same area in times of drought and rain, or when different plants are producing food, overlapping one another. Many Westerners want to know the story of a painting, but often there just isn't one, or the artist may be forbidden by tribal law to explain it.

The power of Aboriginal art is reflected in the demand for it around the world. Collectors flock to exhibitions, and auctions are conducted by satellite video link, with works in central Australian deserts being shown on-screen to buyers in major galleries.

European Art: The main achievement of 200 years of European art in Australia is the appreciation for the beauty of the environment in which it is created. The dark and tormented soul of the artist is certainly present, but on balance the great artists of Australia have concentrated on mythologizing the landscape and its people.

From the beginning of the settlement, artists documented the foundation of the colony and the country's unique flora and fauna. In so doing, they found a quality of light and texture in the landscape that challenged their traditional artistic training. The response was the evolution of a uniquely Australian approach within conventional forms, and this process of discovery is visible in practically all the large galleries in Australia.

Crucial in the development was the Heidelberg school—a circle of artists, including Tom Roberts (who toured Europe in the 1880s), Frederick McCubbin, Arthur Streeton, Charles Conder, and Hans Heysen. They painted in the bucolic township of Heidelberg in Victoria between 1888 and 1901, bringing an impressionist's eye to the heroism of Australian life and history at a time when the country was approaching nationhood. The movement was greatly assisted by Sydney artist Julian Ashton (1851–1942), whose art school trained many of the country's artists and who helped establish the Heidelberg school's influence that is still felt today.

The dark and tormented soul of the artist is certainly present, but on balance the great artists of Australia have concentrated on mythologizing the landscape and its people.

However, it was the work of Norman Lindsay (1876–1969), before World War I, that achieved the most notoriety, at least for a while. The combination of his nudes, which celebrated the pleasures of the flesh, and his determination broke down the barriers of a prudishness that, at the time, saw separate beaches for men and women.

Between the two World Wars, several artists were responsible for bringing contemporary art to the fore. They include the internationally recognized Australian artist Sidney Nolan (1917–1992), Albert Tucker (1914–1999), whose macabre, surrealist works were charged with symbolism, William Dobell (1899–1970), a student of Julian Ashton and an outstanding portrait painter, and Russell Drysdale (1912–1981), whose desolate landscapes and gaunt figures broke with the Heidelberg romanticism. They built on the Heidelberg school's interpretation of light and used surreal perspectives in a local context. In their work, you can see the real Australia and its people—sunburned, withered, and yet resilient.

For postwar impressions of the Australian landscape, Frederick (Fred) Williams (1927–1982) is hard to beat. A gentle, thoughtful man, his sensitivity to the sparse vegetation of the arid interior forms an eloquent bridge to the pointillism of Aboriginal art. For sheer love of color and light, seek out Margaret Olley's (1923–2011) still lifes and luxuriate in the richness of her art.

Color, light, and texture—embodied, for example, in the witty and sensuous work of Brett Whiteley (1939–1992), the hyperrealist urban alienation of Jeffrey Smart (1921–), or even the populist art-on-a-T-shirt of Ken Done—now form the palette of modern Australian art, where innovation continues within relatively conservative and conventional forms. The country's best known art prize, the Archibald Prize, presented at the Art Gallery of New South Wales, is for portraiture, but a host of artists and styles bears testament to the breadth of expression to be found in Australian art.

Literature

Even before the arrival of the First Fleet, the seeds of Australia's literary heritage had been sown. The plan to colonize New South Wales had provoked considerable interest, and before they set sail, several of the senior officers had signed book deals with London publishers. One of the best of these is still available in print: *1788,* by Watkin Tench, is a lively and vivid account of the early years of Sydney and its environs. In the colony's second year of existence, convicts performed its first play, *The Recruiting Officer,* by Irish playwright George Farquhar (circa 1677–1707).

The first golden age of Australian literary life spanned the years leading to Australia's federation in 1901. Balladeers and storytellers Henry Lawson (1867–1922) and Banjo Paterson (also known as A. B.—Andrew Barton—Paterson, 1864–1941) were engaged in lively debate about the merits of city and country life. Ethel Turner's (1872–1958) *Seven Little Australians* was the Australian equivalent of *Little Women* by American writer Louisa May Alcott.

The richness of Sydney's poetry is embodied in the collection *Sydney's Poems,* issued in 1992 to mark the 150th anniversary of Sydney's incorporation as a city. It includes Kenneth Slessor's (1901–1971) "Five Bells," inspired by the drowning of a friend who fell off a ferry to Kirribilli on the way to a party.

Sydney's most famous literary figure is Patrick White (1912–1990), winner of the Nobel Prize for literature in 1973. His works include *Voss* (set in part in Sydney and inspired by explorer Ludwig Leichhardt) and *The Tree of Man* (set on Sydney's outskirts and tracing the hardships of a family struggling to survive).

Robert Drewe's *Bodysurfers* (published in 1983) is a collection of short stories set in Sydney and other locations that captures the hedonism and guilty pleasures of contemporary Australia. Sydneysider Thomas Keneally (1935–) is best known for his Booker Prize–winning *Shindler's Ark* (filmed as *Shindler's List*), but Sydney features prominently in many of his works, fiction and nonfiction. Meanwhile, Australian novelist Peter Carey (1935–) penned a skillfully observed memoir/homage to Sydney after ten years away in New York, *30 Days in Sydney* (2001). ■

Aussiewood

Australia is immensely proud of its many actors, directors, cinematographers, and other film technicians that have made it in Hollywood. Dubbed the Gumleaf Mafia, national pride swells when the likes of Nicole Kidman, Russell Crowe, Cate Blanchett, Naomi Watts, Hugh Jackman, Eric Bana, Geoffrey Rush, and Mel Gibson shine at the Oscars. Many well-known actors, like Gibson, are graduates of the prestigious National Institute of Dramatic Arts in Sydney, and film schools across the country continue to pump out graduates who eye Hollywood as the main prize.

The Opera House, the Royal Botanic Gardens, and the Art Gallery of New South Wales, plus sights of historic interest

Circular Quay & East

Introduction & Map 44–45

Sydney Opera House 46–49

Around Circular Quay 50–53

Experience: Take an Urban Art Time-Out 51

Royal Botanic Gardens & the Domain 54–57

Experience: New Year's Eve in the Gardens 57

A Walk From Hyde Park to Circular Quay 58–60

Art Gallery of New South Wales 61–65

Feature: Artists' Views of Sydney Harbour 64

Australian Museum 66–67

Macquarie Street 68–70

Hotels & Restaurants 238–240

Water lily, Royal Botanic Gardens

Circular Quay & East

Circular Quay, the main ferry terminal, effectively acts as a division between the two sides of the city. The eastern side presents Sydney's most impressive face: The Opera House, the Royal Botanic Gardens, the Domain, Macquarie Street, and Hyde Park stretch back from the harbor. There are also art galleries, cathedrals, and major museums, all on a grand scale. The gardens are among the best in the world and offer spectacular views of the harbor alongside a dazzling and beautiful range of trees and plants.

At Circular Quay, ferries set out for waterside suburbs and ocean liners still berth.

In contrast, the western side, with The Rocks and the docks of Darling Harbour that once housed the convicts from England and where ships loaded or unloaded cargo, is where the daily hustle and bustle of city life takes place.

And it has always been this way. The first Government House was built on the eastern side of the city, and the Royal Botanic Gardens take in the area of the first farm in the colony, itself established on the site of an Aboriginal initiation area.

What is most remarkable is that all these points of interest are contained in an incredibly compact space. A two-hour walk can take you around all the major sights, but, as you will find, you can easily spend several days discovering what this area has to offer. ■

NOT TO BE MISSED:

A tour or a performance at the Sydney Opera House **46–49**

Exploring the diverse habitats of the Royal Botanic Gardens **54–56**

Walking through historic Hyde Park to the Anzac Memorial **58–59**

Seeing the best of Australian art at the Art Gallery of New South Wales **61–65**

The Aboriginal collection at the Australian Museum **66–67**

Experiencing convict Sydney at Hyde Park Barracks **69**

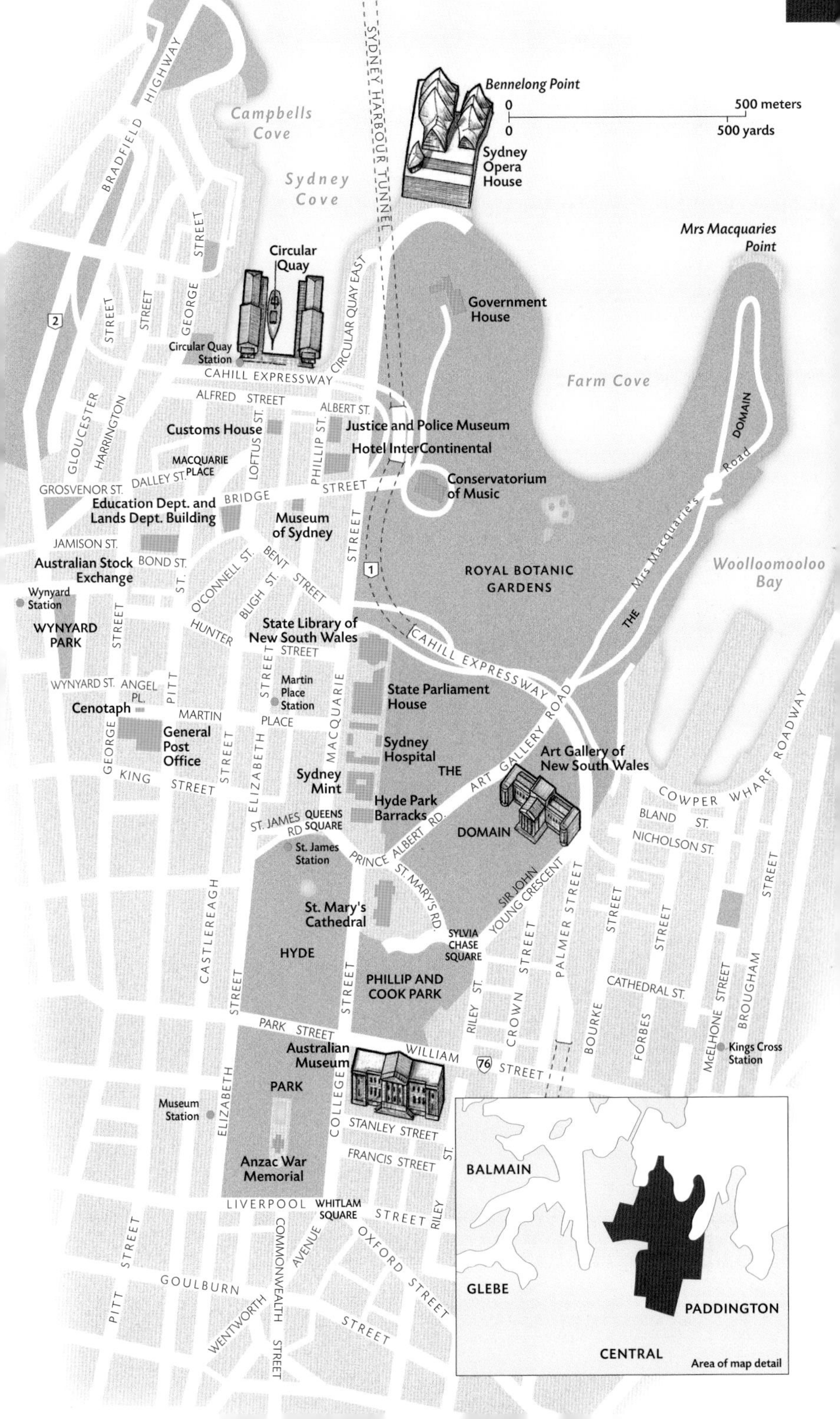
Bennelong Point
0
500 meters
0
500 yards
Sydney Opera House
Campbells Cove
Sydney Cove
SYDNEY HARBOUR TUNNEL
BRADFIELD HIGHWAY
Circular Quay
Circular Quay Station
Mrs Macquaries Point
Government House
Farm Cove
CAHILL EXPRESSWAY
CIRCULAR QUAY EAST
ALFRED STREET
ALBERT ST.
Customs House
Justice and Police Museum
Hotel InterContinental
MACQUARIE PLACE
Conservatorium of Music
GROSVENOR ST.
DALLEY ST.
BRIDGE STREET
Education Dept. and Lands Dept. Building
Museum of Sydney
JAMISON ST.
Australian Stock Exchange
BOND ST.
O'CONNELL ST.
BENT STREET
BLIGH ST.
ROYAL BOTANIC GARDENS
THE Mrs Macquarie's Road
DOMAIN
Woolloomooloo Bay
Wynyard Station
WYNYARD PARK
HUNTER
State Library of New South Wales
STREET
CAHILL EXPRESSWAY
WYNYARD ST.
ANGEL PL.
Martin Place Station
State Parliament House
Cenotaph
MARTIN PLACE
General Post Office
Sydney Hospital
Art Gallery of New South Wales
ART GALLERY ROAD
GEORGE STREET
PITT STREET
KING STREET
ELIZABETH STREET
MACQUARIE STREET
Sydney Mint
THE DOMAIN
Hyde Park Barracks
COWPER WHARF ROADWAY
ST. JAMES RD
QUEENS SQUARE
BLAND ST.
NICHOLSON ST.
St. James Station
PRINCE ALBERT RD.
ST. MARY'S RD.
SIR JOHN YOUNG CRESCENT
CASTLEREAGH STREET
St. Mary's Cathedral
HYDE
SYLVIA CHASE SQUARE
PHILLIP AND COOK PARK
CATHEDRAL ST.
PALMER STREET
CROWN STREET
RILEY ST.
BOURKE STREET
FORBES STREET
McELHONE STREET
BROUGHAM STREET
PARK STREET
Australian Museum
WILLIAM STREET
Kings Cross Station
PARK
Museum Station
COLLEGE
STANLEY STREET
FRANCIS STREET
Anzac War Memorial
LIVERPOOL STREET
WHITLAM SQUARE
OXFORD STREET
AVENUE
COMMONWEALTH STREET
GOULBURN
WENTWORTH
BALMAIN
GLEBE
PADDINGTON
CENTRAL
Area of map detail

Sydney Opera House

It is as much a work of art as a building. Certainly it is one of the greatest architectural statements of the 20th century, not only the hub of the artistic life of the city but an expression of its very soul. One million Swedish ceramic tiles form the seamed pattern covering the distinctive "sails" or "shells," and from a distance the building appears to be voyaging on the harbor water.

The Sydney Opera House, with its billowing sail roofs, is one of the most potent symbols of Australia.

An Unparalleled Design

Construction commenced in 1959 and was expected to take three to four years to complete, at a cost of A$7 million. However, things didn't go quite to plan, and the building was opened in 1973 by Queen Elizabeth II at a final cost of A$102 million. Along the way, Danish architect Jørn Utzon (who had won the competition to design the building in 1957) resigned in the face of constant pressure from engineers, builders, and governments who were becoming increasingly concerned at the cost. Utzon left Australia and never returned to see the completed building, although in 1999, he was named design consultant for remodeling the Opera House. The University of Sydney awarded Utzon an honorary doctorate in 2003, accepted by his son Jan when Utzon was too ill to travel to Australia. Utzon died, age 90, in 2008.

On a sad note related to the building's construction was the Graeme Thorne kidnapping: When the building first began, lotteries were held to raise some money to cover the shortfall (first prize was U.S.$160,000). Thorne, the eight-year-old son of one of the lottery winners, was

Sydney Festival

In January, during the Sydney Festival (see p. 230), free performances are often held on the Monumental Steps. Arrive early and bring a cushion and a sun umbrella, because the events are very popular and the steps and setting sun can be uncomfortable.

kidnapped after the news of his family's good fortune became public. He disappeared on July 7, 1960, and was found, murdered, on August 16, 1960, after a ransom was paid.

The Opera House actually consists of three separate buildings—the proscenium-style **Opera Theatre,** fully rigged under the sails on the eastern side; the cathedral-like **Concert Hall** in the sails on the western side; and the much vaunted **Guillaume at Bennelong** restaurant on the city (southern) side. Smaller performance spaces—the Drama Theatre, Playhouse, and Studio—lie underneath the Concert Hall on the western side, and other restaurants and cafés extend along the western boardwalk to the Harbour Restaurant facing Kirribilli to the north.

In front of the white sails is a giant forecourt, which doubles as an outdoor performance venue, behind which are the nearly 325-foot-wide (100 m) Monumental Steps, a flight of granite stairs that lead up to the performance arts complex.

Each year more than 2,500 performances are staged in the complex, making it one of the busiest arts centers in the world.

The Grand Venues

If visiting the Opera House during the day, you can view the foyers, with their massive concrete arches disappearing into the void above, simply by ascending the Monumental Steps and stepping into them. But to see the rest of the interiors, you will need to take a one-hour guided tour, on which you'll learn the history of the Opera House and see some exquisite designwork. Then take a walk around the base of the building along the eastern and western sides and you'll come across stairs ascending the exterior of the building. These take you up to balconies on the front of the Concert Hall and Opera Theatre sails, with good views of the harbor.

INSIDER TIP:

Avoid the tourist traffic and join the office workers for predinner drinks (and fabulous waterfront views) at the Opera Bar, outside the front of the spectacular Opera House.

—PETER TURNER
National Geographic author

Sydney Opera House

- Map p. 45
- Bennelong Point
- 9250 7111, 9250 7777 (box office)
- Tours $$$$$ (every 30 min., 9 a.m.–5 p.m.)

www.soh.nsw.gov.au

Sydney Opera House

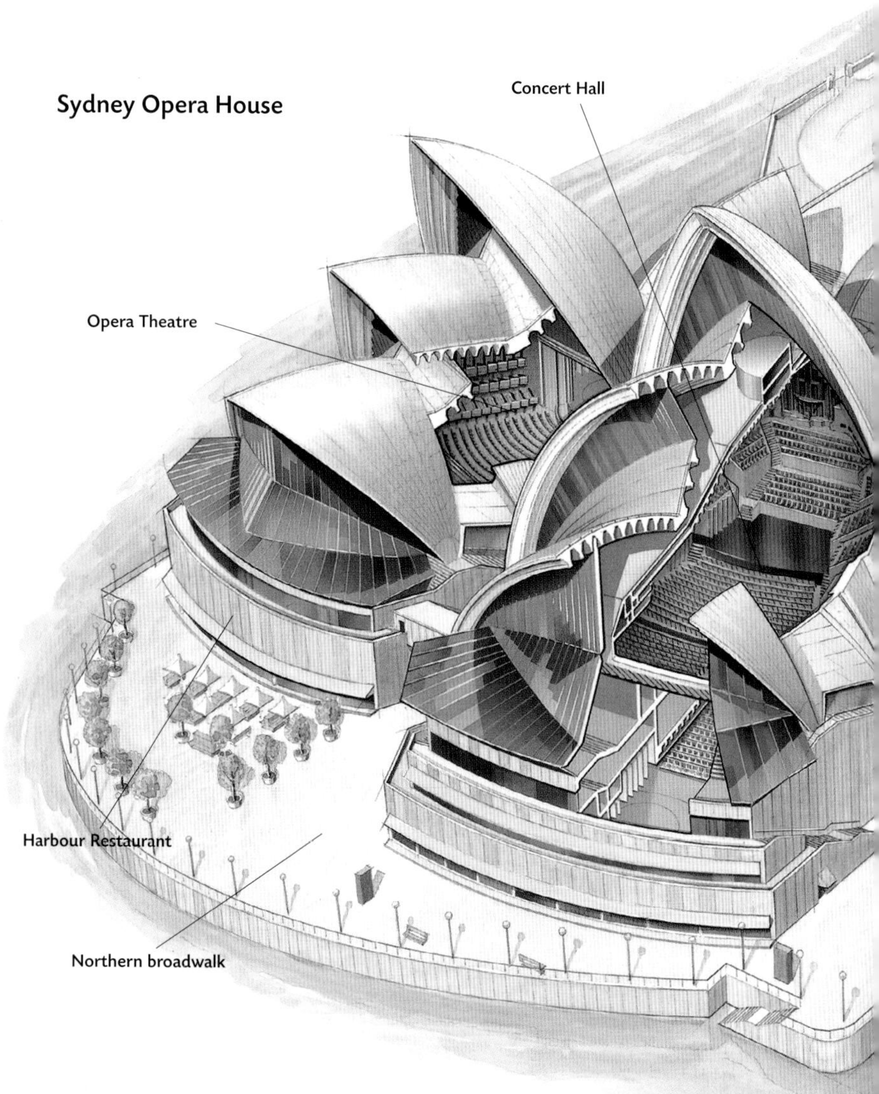

If attending a performance in the Concert Hall—the largest of the Opera House's performance venues, capable of seating 2,679 people—note the 18 large acoustic discs suspended above the stage and the elaborate Australian wood paneling.

During an intermission in performances in the Concert Hall or Opera Theatre, head up to the northern foyers of both buildings. Refreshments are available here, but you'll find the main attraction is the view through the massive glass panes under the sails. It feels like you're on the bridge of a large ship—which is exactly what Utzon intended. ■

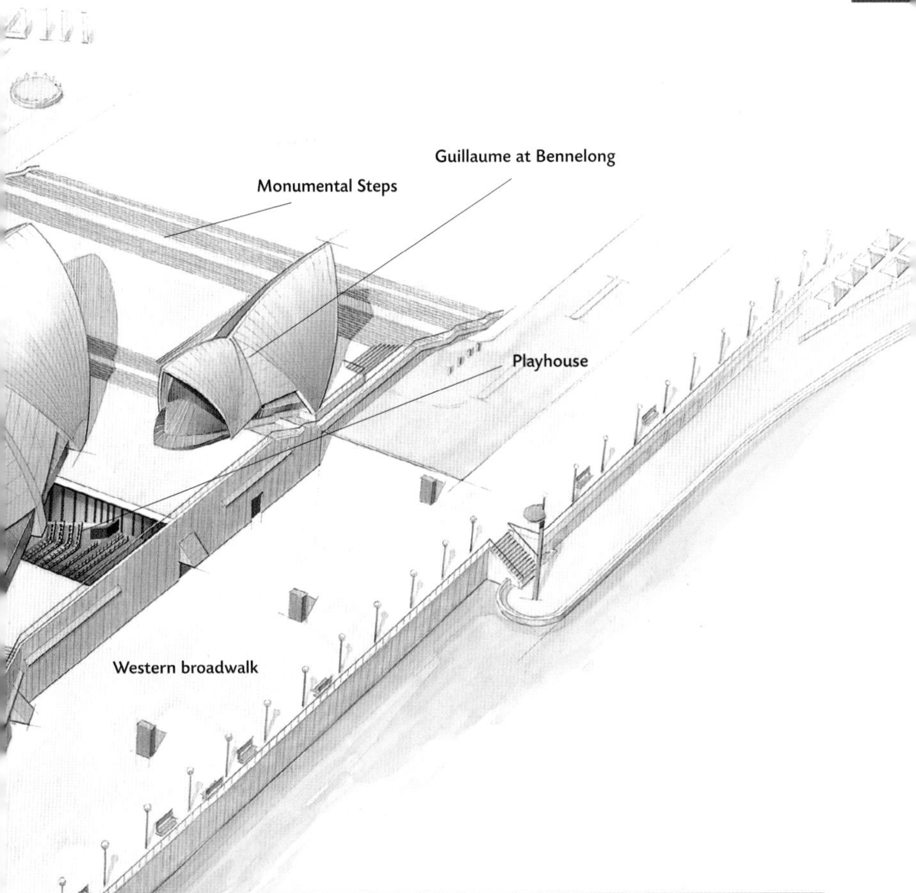

The Opera House dominates the view as visitors idle in cafés lining the Circular Quay promenade.

Around Circular Quay

At first sight, the area directly behind Circular Quay—the main ferry terminal—may appear to be nothing but a concrete jungle, but in fact it is sprinkled with a number of gems that you can explore in as little as two hours or a leisurely day. On the walkway leading to the Opera House, notice the metal plates set into the ground. This is Writers' Walk, commemorating the writings of famous authors, poets, and playwrights who have either visited the city or lived in it.

Of historic and cultural interest, the Customs House sits behind the wharves of Circular Quay.

Circular Quay
Map p. 45
Alfred St.

Circular Quay

Circular Quay is the terminal for all public ferries plying the waters of Sydney Harbour. Bustling from early morning to midnight, as it services both tourists and commuters, it is surrounded by cafés, which are popular places to sit back and watch all the comings and goings of the ferries.

Customs House

Behind Circular Quay is the Customs House, an imposing structure begun in the 1840s and continually added to until 1917. For much of the 19th and 20th centuries, the Customs House served as the primary gateway for most goods and people entering Sydney (and by extension, Australia). It

INSIDER TIP:

Catch a ferry from Circular Quay to just about anywhere in Sydney Harbour. It's a cheap but great way to get on the water, see the Opera House, and check out all the other harbor boats.

—SADIE QUARRIER
National Geographic
magazine photo editor

continued to house the Australian Customs Service until 1990. Now under the purview of the city, the building is multifunctional, with cafés, shops, a library with a good selection of overseas newspapers to browse, and a 1:500 scale model of the city under the glass floor of the atrium. The Aboriginal flag is flown from the building, but it is believed the English flag was first raised in the settlement on this spot.

Justice & Police Museum

A block to the east, on the left as you face the Customs House, is the interesting Justice and Police Museum. It is housed in an attractive collection of former law enforcement buildings that includes the imposing Water Police Court (1856), a single-story classical revival courthouse built of sandstone that became a prototype for other courthouses.

The museum explores the colorful interaction between the constabulary and wrongdoers throughout Sydney and New South Wales. Some of the museum's exhibits are staged in the Corridor of Cells, where prisoners were held, sometimes for days, while awaiting their court appearance or transportation to and from jail. Be sure to visit the Charge Room, where, as it sounds, offenders were charged with their

Customs House

Map p. 45
31 Alfred St.
9242 8551

www.cityofsydney.nsw.gov.au/customshouse

Justice & Police Museum

Map p. 45
1 Albert St.
9252 1144
Closed Mon.–Fri. Feb.–Dec.
$$

www.hht.net.au

EXPERIENCE: Take an Urban Art Time-Out

As you tour the city, step away from Sydney's streets and into its laneways for brief art experiences of the eye-popping, thought-provoking, or merely whimsical variety—depending on which laneway you find yourself in. Once the haunt of backdoor deliveries, garbage bins, alley cats, and shady deals, the labyrinth of laneways that lace the city center are being transformed into art spaces, taking street art to a whole new level, with new dining and drinking venues following. At the forefront of the rejuvenation is the City of Sydney's street art program, installing murals and rotating artworks throughout the laneways. Pick up "City Art" brochures from the Sydney Visitor Centre or the Town Hall for their locations. Keep an eye out also for yearlong Laneway Art installations put up each year as part of the Sydney Art & About Festival *(www.artandabout.com.au)* held around October. In 2012, you could peer through giant, yellow periscopes for unique local views, lounge on inflatable modular furniture, and marvel at an optical illusion.

Museum of Sydney
- Map p. 45
- Bridge & Phillip Sts.
- 9251 5988
- $$

www.hht.net.au

crimes; it has been returned to its 1890s appearance.

Museum of Sydney

Walk a block back from the harbor to the Museum of Sydney (MOS). This small museum is justifiably proud of the fact that it is part of the city's history, built on the site of the colony's first Government House (1788). Initially a prefabricated structure, the foundations of a later, more permanent Government House (demolished in 1846) are still visible through glass panels in the floor. It was the scene of the Rum Rebellion (see p. 30).

Themed areas and rotating exhibits illustrating the history of the city from pre-1788 to recent times include Gadigal Place, chronicling the indigenous people of the Sydney area; Sydney Visionaries, about the people who shaped the city; the Trade Wall, looking at items for sale in early Sydney; and models and the story of the First Fleet ships. When you open the drawers of the "Collectors Chest," you are taken on a journey via images, objects, and text that reflects Sydney's past.

Macquarie Place

Going west from the museum along Bridge Street, you'll find Macquarie Place, yet another of the places the pivotal if egotistical Gov. Lachlan Macquarie

Inside the Museum of Sydney, visitors pore over images that help relate Sydney's history.

named after himself. On Bridge Street, take a moment to admire two buildings on the left: the **Education Department Building** (1913) and the **Lands Department Building** (1876–1890) designed by James Barnet (colonial architect). Here the statues in the porticoes commemorate famous Australian explorers and legislators; the empty spaces await future luminaries. Macquarie Place, a popular spot for workers to have lunch, has an anchor and cannon from the First Fleet's flagship, H.M.A.S. *Sirius.* In one corner of the postage-stamp-size park is a Francis Greenway–designed obelisk, erected in 1818. It is the point from which road distances to the rest of Australia are measured.

Follow Bridge Street across to Pitt Street and you'll be standing above the **Tank Stream,** a watercourse that once supplied the original colony with water and now runs underground into Sydney Cove. Bridge Street was so named because it was the site of the first bridge in the colony, built in 1788 across the mudflats. Along Pitt Street, you'll pass the **Australian Securities Exchange.** The floor is quiet in these electronic trading times, but lectures on investment are frequently held for the public.

Martin Place

Continue two blocks along Pitt Street, away from the harbor. This takes you through the financial section of the Central Business District to Martin Place. Here you'll find the old **General Post Office,** which now houses shops, restaurants, and a hotel. It caused as much controversy over its cost in the 1880s as the Opera House did nearly a hundred years later. Designed by Barnet, the building was begun in 1866 and completed in 1887, in time for the colony's centenary in 1888. The 200-foot (61 m) clock tower, dismantled in 1942 because of fears it would be used as a navigation aid by Japanese bombers, was rebuilt after the war. Martin Place is also the site of the **Cenotaph,** where the memories of those lost in war are honored on Anzac Day (April 25) and Remembrance Day (November 11). ■

Sea Horses

Among the exotic creatures that abound in and around Sydney, one of the most beautiful is the sea horse *(Hippocampus whitei)*, which lives in seagrass beds in the many small bays of the harbor. However, they are usually incredibly well camouflaged. One location where sea horses of a different kind can be easily spotted is Circular Quay. Here ornamental sea horses decorate the railings at the water's edge, and you'll also find some in sculptures in the entrance to the Circular Quay rail station.

Royal Botanic Gardens & the Domain

After visiting the Opera House, consider taking a look at the Royal Botanic Gardens, which sweep around the bay of Farm Cove to the east. Apart from the 7,500 species of trees and plants, there are several food outlets, ranging from a kiosk to the well-established and very satisfying Botanic Gardens Restaurant. The balcony is a lovely spot for a post-visit lunch.

"Love Led Them," a bronze Cupid, graces the central pond of the Pioneer Memorial Garden.

Royal Botanic Gardens

Map p. 45

Mrs Macquaries Rd.

9231 8125

www.rbgsyd.nsw.gov.au

Royal Botanic Gardens

The 75-acre (30 ha) Royal Botanic Gardens, the oldest scientific institution in the country, were established in 1816 by Governor Macquarie on the site of the first farm in the colony. Stunning examples of the flora of Sydney and the surrounding region are set against enchanting views of the city and Sydney Harbour. Numerous sculptures enhance the ambience.

On summer evenings, outdoor performances of William Shakespeare's *A Midsummer Night's Dream (information and tickets available at the botanic gardens shop)* attract audiences who bring champagne picnics with them.

A special feature of the gardens is the **Sydney Tropical Centre,** which consists of two glasshouses, the Pyramid and the Arc. These maintain the humidity and warmth necessary to nurture tropical and native vegetation. At times, the automatic shutters are wide open, which says quite a bit about Sydney's summer.

INSIDER TIP:

Sign up for an Aboriginal heritage tour in the botanic gardens. You'll come away with insights on how plants are traditionally used for their medicinal properties as well as get the opportunity to taste some bush foods.

—JEANINE BARONE
National Geographic writer

The **Rose Garden** is full of a mixture of old-fashioned roses and more modern, distinctive varieties. The **Herb Garden** has a fascinating range of herbs and gives details of their medicinal or culinary uses.

The **Succulent Garden** is a walled-in section with a selection of dry-climate plants from around the world, with an emphasis on Australian flora.

Other sections of the gardens to explore include the **National Herbarium of New South Wales,** established in 1985, which has some of the dried specimens collected by Joseph Banks during Captain Cook's visit to Botany Bay in 1770.

Keep an eye out for long famous but unwelcome visitors hanging from the trees. Thousands of flying foxes—fruit bats—roost in the gardens, killing the trees, but so far all attempts to relocate the bats have failed.

A visitor information center and shop provides leaflets detailing walks and features of the gardens. Free guided walks leave the center at 10:30 a.m., and a "train" runs around the gardens.

Government House: In the gardens just south of the Opera House is Government House, formerly the official residence of the governor of New South Wales. Designed by Edward Blore, it was constructed between 1837 and 1845 in the Gothic Revival style. It replaced the original Government House, whose foundations

Government House

Map p. 45
Royal Botanic Gardens
9931 5222
Tours Fri.–Sun.
www.hht.net.au

Wollemi Pine

One of the most prized specimens in the gardens is found in the Rare and Threatened Plants Garden, which was opened in 1998 near the visitor information center. Referred to as the "Jurassic tree" because it is related to trees from that period, the Wollemi pine was thought to have been extinct until 1994, when it was discovered by a national park ranger, David Noble, hiking in the rugged Wollemi National Park near the northern extremity of the city. The director of the Royal Botanic Gardens at the time, Professor Carrick Chambers, compared the discovery to finding a "small dinosaur still alive on Earth."

Less than 100 mature trees—growing up to 129 feet (40 m) tall—survive in Wollemi National Park (in three locations that are kept secret), but propagation has ensured that the dangers of flood and bush fire will not mean the loss of the species.

The Domain
Map p. 45
www.rbgsyd.nsw.gov.au

can be seen at the Museum of Sydney (see p. 52).

Far grander are the stables (situated on the approach road from Conservatorium Road) designed by Francis Greenway. They were a cause of controversy when Commissioner J. T. Bigge arrived in 1819 to examine Macquarie's spending and questioned the construction of "such a palace for horses." The stable buildings now house the **Conservatorium of Music** *(tel 9351 1263),* a music school. The grounds are open daily, or free tours of the house run Friday to Sunday, 10:30 a.m.–3 p.m., subject to official functions being held.

The Domain

Pass through it at the wrong time of the year, or even the wrong time of day, and the Domain doesn't look like much at all. It's just a big field. However, the fact is that since the city's early days, the Domain has been, well, special. As Banjo Patterson claims in his 1902 poem "It's Grand": "It's grand to be an unemployed / And lie in The Domain, / And wake up every second day / And go to sleep again."

At certain times, up to a quarter of a million people can throng this field–attending a massive open-air concert as part of the annual Sydney Festival (see Travelwise p. 230), for example. People have gathered here since the area was made part of the "public domain" in 1810.

Originally it was fenced in (you can still see the gates, dating

Amateur sports league teams flock to the Domain to take advantage of its wide-open spaces.

EXPERIENCE: New Year's Eve in the Gardens

Find a spot at the waterfront Royal Botanic Gardens on December 31 and be among the first in the world to celebrate the New Year. Sydney uses its geographic advantages to spectacular effect. Its celebrations focus on the Harbour Bridge, its arch bursting with color, while a supporting act of shooting stars launches from city buildings and barges on the harbor, setting the night sky ablaze with 7,000 tons of fireworks, shot off in two displays: the family-friendly 9 p.m. fireworks and the midnight extravaganza.

The gardens offers two catered events and two public viewing areas. You can dine under the stars on a three-course meal at the **Midnight at the Oasis** event, or you can dig into a gourmet picnic basket at the **Lawn With a View** event (bring your own blanket); tickets to both events sell out weeks ahead *(www.rbgsyd.nsw.gov.au, $$$$$)*. The public viewpoints—Mrs Macquaries Point and Tarpeian Precinct—begin filling well before showtime, so arrive early to claim to your spot and join the thousands of others picnicking and socializing in the hours prior to the fireworks.

If the gardens aren't for you, there are many other designated public viewpoints around Sydney; a map can be found at the official website *(www.sydneynewyearseve.com)*. The islands and parks of Sydney Harbour National Park are also prime real estate for the display. Or take to the water: Sydney Ferries offers a cruise (*tickets on sale early November; www.sydneyferries.info*) and other more expensive cruises operate (see pp. 88–89).

from 1817, which flank the road on the southern side) and was open during daylight hours only. Since 1860, it has remained open 24 hours a day, at times serving as a resting place for the destitute, as poet Paterson attests. The Domain was also the venue for cricket matches, once nearby Hyde Park became too congested.

It was and still is a venue for rallies, protests, and public meetings that have shaped the future of the city and the nation. On Sundays, it is a "speakers' corner," with pundits declaiming from boxes.

At lunchtime, the Domain is very much alive with soccer players and joggers. In December and January, the park becomes one of the major venues for Christmas and New Year's celebrations. Carols are sung by candlelight in late December, and in January, every Saturday, jazz, country and western, pop, classical, and opera concerts are staged—all free. Giant video screens and an all-encompassing sound system ensure everyone can see and hear the performances. A highlight of the classical music concert is Tchaikovsky's *1812 Overture,* complete with cannon, fireworks, and the sound of the bells of St. Mary's Cathedral on nearby College Street.

However, it is the pleasure of an evening of entertainment under twinkling stars that is the main attraction. As Dorothea Mackellar wrote in a poem about a group of children from Woolloomooloo she had seen in the Domain: "Elf-light, owl-light, / Elfin-green sky; / Under the fig trees / Bats flit by" ("Dusk in the Domain," 1919).

It's still like that. ■

A Walk From Hyde Park to Circular Quay

This itinerary is one of Sydney's best walks, taking in the grand central boulevard of Hyde Park, the historic buildings of Macquarie Street, and the Art Gallery of New South Wales. Finally, the harbor esplanade winds through the Royal Botanic Gardens to Sydney Opera House. And it's all downhill.

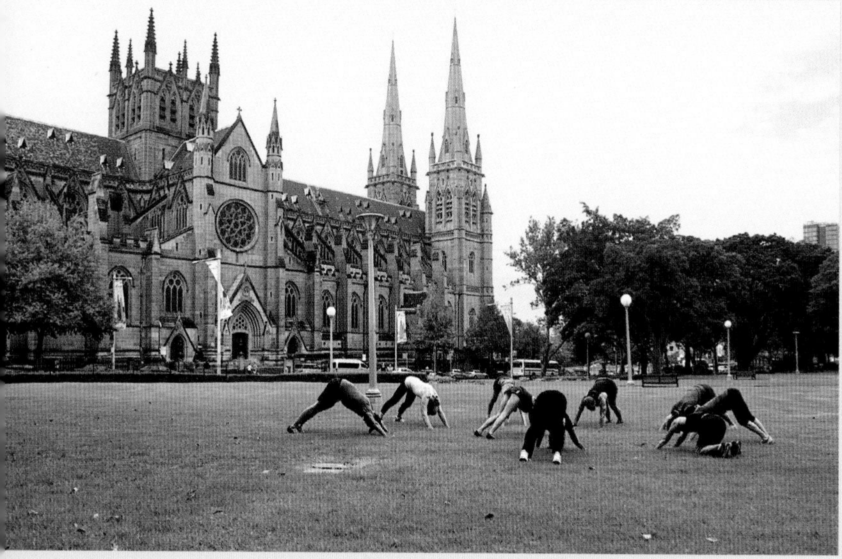

In the shadow of St. Mary's Cathedral, yogis practice their downward dog in Hyde Park.

From behind Museum Station in Hyde Park, walk to the 98-foot (30 m) art deco **Anzac War Memorial** ❶, erected in 1934 to commemorate those who died in World War I. Inside is a museum dedicated to Australian military campaigns from WWI to Iraq.

The **Pool of Reflection** next to the memorial is usually used as a birdbath by seagulls, Pacific or black ducks, ibis, and water hens. Hyde Park was the city's first public space, and Australia's first recorded cricket matches were played here in 1804. The matches subsequently moved to the Domain (see pp. 56–57) when space in the park became restricted.

NOT TO BE MISSED:

Anzac War Memorial • St. Mary's Cathedral • Sydney Hospital

From the memorial, amble north along the park's central avenue and cross Park Street. On the right, a wisteria grove in the **Sandringham Memorial Garden** ❷ provides a heady perfume in the summer months. The gardens were opened in 1954 by Queen Elizabeth II in memory of King George V and King George VI.

Return to the central avenue and continue northward to arrive at the **Archibald Fountain** ❸, which dates from 1932. J. F. Archibald founded the *Bulletin* magazine (Australia's version of *Time*) and established the Archibald Prize for portraiture in 1920. Just west of the fountain on the city (left) side is a giant outdoor chess set, generally in use every lunchtime during the week. The central avenue is lit up with fairy lights at night, and visitors may spy possums scurrying across the lawns after dusk falls.

On College Street, which runs parallel to the central path on the east side of the park, is **St. Mary's Cathedral** *(College & Cathedral Sts., tel 9220 0400)*. Free tours on Sundays at noon include the extraordinary mosaic floor

- See also map inside front cover C2
- ➤ Museum Station, Hyde Park
- Allow 2 hours to half a day
- 3 miles (5 km)
- ➤ Circular Quay

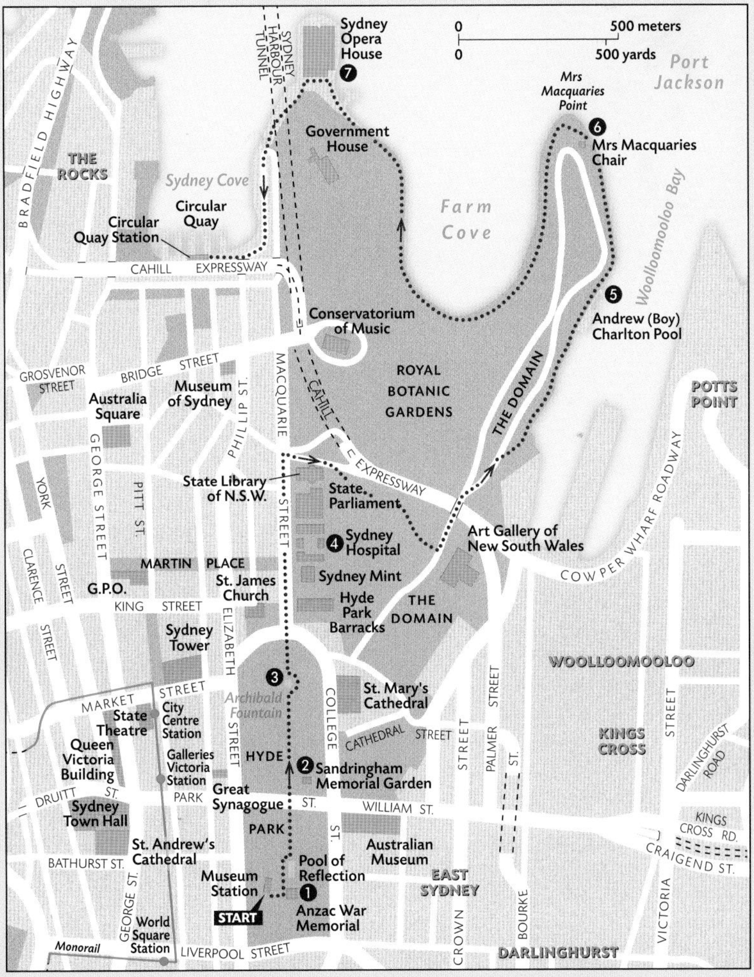

of the cathedral's crypt. It took dedicated local artisans, the Melocco brothers, 16 years (1930–1946) to complete. They also created the floor of the Mitchell and Dixson Libraries foyer within the State Library of N.S.W. (see p. 69), farther along Macquarie Street, and the State Theatre foyer. Also on College Street is the Australian Museum (see pp. 66–67).

Beyond Hyde Park

At the northern end of the park, enter Macquarie Street, with statues of Queen Victoria and her husband, Prince Albert, on the left and right, respectively. Francis Greenway's **St. James Church** (1822) is on the left, and his **Hyde Park Barracks** (see p. 69) are on the right. The former **Sydney Mint** (see p. 70) stands next door to the barracks.

On the other side of the Sydney Mint is the **Sydney Hospital ❹**. Outside is "Il Porcellino," a reproduction of the boar in Florence's Mercato Nuovo; it was donated to Sydney by a family of Italian surgeons who worked in the city. The bronze animal has a shiny nose that people rub for luck . . . well, it's worth a try. The hospital itself has a beautiful central courtyard and fountain overlooked by the Nightingale Wing (1869), built to house Australia's first professional nurses.

Continue through the hospital courtyard into the Domain, or walk to the end of the block to visit the other Macquarie Street buildings (see pp. 68–70) and continue around the State Library of New South Wales to the northern end of the Domain. Cross the Domain to the Art Gallery of New South Wales (see pp. 61–65) on the east side, then follow the path to the left over the Cahill Expressway into the Royal Botanic Gardens (see pp. 54–56).

Keep to the path to the right, overlooking the water, to reach the **Andrew (Boy) Charlton Pool ❺**. Charlton, a revered champion swimmer, was a gold medalist in the 1,500 meters race of the 1924 Paris Olympics.

From the pool, the path leads northward to the water's edge to **Mrs. Macquarie's Chair ❻**, a large seat carved out of the rock for the governor's wife, Elizabeth. Follow the path around the grand sweep of Farm Cove, exit through the gates of the botanic gardens, and carry on around the base of the **Sydney Opera House ❼** (see pp. 46–49).

Westward, you can get a plate of oysters and a glass of sparkling wine or orange juice at the Sydney Cove Oyster Bar *(1 Circular Quay East, tel 9247 2937)*.

The walk concludes at the bus, train, ferry, and taxi terminus of Circular Quay.

Great Synagogue

Amid all the commercial activity in the center of the city, the Great Synagogue *(187 Elizabeth St., tel 9267 2477, www.greatsynagogue.org.au)* offers a respite from the shops and traffic. Facing Hyde Park, the synagogue was consecrated in 1878, although the history of Australian Judaism reaches back to a small number of Jews who arrived with the First Fleet in 1788. It was designed by Thomas Rowe in Byzantine style. Special features are the wrought-iron gate and railings, whose design is repeated in the wheel window above, and the decoration of the interior. Tours of the synagogue and a visit to a small museum (entry from Elizabeth St.), are conducted on Tuesdays and Thursdays at noon *($$)*. The tour is a great opportunity to see the interior of the synagogue. Look at the star-speckled ceiling in particular. The volunteer guides are very knowledgeable and willing to answer any number of questions.

Note that before and during World War II many Jews fled to Australia to escape persecution. Their story and more of the history of Australian Jews is told at the Sydney Jewish Museum (see p. 147).

Art Gallery of New South Wales

Established in 1874, the Art Gallery of New South Wales has one of the premier art collections in the country. Its emphasis, as you would expect, is on Australian art, from all periods, but there are also notable pieces of Impressionist and Asian art—a legacy of the local Asian community and generous Asian patrons who have close business relationships with Australia.

Exhibitions from overseas galleries are also mounted in the museum, many involving the cream of the art world, and other exhibits present retrospectives by local artists. Annually, entries in three of Australia's leading art prizes—the Archibald (named after Jules François Archibald, 1856–1919) for portraiture, the Wynne (Richard Wynne, died 1895) for landscape, and the Sulman (Sir John Sulman, 1849–1934) for watercolor—are displayed and judged, often controversially.

Designed by colonial architect W. L. Vernon, the gallery (extended in 1988) is built on a hillside in the Domain. The collection exhibits are spread over five levels, ascending and descending from the ground level. Guides and floorplans to the gallery can be obtained from the visitor information desk on the ground level. The upper level holds temporary exhibitions, while Lower Level 3 houses the exceptional **Yiribana Aboriginal and Torres Strait Islander Gallery** (see pp. 136–137), opened in 1994, dedicated to Australian Aboriginal art.

Henry Moore's sculpture "Reclining Figure, Angles" (1980), outside the Art Gallery of New South Wales

Free Sydney

The Art Gallery of New South Wales is just one of Sydney's many stellar free attractions in what can be otherwise an expensive city to visit. Here are others to enjoy:

- **Any of Sydney's wonderful beaches**
- **Museum of Contemporary Art**
- **Royal Botanic Gardens**
- **Sydney Harbour National Park (try Bradleys Head walk, or visit Middle Head Fort)**
- **Sydney's markets (Paddy's Markets, The Rocks Markets, and Paddington Markets top the list.)**
- **Sydney Observatory**
- **The Rocks Discovery Museum**
- **Walks (As well as the walking tours in this book, the walk from Bondi to Tamarama or Coogee is a must, or the Harbour Circle Walk has one- to four-day options.)**

Art Gallery of New South Wales

Map p. 45

Art Gallery Rd., The Domain

9225 1744

Sydney Explorer, Martin Place Station

www.artgallery.nsw.gov.au

Ground Level

The entrance to the building is on this floor, and what an entry it is. Take a moment to admire the grand ceiling before moving on to the 19th-century European and Australian art galleries and the 20th- and 21st-century Australian collection, where one of the must-sees is Elioth Gruner's "Spring Frost," which won the Wynne Prize in 1919. You'll also find the gallery gift shop and a restaurant serving modern Australian cuisine on this level. Ask at the main information desk for details of talks and visiting exhibitions.

The **19th-Century European Gallery** is small, but it contains many outstanding pieces of art. Those of particular interest are James Whistler's "Nocturne in Grey and Silver" and works by several of the Impressionists, including Camille Pissarro, Claude Monet, and Henri Toulouse-Lautrec.

From here, you can walk straight through to the **19th-Century Australian Gallery,** which presents some of the most revered works in the country. Arthur Streeton's "Fire's On" (1891) depicts a railway tunnel blast, but the landscape dominates the painting. Tom Roberts's classic "The Golden Fleece" (1894) is another must-see.

INSIDER TIP:

For free cultural entertainment, head to the Art Gallery of New South Wales for its Art After Hours program, held Wednesday evenings. Doors stay open until 9 p.m. for films, talks, and performances among the exhibits.

—VALENTINE QUADRAT
National Geographic Channel

Lower Level 1

Head down the escalators to Lower Level 1 and you'll be among the Asian collections. The Asian collection, comprising art, sculpture, tapestries, and pottery, is well worth a visit. There are exquisite pieces from across Southeast Asia, China, and Japan. You'll

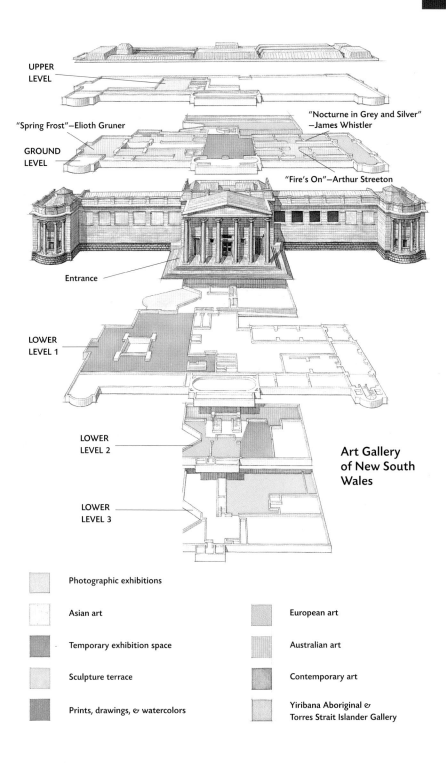

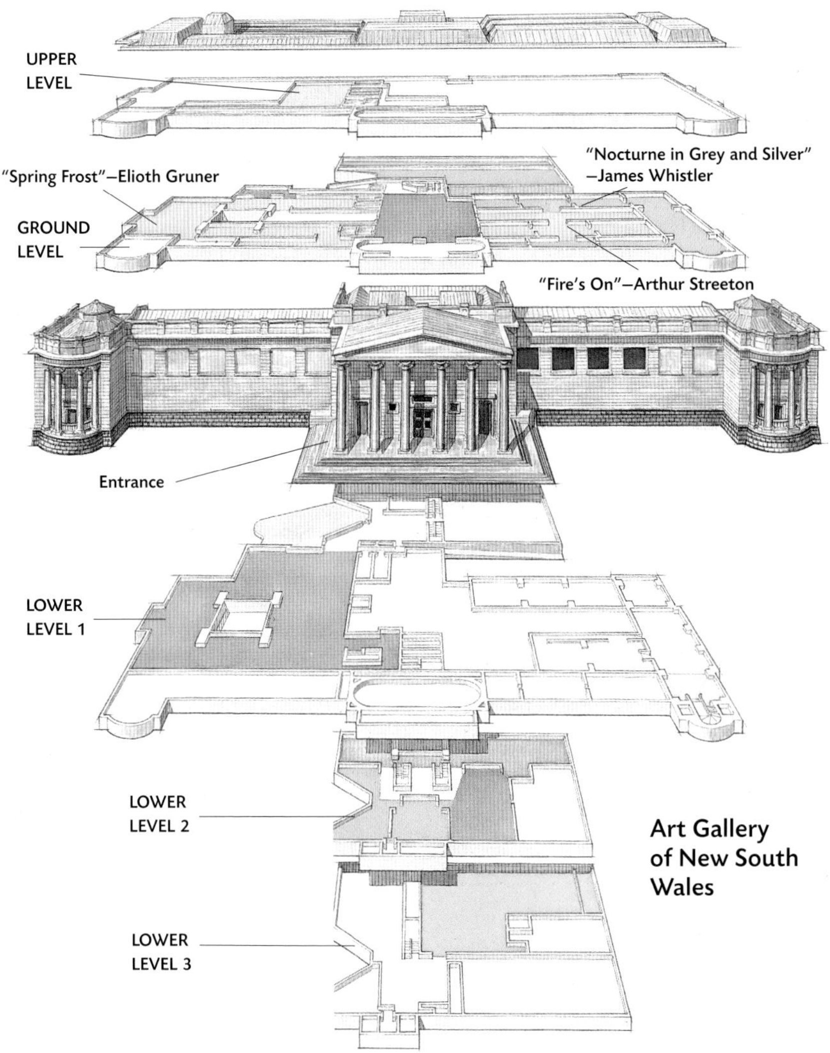

Art Gallery of New South Wales

Photographic exhibitions

Asian art

Temporary exhibition space

Sculpture terrace

Prints, drawings, & watercolors

European art

Australian art

Contemporary art

Yiribana Aboriginal & Torres Strait Islander Gallery

Artists' Views of Sydney Harbour

When the First Fleet sailed into Sydney Harbour, painters were on board ready to record one of the most momentous events in English history. They started a documentary process that has continued in Australian art for more than 200 years. Charles Gore, for example, recorded the fleet entering Botany Bay in 1788, and a watercolor by William Bradley, first lieutenant aboard the *Sirius,* shows the fleet entering Port Jackson.

Grace Cossington Smith's "The Bridge in Curve"

You can see these and other representations of the harbor at the State Library of New South Wales (see pp. 69–70) and Art Gallery of New South Wales (see pp. 61–65). If you tour through the galleries of 19th- and 20th-century art, you can trace the development of the city and the harbor through the eyes of some of Australia's best known artists.

In 1865, Eugène Von Guérard (1811–1901) painted "Sydney Heads," a luminous work whose setting (although considerably changed) is partly visible from the gallery itself. Two works from 1888 reveal a quite different view of the city—that of a busy working port. Charles Conder (1868–1909) painted "Departure of the *Orient,* Circular Quay," which shows the arrival of the steam age and the area where the Opera House is now located, while Tom Roberts (1856–1931) painted "Autumn Morning, Milsons Point," with the mist punctuated by the comings and goings of passenger ferries.

Heidelberg School

Near these two works are some of the best known paintings by artists of the Heidelberg school, a group of painters who had a major influence on Australian art (see p. 41). The painting directly above Roberts's is by Arthur Streeton; it depicts the countryside of Heidelberg in Victoria. Another Streeton in the gallery, "Cremorne Pastoral," painted in 1895, reflects the school's interest in romanticizing and mythologizing the Australian landscape, but in a harborside context.

While walking from one room to the other, you can see the changes both in the harbor and in painting styles during the intervening years. The paintings in the 20th- and 21st-Century Australian Gallery can rotate, but regulars such as Roland Wakelin's "Down the Hill to Berry's Bay" (1916) and Grace Cossington Smith's muscular "The Curve of the Bridge" (1928–1929) show the strong influence of Impressionism. Cossington Smith's work, painted while the bridge was under construction, again captures the changing face of the harbor. From the same period, the work of Margaret Preston (1875–1963) shows the harbor as it is more often seen—fringed with the leaves of Moreton Bay figs or eucalyptuses, providing shadowy glimpses of water at dawn and dusk. The gallery also has several works by Lloyd Rees, one of Australia's most eloquent and gifted artists, including "City Skyline" (1935) and "Sydney Harbour" (1936), which show the harbor almost as French artist Paul Cézanne might have painted it. They provide a marked contrast with Rees's work from 1950, "The Harbour From McMahon's Point."

find Japanese sculpture from the 12th century, and as you walk around the gallery, the objects get much older. The Tang tomb guardian figures are youthful seventh-century works, whereas the Han figures date from the second century. Don't miss the ceremonial vases from the Zhou dynasty (1000–700 B.C.) and pottery from the Shang dynasty (2200–1700 B.C.).

Let yourself be tempted by the café on this level, which offers both harbor views and outdoor seating.

Lower Level 2

Much of the space on Lower Level 2 is devoted to temporary exhibits (usually of contemporary art). Among the contemporary galleries is the small Contemporary Project Space, which showcases new art by living artists; featured artists have included Australian Simone Mangos. There's also the new John Kaldor Family Gallery.

The more permanent areas of Lower Level 2 concentrate on late 19th- and 20th-century British and European art. Examples of the gallery's collection of works by Bacon, Braque, Degas, Magritte, Picasso, Renoir, and others are usually on display. Exhibitions of prints, drawings, watercolors, and photographs are also held in this area. ■

Detail of Sol LeWitt's 2003 "Wall Drawing #1091: Arcs, Circles, and Bands (Room)," an installation exhibited in the John Kaldor Family Gallery, a contemporary gallery on Lower Level 2

Australian Museum

The Australian Museum has been collecting specimens of the natural and indigenous history of Australia since 1827. The first buildings were erected in the 1840s, although the present edifice on College Street wasn't completed until 1868. This was the first project to be undertaken in New South Wales by government architect James Barnet.

Jumbo the elephant takes center stage in the Australian Museum's Skeletons gallery.

Australian Museum
Map p. 45
6 College St.
9320 6000
$$
Museum Station
www.australianmuseum.net.au

The museum features many stimulating displays and hands-on exhibits. Its major emphasis is on indigenous culture, ranging from spirituality and cultural heritage to themes of social justice. Regular exhibitions are staged, including dinosaurs, spiders, insects, and Egyptian antiquities, often presented with incredible giant-scale animatronic displays.

Level G (Ground Level)

The recently revamped **Skeletons** gallery provides a fascinating look at the skeletal systems of numerous creatures, including humans, kangaroos, and koalas, plus crocodiles, elephants, lions, giraffes, fish, snakes, and whales. A skeletal rider on a rearing horse is called the Bone Ranger, and a cycle machine with a skeleton shows how your bones move when you pedal.

The **Indigenous Australians** gallery showcases the history and culture of Aboriginals and Torres Strait Islanders. Boomerangs, didgeridoos, and a wide range of artifacts are on show, while Dreamtime (see sidebar p. 39) stories are told in a reconstructed cave. Other displays highlight the Aboriginal political struggle.

In addition, there is a café and a comprehensive book and gift shop here selling Aboriginal publications and artifacts.

Level 1

On Level 1 you'll find the **Planet of Minerals** and the **Chapman Mineral Collection.** The Planet of Minerals hall illuminates the vast wealth of minerals that have been found across Australia. Of particular interest are the reproductions of some of the enormous nuggets that have been found at Australian gold-fields. The Chapman collection is the bequest of Albert Chapman (1912–1996), a local builder and mineral hobbyist, who built an impressive collection of over 800 pieces of the most beautiful crystals to be found anywhere in the world.

Level 2

Directly above the Planet of Minerals is the **Bird and Insect Hall,** with particular emphasis on Australia's wide range of species. Nearby is **Search and Discover,** an area that allows you to browse through the museum's computer databases, online resources, books, magazines, and many specimens that can be handled, looked at through microscopes, and generally experienced at close range.

Also on Level 2 is the popular **Dinosaurs** exhibition *($$)*. Eighteen giants of the dinosaur world are on display, including a *Stegosaurus,* a *Tyrannosaurus rex,* the birdlike bambiraptor, and a 70-foot (22 m) *Jobaria* sauropod.

INSIDER TIP:

Be sure to visit the Australian Museum's Skeletons and Dinosaurs exhibits—perfect if you have kids.

—JILL SCHNEIDER
National Geographic photographer

Numerous fossils of some of the earliest life-forms can also be seen, as well as Eric, the opalized plesiosaur. When Eric was found, he was in danger of being sold to overseas collectors, but a public appeal raised enough money to keep him in Australia.

Surviving Australia takes a different look at Australia's weird and varied animals. On show are examples of Australia's megafauna—giant kangaroos (with fangs), giant wombats, and emus. Displays on the country's top ten venomous snakes will teach you what to avoid, along with other nasties such as sharks and poisonous spiders. The freshwater habitats have live animals, including baby crocodiles and turtles, while stories of less successful adaptations include the legendary, extinct Tasmanian tiger. The interactive table is always a hit with children.

Kidspace is devoted to children under age five, with magnifying glasses, light tables, and pods that children can enter to explore bugs, marine animals, and habitats with plenty of interactive activities.

Level 3

Level 3 is the research library, which is open to the public. ■

Macquarie Street

This is very much the "Establishment" street of Sydney, with Government House and the Conservatorium of Music (see pp. 55–56) off to the east at the northern end, and government buildings, the State Parliament House, the State Library of New South Wales, Sydney Hospital, and several other historic buildings at the southern end.

Sydney's ceremonial boulevard, Macquarie Street sees many parades, including the Anzac Day march.

Across Macquarie Street from the second set of gates to the Royal Botanic Gardens are several noteworthy buildings. The **British Medical Association House** at Nos. 135–137 stands out. Built in 1929, it features griffins, shield-bearing lions, and knights guarding the top of the building. Next door, at No. 133, is **History House.** It is part of a row of grand terraced houses that used to grace Macquarie Street, now one of the few remaining Victorian terraces in the Central Business District. History House was completed in 1872 and is now used both as a functions and meetings center and headquarters for the Royal Australian Historical Society. A reference library, which the public is welcome to use, includes records of convict transportation. Helpful staff is ready to assist and provide details of the society's program of lectures.

At the corner of Bridge and Macquarie Streets are two of the city's most impressive buildings. Take a while to admire the statuary and stone carving on the former Colonial Secretary's Building, now the **Public Works Minister's**

INSIDER TIP:

At the Hyde Park Barracks, you can get a sense of convict living by trying on a pair of leg shackles.

—JANE SUNDERLAND
National Geographic contributor

Office. Dating from the 1870s, it was designed by colonial architect James Barnet.

On the opposite corner of Bridge Street from the works office building, the **Hotel Inter-Continental** *(117 Macquarie St., tel 9253 9000)* rises above the facade of the former Treasury Building, completed in 1851 and designed by colonial architect Mortimer Lewis (1796–1879). Constructed on a slightly less imposing scale than the works office, it nevertheless incorporates some fine stonework on the front facade. Inside is a large atrium with a café and, of course, the entrance to the hotel, which has splendid views of the Royal Botanic Gardens and harbor. There is an interesting connection between this building and the birth of Australian viticulture (see p. 210).

State Library of New South Wales

Farther south, just beyond Bent Street, the State Library of New South Wales may not strike visitors immediately as the most enthralling of destinations, but it contains a number of items of interest. The Mitchell Library, housed in the oldest part of the building (which dates from 1910, although the library has existed since 1826), has the country's greatest collection of Australiana. You can see items such as Captain Cook's diaries, eight of the ten known diaries written by First Fleeters, and numerous paintings dating from 1788. The general collection is housed in a new annex featuring changing displays that often include some of the library's rare treasures.

Worth a visit in itself is the foyer of the Mitchell Library, which has a stunning mosaic floor (1941) of marble and brass by Sydney's Melocco brothers. It presents a map of Dutch explorer Abel Tasman's voyages to Terra Australis ("great south land") in 1642 and 1643. To see other

State Library of New South Wales

Map p. 45
Macquarie St.
9273 1414

www.sl.nsw.gov.au

Hyde Park Barracks

Map p. 45
Queens Sq., Macquarie St.
8239 2311
$$

www.hht.net.au

Hyde Park Barracks

At the southernmost end of Macquarie Street, the Hyde Park Barracks was designed by convict architect Francis Greenway and built in 1819 to house the city's male convicts. Between 1848 and 1886, it became an immigration depot for single women, and the hammocks were replaced with iron beds. Destitute elderly women were cared for in the upper story. The surrounding buildings were variously used as the Government Printer, the Vaccine Institute, district courts, and the headquarters of the N.S.W. Volunteer Rifles. From 1887 until 1979, the barracks housed courtroom facilities and numerous government departments. Today, it serves as the backdrop of a museum devoted to convict Sydney. A display case with rats in it provides atmosphere, and groups can book to spend the night convict style in a dormitory complete with hammock (inquire of the staff).

State Parliament House
Map p. 45
6 Macquarie St.
9230 2111
www.parliament.nsw.gov.au

impressive examples of the brothers' work, visit the crypt of St. Mary's Cathedral (see pp. 59–60) and the State Theatre foyer (see pp. 111–113).

Rum Hospital

The buildings south of the State Library, comprising the Sydney Mint, Sydney Hospital, and State Parliament House, were originally all part of what was known as the Rum Hospital (built 1810–1816). It was financed by Macquarie giving the builders a monopoly on the lucrative rum trade in the colony, a move that made the governor very unpopular. However, Macquarie silenced his critics when he revealed that the government had profited on the deal to the tune of about U.S.$11,000.

The **Sydney Mint** *(www.hht.net.au)* is now in the hands of the Historic Houses Trust, but in the 1850s it was used to process bullion from the Australian goldfields.

Sydney Hospital next door is on the site of the central building of the Rum Hospital. The original building fell into disrepair and was demolished in 1879. A new hospital was built in its place in the 1880s with features that include marble floors, a baroque staircase, and magnificent floral stained-glass windows.

An art deco fountain, courtyard of Sydney Hospital

State Parliament House:

The third of the Rum Hospital buildings is now the seat of the State Parliament. There are three tiers of Australian government: federal, state, and local.

The New South Wales State Parliament's lower chamber is known locally as the "Bear Pit" (visit when the honorable members' fur is flying to see why). The parliament is open to the public during the week *(9:30 a.m.–4 p.m.)*, and free tours operate whenever the House isn't sitting; the public gallery is open when the parliament is sitting.

Pick up a free pamphlet on the House in the foyer and view the rotating exhibitions. The Jubilee Room lined with leather-bound volumes is worth a look, and near the main entry, a glass case displays the scissors used to open the Harbour Bridge in 1932. ■

Sydney's oldest suburb, today a lively tourist enclave with plenty of shops, galleries, restaurants, and historic pubs

The Rocks

Introduction & Map 72–73

Foreshore 74–75

The Rocks Walk 76–79

Experience: Cooking Aussie Style 78

Observatory Hill 80–84

Feature: Architectural Sydney 82–83

Experience: Gain an Architectural Education 83

Hotels & Restaurants 240–242

The ASN Company Building (1884), built on The Rocks' foreshore

The Rocks

The Rocks was once the working-class area to the west of Circular Quay. Here, starting in 1788, convicts were originally held in tents and the first ramshackle houses were built. Much of the work of the port was carried out here during the colony's early days, as is evident by the many warehouses that reach around the waterfront beyond the imposing facades of the Museum of Contemporary Art and the Overseas Passenger Terminal.

Numerous historic buildings line George Street, the first street laid down in The Rocks.

NOT TO BE MISSED:

The latest exhibit at the Museum of Contemporary Art **74–75**

Cadman's Cottage, Sydney's oldest house **75**

Having a pint at Lord Nelson Brewery Hotel, Sydney's oldest pub **77**

Shopping for souvenirs at The Rocks Markets on weekends **78**

Wandering cobbled lanes, such as Nurses Walk **79**

Observing the night sky at Sydney Observatory **81**

Behind them, tiny cottages cluster together in narrow avenues, and there is a pub on nearly every street corner. These days, the area has been turned over almost entirely to tourism, with dozens of gift shops and eateries ranging from cheap and cheerful cafés to restaurants serving the finest fare. There are also several hotels and a few small museums, and the area is the base of the Sydney Theatre Company.

While most of the land between Sydney Cove and Darling Harbour is referred to as The Rocks, the western side of the promontory is known as Millers Point. Here cheek-to-jowl terrace houses tell of the working-class origins of the area. ■

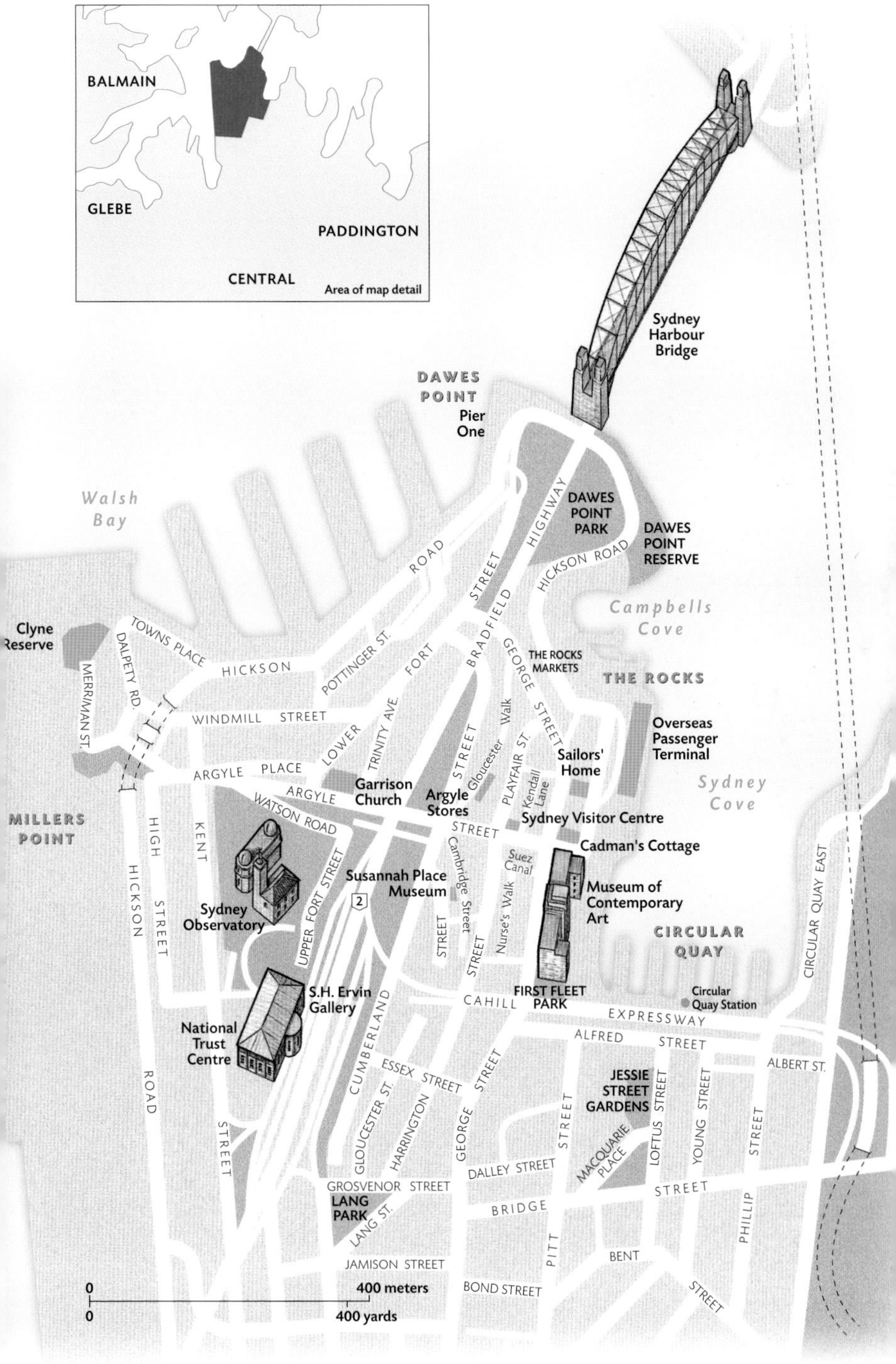
BALMAIN
GLEBE
PADDINGTON
CENTRAL
Area of map detail
Sydney Harbour Bridge
DAWES POINT
Pier One
Walsh Bay
DAWES POINT PARK
DAWES POINT RESERVE
HICKSON ROAD
Campbells Cove
THE ROCKS MARKETS
THE ROCKS
Overseas Passenger Terminal
Sydney Cove
Clyne Reserve
TOWNS PLACE
DALPETY RD.
MERRIMAN ST.
HICKSON
POTTINGER ST.
FORT
BRADFIELD
HIGHWAY
STREET
GEORGE STREET
WINDMILL STREET
LOWER
TRINITY AVE.
Gloucester Walk
PLAYFAIR ST.
Kendall Lane
Sailors' Home
ARGYLE PLACE
ARGYLE
STREET
Garrison Church
Argyle Stores
Sydney Visitor Centre
MILLERS POINT
WATSON ROAD
Cadman's Cottage
Suez Canal
Cambridge Street
Nurse's Walk
Museum of Contemporary Art
CIRCULAR QUAY
CIRCULAR QUAY EAST
HICKSON ROAD
HIGH STREET
KENT STREET
Sydney Observatory
UPPER FORT STREET
Susannah Place Museum
2
S.H. Ervin Gallery
National Trust Centre
CUMBERLAND
CAHILL EXPRESSWAY
FIRST FLEET PARK
Circular Quay Station
ALFRED STREET
ALBERT ST.
ESSEX STREET
GLOUCESTER ST.
HARRINGTON
GEORGE
JESSIE STREET GARDENS
LOFTUS STREET
YOUNG STREET
PHILLIP STREET
PITT STREET
MACQUARIE PLACE
DALLEY STREET
GROSVENOR STREET
LANG PARK
LANG ST.
BRIDGE STREET
BENT STREET
JAMISON STREET
BOND STREET
0
400 meters
0
400 yards

Foreshore

Since the start of the colony of Sydney in 1788, the stretch of shore on the western side of Circular Quay has been busy with the commercial activity of the city. These days, it throngs with visitors, street musicians, and vendors, while its buildings present a mixture of styles spanning the entire history of Australia.

Ever since it opened, the MCA has been one of Sydney's most vibrant centers for the arts.

Museum of Contemporary Art

- Map p. 73
- 140 George St.
- 9245 2400
- Circular Quay Station
- Circular Quay

www.mca.com.au

Museum of Contemporary Art

The Museum of Contemporary Art (MCA) is housed in the former Maritime Services Board building west of Circular Quay. Dating from the 1930s, it is a huge art deco edifice. The MCA, established in 1989 by the University of Sydney, has been operating since 1991.

The museum underwent major renovations in 2011–2012, adding a modern wing with rooftop venues and expanded gallery space. It is Australia's only major institution dedicated to contemporary art, but because the amount of work it holds is so great (over 4,000 pieces), no one piece of the collection is on permanent display. So, while the MCA has works by internationally known artists such as Pablo Picasso and Henry Moore, as well as such local artists as Brett Whiteley and Maria Kozic, it is a matter of luck as to which works you'll see.

Even the walls don't stay in the same places—they're constantly being shifted and shaped to accommodate the diverse range of work that appears in the gallery.

In presenting contemporary art, which tests the edges of what does and doesn't work in the public and artistic consciousness, the MCA has created more than its fair share of headlines. There is a reasonable expectation, therefore, that any visit will yield experiences that are stimulating, challenging, shocking, amusing, and exciting.

The MCA also houses a very popular café with wonderful views of the harbor, along with a well-appointed gift shop.

Foreshore

Next to the MCA is **Cadman's Cottage,** built in 1816 for John Cadman, a convict transported to New South Wales for stealing a horse. This simple, two-story building is the oldest surviving house in the city. Cadman was eventually pardoned and went on to become the superintendent of government boats. The cottage is now an information center for the New South Wales National Parks and Wildlife Service; it's also the reservations center and meeting place for tours to several of the harbor's islands (see pp. 98–99).

Just beside Cadman's Cottage is the old **Sailors' Home,** now a popular Thai restaurant. It was built in 1864 to provide visiting sailors with decent lodgings while they were in port, a function it served until 1980. For many years, it housed the Sydney Visitor Centre, which has now moved a block back from the harbor.

Continue on the foreshore to reach the **Overseas Passenger Terminal** and take the escalator to the top level for great views across to the Opera House. There are various eateries in and around the terminal, which is also a major bus tour departure point; the tour office is at the southern end.

On the northern side of the terminal, past the tower of the ASN Company Building (1884), is **Campbells Cove.** The first wharves were built here in the early 1800s by a merchant, Robert Campbell, who also built the dockside warehouses (Campbells Storehouses) that now house a collection of restaurants with wonderful harbor views. Cruises of the harbor are conducted by Sydney Harbour Tall Ships' reproduction of an 1850s square-rigger moored at the wharf.

INSIDER TIP:

In late July, the annual Rocks Aroma Festival is staged throughout The Rocks. You can sample (for a small fee) coffee brewed by 20-some top Australian roasters and learn how they make the perfect cup.

—JEANINE BARONE
National Geographic writer

The sweep of new buildings beyond Campbells Storehouses is the Park Hyatt Sydney. Continue around the boardwalk to Dawes Point (see p. 76), where Sydney Harbour Bridge vaults across to North Sydney at the narrowest point in the main harbor. ■

Cadman's Cottage

Map p. 73
110 George St.
9247 5033

Sydney Visitor Centre

Map p. 73
Argyle & Playfair Sts.
9240 8788

Rocks Aroma Festival

www.therocks.com

The Rocks Walk

A short stroll though The Rocks provides an excellent snapshot of the social, commercial, and maritime history of Sydney, plus wonderful views of Sydney Opera House, Sydney Harbour Bridge, and the harbor. This extremely compact area is jammed with historic buildings, shops, galleries, and countless restaurants and pubs. Around every corner, you'll find plenty of surprises that can turn an hour-long walk into a whole day's outing.

The Friday food market at The Rocks serves up a cornucopia of delectable dishes and produce.

From **Circular Quay ❶** (see pp. 50–53), follow the foreshore to the west, then north to **Dawes Point ❷**. The point was named after Lt. William Dawes, an officer of the First Fleet who established Australia's first observatory (initially for the purpose of observing Maskelyne's comet). Dawes fixed the exact position of Sydney in latitude and longitude with more than 300 observations, and he was one of the first Europeans to record much of the language of the local Aborigine.

Just to the west of the Harbour Bridge is **Pier One ❸**, an upmarket hotel with restaurants, bars, function rooms, and some impressive inner harbor views. This is the first of four finger wharves that were built in Walsh Bay in the 1920s. The others have been converted into prestige apartments and

NOT TO BE MISSED:

Dawes Point • Lord Nelson Brewery Hotel • Garrison Church • The Rocks Markets • Susannah Place Museum

offices, with a selection of cafés and bars. If you continue past Pier One, Pier 4/5 is home to the Sydney Theatre Company's **Wharf Theatre** *(Pier 4, Hickson Rd., Walsh Bay, tel 9250 1777)*. On the same wharf, you'll find two of the city's premier dance companies: Sydney Dance Company and Bangarra Dance Theatre. There are restaurants here, too, and a bar with wonderful harbor views, or drop in for a dance class (beginners welcome).

Backtrack to a path that leads up to **Dawes Point Park ❹**, directly beneath the bridge, where a battery of cannon from the 1840s is all that remains of a fort built on the site of the first observatory, established by Dawes. Cutting through the park is Lower Fort Street, with a row of Victorian terraces that dominated the heights of The Rocks before the Harbour Bridge was built.

Lower Fort Street to Argyle Cut

Farther along Lower Fort Street, the **Hero of Waterloo ❺** *(tel 9252 4553)* is one of the typical pubs of the area. Built in 1884, it is one of the city's oldest hotels. Another old-timer, the **Lord Nelson Brewery Hotel,** around the corner on Kent Street in Millers Point, is well worth a detour for the atmospheric bar and the many beers for which it is famous. Built in 1834 and licensed in 1841, it claims to be the oldest licensed pub in Sydney (but don't mention that if you go into the Fortune of War Hotel, 137 George Street, which claims a lineage back to 1828).

Back on Lower Fort Street, continue to the end and turn left onto Argyle Street. Well worth a visit is the **Garrison Church ❻** (Holy Trinity Church, 1840), on the left, with a fine stained-glass east window. The church was designed by Edmund Blacket (1817–1873) and built from stone quarried from the **Argyle Cut ❼**, just down the hill on Argyle Street. The cut

See also map inside front cover C5
- ➤ Circular Quay
- Allow 1.5 hours
- 1.5 miles (2.4 km)
- ➤ Circular Quay

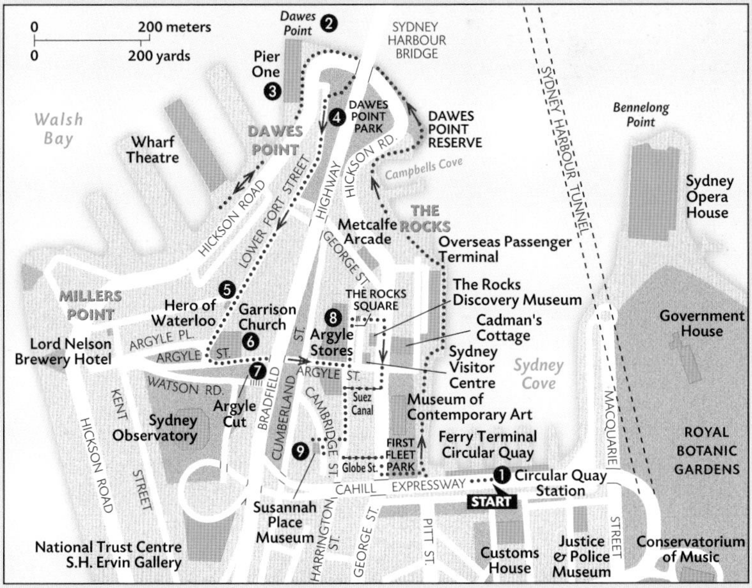

EXPERIENCE: Cooking Aussie Style

Sydney is a great place to try your hand at cooking Aussie style, especially focusing on two important culinary influences: Asian cuisine and seafood. At Sailors Thai *(106 George St., tel 9251 2610, www.sailorsthai.com.au)*, a Rocks restaurant well known for innovative Thai food, you can learn some of the finer arts involved in cooking Thai with an Australian twist. It passes on some of its secrets on the first Saturday of every month in a four-hour class *($$$$$)*, with the menu based on seasonally available local produce, maybe including seafood. There's no maybe about seafood being on the menu at the Sydney Seafood School *(tel 9004 1111, www.sydneyfishmarket.com.au)*, however. Located at the fish market in Pyrmont, this school will instruct you in more than just throwing shrimp on the barbie, delving deep into the sea for such ingredients as octopus, sea snail, and red mullet. Renowned visiting chefs demonstrate how to prepare the dishes, and then you re-create them. A two-, three-, or four-hour class *($$$$$)* is offered most days of the week. Check the website for details.

was carved through solid rock by convicts in 1843 and completed by free labor in 1859; you can still see the marks of the chisels.

At the bottom of the cut, the Argyle Stairs lead up to Cumberland Street and the start of the walk across the Harbour Bridge (see pp. 94–95). At the top of the stairs, you can continue past the **Glenmore Hotel** (which has a rooftop beer garden with great harbor views) to **Gloucester Walk** (see sidebar opposite), or if you want to end your walk at this point, continue east along Argyle Street into the heart of The Rocks, down to the harbor, and back to Circular Quay.

Alternatively, continue to walk along Argyle Street to reach the four-story **Argyle Stores** on your left. These converted warehouses were built in 1828 as bond stores and are now dominated by the Argyle, a sprawling bar/entertainment venue.

The Heart of The Rocks

On the next corner at Playfair Street is the Sydney Visitor Centre *(tel 9240 8788)*. Turn left into Playfair Street, which leads to **The Rocks Square ❽.** Here there is plenty of weekend entertainment and you can see the "First Impressions" sculpture, a sandstone monument to the convicts, soldiers, and free settlers of the early colony.

Drop down from the square and you'll find yourself on Kendall Lane, near the stores and restaurants of **The Rocks Centre** and **The Rocks Discovery Museum** *(tel 9240 8680)*. The latter explores the area's history from the Aboriginal Cadigal people through the early days of the colony to the 1970s. Stroll down farther still and you'll be on George Street. If it's the weekend, you'll have noticed—and probably been diverted north by—**The Rocks Markets,** which sets up stalls at the top of George Street. Here you'll find ceramics, original artworks, photographs, jewelry, handmade soaps, and plenty of food. On Fridays, a food market sets up. On the east side of George Street is the **Metcalfe Arcade,** former bond stores that house several major galleries and boutiques. Farther south on the corner of Hickson Road, the **ASN Company Building** is a grand edifice built for a steamship company in 1884. It houses the gallery of artist Ken Done, famous for his colorful portraits of Sydney.

George Street, the major street of The Rocks, was the first road to be built in the area. It replaced the track that ran from the western side of the Tank Stream (see p. 53) out to Lieutenant Dawes's observatory and gun battery on Dawes Point (see p. 76). Originally known as Spring Row, George Street was renamed in 1810 to commemorate King George III and boasts some of the most important heritage buildings in Australia. These include Cadman's Cottage (see p. 75), the former Police Station (1882), and the Mariner's Church (1856).

Just after crossing Argyle Street, keep an eye out for an alley heading off George Street to the right. Known as the **Suez Canal** because of the river of water that used to flow down it during a heavy rain, this narrow lane is much as it was in the 1850s. The Rocks used to be full of such lanes, the haunt of gangs who preyed on the unwary, among them sailors who often found themselves kidnapped and sold to other ships.

Harrington Street & Beyond

The Suez Canal links through to Harrington Street. Halfway along the street is **Nurses Walk,** another cobbled lane that looks much as it did in the 19th century, and which offers interesting shops and restaurants in a quiet pedestrianized area. Harrington Street is a busy shopping and hotel area that contains **Reynolds Cottage,** one of the city's earliest two-story houses at No. 28–30, built in 1830 by Irish blacksmith William Reynolds; it now houses Bonza Bike Tours.

Just west of Harrington Street is **Susannah Place Museum** ⑨ *(58–64 Gloucester St., tel 9241 1893, closed Mon.–Fri., except Jan.),* a row of four terraced houses and a corner store dating from 1844. The buildings now house a small museum of 19th-century inner-city life.

The Harbour Bridge arcs from The Rocks to North Sydney, across the harbor's narrowest point.

From Susannah Place, turn right onto Harrington Street, then take a left to Globe Street, which will take you back to the main thoroughfare of George Street. Turn left into **First Fleet Park,** a good place to rest your weary legs before returning to Circular Quay.

Gloucester Walk

Of all the lanes in The Rocks, be sure to stroll along Gloucester Walk. From the northern end of George Street, climb westward across the top of a cliff that looks down into the gardens of the pubs and shops on George Street.

Information boards detail the earliest history of the area, which is known as Bunker's Hill, after a U.S. skipper, Capt. Eber Bunker (from Plymouth, Massachusetts), who was involved in the first whaling operations in New South Wales. A desirable residential area in the 1820s, the houses of Gloucester Walk, formerly Gloucester Street, were demolished after an outbreak of plague at the turn of the 20th century.

In a short distance, you will reach Foundation Park, with all that remains of some of the earliest houses in Australia. The sidewalk bears the numbers of the houses, and modern sculptures re-create some of the atmosphere of previous eras. From the park, it is just a short walk to the small flight of steps that leads to the top of the Argyle Stairs.

Observatory Hill

On the western side of The Rocks, Observatory Hill towers over central Sydney and was a strategic site for the early colony. This vistaed retreat from the downtown bustle is home to the Sydney Observatory, once a fort on the highest point in the city, and the National Trust Centre, housed in a former military hospital. At the northwestern foot of the hill lies Millers Point, a quiet district of workers' cottages and warehouses, several now converted into apartments or hotels.

Assorted buildings of the Sydney Observatory—note the time ball at the base of the weathervane.

Sydney Observatory

- Map p. 73
- Watson Rd., Observatory Hill
- 9921 3485
- Free. Viewing sessions $\$\$$–$\$\$\$$
- Bus 431 or 432, or City Sightseeing bus

www.sydney observatory.com.au

Observatory Hill, the highest point in the Sydney area at 140 feet (43 m), was formerly known as Windmill Hill because the first windmill to be built in the colony in 1795 originally stood on the site. A few years later, in 1804, the construction of Fort Phillip was begun on the hill so the government would have somewhere to retreat in the event of an uprising.

As it turned out, four years after Fort Phillip was built, there actually was an uprising. However, the governor at the time, Capt. William Bligh, retreated not to the redoubt but under his bed and was placed under house arrest. Two of the fort's walls now form part of the observatory, which replaces the smaller one built on Dawes Point (see p. 76) in the early years of the colony.

To get an overview of Millers Point, from the Lord Nelson Brewery Hotel (see p. 77), cross Hickson Road to the elegant

INSIDER TIP:

Grab lunch to go at the Fine Food Store *(Mill & Kendall Lns.)* and head to the National Trust Centre to picnic on the grass with a spectacular view of the Sydney Harbour Bridge.

—JILL SCHNEIDER
National Geographic photographer

Palisade Hotel on Bettington Street. Continue northward onto Merriman Street, where you can look across to the west of Darling Harbour. Plans for residential and business development include making this a financial center modeled on Wall Street.

Sydney Observatory

Established in 1858 in Italian Renaissance–style buildings, the observatory took some of the first astronomical photographs of the southern sky, as part of an international project to produce the first complete atlas of the night sky. It operated until the 1980s, when the bright lights of the city made use of the telescopes impractical. Sydney's rainfall is still measured on the site, however.

There is no charge to wander around the grounds and view the observatory exhibitions. Along with telescopes, videos, and hands-on astronomical exhibits, the museum has information about the site's history and its contribution to astronomy. For a fee you can view films in the 3D space theater, visit the planetarium and telescope tower, and attend day and night telescope viewing sessions. The evening telescope sessions, during which you study the night sky to view planets, must be reserved online or by phone.

The park surrounding the observatory has an elegant band rotunda, with some harbor views, but the noise from the traffic on the Harbour Bridge detracts from the ambience.

National Trust Centre
- Map p. 73
- Observatory Hill
- 9258 0123
- Closed Mon.
- $$
- Bus 431 or 432, or City Sightseeing bus

www.nationaltrust.com.au

The Time Ball

In the 19th century, a vital function of the Sydney Observatory was the daily dropping of the time ball. Located in the observatory tower, the ball was dropped at the stroke of 1 p.m. (cued by the observatory's highly reliable timepieces) to signal the firing of a cannon at Fort Denison. This allowed ships to check the accuracy of their chronometers, which were crucial for navigation. The firing of the gun was stopped during World War II after an attack on the harbor by a Japanese midget submarine; several people were killed, and Sydney's residents became fearful of gunfire. The practice of firing the gun daily was resumed in 1986, and the time ball is dropped if staff are available. So, if you're in the vicinity at 1 p.m., set your watch.

National Trust Centre

The New South Wales headquarters of the National Trust of Australia, a conservation organization focused on the built, cultural, and natural heritage of the country, is housed in Governor Macquarie's military

(continued on p. 84)

Architectural Sydney

As Australia's oldest city, Sydney is the best repository of the country's architectural styles from Georgian to postmodern. Though much of the city center is dominated by modern skyscrapers, whole heritage streetscapes remain preserved.

Gothic Revival–style Government House, the official residence of the governor of New South Wales

Georgian & Victorian Years

The city's early development was haphazard and unplanned, with shoddy building standards. No buildings survive from the first years of the colony established in 1788 at Sydney Cove (present-day Circular Quay). For the earliest extant architecture, head west to Parramatta, where you'll find the oldest house in the country, Elizabeth Farm (1793), an Indian-bungalow-style homestead with wide verandas, and Old Government House (1799), a fine example of old colonial Georgian architecture.

It was not until Lachlan Macquarie became governor in 1810 that the colony assumed some order and significant public buildings were commissioned. Many were designed by architect Francis Greenway (1777–1837), a convict transported for forgery, whose achievements include Hyde Park Barracks (1819; see p. 69), St. James Church, and the neo-Gothic Conservatorium of Music (1821; see p. 56). Greenway also played a role in the construction of Cadman's Cottage (1816) in The Rocks, the oldest surviving house in Sydney.

The Rocks was established soon after colonial settlement and has some of Sydney's oldest buildings, many built of the sandstone that gave the area its name. Early houses such as the Susannah Place Museum (1844; see p. 79) remain, though some of the oldest buildings are pubs like the Lord Nelson (1836) and the Hero of Waterloo (1843; see p. 77 for both). Elsewhere in the city center, the Gothic Revival style dominated public architecture, at its best in Government House (1845; see pp. 55–56) and such private mansions as Vaucluse House (1830s; see p. 158) and Bronte House (1845), the work of prolific architect Mortimer Lewis (1796–1879).

The colony boomed during Victorian times, as wealth from agriculture and then gold delivered imposing buildings. James Barnet (1827–1904), colonial architect from 1862 to 1890, was responsible for the General Post Office (1890; see p. 53), the Australian Museum (1864; see pp. 66–67), the Customs House (1884; see pp. 50–51), and scores of other buildings. The diversity of styles also boomed, from Italianate to Gothic, Tudor to Queen Anne, Moorish to Anglo-Dutch.

20th Century

American architect Walter Burley Griffin (1876–1937) found fame as the designer of Australia's spacious capital Canberra in 1913. In 1920s Sydney, he applied his Prairie School principles and unique vision to the model suburb of Castlecrag, where he designed an estate and stone houses to blend with the natural bushland of Middle Harbour. Some of the most delightful architecture of the art deco era can be found at Sydney's bathing pavilions, such as those at Bondi (1929) and Balmoral (1929) beaches.

Office towers such as the skyscraper-Gothic Sun Building in Phillip Street mushroomed in the city center in the latter half of the century, and high-rise apartments grabbed prime harbor-view sites. A building boom in the 1960s threatened the city's rich architectural heritage, but much of The Rocks and the Victorian streetscapes of the inner suburbs escaped the wrecker's ball thanks to resident action groups backed by building union "green bans" in the 1970s.

During this period, Harry Seidler (1923–2006) was the city's leading light of modernism. Of his nearly 200 buildings, most notable are the MLC Centre skyscraper (1977) and the Rose Seidler House (1950) in the suburb of Wahroonga, built for his parents and now a museum.

Above all, Jørn Utzon (1918–2008) steals the prize for Sydney architecture, even though he designed only one building and left the country in disgust before it was finished. Utzon never did see his completed Sydney Opera House (see pp. 46–49), but his stunning vision, years ahead of its time and construction techniques, changed the image of the city forever.

EXPERIENCE: Gain an Architectural Education

Gain a greater understanding of Sydney's character by studying its architectural evolution on any number of walking tours. Wander the warren of streets in The Rocks, stroll down ceremonial Macquarie Street, and duck into laneways and elegant shopping arcades to discover how Sydney's grand and not-so-grand buildings form the perfect backdrop for the city's vibrant yet laid-back attitude. You can explore on your own, using the excellent series of Historical Walking Tour brochures produced by the City of Sydney—available at the Sydney Visitor Centre (see p. 75) or Sydney Town Hall (see pp. 114–115)—but you'll find guided walks more entertaining.

Sydney Architecture Walks *(www.sydneyarchitecture.org, $$$$$)* offers architect-led, two-hour tours that explore the architectural themes of selected city buildings, as well as a harbor walking tour and a tour focusing on the Opera House. The **Australian Architecture Association** *(www.architecture.org.au, $$$$$)* takes a look at the city's skyscrapers and the adaptive reuse of heritage buildings in its informative two-hour Sydney City Walk on Saturday mornings and occasionally runs other tours.

A number of general walking tours also cover the history and architecture of Sydney. Operators include **The Rocks Walking Tours** *(www.rockswalkingtours.com.au)*, **Sydney Walking Tours** *(www.citywalkingtours.com.au)*, and **Secrets of Sydney Walking Tours** *(www.secretsofsydney.com.au)*.

Salon des Refusés

An annual Australian autumn highlight of the S. H. Ervin Gallery, the Salon des Refusés (Salon of the Rejected) exhibits the best of the paintings that didn't make the cut for the prestigious Archibald (portraiture) and Wynne (landscape) Prizes (see p. 61). Named after the 19th-century event in Paris that gave artists such as Manet and Pissarro a public viewing after being rejected by the French Academy as too radical, it similarly highlights alternative works and showcases emerging artists.

hospital of 1815. Situated just behind the observatory, the building was used by the soldiers quartered in George Street until it moved to Victoria Barracks in Paddington in 1848. The building, with its neoclassical facade added in 1871, operated as a school until 1974. The National Trust moved into the premises in 1975 and has information relating to the many significant buildings in Sydney and New South Wales.

S. H. Ervin Gallery: Don't miss the S. H. Ervin Gallery, which occupies an annex of the military hospital, built in 1841, and operates on a similar but much smaller scale to the Art Gallery of New South Wales (see pp. 61–65) or the MCA (see pp. 74–75).

The gallery opened in 1978 and has been consistent in bringing interesting and easily digestible exhibitions for the public. In keeping with its relationship with the National Trust, its constantly changing exhibitions often have a historical theme relating to Australia's cultural heritage, both European and Aboriginal.

The traditional tearooms on the premises provide refreshments. ■

The grounds of the National Trust Centre command impressive views of Sydney Harbour.

The jewel of the city, with spectacular coves, bays, islands, and, just a ferry ride away, the beach resort of Manly

Sydney Harbour

Introduction & Map 86–87

Cruises 88–89

Sydney Harbour Bridge 90–93

Experience: Scale the Harbour Bridge 91

Harbour Bridge Walk 94–95

Taronga Zoo 96–97

Experience: Walk Out to Bradleys Head 97

Harbor Islands 98–99

Feature: Shipwrecks 100

Manly 101–104

A Walk From The Spit to Manly 102–103

Experience: Surf Sydney's Waters 105

More Places to Visit Around Sydney Harbour 106

Hotels & Restaurants 242–243

New Year's Eve fireworks explode off the Harbour Bridge.

Sydney Harbour

When Governor Phillip first entered Sydney Harbour in 1788, he wasn't exaggerating when he claimed "a thousand ships of the line could safely shelter in it / There'd be room to spare." The harbor was named Port Jackson by Captain Cook when he sailed past North Head and South Head in 1770, and it has been seducing visitors ever since. A very safe waterway, it has only one reef in the main harbor and deep water nearly everywhere else.

One of the main attractions is that, although surrounded by the most populous city in Australia, the harbor has managed to retain much of its natural beauty. Sydney Harbour National Park takes in many of the headlands and islands, and plenty of short walks snake through the harborside suburbs and bushland, with places to stop for a leisurely picnic.

The harbor, a drowned river valley covering 22 square miles (57 sq km) with 150 miles (240 km) of shoreline, comprises three main arms: North Harbour is the smallest, Middle Harbour reaches into the hilly terrain of the northern suburbs, and Port Jackson itself is navigable all the way to Parramatta, 15 miles (24 km) inland.

Options for exploring these waterways abound. You can walk around them, sail on them, take off and land on them in seaplanes, cross Harbour Bridge, or rent kayaks and paddle along some of the more sheltered parts. ■

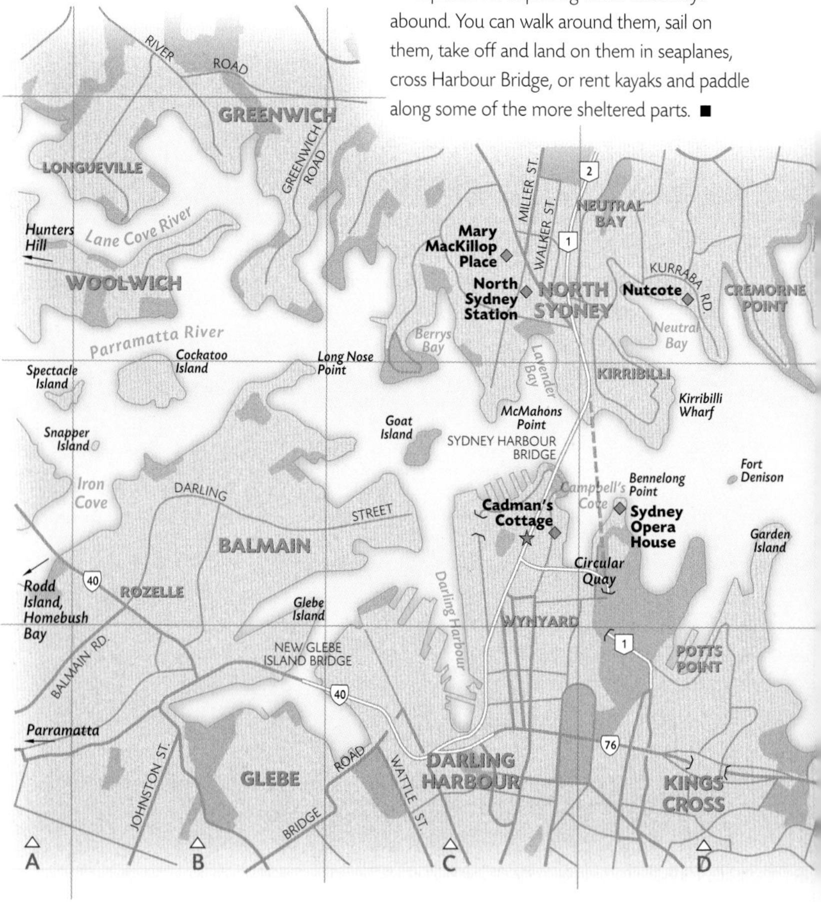

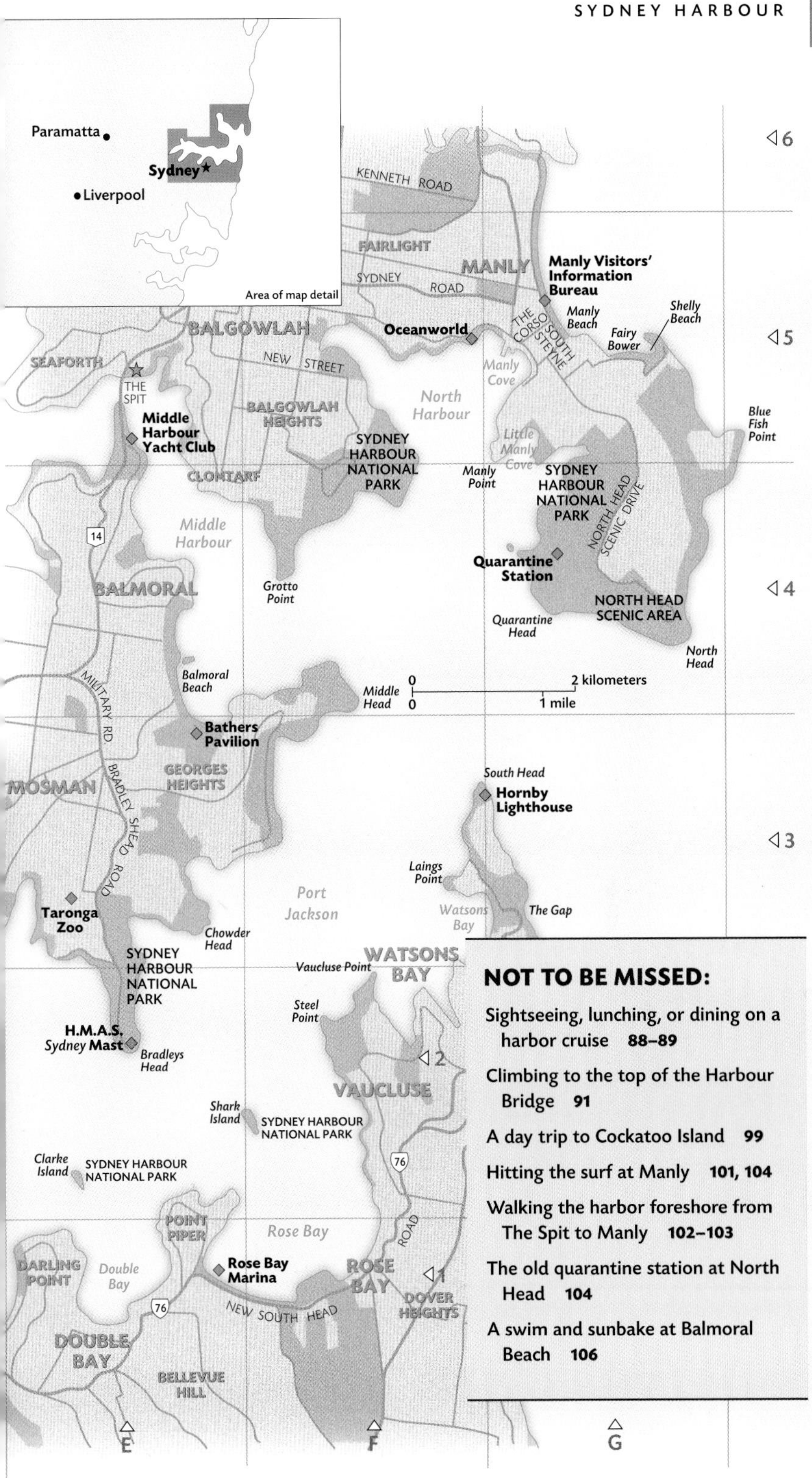

NOT TO BE MISSED:

Sightseeing, lunching, or dining on a harbor cruise **88–89**

Climbing to the top of the Harbour Bridge **91**

A day trip to Cockatoo Island **99**

Hitting the surf at Manly **101, 104**

Walking the harbor foreshore from The Spit to Manly **102–103**

The old quarantine station at North Head **104**

A swim and sunbake at Balmoral Beach **106**

Cruises

You can't say you've been to Sydney until you've taken a trip on its world-famous harbor, even for the briefest of passages. And, unsurprisingly, there are a number of ways to do just that. So many, in fact, that it can be confusing. Take a moment to work out what you'd like to see—the classic journey from Circular Quay to Manly on a regular ferry, perhaps, a lunch or dinner cruise, a harbor lights cruise, or a short trip on a square-rigger. Then it's bon voyage.

Regardless of the weather, a ferry ride on Sydney Harbour never disappoints.

Sydney Ferries
☎ 131 500
www.sydneyferries.info

Sydney Ferries

Sydney Ferries operates from Circular Quay and services Manly, Kirribilli, Neutral Bay, Cremorne, Mosman and Taronga Zoo, Watsons Bay, and Rose Bay east of the bridge; and Balmain, Darling Harbour, Woolwich, and Parramatta to the west. The Manly trip is a must, but a run on the RiverCat to Parramatta (see pp. 186–187) takes in some of the idyllic harborside suburbs, wharf areas, and waterfront industries of the working port. It also passes the Olympic site at Homebush.

Tour Operators

Numerous companies operate a wide selection of tours. The major operators are **Captain Cook Cruises, Vagabond Cruises,** and **Magistic Cruises.** Cruise details are available from booths at Darling Harbour and Circular Quay and from the tourist office. All three companies offer cruises ranging from one to three hours with a choice of morning tea, lunch, or dinner, priced accordingly.

All three companies operate cruises from King Street Wharf, at the northern end of Darling

Harbour, and at Circular Quay, usually picking up at both destinations.

Captain Cook, the biggest operator, also runs the Sydney Harbour Explorer from Pier 26 near the aquarium at Darling Harbour every 45 minutes, stopping at Circular Quay, Fort Denison, Taronga Zoo, Shark Island, Watsons Bay, and Luna Park. Passengers can embark and disembark at their leisure from 9:30 a.m. to 6 p.m. As well as a Zoo Express service that includes entry to the zoo, Captain Cook also has two-night weekender harbor cruises on a small cruise liner.

Alternatives proliferate, with many companies offering specialized cruises. The paddle steamers of **Sydney Showboats** depart from King Street Wharf 5 at 7 p.m. for an all-singing, all-dancing dinner show; they also offer sunset happy-hour cruises from 5 p.m. Vagabond has jazz luncheon cruises and an Aqua Latino floor show and dinner cruise.

Sydney Harbour Tall Ships' reproduction of an 1850s square-rigger leaves Campbells Cove north of Circular Quay near the Park Hyatt Hotel. This considerably more rustic vessel provides plenty of photo opportunities and offers mast-climbing experiences as well as a host of cruises.

For those who like to combine thrills with their sightseeing, **Jet Cruiser** tours the inner harbor before unleashing its high-speed engines. It also runs a cruise through the heads to Bondi and back.

Yachts & Charters

Sailing enthusiasts, and those who just want to get out onto the water and have a bit more control, are well catered for, too. **Sydney by Sail** has three-hour yachting tours that also teach sailing basics. It is based at the Australian National Maritime Museum (see pp. 128–129), where several interesting vessels also conduct short cruises.

There are many yacht, sailboat, and cruiser charter companies, with or without skippers. These include **Ausail** and **Eastsail,** which provide self-sailing or sailing with a skipper. Waking up on a yacht moored in a cove of Sydney Harbor could well be a highlight of your visit.

If a small catamaran, sailboat, or dinghy with outboard is more to your liking, try **Balmoral Boatshed** at Middle Harbour. On the south side, try **Rose Bay Marina** or **Rose Bay Aquatic Hire.** ■

Slip, Slop, Slap

This enduring health campaign slogan delivers the message to "slip on a shirt, slop on sunscreen, and slap on a hat" to avoid skin cancer. Surrounded by wonderful beaches, blessed with a warm climate and abundant sunshine, Australians reveled in their sun-bronzed image until health studies showed Australia had one the world's highest skin cancer rates. Visitors are also advised to follow the slogan.

Tour Operators

Capt. Cook Cruises
☎ 9206 1111
www.captaincook.com.au

Vagabond Cruises
☎ 9660 0388
www.cvagabond.com.au

Magistic Cruises
☎ 8296 7222
www.magisticcruises.com.au

Sydney Showboats
☎ 8296 2700
www.sydneyshowboats.com.au

Sydney Harbour Tall Ships
☎ 8243 7961
www.sydneytallships.com.au

Jet Cruiser
☎ 9807 1999
www.jetcruiser.com

Yachts & Charters

Sydney by Sail
☎ 9280 1110
www.sydneysail.com

Ausail
☎ 9960 5511
www.ausail.com.au

Eastsail
☎ 9327 1166
www.eastsail.com.au

Balmoral Boatshed
☎ 9969 6006
www.balmoralboatshed.com.au

Rose Bay Marina
☎ 9363 5930

Rose Bay Aquatic Hire
☎ 9371 7036

Sydney Harbour Bridge

Along with the Opera House, the Sydney Harbour Bridge is an instantly recognizable icon that says "Sydney." For 30 years, it was the tallest structure in the city, and even now it dominates the harbor. It is one of the architectural and engineering wonders of Australia and, like the Opera House, you may find it has a surprise in store. When you see it for the first time, you'll discover that it's far grander than any photograph can convey.

The Harbour Bridge spans the harbor's narrowest point, connecting The Rocks and Milsons Point.

Sydney Harbour Bridge
Map 86 C2
$ Bradfield Hwy. toll $. Free to cyclists & pedestrians

Known locally as the "Coat Hanger," the bridge was designed by Dorman Long and Co. of England to specifications of its chief engineer, Dr. John Bradfield (1867–1943). It carries eight lanes of traffic, two railroads, and two walkways—pedestrians are permitted on the eastern walkway and cyclists on the western walkway—on a deck that is 161 feet (49 m) wide.

Prior to the construction of the bridge, travel between north and south Sydney was by ferry or a 12.5-mile (20 km) road journey skirting the harbor. The decision to build the bridge was a welcome relief to the struggling ferries, and its opening triggered a building boom on the north side of the harbor.

EXPERIENCE: Scale the Harbour Bridge

If you've got a good head for heights, you'll want to tackle one of Sydney's premier experiences: the tour to the top of the Harbour Bridge arch with BridgeClimb *(5 Cumberland St., The Rocks, tel 8274 7777, www.bridgeclimb.com, $$$$$)*. Judging by the celebrity photos, everyone has done it, and the jumpsuits all climbers don are a great fashion leveler. Other gear includes a belt and slider clip that attaches to a safety wire, and military headsets to hear the climb leader's commentary, which is often riveting (yes, that's a pun).

The climb up and down the arch's catwalks and ladders is not overly taxing, with plenty of stops on the way, and the views from the top are fantastic, right across to the Blue Mountains and over the Pacific on a clear day. The only drawback is that you cannot bring loose objects, including cameras, on the climb, but free group shots are given out, or you can buy solo pics. You have a choice of three tours: Express (2.25 hours), Bridge, and Discovery (the latter two both 3.5 hours long), offered from dawn to dusk as well as at nighttime.

Bridge work started in 1923 when the city was enjoying prosperity, but was completed during the Depression in 1932. In these difficult years, the bridge became a symbol of hope for the future.

The opening ceremony in March 1932 was interrupted when an anticommunist, Francis de Groot, rode forward on his horse and slashed the opening ribbon with a sword before it could be cut officially by the Labour premier, Jack Lang. After de Groot had been led away by the police, the ribbon was quickly rejoined and the official ceremony continued.

INSIDER TIP:

The Harbour Bridge climb is worth the splurge: It's a novel experience and it offers epic views. Try to go at dusk, when the city lights start to come on.

—SADIE QUARRIER
National Geographic
magazine photo editor

Vital Statistics

The bridge weighs 58,200 tons (52,800 tonnes); when it was built it was the widest long-span bridge in the world (over 1,650 feet/503 m). The bridge was originally designed to carry up to 6,000 cars an hour, but now tops 15,000 at peak times. Sixty years after the bridge's opening, the Sydney Harbour Tunnel was built to help cope with the increasing volume of traffic between the north and south shores.

Of the 1,400 workers employed in the construction of the bridge, 16 were killed in accidents, mostly due to the absence of safety rails.

Today, maintaining the steel structure is an endless job: A single coat of paint requires 8,000 gallons (30,000 liters) and takes a team of bridge painters around ten years to apply—at the end of which it's time to start again.

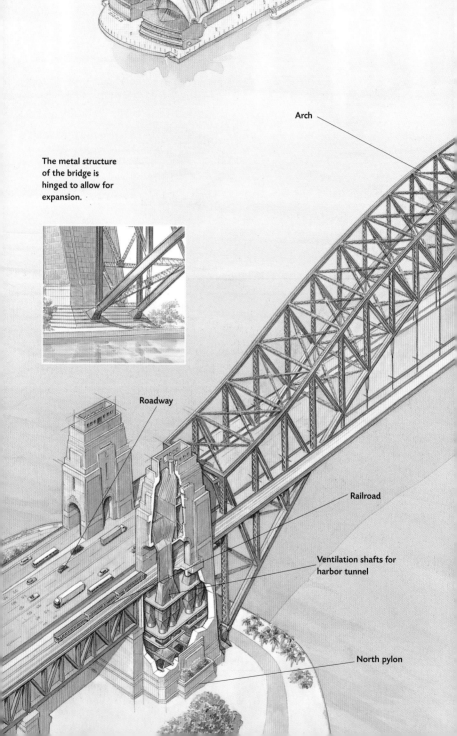

The metal structure of the bridge is hinged to allow for expansion.

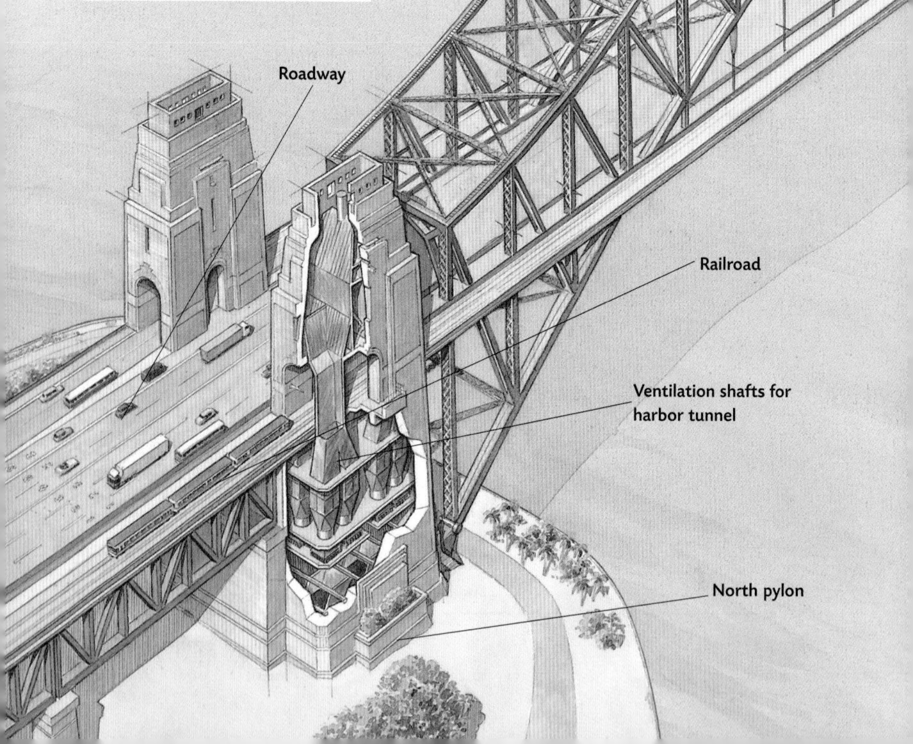

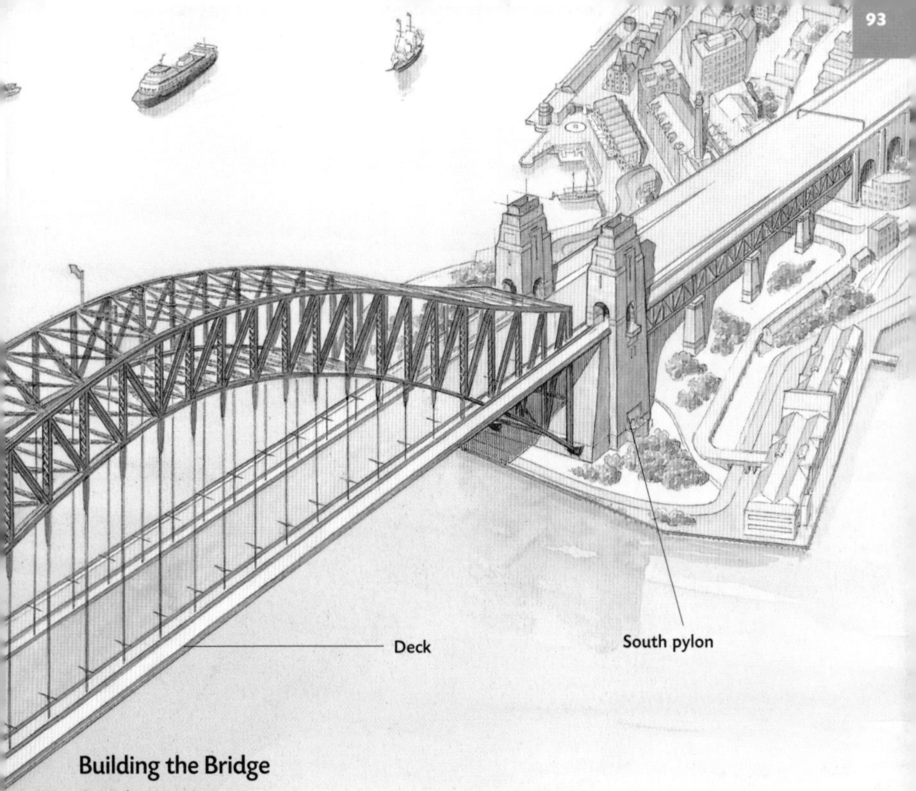

Building the Bridge

On July 28, 1923, construction on Sydney Harbour Bridge began with the ceremony of the "Turning of the First Sod" at North Sydney. At the time, the final design had yet to be chosen, and it was not until March 24, 1924, that the offer of Dorman Long and Co. was accepted.

Once the foundations had been built, work on erecting the two halves of the arch, using creeper cranes, commenced in October 1928. Each half was firmly anchored by steel cables fixed in horseshoe-shaped tunnels dug into rock. By August 1930, the two half arches were ready to be joined, the gap between them just 3.5 feet (1.07 m) apart.

Later that year, the deck was hung from the center outward, and by April 1931, both arch and deck were complete. ■

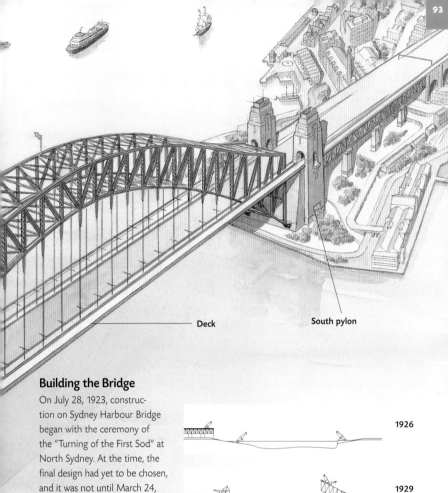

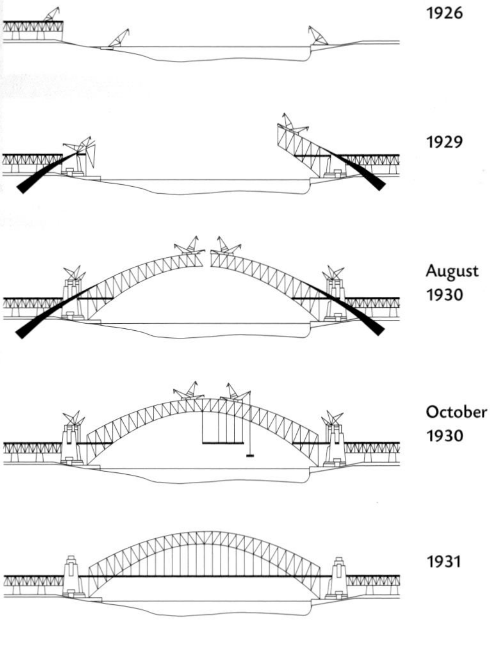

Harbour Bridge Walk

This short walk across the bridge from the city to Kirribilli and Milsons Point provides spectacular views of the harbor. If you want to make a longer route, combine it with The Rocks Walk (see pp. 76–79).

Start on the south side of the bridge at the entrance to the pedestrian walkway, located on the other side of the street from the Argyle Stairs that climb to the top of the Argyle Cut on Argyle Street (see p. 77).

As you move onto the Sydney Harbour Bridge, one of the most wonderful views imaginable unfolds around you. Almost directly below are The Rocks, Circular Quay, and Sydney Cove. You have a bird's-eye view of the Opera House on Bennelong Point. Beyond it, you'll see the sandstone structure of Fort Denison (see pp. 98–99) rising straight out of the harbor. Behind that and to the right, the high-rise apartments of Darling Point stand on the water's edge, with Rose Bay and Vaucluse behind them. On the left are Kirribilli, Cremorne, and Mosman, with the bush-clad promontory of Bradleys Head.

A harborfront amusement park, Luna Park has been a Sydney attraction since 1935.

NOT TO BE MISSED:

Pylon Lookout • North Sydney Olympic Pool • Bradfield Park

The **Pylon Lookout** ❶ *(tel 9240 1100, $$$)* on the city side of the bridge is well worth a visit (pedestrian access only). Not only are the views from the lookout itself—a 200-step climb—among the best in the city, but there are displays of photographs and information about the construction of the bridge in the lower levels in the base of the pylon.

Those with a good head for heights can brave the three-hour walking tour to the top of the bridge arch with BridgeClimb (see sidebar p. 91). The views are fantastic.

Kirribilli & Milsons Point

Continuing to the far side of the bridge, descend the steps and double back under the bridge to Milsons Point. From here, walk down the hill to the harbor and the **North Sydney Olympic Pool** ❷, a popular spot for a refreshing swim with spectacular views. Although it is no longer used for international competition, it has a rich heritage, with 86 world records set at this pool. This is due to the extra buoyancy, and

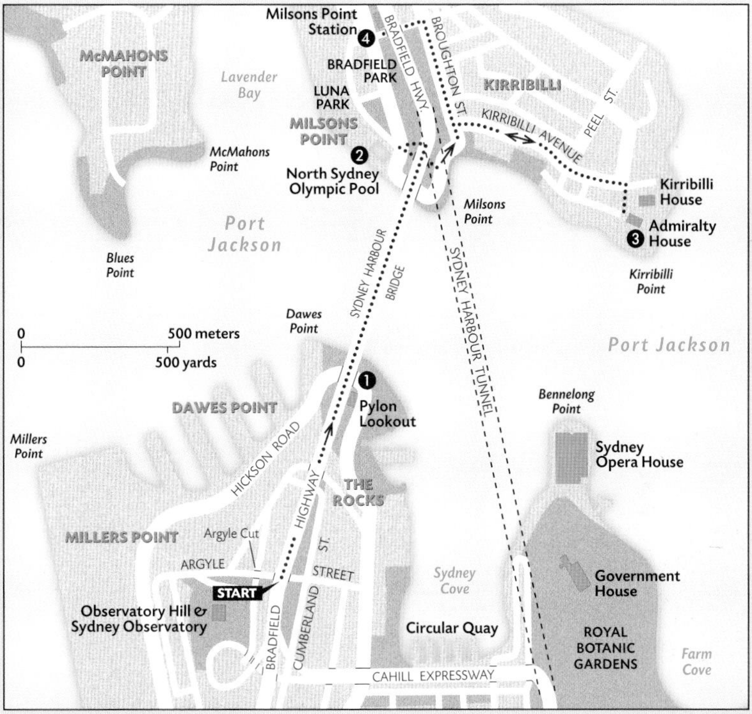

therefore speed, afforded to swimmers by the saltwater.

On the far side of the pool, the large, laughing face over the entrance to **Luna Park** *(tel 9033 7676)* is a Sydney landmark. Based on its Coney Island cousin, this delightfully old-fashioned amusement park opened in 1935 and thrilled generations of Sydneysiders until it closed in 1979 after a fire. After ongoing campaigns and failed business proposals, it finally sputtered back to life in 2004, minus its prime roller coaster ride, the Big Dipper, due to resident complaints about noise. Work continues, but most of the old rides have now been restored. Entry is free, and a variety of ride tickets will delight children young and old.

Walk back under the Sydney Harbour Bridge to **Bradfield Park,** where there is an unobstructed view across to the Opera House and city. When you head back up the hill, the road to the right, Kirribilli Avenue, winds around to **Kirribilli House** (the Australian prime minister's Sydney pile) and **Admiralty House** ❸ (the governor-general's Sydney residence). These are only open to the public on special occasions.

Retrace your steps along Kirribilli Avenue and then head up Broughton Street, where there are a number of cafés. Cross Broughton Street to **Milsons Point** ❹ and go under the bridge to the railway station. Alternatively, walk back across the bridge or take a ferry from Luna Park.

- See also map inside front cover C5
- ➤ Entrance to pedestrian walkway, south side of bridge
- Allow 2 hours
- 1.5 miles (2.4 km)
- ➤ Milsons Point

Taronga Zoo

One of the quickest and easiest ways to get acquainted with the wildlife of Australia is to visit Taronga Zoo, one of the country's largest collection of native and exotic animals. As a bonus, it is superbly located on a hilltop position overlooking the city and the harbor (*taronga* is Aboriginal for "water view").

The Tasmanian devil and other native Australian fauna are popular draws at Taronga Zoo.

From the ferry, the best option is to take the cable car or a bus up to the top entrance of the zoo and gradually make your way down. The cable car passes right over the elephants, so have your camera ready. Comprehensive guides to the zoo are available at the entrances.

As you make your way downhill, you pass koalas and native birds, including talkative cockatoos, before reaching **Reptile World,** where you see some of Australia's most dangerous creatures.

Animals are kept in environments that are as similar to their natural habitats as possible, and this can be seen in many of the African and Asian animal enclosures that mostly populate the western half of the zoo. Taronga has a strong reputation for wildlife conservation and an active endangered species breeding program. Be sure to see the gorilla rain forest, the chimpanzee park, and the Sumatran tigers (the latter are one of the zoo's captive breeding successes). The seals are always fun, and the zoo has a large collection of marine mammals.

Australian animals hold the most interest for international visitors, and the eastern part of the zoo has large enclosures and walk-through areas to get up close to kangaroos, wallabies, emus, and other indigenous creatures. The **Australian Nightlife** pavilion introduces nocturnal creatures, while the platypus pools and Australian rain forest aviary are other must-sees. The main koala enclosure features a walkway that winds up to the creatures in the treetops. Always a zoo favorite, you can book an up close encounter with these cuddly marsupials.

INSIDER TIP:

At Taronga Zoo, make sure to catch the bird and gorilla shows, both something someone at any age would love.

—JILL SCHNEIDER
National Geographic photographer

Zoo Events

Children can see and touch farm animals in the **Farm Playground.** There is also a seal show that is as educational as it is entertaining, a bird show, and talks on Tasmanian devils, gorillas, and the big cats, to name but a few.

The zoo offers guided tours with an emphasis on Australian wildlife, or you can camp out in upmarket safari tents to see the animals at night and wake up to spectacular sunrise views of the city. Contact the zoo for details. ■

Taronga Zoo
87 E3
Bradleys Head Rd., Mosman
9969 2777
$$$$$
Taronga Zoo
taronga.org.au

ZOOPASS: From any Sydney Ferries ticket office at Circular Quay Station, you can buy a travel-and-zoo ticket that includes the ferry across to Taronga Zoo at Mosman. Buying an all-in-one ticket is cheaper than buying tickets individually. Captain Cook Cruises and Vagabond also offer discounted cruise and zoo deals.

EXPERIENCE: Walk Out to Bradleys Head

After a few hours spent at Taronga Zoo, seek out the peace and quiet of Bradleys Head, just a short walk south from the zoo's lower entrance. Now part of Sydney Harbour National Park, the headland was named after Lt. William Bradley, a cartographer with the First Fleet. Tiny pockets of rain forest where colorful parrots fly lie in the valleys.

From the ferry wharf at Mosman, walk about 200 yards (180 m) up the road to a path on the right, which weaves 3 miles (5 km) through largely unspoiled bushland to the headland. Along the way of this easy walk, there are good views back toward the city and several nice spots for a dip or picnic. You can download an mp3 walking tour from the website of the **National Parks and Wildlife Service** *(tel 9247 5033, www.nationalparks.nsw.gov.au).*

At the point, you will see several cannon dating from 1871—part of the harbor defenses built to protect the city from the perceived threat of the Russian fleet—and the mast from the H.M.A.S. *Sydney,* a cruiser that participated in Australia's first naval engagement, sinking the German raider *Emden* in 1914. Note the lighthouse, one of many that dot the harbor. These include the Wedding Cakes, visible offshore from the headland, which mark the east and west channels in the main harbor. The headland is a great spot to watch freighters putting out to sea.

Retrace your steps along the path you came on to return to the city.

Harbor Islands

Scattered the length of the harbor, Sydney's islands are great places to explore the different faces of a working port. Visit a fort one day, a shipyard the next, an idyllic picnic spot the day after that. Some of the islands are no longer recognizable as such, having been bridged to the mainland, and only their names betray their previous existence—Glebe Island, west of the city, and Garden Island to the east, for example.

Now popular with picnickers, Shark Island was once used as a quarantine station for animals.

Several of the islands form part of **Sydney Harbour National Park.** The best known and most striking of these is **Fort Denison,** in the center of the main harbor. The First Fleeters named it Rock Island and banished particularly recalcitrant convicts to it with scarcely enough to eat, thus earning it the nickname "Pinchgut."

The island's golden-yellow sandstone fort was built in the 1840s and '50s after two U.S. merchant vessels were discovered at anchor in the harbor one morning, having arrived undetected and unchallenged during the night. Work on the fort wasn't completed until 1857, when it was named after the governor in office, Sir William Denison. The fort has never had to fire a defensive shot, although it fires a gun every day at 1 p.m., originally on a cue from the time ball at the Sydney Observatory (see sidebar p. 81). You can wander the fort or book a National Parks and Wildlife Service (NPWS) tour of the island and its museum. There is a café and a restaurant.

NPWS tours run on Sundays to **Goat Island,** west of the Harbour Bridge. The island was given the name by convicts because it was where goats, and later sheep, were kept. Like Rock Island, it was also where troublesome convicts sometimes found themselves. One of them, Charles "Bony" Anderson, was chained to a sandstone ledge, the "Convict Couch," for two years.

Cockatoo Island, once a prison, then a shipbuilding yard, is the largest of the harbor's islands. You can tour the convict buildings and dockyards. A bar opens in summer, and regular art exhibitions are held.

The NPWS also administers **Clarke** and **Shark Islands,** east of the bridge, and **Rodd Island,** tucked well into the harbor in Iron Cove. Shark Island, between Bradleys Head and Rose Bay, has great views up to Manly and down to the city and a small beach. Rodd Island has been popular for picnics since the early days of the colony; it has three Edwardian gazebos and a reception hall.

Getting to the Islands

Captain Cook Cruises *(tel 9206 1111)* runs ferries from Darling Harbour and Circular Quay to Fort Denison and Shark Island every 45 minutes from 9:30 a.m., and daily ferries run to Goat Island in January only. Alternatively, take a water taxi. Reservations are essential for all NPWS tours. Access to Cockatoo Island is via Sydney Ferries.

Keep an eye out for special events held on all the islands, particularly during school vacations. ■

Fort Denison

86 D2

Visitor Information

National Parks and Wildlife Service, Cadman's Cottage, The Rocks

9247 5033

www.nationalparks.nsw.gov.au

Garden Island

Garden Island, at the end of Potts Point in the Kings Cross precinct, is part of Australia's major naval base. Since 2002, part of the base has been open to the public daily from 9:30 a.m. to 3:30 p.m. Access is by Sydney Ferries only.

Here, you can view colonial fortifications, Australia's first grass tennis court, heritage rose gardens, and the former Main Signal Building. The latter once directed all naval shipping; its converted viewing platform has spectacular 360-degree views of Sydney Harbour.

The Naval Heritage Centre is full of interesting relics from visiting vessels dating back to the First Fleet, including one of the midget submarines that attacked Sydney in World War II.

You can also see the initials and date "1788" carved by one of the mariners from the First Fleet when vegetable gardens were established on the island (hence the name). Due to land reclamation, the island now abuts the mainland.

Shipwrecks

On a sparkling summer's day, when hundreds of boats flit across the surface of Sydney Harbour, the scene is idyllic. But while the harbor may be a safe haven today, several tales of disaster and woe are associated with it. One of the first vessels to visit the harbor, the First Fleet flagship *Sirius,* was wrecked off Norfolk Island in 1790. In 1834, 12 people died when the fully rigged *Edward Lombe* was wrecked on Middle Head, inside the harbor.

A memorial to the *Dunbar,* Watsons Bay

One of the blackest years in the city's maritime history was 1857. On the night of August 20, the crew of the clipper *Dunbar* mistook the lower cliffs of The Gap for the entrance to the harbor, and the ship foundered, sending 121 people to a watery grave. Just two months later, the clipper *Catherine Adamson* was wrecked on inner North Head, with 21 fatalities. The traumatic effect of these disasters was far reaching, and the following year the Hornby Lighthouse was constructed to more clearly mark the entrance to the harbor at the end of South Head.

Harbor Disasters

Tragedy has also occurred within the harbor itself. On November 3, 1927, the steamship *Tahiti,* running too fast as it rounded Bradleys Head, struck and sank the ferry *Greycliffe.* Among the 40 who drowned were many children on their way home from school.

In 1938, the small ferry *Rodney* was chartered to bid farewell to the visiting U.S. ship *Louisville.* Again off Bradleys Head, the overloaded ferry, listing to one side, capsized and 19 people were drowned.

Mystery surrounds the fate of one of the midget submarines involved in the attack on Sydney on the night of May 31, 1942. One was sunk, one became entangled in antisubmarine nets, but a third disappeared without trace. It may have been sunk somewhere in the harbor, but it has never been located, despite extensive searches with metal detectors.

Another mysterious and well-known tragedy involved just one life. One evening in the 1930s, an artist named Joe Lynch boarded a ferry with a group of friends; he was bound for a party on the North Shore, his pockets laden with bottles of beer. Lynch was last seen sitting on the rail of the boat and presumably fell overboard. No trace of him was ever found. The loss prompted his friend Kenneth Slessor to write the poem "Five Bells," which captures both the harbor's beauty and a poignant sense of mourning. The full text is in Slessor's *Selected Poems.*

I looked out of my window in the dark
At waves with diamond quills and combs of light
That arched their mackerel-backs and smacked
the sand
In the moon's drench, that straight enormous glaze,
And ships far off asleep, and Harbour-buoys
Tossing their fireballs wearily each to each,
And tried to hear your voice, but all I heard
Was a boat's whistle, and the scraping squeal
Of seabirds' voices far away, and bells,
Five bells. Five bells coldly ringing out.
Five Bells.

–Kenneth Slessor, "Five Bells" (1939)

Manly

Manly's slogan has long been "Seven miles from Sydney and a thousand miles from care." That just about sums up the shift that occurs when passengers disembark from the ferries or Fast Ferry catamarans from Circular Quay with surfboards or towels tucked under their arms. The curious name came about because of the "manly" bearing of the Aborigines noted by Governor Phillip when he encountered them on a visit there.

Queenscliff Beach, the far northern end of the same stretch of sand that comprises Manly Beach

A visit to Manly is a must-do, not least because of the trip there. As the ferry approaches the heads, you may spot dolphins, or little penguins from the colony near Manly Cove.

The obvious attraction of Manly is its beach, a short stroll from the ferry wharf through the pedestrian walkway called **The Corso.** This is a lively strip lined with shops and pubs, bearing little resemblance to its namesake in Italy. On weekends, there is an open-air market. Most of the cafés and restaurants are on the street facing the famous surf beach.

If a plunge in the high surf here isn't appealing, turn right at the beach for a short walk to the much calmer **Fairy Bower,** a small cove well protected by the headland opposite. Farther on, tucked under the headland, is **Shelly Beach,** one of the only two

(continued on p. 104)

Manly

Map 87 G5

Visitor Information

Manly Wharf

9976 1430

A Walk From The Spit to Manly

Known as the Manly Scenic Walkway, this popular 6-mile (9.5 km) walk in the Sydney area can be joined at several points along the route. It explores beautiful scenery, offers great views, and passes several small coves and arms of the harbor. You'll find plenty of opportunities for safe swimming along the way and a choice of cafés at Manly.

You can start the walk from either end, but the best option is to take the ferry to Manly and then catch a bus or taxi back to The Spit Bridge. Alternatively, buses from Wynyard in the city go to The Spit *(tel 131 500 for timetable information).*

Start in the park at the northeastern (higher) end of **The Spit Bridge.** From here, follow the path through to the harborside suburb of **Clontarf** and on to sandy **Clontarf Beach ❶.** There is a harbor pool here if you fancy a swim, plus Clonny's café-restaurant.

At the far end of the beach, follow the path into the bush once more, passing several small coves that are reasonably safe for swimming, though caution should be exercised.

Eventually you start to climb away from the water toward the heights of Dobroyd

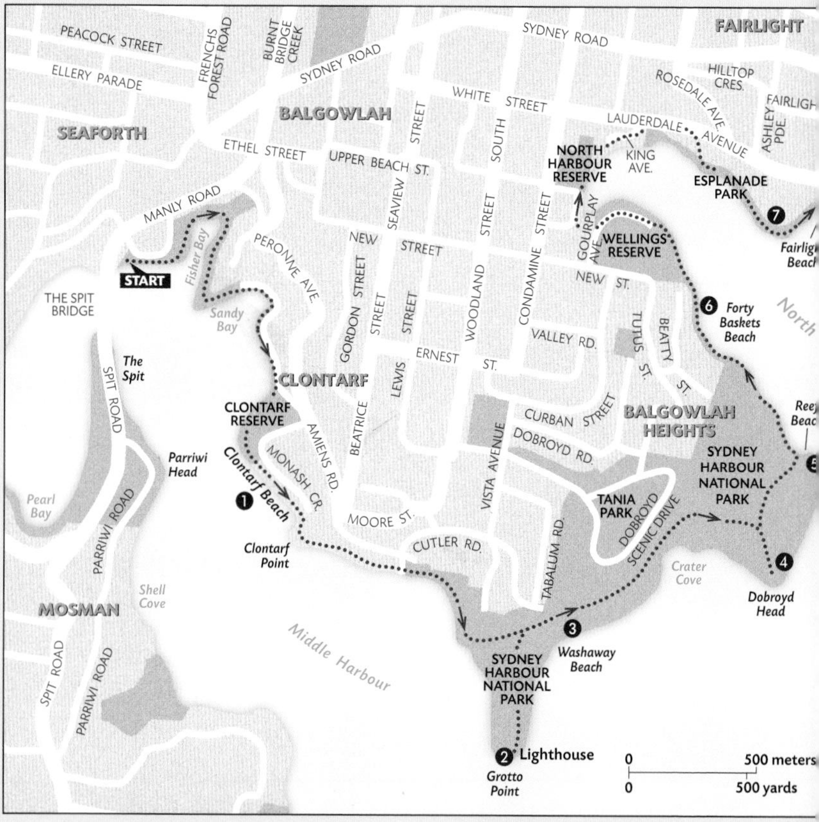

NOT TO BE MISSED:

Lighthouse on Grotto Point • Washaway Beach • Dobroyd Head • Forty Baskets Beach

Head; a branch track, lined with colorful plants and flowers, runs down to the beautiful little lighthouse of **Grotto Point ❷**. Close by Grotto Point is secluded **Washaway Beach ❸,** which faces the harbor heads and open ocean.

Up on **Dobroyd Head ❹,** the view over the harbor to Manly is worth the long uphill haul. Far below, near the water's edge, you may be able to make out ramshackle fishermen's huts that date from the Depression years and now form a small alternative-lifestyle enclave.

Follow the path away from the parking lot down to the end of the headland. From here, wind your way back to the sheltered area of North Harbour and across the sands of **Reef Beach ❺,** once a nude beach.

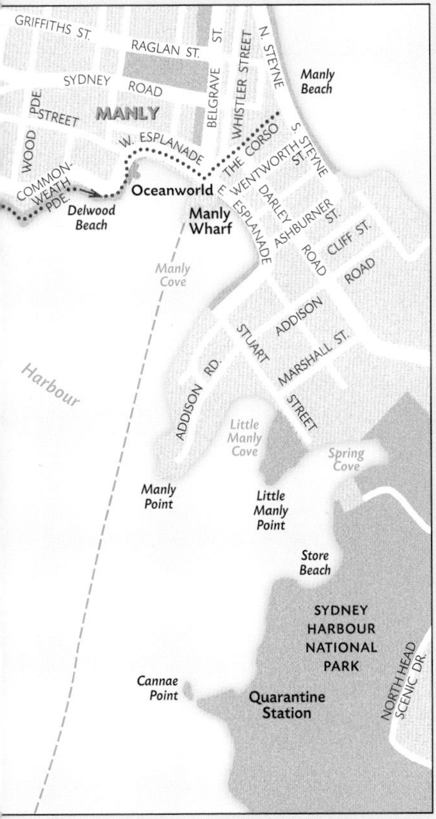

Along the Shore of North Harbour

A short distance farther on is **Forty Baskets Beach ❻,** a former fishing enclave with a harbor pool and some very exclusive real estate. The beach is so named because a catch made here of 40 baskets of fish was sent to some Sudanese troops being held at the Quarantine Station (see p. 104) in 1885. Just past Forty Baskets is a small marina.

Follow the road up past the parking lot, turn right down a path that crosses a small bridge to reach the suburb of Balgowlah, then drop down to the park at the bottom. Cross the park, with the sand flats of North Harbour Reserve on the right. Continue up the other side to King Avenue. Follow it to Lauderdale Avenue and turn right. After a short distance, branch off to the right and pass the apartments and houses of Fairlight, with their marvelous views over North Harbour.

At **Fairlight Beach ❼,** there is a harbor pool and another beach. Shortly afterward, Manly comes into view around a headland, and you drop down to the aquarium complex of **Oceanworld** (see p. 104). The bright lights of civilization await at the ferry end of the esplanade. You can take a ferry back to the city or continue along The Corso to reach Manly Beach.

- See also map p. 87 E5
- ➤ The Spit Bridge
- Allow 3–4 hours (don't forget to carry water)
- 6 miles (9.5 km)
- ➤ Manly Wharf

Quarantine Station

Just above Spring Cove, on the way to North Head, you'll find the old Quarantine Station *(off North Head Scenic Dr., tel 9466 1500, www.qstation.com.au, access by car or bus 135 from Manly Wharf).* Its attractive buildings belie a grim history, as this was where ships that could have been carrying epidemic diseases such as smallpox, Spanish influenza, and bubonic plague docked. On arrival, the passengers and crew were quarantined for several weeks. The station opened in 1832 and continued operating until 1984, when it became part of Sydney Harbour National Park. Now run by Mirvac Hotels, it offers accommodations, the Boilerhouse restaurant, and a host of tours *(reservations essential, $$$–$$$$$).*

Daytime historical tours of the station are conducted daily. They take in the hospital, the mortuary, the disinfecting showers, and the housing.

Four nights a week *(Wed.–Sun.),* a very popular tour includes ghostly tales of the supposedly haunted buildings. It can be combined with a dinner package.

The tour unit operates a number of other ghost experiences and even a spirit investigator tour using instruments to detect paranormal activity. The pinnacle of ghostliness is a ghost sleepover, in what is allegedly one of the most haunted precincts of the station.

Oceanworld
West Esplanade
8251 7877
$$$$
www.oceanworld.com.au

west-facing beaches on the east coast of Australia.

North Head, where sheer cliffs form a dramatic entrance to the harbor, has sweeping ocean and harbor views. It is accessible by foot, or there is a loop road. Buses (route 135) and short tours from Manly Wharf are available.

Oceanworld

A prime attraction in Manly, Oceanworld lies just along the esplanade from the ferry wharf. Take a seabed walk to see thousands of marine animals, including sharks—grey nurse, wobegong, white-tipped reef, and Port Jackson, among them—in the main tank. There are feeding tours, talks, and a variety of activities for children. Don't miss the exquisite coral reefs or touch pool (with guides) that provides hands-on experience of the local ecology.

INSIDER TIP:

Become a true local by signing up for surfing lessons at any of Sydney's popular beaches. Be prepared to be sore the next day—it's great exercise! The best surfing beaches are Bondi and Manly.

—FARNOUSH AFARINESH
National Geographic Channels International

The emphasis has become getting into the tanks with the sealife, and the big attraction is diving with the sharks. After an introduction to scuba diving, you spend 30 minutes in the tanks. Snorkeling and mermaid camps give children a chance to get into the water. ■

EXPERIENCE: Surf Sydney's Waters

Sydney's strong surf culture has bred a host of world champions—not surprising, given the variety and easy access to dozens of world-class waves within the city's boundaries. Experienced surfers will find a huge choice, and beginners can learn on some of the world's most famous surf beaches. The northern beaches have the best swells, but the south has some good options and big barrels—waves that create a "tube" when they break—for experienced surfers.

Northern Beaches

The long stretch of sand at **Manly** comprises Manly, North Steyne, and Queenscliff Beaches. Manly Beach is best in summer and is popular for beginners' classes. Swells increase farther north up the beach, where the first world championships were held in 1964. Just north of Manly, **Freshwater Beach** earned its place in history in 1915 when legendary Duke Kahanamoku kick-started the local scene with an exhibition of Hawaiian surfing.

Continuing northward, **Long Reef** has good surf when the westerly is blowing and is also popular with kite surfers. **Curl Curl** has reliable swells. **Narrabeen** is a long beach best known for the left-hander at North Narrabeen. Farther north, **North Avalon** has right and left beach breaks, while long **Palm Beach** ranges from gentle Kiddie's Corner in the south to some good barrels up near Barrenjoey Head.

Southern Beaches

In the south, **Bondi Beach** is crowded, but has good beginner and intermediate swells—and what an iconic beach for learning to surf. Farther south, small **Tamarama** has better waves but savage rips. **Maroubra** is the pick of the surf beaches, with long waves directly off the beach and a good right-hand break at its southern end, but watch out for the territorial 'Bra Boys surfer gang. **Cronulla,** farther south still but with easy train access, attracts crowds and surfers from all over Sydney and ranges from huge reef barrels such as Voodoo and Shark Island to gentler breaks in the south.

Surf Shops & Lessons

For board and wet suit hire, you can try **Bondi Surf Co.** *(80 Campbell Pde., tel 9365 0870)*, opposite Bondi Beach, or **Dripping Wet** *(2/93–95 N. Steyne, tel 9977 3549)* at Manly Beach. Plenty of others can also arrange dropoff and pickup.

Dozens of companies offer lessons, ranging from two-hour beginner classes, covering safety, paddling, and standing, to more advanced techniques and multilesson sessions. Bondi and Manly are the main centers; two well-known operators are **Let's Go Surfing** *(128 Ramsgate Ave., North Bondi, tel 9365 1800, letsgosurfing.com.au)* and **Manly Surf School** *(tel 9977 6977, www.manlysurfschool.com)* at the North Steyne Surf Lifesaving Club, on the beach opposite Pine Street in Manly.

Taking full advantage of the miles upon miles of nearby excellent wave action, many Sydneysiders learn to surf early.

More Places to Visit Around Sydney Harbour

With its verdant flora, Balmoral's foreshore offers an idyllic setting in which to relax.

Balmoral

One of the finest inner harbor beaches is Balmoral, in Middle Harbour. The area has been popular since a religious group in the 1920s became convinced it was going to be the site for the Second Coming of Jesus Christ. They were wrong, but the amphitheater they built on the site became an ideal entertainment venue. There is a harbor pool and sailboat, dinghy, and kayak rental nearby, plus one of Sydney's great waterside restaurants, the Bathers Pavilion (see Travelwise pp. 242–243).

87 E3–E4 Ferry to Taronga Zoo (see pp. 92–93), then bus 238 or 245 to Balmoral

Mary MacKillop Place

At Mary MacKillop Place, you learn about Australia's only saint, Sister Mary MacKillop (1842–1909). Her tomb is also here. She did a great deal for the poor in Australia and was canonized in 2010. To reach the museum, walk up the hill from North Sydney Station to Miller Street, then turn right. Two blocks later, turn left onto Mount Street.

86 C3 7 Mount St., North Sydney
8912 4878

Mosman

Mosman, easily reached from the city, is the north side's answer to the south side's fashionable Double Bay (see p. 155). The shops along the main thoroughfare, Military Road, are a mix of elegant clothing boutiques, antiques shops, and sophisticated cafés and restaurants. Many of the nearby houses are stately federation-style residences surrounded by land acquired when values were lower—before the Harbour Bridge was built.

87 E3 Bus 244 or 247 from the city
Ferry to Taronga Zoo then bus 238, or ferry to Mosman Wharf and bus 230 or 236

Nutcote

Nutcote belonged to children's author May Gibbs (1877–1969), whose characters were inspired by life in the Australian bush. Two "gumnut children," Snugglepot and Cuddlepie, are the main heroes of her stories. To reach the beautiful harborside house from Kurraba Point Wharf, turn left onto Kurraba Road, then turn left again and wind your way through to Wallaringa Avenue.

86 D3 5 Wallaringa Ave., Neutral Bay
9953 4453 Closed Mon.–Tues.

Stunningly beautiful buildings in the city center, plus the delights of Chinatown and the lively Spanish Quarter farther south

City Center & South

Introduction & Map 108–109

Market Street Area 110–113

Experience: Pick the Perfect Opal 112

Sydney Town Hall & Around 114–115

City South 116

Chinatown & Around 117–120

A Walk to the Chinese Garden of Friendship 118–119

Experience: Wander Sydney's Markets 120

Hotels & Restaurants 243–245

Allegorical statuary above the George Street entrance to the Queen Victoria Building

City Center & South

The commerce of the city has always been squeezed into the narrow strip of land known as the Central Business District (CBD), an area bordered by Hyde Park on one side and Darling Harbour on the other. At times, the focus of business activity has been at the southern end; at others, nearer the harbor.

Willows and ornamentals surround the Lotus Pond of the Chinese Garden of Friendship.

The result of this shifting is that the CBD has different "centers" with opulent buildings in areas that have seen their heyday. However, recent prosperity after the revamp for the 2000 Olympics has breathed new life into the older areas of the city, with high-rise apartments, restaurants, shops, and bars springing everywhere.

These days, much of the city's finance sector is found between Martin Place and Circular Quay, while the shopping is between St. James Station and the Town Hall, focused on Pitt Street. Between the Town Hall and Central Station, there are food and entertainment venues. Down the hill from the Town Hall, you find movie theaters, Chinatown, and the Spanish Quarter. The Capitol Theatre, Her Majesty's Theatre, and the Entertainment Centre account for the crowds grabbing a quick bowl of noodles before heading to a show.

The central and southern part of the CBD is the place to shop, spend a night out, or sightsee, with some of the city's most interesting buildings nestled beside huge towers offering incredible panoramas of the city and beyond. ■

NOT TO BE MISSED:

Sydney Tower for the city's best views **110–111**

Touring the majestic State Theatre **111–113**

The ornate Queen Victoria Building **113**

Hearing the mighty organ play at Sydney Town Hall **114–115**

A *yum cha* lunch in Chinatown **117**

Bargain shopping at labyrinthine Paddy's Markets **118, 120**

Escaping from the city bustle at the serene Chinese Garden of Friendship **120**

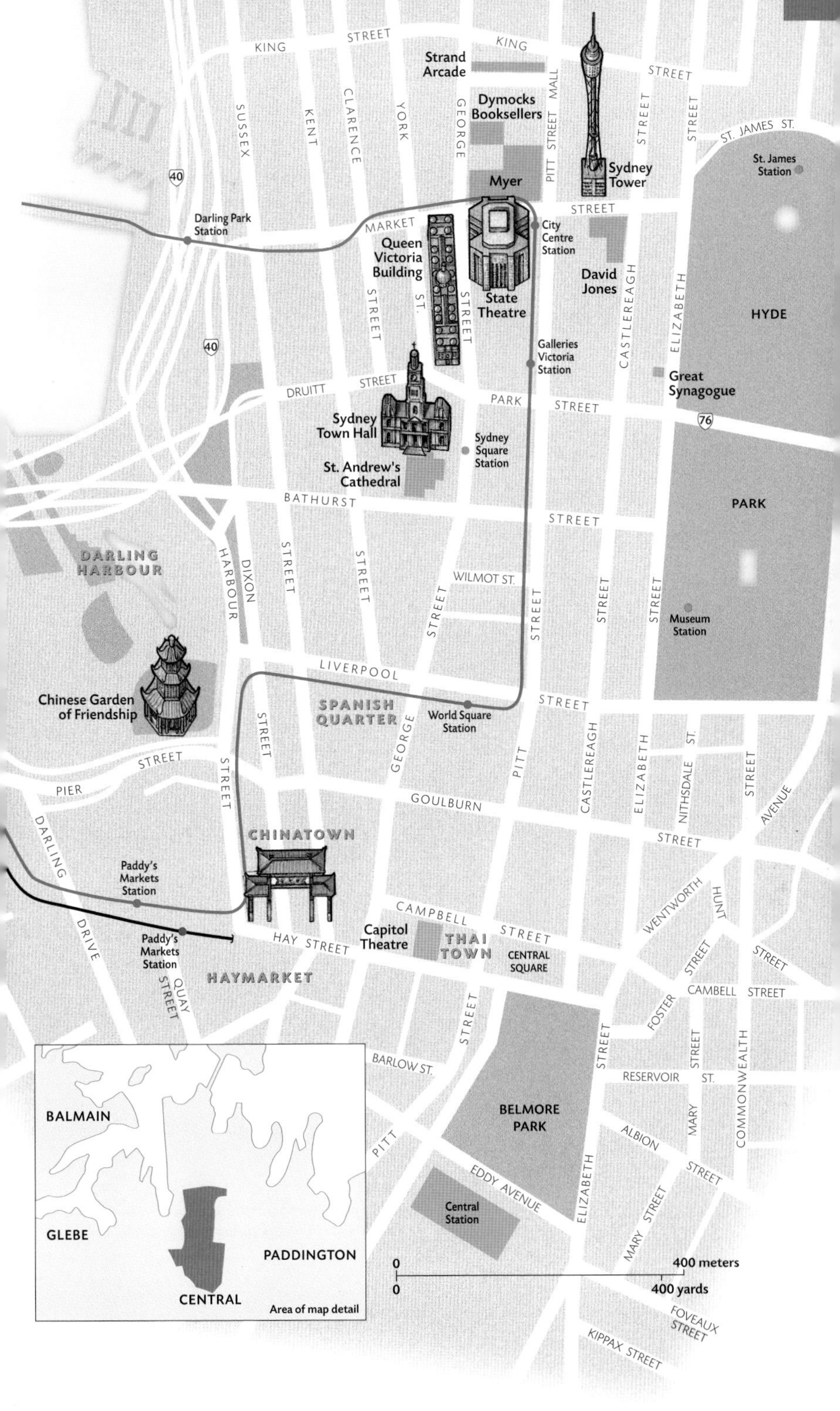

KING STREET
Strand Arcade
Dymocks Booksellers
Myer
Sydney Tower
PITT STREET MALL
ST. JAMES ST.
St. James Station
MARKET STREET
Darling Park Station
City Centre Station
Queen Victoria Building
State Theatre
David Jones
HYDE PARK
Galleries Victoria Station
Great Synagogue
DRUITT STREET
PARK STREET
Sydney Town Hall
St. Andrew's Cathedral
Sydney Square Station
BATHURST STREET
DARLING HARBOUR
WILMOT ST.
Museum Station
LIVERPOOL STREET
Chinese Garden of Friendship
SPANISH QUARTER
World Square Station
PIER STREET
GOULBURN STREET
CHINATOWN
Paddy's Markets Station
CAMPBELL STREET
Capitol Theatre
THAI TOWN
CENTRAL SQUARE
HAY STREET
HAYMARKET
CAMBELL STREET
BARLOW ST.
RESERVOIR ST.
BELMORE PARK
ALBION STREET
EDDY AVENUE
Central Station
FOVEAUX STREET
KIPPAX STREET
SUSSEX
KENT
CLARENCE
YORK
GEORGE
CASTLEREAGH
ELIZABETH
DIXON STREET
HARBOUR STREET
PITT
NITHSDALE ST.
WENTWORTH AVENUE
HUNT STREET
FOSTER STREET
MARY STREET
COMMONWEALTH STREET
DARLING DRIVE
QUAY STREET
0 400 meters
0 400 yards
BALMAIN
GLEBE
PADDINGTON
CENTRAL
Area of map detail

Market Street Area

Away from its dazzling waterfront, Sydney's glass-and-concrete canyons and traffic-clogged streets resemble those of cities the world over. Nevertheless, a stroll down Market Street, in the heart of the Central Business District, takes you shopping and sightseeing around a uniquely Australian downtown.

The Sydney Tower is the most prominent landmark on the skyline and often serves as a backdrop for fireworks displays.

Sydney Tower

It's had more name changes than Puff Daddy, but ask a taxi driver to take you to the Sydney Tower or Centrepoint and you'll be at the corner of Pitt Street Mall and Market Street in a trice. At 1,014 feet (309 m) the tower is the tallest structure in Sydney. It rises above the sprawling Westfield Sydney (aka Centrepoint) mall, an ever expanding labyrinth of clothing, jewelry, food, and other outlets and the focal point of the city's main shopping area.

Built in 1981, the tower's central spike is made up of 46 stacked barrels, with a golden turret on top that is anchored to the ground by 56 cables weighing 7 tons each. This top section weighs 2,000 tons, much of the weight being provided by more than 35,000 gallons (160,000 liters) of water. It acts as a counterbalance to any gust of wind, with the result that this "intelligent" building hardly sways at all, even in the strongest winds.

In the turret, you'll find an observation deck on level 4, two revolving restaurants—one each on levels 1 and level 2—and a coffee shop on level 3. In just 40 seconds, by way of high-speed elevators, you leave the bustle and noise of the street far below and replace them with wonderful 360-degree views over the whole Sydney urban sprawl on a clear day.

The experience has been rebranded the **Sydney Tower Eye,** with plenty of value-added products such as a "4D" cinema and Skywalk, which is a guided tour out onto a glass platform overhang. A profusion of ticket combos and discounts exist, though it is generally cheaper to book online.

Downtown Shopping: The area around Sydney Tower is prime shopping territory, but the following are worth visiting for their aesthetic value alone. First is **Pitt Street Mall,** running off Market Street outside Westfield Sydney. The pedestrianized section of the street features some excellent examples of Victorian architecture and is one of the city's busiest shopping precincts. Pitt Street was named after English prime minister William Pitt the Younger (1759–1806), who was responsible for the establishment of the colony of Sydney.

Halfway along the mall is the **Strand Arcade,** the most beautiful arcade in the city. It opened in 1892 and features much of the wrought-iron lacework, colored glass, and detailing typical of Victorian storefronts. Badly damaged by a fire in 1976, it held such a place in the heart of the city and the shopkeepers that it was carefully restored to its original condition. At the George Street end of the Strand is **Dymocks Booksellers,** one of the biggest bookshops in Sydney, just behind Kinokuniya at 500 George Street.

On the corner of Pitt and Market Streets is **Myer** department store, and on the other side of Westfield Sydney is the elegant **David Jones,** comprising two stores on diagonal corners: Market Street and Elizabeth Street. Enter the latter (opposite Hyde Park) at ground level to find gray marble, mirrors, huge sprays of flowers, and, usually, live piano music.

Across Market Street, go downstairs to discover the David Jones Food Hall, a food lover's paradise. The oyster bar is especially good.

INSIDER TIP:

The bar Grasshopper *(tel 9947 9025)* is a favorite for its cocktails, industrial decor, and ironic address: 1 Temperance Lane *(near Strand Arcade, off George St. bet. King & Market Sts.).*

—PETER TURNER
National Geographic author

State Theatre

Along Market Street, the State Theatre is a grand motion-picture palace from the silent movie era. When it was opened in 1929, the deputy premier declared that no words of his could do justice to the beauty of the interior. The theater is now a popular venue for

Sydney Tower Eye

Map p. 109
100 Market St.
9333 9222
$$$–$$$$$
St. James Station

www.sydneytowereye.com.au

State Theatre

Map p. 109
49 Market St.
9373 6655
St. James Station

www.statetheatre.com.au

drama, concerts, and the annual two-week Sydney Film Festival *(tel 9690 5333, www.sff.org.au)* held in June.

The aim of the theater's architect, Henry White, and the managing director of Union Theatres at the time, Stuart Doyle, was to bring many of the architectural styles of Europe (especially Gothic and rococo) to the largely untraveled Sydney public. Particularly splendid is the domed Grand Assembly Room, with marble staircases sweeping up to a marble balcony. On the floor, a mosaic by the Melocco brothers depicts St. George doing battle with the dragon, and there is another St. George scene over the doors in the entrance foyer. The foyer's bronze fan ceiling is modeled on Henry VIII's chapel in Westminster Cathedral, London. Also note the dress circle foyer, which incorporates an art gallery with works by portrait painter Sir William Dobell (1899–1970), Thea Proctor (1879–1966), and others.

Inside the auditorium are busts of famous historical figures, and the stage is dressed by the Golden Arch—surmounted by the Crown of England—and flanked by Aboriginal maidens. The domed ceiling is made up of plaster octagons each containing a patterned snowflake. The pièce de résistance, however, is the second largest cut-glass chandelier in the world (the largest is in the Hofburg Palace, Vienna), with 321 lights and 17,363 pieces of glass.

Interesting two-hour tours of the theater are available Monday through Wednesday at 10 a.m. and 1 p.m. *($$$$, reserve at theater box office or tel 136 100).*

EXPERIENCE: Pick the Perfect Opal

Australia's fiery opals are lovely and make wonderful souvenirs, but take care when buying, as many are not of gemstone quality. Still, cheaper opals can make attractive, inexpensive jewelry and souvenirs. Knowing what to look for in quality and cut will help you pick the best opal for you.

The **National Opal Collection** *(60 Pitt St., tel 9247 6344, www.nationalopal.com)* in the city center is a good place to start your education. It has opal jewelry, loose opals, and a museum where you'll learn, among other things, that Australia produces 95 percent of the world's opals. Most come from the South Australian opal fields of Coober Pedy and Andamooka and from Lightning Ridge in New South Wales.

Opal is made of layers of silica that refract light like a prism and give the stone its distinctive sparkle. Like other gems, opals are valued by their size, the strength and brilliance of color, and clarity. The brighter and clearer the stone, the higher the value. Black and crystal opals are the most valuable. Milky opals, though still pretty, lack that special dark fire and are the cheapest.

Shape is also very important. The categories in descending order of value are cabochon, a solid domed piece; doublet, a thin wafer of opal against a dark background; and triplet, which has a quartz lens.

Test your opal knowledge at well-known Sydney dealers such as **Flame Opals** and **Opal Fields,** both on George Street in The Rocks (see Travelwise p. 260), as well as in jewelers found in the Queen Victoria Building and the Strand Arcade.

Alternatively, attend a show and have a good look around at the same time.

Queen Victoria Building

Another fine example of late 19th-century architecture is the Queen Victoria Building (QVB), on Market Street at the corner of George Street. While the Town Hall was constructed in a period of prosperity, the QVB, built to commemorate Queen Victoria's Golden Jubilee, was completed in 1898, during a period of depression.

As a means of providing work for unemployed craftsmen—especially stonemasons and stained-glass artists—it was a great success, and at the same time it provided the city with a stunning building. French fashion designer Pierre Cardin is reported to have called it the "most beautiful shopping center in the world."

Over the years, the QVB has had many functions—it housed the city's produce markets in the 19th century and was subsequently used as offices and the city library—and yet, unbelievably, in the 1950s the authorities considered tearing it down. Fortunately, it survived and in the 1980s, courtesy of a Malaysian company, underwent a massive restoration program and was converted into a shopping gallery, with another major refurbishment in 2009.

Inside and out, it is breathtaking. Note the patterned tiled floors, polished woodwork, and elegant storefronts. Particularly striking is the central glass dome, with beautiful stained-glass windows on either side, which creates a dramatic space between the multiple levels of stores. There are nearly 200 stores, including plenty of big brand names. On the lowest level, you'll find plenty of stylish cafés and eateries.

If you walk through to the far end of the QVB, a block along George Street, you'll come to the imposing statue of Queen Victoria herself, in the main forecourt of the building. And across Druitt Street, you'll see yet another great Victorian building, the Sydney Town Hall (see pp. 114–115). ■

The Queen Victoria Building's Royal Clock displays scenes from the lives of English kings and queens on the hour.

Queen Victoria Building

- Map p. 109
- Market & George Sts.
- 9283 5211
- Town Hall Station

www.qvb.com.au

Sydney Town Hall & Around

Seat of the City of Sydney government, the centrally sited Town Hall is a glorious building built of golden sandstone. Its steps serve as a popular gathering point. The hall nicely complements Australia's oldest cathedral, St. Andrew's, standing alongside it.

The Sydney Town Hall and its adjacent square have been a social hub of the city since 1889.

Sydney Town Hall

Map p. 109

George & Druitt Sts.

9265 9189

www.cityofsydney.nsw.gov.gau/sydneytownhall

Sydney Town Hall

Built in stages between 1868 and 1889 on the site of the old Sydney Burial Ground, the Town Hall is another beautiful Victorian building. Its foundation stone was laid in 1868 by Prince Alfred, Queen Victoria's son.

The interior is one of the finest examples of high Victorian decoration in Australia. Note particularly the vestibule, with its 1,952-piece crystal chandelier and stained-glass ceiling panels depicting the four elements and eight virtues.

The **Centennial Hall** was the home of the Sydney Symphony Orchestra until the company moved to the Opera House in the 1970s, but is still used for concerts and large public meetings. Constructed in 1890, the organ, with nearly 9,000 pipes, is one of the largest ever built. The ceiling of the hall—the largest pressed-zinc ceiling in Australia—is specially designed to withstand the vibrations the organ causes. Recitals are held on a regular basis, and there are free lunchtime concerts about once a month. Details of these and other events are available on the Town Hall website or in the foyer. Here you can also find out about guided tours or pick up a leaflet showing you where to find such curios as a marble sculpture of diva Dame Joan Sutherland's ear.

Meetings of the Sydney City Council are still held at the Town Hall, with the Lord Mayor usually presiding in ceremonial regalia. The public is welcome to attend.

St. Andrew's Cathedral

Situated alongside the Town Hall, St. Andrew's Cathedral is the oldest cathedral in Australia. Its foundation stone was laid in 1819 by Lachlan Macquarie, but construction was delayed by the fiscal rectitude of the governor's nemesis, Commissioner Bigge. The building was eventually consecrated in 1868.

Immortality

One of Sydney's most unusual sights lies between the Town Hall and St. Andrew's Cathedral. From Sydney Square, descend the steps to a small courtyard. Here, on the ground in front of the fountain, you'll find the word "Eternity" cast in metal. What does it mean? For 30-odd years, reformed alcoholic Arthur Stace (1885–1967) chalked the word all over the city during the night. He had been helped by a Baptist preacher and in turn wanted people to think beyond the present.

INSIDER TIP:

The Australian Architecture Association (*www.architecture.org.au*) offers myriad tours that will acquaint you with the works of renowned architects, whether on a suburban walk or a nighttime stroll in the city center.

—JEANINE BARONE
National Geographic writer

Built in late Gothic style, it was designed by Edmund Blacket (1817–1883). When Blacket died, he was buried in Balmain Cemetery, but after the cemetery was turned into a park, his ashes were reinterred under the cathedral's floor.

The cathedral's organ dates from 1866 (recitals are usually held twice a week), and there are a number of icons from Australian history within the building. Of significance to Australians is a flag from Gallipoli, where, in 1915, thousands perished storming the Turkish ramparts and the newly independent country of Australia had its first baptism of fire. There is also a memorial to Samuel Marsden, the colony's first parson.

Other notable features in the cathedral include the original choir stalls that are carved in American oak; the Great Bible, dating from the 16th century; and a Union flag that was held by prisoners under the Japanese at Changi prison camp in Singapore. The marble floor in the side chapel came from St. Paul's Cathedral in London. ■

St. Andrew's Cathedral

Map p. 109

Sydney Sq., George St.

9265 1670

City South

The roots of Sydney may be firmly sunk into the ground around Circular Quay, but as the city grew, it spread south, away from the harbor. The southern end of the long finger of the CBD is where the locals generally gather to spend their free time.

Capitol Theatre
Map p. 109
13 Campbell St.
9320 5000 (inquiries)

The block of Liverpool Street west off George Street is sometimes called the **Spanish Quarter.** Among the Spanish restaurants here (and around the corner on Kent Street) is the Spanish Club, the focus of a small but very active Spanish community and a number of Latin American communities. There is dancing, food, and music, and visitors are welcome.

A block farther down George Street from the Spanish Quarter is the more substantial **Chinatown** (see pp. 117–120).

INSIDER TIP:

Head to the Spanish Quarter for tapas! With many restaurants to choose from, sample from a few.

—JILL SCHNEIDER
National Geographic photographer

Continue to the bottom of the hill and you will come across tram tracks, the remnants of the city's once extensive tram system. Trams have made their return in the form of the Metro Light Rail, ferrying passengers from Central Station to Darling Harbour and the Sydney Fish Market at Pyrmont.

Turn left and follow the tracks to reach the **Capitol Theatre** on Campbell Street. During the 1890s, a market was held here, and later the site was used as an open-air theater and hippodrome. The existing theater was built in 1928 by John Eberson. Its beautiful interior is themed as a Florentine garden at night, complete with shining stars reflecting the southern sky and drifting shadow clouds. The theater was faithfully restored to Eberson's original specifications in the mid-1990s and reopened to stage large musicals, such as those imported from Broadway. It is worth seeing a show to appreciate the interior, but tours can also be booked *(tel 9320 5005, $$$)*.

Around the Capitol Theatre, on Campbell, **Thai Town** has sprung up in recent years, with many Thai restaurants and grocery stores moving in.

Continue following the tram tracks to reach **Belmore Park,** with its band rotunda and spreading Moreton Bay fig trees. At the park's far end is the grand Renaissance-style **Central Station,** built in 1906. The arrival hall is the must-see feature here, excepting the video destination screens. The original destination board is now in the Powerhouse Museum (see pp. 124–126). In the railway bar off the main hall is yet another Melocco brothers mosaic floor. ■

Chinatown & Around

Sydney can claim to have had a Chinese community ever since two Chinese cooks arrived with the First Fleet. Shortly after its foundation, the colony's trade with Hong Kong and other Asian centers saw rising numbers of Chinese people coming to Australia, futher increasing with the gold rushes from the 1850s onward.

A Chinese gate stands at each end of pedestrians-only Dixon Street, the heart of Chinatown.

Chinatown consists of a handful of streets around Dixon Street, although a stroll through the nearby suburbs of Surry Hills and Pyrmont will also reveal many Chinese shops and houses. Here you can get a good meal, a massage, Chinese herbs and remedies, and plenty of the exotic flavor of Australia's Asian neighbors. The district also has a scattering of Japanese and other Asian restaurants.

Off Harbour Street, the pedestrian mall of Dixon Street, and Sussex Street, food halls can be found on several stories of quite a few buildings. Specialties include "steamboat" (you broil food at your table) and *yum cha* (dozens of help-yourself trolleys are wheeled past your table). Good places for yum cha include Nine Dragons *(39 Dixon St.)* or East Ocean *(421 Sussex St.)*.

At the bottom of Dixon Street, turn left and head up to Campbell Street at the front of the Capitol Theatre, where Thai restaurants and businesses have moved in to create Thai Town. Check out Lucky Thai at No. 40, one of the best stocked Asian groceries in the area; its sweet shop next door sells delicious *khanom buang* pancakes.

(continued on p. 120)

Chinatown

Map p. 109

A Walk to the Chinese Garden of Friendship

This is a short, mostly downhill or level walk from Central Station through Chinatown to the Chinese Garden of Friendship and Darling Harbour. Walking time is only 30 minutes, but there are plenty of distractions along the way. It is possible to cover most of the route from the comfort of the Metro Light Rail system, hopping on and off as various sights attract your interest.

The Chinese Garden of Friendship teahouse offers both sustenance and peaceful surroundings.

From Central Station, take the path that follows the tram tracks past **Belmore Park** ❶ (see p. 116) and then turn left onto Hay Street. Having crossed George Street, enter Chinatown proper (see p. 117), with Sussex Street and the pedestrian walkway of Dixon Street to the right.

On the left is one of Sydney's institutions—**Paddy's Markets** ❷ *(Thomas & Hay Sts., Haymarket, tel 9325 6200, www.paddysmarkets.com.au, closed Mon.–Tues.)*, here since the mid-19th century, moving only while the Market City mall that now towers over the site was under construction. It sells everything from leather jackets to luggage, from fruit and vegetables to souvenirs and cheap seafood. The three-story mall above also sells discount clothing from factory outlets and has restaurants and two good Asian food courts.

Next, stroll north along Dixon Street, where there are lots of places to eat. At the top of the street, turn left and take the walkway across Harbour Street, then spiral down the path to the side of the **Sydney Entertainment Centre**

NOT TO BE MISSED:

Belmore Park • Paddy's Markets • Sydney Entertainment Centre • Chinese Garden of Friendship

---

❸ *(Harbour St., Haymarket, tel 9320 4200).* This is the largest indoor complex in the city, seating up to 12,500. It is the venue for major international rock concerts, and the Sydney Kings basketball team also plays here.

Keeping the center on the left, follow Little Pier Street to the **Pumphouse Bar** ❹ *(17 Little Pier St., tel 8217 4100).* Originally, the 1891 building provided hydraulic pressure to operate the elevators of the city; it was then converted into a pub, with brewing facilities and many boutique beers, and is now part of a luxury hotel.

Just past the front of the Pumphouse Hotel, you will come across the walkway that passes under Pier Street. If you look up, you'll notice a long pipe running across the bottom of the road bridge that releases a curtain of water with unpredictable regularity. Kids love it and wait around in groups for the next soaking.

Just beyond the waterfall, Darling Harbour starts, although the **Chinese Garden of Friendship** ❺ (see p. 120) marks the boundary of Chinatown. You can either end the walk here with traditional Chinese tea and cakes in the teahouse or continue by following the Darling Harbour walk (see pp. 128–129), which ends at the Sydney Fish Market, an ideal place to stop for lunch.

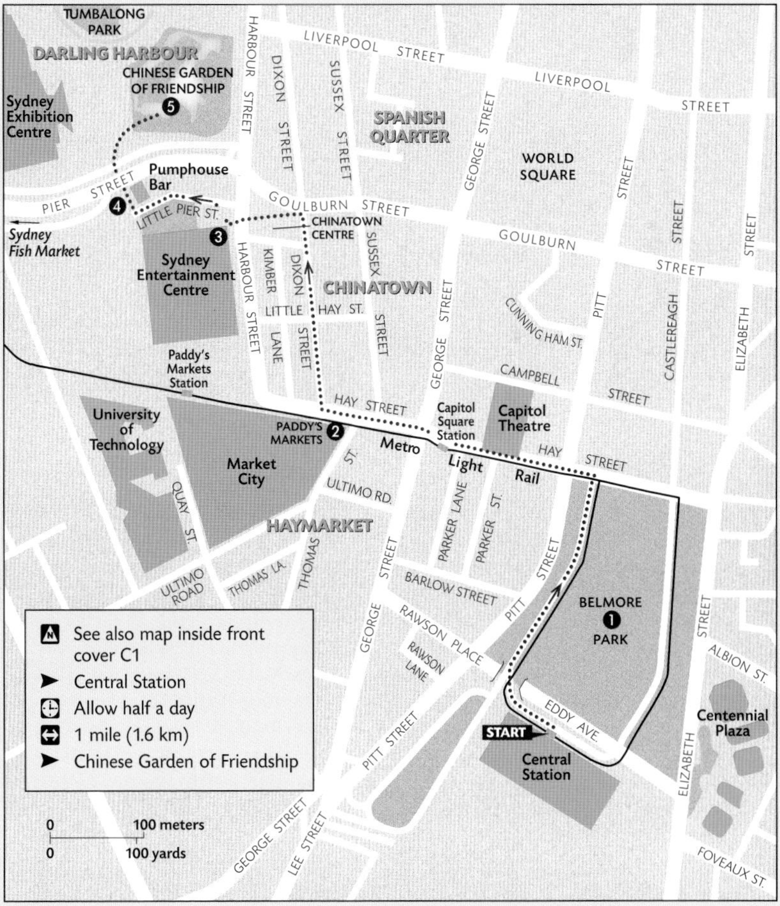

Chinese Garden of Friendship

Map p. 109

Pier & Harbour Sts., bet. Darling Harbour & Chinatown

9240 8888

$

Paddy's Markets, or City Sightseeing bus

Chinese Garden of Friendship

During Australia's Bicentennial, in 1988, marking 200 years of European settlement, Sydney and other Australian cities received gifts from countries around the world. One of Sydney's presents was the Chinese Garden of Friendship, a gift from Guangdong Province in China.

The walled 2.5-acre (1 ha) garden, the largest of its type outside China, is designed according to southern Chinese tradition. It combines pavilions, lakes, waterfalls, and winding paths with lush vegetation, cherry and lychee trees, and scented flowers, including many gardenias. The system of waterways is well stocked with fish, and shoals often congregate in the canal outside the entrance waiting to be fed (bring bread with you).

A traditional two-story *gurr* (pavilion) on a high point of the garden sets the scene, but there are also many small rooms, gazebos, and walls that enhance the plants and rockeries. Notice, too, the elaborate wood carvings and statues that include lions, dragons, and chubby infants in repose. Don't miss the fabulous bridal carriage carved from 30 tons of jade. Traditional-style tearooms make the garden an ideal place to wind up at the end of a walk.

It doesn't take long to walk around, but the garden's design tempts you to linger, to enjoy this oasis of peace in a bustling city. ■

EXPERIENCE: Wander Sydney's Markets

Partake in a slice of Sydney life by roaming the stalls of one or more of the city's lively markets. As you rub shoulders with Sydneysiders doing their shopping, you'll find each market has its own character, but they are all great for souvenirs, gifts, fashion, people-watching, music, or a quick bite.

You are unlikely to find haute couture at **Paddy's Markets** (see p. 118; *9 a.m.–5 p.m.*), but Sydney's biggest market is crammed with just about everything else at bargain prices, and it is always a fun place to browse.

The Rocks Markets, held weekends (*10 a.m.–4 p.m.*) at the top end of George Street, is a perennial tourist favorite. You'll find arts and crafts, jewelry, homewares, and everything from designer T-shirts to boomerangs. A new offshoot, the Foodies Market on Fridays, has condiments, olive oils, flowers, fruit, and a host of ready-to-eat treats.

Crowds flock to the Saturday-only **Paddington Markets** (see p. 144; *10 a.m.–4 p.m., www.paddingtonmarkets.com.au*). Around 250 stalls set up, with arts and crafts, bric-a-brac, jewelry, and vintage and young designer fashion.

Bondi Markets (*www.bondimarkets.com.au*) competes for young designer fashions and many of the city's best fashion outlets started here. Plenty of other stalls round out this Sunday market (*10 a.m.–4 p.m.*), on the beachfront grounds of Bondi Beach Public School on Campbell Parade.

Glebe Markets (*www.glebemarkets.com.au*), in the Glebe Public School on Glebe Point Road, is another Saturday favorite (*10 a.m.–4 p.m.*). Laid-back and popular with students and urban hippies, vendors sell secondhand goods, books, records, furniture, arts, crafts, and clothing, while musicians entertain the crowds.

A bustling tourist area with museums, an aquarium, restaurants, shopping, parks, and gardens—something for everyone

Darling Harbour

Introduction & Map 122–123

Powerhouse Museum 124–126

Sydney Aquarium 127–132

A Walk to Sydney Fish Market 128–130

Experience: Steep Yourself in Aboriginal Culture 133

Feature: Indigenous Sydney 134–137

Australian National Maritime Museum 138–140

Hotels & Restaurants 245–247

Sharks and other marine life glide overhead at the Sydney Aquarium.

Darling Harbour

Darling Harbour encompasses both the old and the new faces of Sydney: Old because it was where ships were unloaded from the early 19th century on; new because a large part of it was converted into a complex of stores, convention centers, exhibition halls, and entertainment facilities for the 1988 Bicentennial. Some wharves still await development, but the rest of the area has been completely revamped to become a prime tourist center.

Cockle Bay, Darling Harbour's innermost bay

On all sides, hotels, high-rise apartments, and restaurants have sprung up. The precinct feels more like a theme park than any other part of Sydney—which may be a plus or a minus, depending on taste. But even if such amusements don't appeal, you will find some interesting and enjoyable alternatives.

Among the possibilities are the largest museum in the country, the Powerhouse, and the Australian National Maritime Museum, which contains significant relics from Australian seafaring history. Pyrmont Bridge, the swing bridge spanning the center of Darling Harbour, is a beautiful piece of engineering, and one of the early Manly ferries, the *South Steyne,* now a floating restaurant, is permanently moored at the docks. A very pleasant walk around the waterfront areas brings you to the Sydney Fish Market—a great place for lunch. If you want to see the fish (and sharks) while they're still swimming, visit the nearby Sydney Aquarium. Adjacent Wild Life Sydney offers a taste of exotic Australian fauna.

Numerous other amusements include an IMAX theater, Madame Tussauds, and the Star, Sydney's casino. A variety of restaurants caters to nearly every taste and budget, and the shopping area is geared to visitors.

In addition, you can enjoy a full calendar of special events and free entertainment, staged in amphitheaters and on floating stages year-round. Outdoor entertainment increases in the summer, and the place positively hums during the Christmas and January school vacations. ■

NOT TO BE MISSED:

Browsing for hours in the Powerhouse Museum 124–126

Shark-gazing while walking through the glass tunnel in the Sydney Aquarium 127–132

The celebrity waxworks at Madame Tussauds 130

Wild Life Sydney for an introduction to Australian animals 132

Stepping aboard the old rigger at the Australian National Maritime Museum 138–140

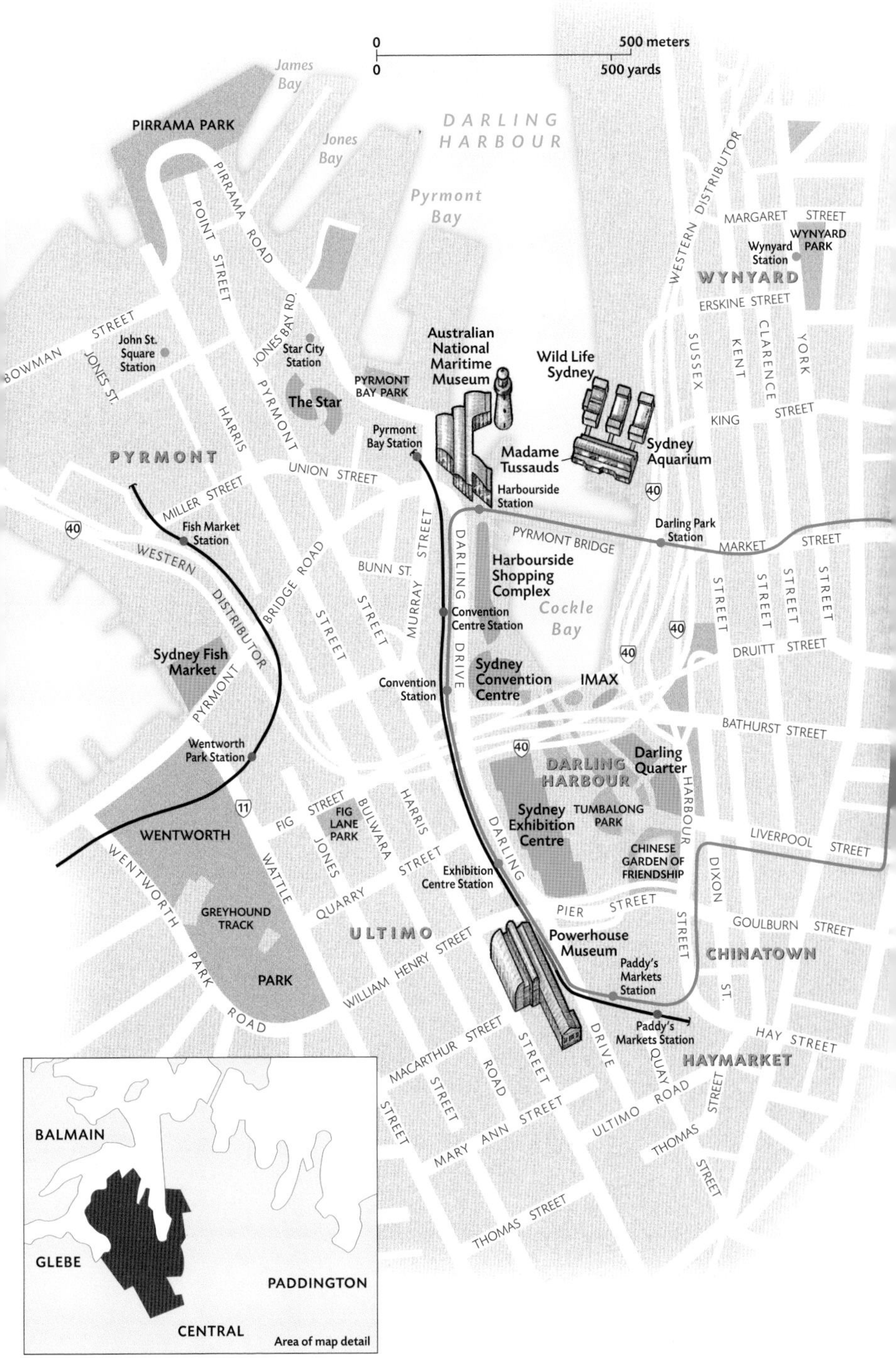
0
500 meters
0
500 yards
James Bay
PIRRAMA PARK
Jones Bay
DARLING HARBOUR
Pyrmont Bay
PIRRAMA ROAD
POINT STREET
WESTERN DISTRIBUTOR
MARGARET STREET
Wynyard Station
WYNYARD PARK
WYNYARD
ERSKINE STREET
BOWMAN STREET
John St. Square Station
JONES ST.
JONES BAY RD.
Star City Station
Australian National Maritime Museum
Wild Life Sydney
SUSSEX
KENT
CLARENCE
YORK
PYRMONT BAY PARK
The Star
HARRIS
PYRMONT
KING STREET
Pyrmont Bay Station
PYRMONT
Madame Tussauds
Sydney Aquarium
UNION STREET
MILLER STREET
Harbourside Station
40
Fish Market Station
Darling Park Station
PYRMONT BRIDGE
MARKET STREET
WESTERN DISTRIBUTOR
BRIDGE ROAD
STREET
BUNN ST.
STREET
MURRAY STREET
DARLING DRIVE
Harbourside Shopping Complex
Cockle Bay
STREET
STREET
STREET
STREET
Convention Centre Station
Sydney Fish Market
PYRMONT
Convention Station
Sydney Convention Centre
IMAX
DRUITT STREET
BATHURST STREET
Wentworth Park Station
DARLING HARBOUR
Darling Quarter
HARBOUR
11
FIG STREET
FIG LANE PARK
BULWARA
HARRIS
JONES
Sydney Exhibition Centre
TUMBALONG PARK
WENTWORTH
LIVERPOOL STREET
WENTWORTH
WATTLE
STREET
DARLING
Exhibition Centre Station
CHINESE GARDEN OF FRIENDSHIP
DIXON
QUARRY
GREYHOUND TRACK
PIER STREET
GOULBURN STREET
ULTIMO
Powerhouse Museum
STREET
CHINATOWN
WILLIAM HENRY STREET
PARK
Paddy's Markets Station
ST.
PARK
ROAD
Paddy's Markets Station
MACARTHUR STREET
ROAD
STREET
DRIVE
QUAY
HAY STREET
HAYMARKET
STREET
STREET
MARY ANN STREET
ULTIMO ROAD
THOMAS
STREET
THOMAS STREET
BALMAIN
GLEBE
PADDINGTON
CENTRAL
Area of map detail

Powerhouse Museum

So called because it occupies the shell of the turn-of-the-20th-century Ultimo Power Station, the Powerhouse Museum is the largest museum in the country. It houses a collection that was begun more than 130 years ago and now comprises 380,000 items (not all are on display at once!). Despite its long history, the museum has a modern approach to the presentation of its material, and the emphasis is on interactivity.

In the Powerhouse's Zero Gravity Space Lab, special effects create the illusion of weightlessness.

The Powerhouse Museum's exhibits are displayed thematically on four levels, covering the main topics of steam engines, flight and space exploration, decorative arts and design, and Australian social history. In addition, continually changing exhibitions take place throughout the museum from its collections of porcelain, military memorabilia, furniture, clocks, relics of Sydney's history, music, and Aboriginal culture.

At any one time, only a fraction of the museum's collection is on display, and the museum has a regular program of rotating exhibitions, ranging from popular blockbusters like "Harry Potter" to homegrown heroes such as "The Wiggles." Most of the collection is stored at the **Powerhouse Discovery Centre** at Castle Hill, 18.5 miles (30 km) northwest of the city center, in a series of huge sheds open to the public *(reservations tel 9762 1300)* since 2006.

Level 1 (Courtyard Level)

There are a number of fascinating exhibits on this level, but you will find it particularly difficult to drag children away from the hands-on **Experimentations** section. It features a wealth of lights, levers, pulleys, knobs, and dials that entice young and old to have a great deal of fun discovering the workings of such things as gravity, electricity, magnetism, heat, and light.

Cyberworlds, next door, is a fascinating look at the history of computer use from military science to the home PC.

Perhaps the most spectacular section of the museum, though, is the **Transport Hall,** where various forms of transport show how transportation has developed and changed our lives. The space section, for example, contains a space shuttle flight deck and a selection of satellites and lunar landers. There are also pieces of equipment from China, Russia, and the United States. The romance of rail travel is evoked by the original destinations board from the grand hall in Central Station (see p. 116). Nearby is an entire switching room, and you can see some of the famous trains from Australia's history. Another highlight of the transport area is the Blériot monoplane suspended from the ceiling. It made the first flight from Sydney to Melbourne in 1914. Nearby is the plane used by the fledgling Qantas airline for its first commercial flight.

One of the smaller sections on Level 1 is **Musical Instruments,** displaying numerous historically significant musical instruments that the museum holds.

For some refreshment, try the outdoor café in the courtyard.

Level 2

This level is devoted to design and contains several special-purpose venues for groups and school parties. The **Kings Cinema,** a wonderfully evocative art deco 1930s theater, shows nonstop news and feature films of the era. Near the Kings Cinema, you will also find rotating displays on significant elements in Australian culture.

INSIDER TIP:

Be sure to go inside the Powerhouse Museum's Zero Gravity Space Lab to experience what it feels like to be in space.

—JILL SCHNEIDER
National Geographic photographer

Here, too, is **Thinkspace,** the museum's digital learning center for media production, and **Love Lace,** a lacemaking study center with regular exhibits.

Permanent exhibits include the **Steam Revolution,** which presents a variety of hands-on displays and historic engines that demonstrate the development of steam and the power available through air pressure.

Level 3

This is the entry and exit level for the museum, with most of its space devoted to temporary

Powerhouse Museum

Map p. 123
500 Harris St., Ultimo
9217 0222
$$
Light rail to Haymarket Station, bus 422 from Circular Quay, or City Sightseeing bus

www.powerhousemuseum.com

Locomotive 1243, on display in the Transport Hall

exhibitions, but there are three particular gems to seek out. Here you can see **Locomotive No. 1,** the first train to run in Australia, in 1863. It was built at Robert Stephenson's factory in Newcastle, England, in 1854, and brought to Sydney, where it ran on the country's first railway line, from Redfern to Parramatta. Just behind the train is the oldest rotative steam engine known to be in existence—the Boulton and Watt steam engine. It was originally installed in a London brewery in 1785, where it ran for more than 100 years. Other railway items of interest are signals and signal boxes.

Near the glass elevator, look for the **Strasburg Clock** (as Strasbourg was spelled when this one-sixth-scale reproduction was built in 1887–1889). It was modeled on the 1354 clock that graces Strasbourg Cathedral in France. The clock swings into action six minutes before the hour with music and commentary before the Apostles make their procession.

Also on this level, hanging from the ceiling, is a replica of **Hargrave's box kite**. Dating from 1894, it was a forerunner of the biplane and an important advance in aeronautics ahead of the first powered flight in 1903.

The gift shop and another café are other Level 3 attractions.

Level 4

The Asian Gallery on Level 4 showcases changing exhibitions of the museum's large collection of Asian cultural items. ■

Goodbye, Sydney Monorail

A Sydney icon, the Sydney Monorail, which runs past the Powerhouse Museum, has shuttled people between Darling Harbour and the city center for more than 25 years, but in a shocking move, the state government announced in 2012 it would tear it down—perhaps in 2013 or 2014. Sydneysiders mostly lauded the decision, as the monorail was always a contentious project. Many declared it an eyesore when it was built in 1988 for the Bicentennial, and most passengers were tourists. The government plans to extend the light rail in its place.

Sydney Aquarium

On the city side of Pyrmont Bridge, the Sydney Aquarium building echoes the design of the Australian National Maritime Museum (see pp. 138–140) and is one of the city's most popular tourist attractions. One of the largest in the world, with submarine walkways 175 yards (160 m) long, the aquarium features a diverse collection of aquatic life from a wide range of marine environments that extends from the Great Barrier Reef and inland waterways of Australia to the southern oceans. There are more than 12,000 sea creatures from 650 species.

The aquarium's underwater walkways give visitors a unique perspective on the enclosed sea life.

Southern & Northern Rivers

Your exploration of the Sydney Aquarium starts with the Southern Rivers area, featuring the freshwater fish in the Murray-Darling River system, Australia's longest waterway, and the coastal rivers of southeastern Australia, including the giant Murray cod, Australia's largest freshwater species.

Also here is the platypus tank, which re-creates the endemic animals' natural river habitat. Low-level lighting simulates dusk, the time when platypuses are naturally at their most active. The Southern Rivers section also features long-finned eels and numerous species of bass, perch, trout, minnow, and turtle. However, don't linger too long,

(continued on p. 131)

Sydney Aquarium

- Map p. 123
- Aquarium Pier, Darling Harbour
- 8251 7800
- $$$$$
- Town Hall Station, or City Sightseeing bus
- Darling Harbour

www.sydneyaquarium.com.au

A Walk to Sydney Fish Market

This is a nice level stroll through Darling Harbour and on to the Sydney Fish Market, passing several of the area's major attractions, including the Sydney Aquarium and the Australian National Maritime Museum. Allow 1.5 hours for walking and the rest of the day for sightseeing. A good idea is to arrive at the fish market for lunch. Note that this walk joins the one from Central Station to the Chinese Garden of Friendship (see pp. 118–119).

Many of the points on this route are accessible from the Metro Light Rail system.

Starting from the **Chinese Garden of Friendship** (see p. 120), walk through **Tumbalong Park ❶**, an open-air performance space, past the newly redeveloped Darling Quarter lined with restaurants, to the IMAX Theatre (see sidebar p. 130). Just before the IMAX, the **Sydney Visitor Centre** can fill you in on the city's attractions and make reservations.

NOT TO BE MISSED:

Sydney Aquarium • Australian National Maritime Museum • Pirrama Park • Sydney Fish Market

Thousands of fish come through the Sydney Fish Market daily, Australia's largest fish market.

Continue along the right-hand side of the bay, past Cockle Bay Wharf–a series of shops and eateries–to the **Sydney Aquarium ❷** (see p. 127); in the same complex is **Wild Life Sydney** (see sidebar p. 132) and **Madame Tussauds** (see sidebar p. 130).

Take the stairs or escalator to the deck of **Pyrmont Bridge ❸**. Opened in 1902, it was the first electrically operated swing-span bridge in the world and was powered by the Ultimo Power Station, which now houses the Powerhouse Museum (see pp. 124–126). The bridge is closed to traffic, though it still opens to allow tall-masted ships access to Darling Harbour. It opens only on demand, so you may or may not be lucky enough to catch it in operation.

Across Pyrmont Bridge

Cross to the other side of the bridge and then either descend to dock level on the left-hand side and be tempted by the stores, restaurants, and entertainments of the Harbourside Shopping Complex or descend to the right to reach the **Australian National Maritime Museum ❹** (see pp. 138–140).

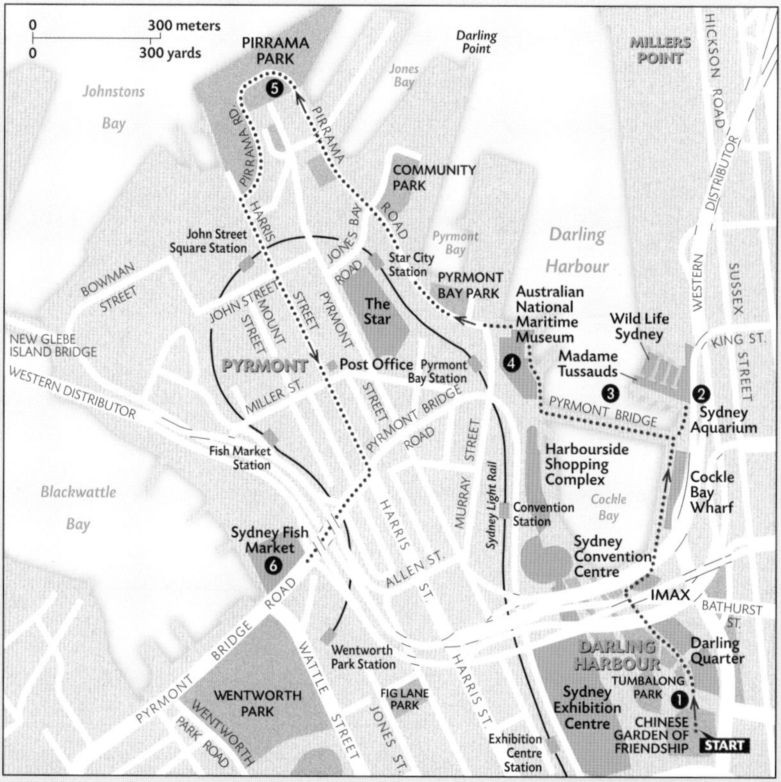

- See also map inside front cover C2
- ➤ Chinese Garden of Friendship
- Allow half a day
- 3 miles (5 km)
- ➤ Sydney Fish Market

Walk along the harbor side of the museum past the museum's assortment of moored vessels. On the far side of the museum, **Pyrmont Bay Park** stretches past the front of the **Star** (see sidebar p. 130), the city's casino. Pirrama Road passes what were once naval facilities and several finger wharves built between 1913 and 1933. Head past the historic Darling Island Road area, now redeveloped and housing mostly offices–including Fairfax, publisher of the *Sydney Morning Herald* newspaper–and on to the renovated **Jones Bay Wharf,** now featuring restaurants, luxury offices, and cruise companies. Note the double-story roadway built out over the bay between parallel wharf sheds to move freight.

Just beyond the wharves is **Pirrama Park ❺.** Opened in 1996 and completely redeveloped a decade later, it features playgrounds, a waterfront promenade, and barbecue areas. Great views of the city, Sydney Harbour Bridge, and New Glebe Island Bridge (opened in 1995) can be enjoyed from here, too.

Follow the road around to Harris Street, passing several of the 1870s pubs and cottages that remain in the area. You'll find several cafés along the street, and on the corner of Scott Street, a signboard highlights the old

The lights of Sydney reflect off Darling Harbour.

INSIDER TIP:

Musically choreographed fireworks explode over Darling Harbour most Saturday evenings June through December.

—VALENTINE QUADRAT
National Geographic Channel

brick tunnel and rail cutting built to service the wharves, now part of the light rail line.

At the old post office (circa 1895, now a bank) on Union Square at the corner of Miller Street, turn right and head down to the Fish Market light rail station. Alternatively, continue along Harris Street to Simon Johnson's Fine Foods, a Sydney institution at No. 181. From there, the **Sydney Fish Market** ❻ *(Bank St. & Pyrmont Bridge Rd., tel 9004 1100)* beckons—just follow the signs.

Each weekday, the market auctions the previous night's catch in the early hours of the morning, finishing at about 8 a.m., and the fish is sold in the surrounding shops. Some of the shops will cook seafood platters for you, or you can try one of the open-air restaurants. A particular pleasure is to take your own picnic supplies out onto the docks and enjoy them at tables while watching the yachts and cruisers coming and going.

Return to the city by Metro Light Rail or walk straight up Pyrmont Bridge Road to Darling Harbour.

Darling Harbour Entertainment

Darling Harbour boasts many entertainment venues that appeal to both young and old. These three stand out.

IMAX Theatre: Located in the massive silver-colored building at the head of Darling Harbour, the IMAX Theatre has the largest screen in the world. Films about wildlife, 3D re-creations of the dinosaurs, and the scenic outdoors predominate. *Southern Promenade, Darling Harbour, tel 9281 3300, www.imax.com.au, $$$$*

Madame Tussauds: This franchise of the famous London attraction sits between the Sydney Aquarium and Wild Life Sydney. Waxwork figures focus on world leaders such as Nelson Mandela and Queen Elizabeth II, pop stars like Lady Gaga, and cultural and Hollywood icons. Australian celebrities such as actors Hugh Jackman and Nicole Kidman feature prominently. *Aquarium Pier, Darling Harbour, tel 9333 9240, www.madametussauds.com.au, $$$*

The Star: Opened in 1995, the Star was the city's first legal gaming house. The casino is open 24/7 year-round and has two large gaming and slot machine areas. The complex also includes theaters, 15 restaurants and bars, shops, and a large hotel/apartment facility. It recently rebranded itself as the Star, but is still widely known by its old name, Star City. *80 Pyrmont St., Pyrmont, tel 9777 9000, www.star.com.au*

because there is a huge amount to see ahead.

The Northern Rivers section showcases the north's tropical mangrove swamps and displays crabs, mudskippers, lungfish, saratoga, and fish of the intertidal zone flooded by monsoon rains, including huge barramundi (they can reach 130 pounds/60 kg), much prized by fishermen.

The aquarium's big tanks draw oohs and aahs, but the smaller tanks hold much of interest, too.

Southern Oceans

The feature of these main tanks is the sharks—Port Jackson, shovelnose, and the gray nurse, one of the aquarium's flagship species, seen up close while strolling through an underwater walkway. Stingrays also glide effortlessly, along with turtles and oddities like sea dragons and pineapple fish.

Among the star attractions, however, are the penguins. In a separate enclosure, the aquarium has a successful breeding colony of little (or fairy) penguins. These small and very cute penguins breed on the southern coastline, where they waddle ashore at dusk to lay their eggs, sometimes in large numbers. The specially designed enclosure re-creates their natural environment with wave action as the penguins dart in the water and glide around you in all three dimensions.

Other facilities include the touch pool, where you can pick up the less harmful creatures of the deep and learn how they

INSIDER TIP:

The aquarium's massive Great Barrier Reef tank is amazing. Linger along the floor-to-ceiling glass walls to watch the sea life swim in and out of view.

—JANE SUNDERLAND
National Geographic contributor

live. The **Sydney & Surrounds** section features the inhabitants of Sydney Harbour and the nearby Pacific coast.

Northern Oceans & Great Barrier Reef

Next along is the Northern Oceans, re-creating the warmer waters of northern Australia, where colorful fish like the clown anemone and giant trevally play among the myriad coral. This section culminates in the Great Barrier Reef display, the highlight of the aquarium.

This is an attempt to produce and sustain a massive piece of tropical coral reef, complete with over 2,000 fish ranging from tiny, coral-dwelling species to tiger sharks. Several smaller tanks allow you to appreciate close-up the beautiful and delicate corals, anemones, and fish life of the reef, but the main tank is simply brilliant. Stocked with some of the most beautiful fish in the world and the various sharks of the reef, the presentation includes floor-to-ceiling glass and grottoes where the smaller fish can keep out of the way of the predators.

And then you come to the huge glass tunnel. As you walk through, fish swim above and you can look straight down the length of the tank while white-tipped reef, black-tipped reef, and leopard sharks swim toward you; stingrays lie on the sand beneath and fish swim all around.

The Sydney Aquarium also features rotating exhibits. It is destined for a new face-lift and rebranding to become Sydney Sea Life Centre. ■

Wild Life Sydney

Next to the Sydney Aquarium, the small indoor zoo Wild Life Sydney *(Aquarium Pier, tel 9333 9288, www.wildlifesydney.com.au, $$$$$)* has wallabies, koalas, nocturnal marsupials, snakes, and birds for a compact glimpse of the weird and wonderful wildlife Australia has on offer.

The popular estuarine crocodile from the Sydney Aquarium has moved to the Kakadu Gorge exhibit here, and a variety of other habitats have been re-created, including the Daintree Rainforest and the outback, which features red kangaroos—the largest of the kangaroo species—emus, and frill-necked lizards. The Nightfall exhibit allows you to see rare nocturnal animals such as the bilby and ghost bat up close, and on the rooftop deck you can pat koalas or breakfast with them.

Some people might prefer the larger spaces at Taronga Zoo (see pp. 96–97), but this popular family attraction is an easy introduction to Australian fauna if your time is limited.

EXPERIENCE: Steep Yourself in Aboriginal Culture

To get anywhere close to a traditional Aboriginal settlement, you will have to venture thousands of miles to the far north or the outback of Australia, but the archaeological sites around Sydney and outings with Aboriginal guides that focus on Aboriginal beliefs, bush activities, and wildlife can be very informative and give you the opportunity to better understand the Aboriginal way of life.

Sydney & Environs

The **Royal Botanic Gardens** (see pp. 54–56) offers an interesting 1.5-hour Aboriginal heritage walk (*$$$$*) on Friday mornings. An Aboriginal guide explains the significance of the grounds to the Cadigal, the original inhabitants of central Sydney, and their use of plants. You'll also taste bush food and learn about traditional music, dance, and artifacts.

At **Taronga Zoo** (see pp. 96–97), you can learn from an Aboriginal guide about the significance and role of wildlife, including koalas, kangaroos, wallabies, and birds, in the Dreamtime stories of creation. The Nura Diya Aboriginal wildlife tour departs at 9:45 a.m. daily.

Several tour companies also incorporate Aboriginal culture into their Sydney tours. **Boutique Tours** (*www.boutiquetoursaustralia.com.au*), for example, stops at the Muru Mittigar Cultural Centre (see pp. 135–136) for traditional stories, bush-food and medicine walks, and boomerang demonstrations.

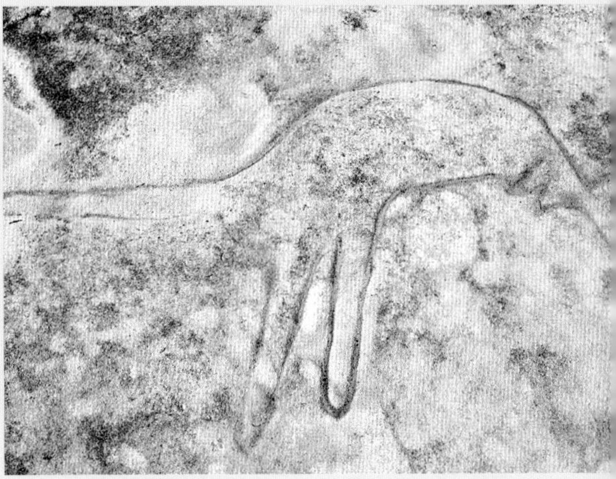

Aboriginal rock carving at Jibbon Headland, Royal National Park

The National Parks

Outside the city, the most significant Aboriginal rock art sites are in the national parks. You can explore them on your own, but an informative, guided walking tour can enhance the experience.

Join the **Jibbon Headland Aboriginal Discovery Tour** (*tel 9542 0649, Wed. & Sat. at 2 p.m., $$$*), organized by the National Parks and Wildlife Service, to visit the sites in Royal National Park (see p. 135). An Aboriginal discovery ranger will guide you from Bundeena along scenic Jibbon Beach to the rock engravings of the Dharawal people at Jibbon Headland. You can also visit Royal with **Understand Down Under** (*www.udu.com.au*), whose cultural tours of the park team up with anthropologists and Dharawal elders for a unique experience.

Ku-ring-gai Chase National Park has the most famous rock art sites around Sydney (see p. 135). **Walkabout Tours** (*www.walkabouttours.com.au*) leads guided walks to the sites.

If you want a little more of a hands-on experience, in the Blue Mountains (see pp. 215–220), Evan Yanna Muru of **Blue Mountains Walkabout** (*tel 0408 443 822*) conducts half- and full-day walking tours that include Darug art and ceremonial sites, Dreamtime stories, ocher bark and body painting, bush-food tastings, wildlife encounters, and sandstone caves.

Indigenous Sydney

Altogether, the Sydney region has some 1,200 known sites where rock engravings, cave paintings, and remains of Aboriginal campsites can be seen, or where Aboriginal ceremonies were held. Sydney's indigenous heritage is one of the richest of any city in the world, and research has shown that as many as 70 percent of visitors to Australia hope to experience this heritage in some form. Many people at the sites described on the following pages will help to take you a step beyond the usual tourist presentations.

A group of Aborigines participates in a ceremony honoring World Youth Day.

The Aboriginal people of Australia have had it hard since the Europeans arrived in 1788, falling victim to disease, massacres, the state-sanctioned separation of children from their parents, and exile to mission stations. For most, the traditional way of life has been overwhelmed, and Aboriginal people have struggled to find a place in the modern world—a situation not helped by the apathy or discrimination of the European settlers. The consequences of unemployment, lack of education, and poor health standards are still widespread.

The good news is that Australia is actively engaged in a process of reconciliation that has placed the delivery of improved health, economic opportunities, and cultural respect and recognition high on the national agenda. There is a very, very long way to go, but some benefits are already beginning to be felt. Perhaps the most significant development is pride; where once some people kept their Aboriginal

The Block

For many Aborigines, the Sydney suburb of Redfern is a modern sacred site, the birthplace of black power and the civil rights struggle in Australia. Centered on the Block—bounded by Eveleigh, Caroline, Louis, and Vine Streets—it was born of protest in the 1970s against landlord eviction of Aboriginal tenants and resulted in the formation of the Aboriginal Housing Company (AHC) to buy houses for the disadvantaged urban Aboriginal population.

A focal point for indigenous activism, the community splintered and violence grew with the heroin epidemic of the 1990s. The Block became a no-go zone, culminating in 2004 riots after an Aboriginal boy died fleeing from police. The government and the Aboriginal-run AHC decided enough was enough and entered into a redevelopment project with private developers, catering for a mixture of nonindigenous and Aboriginal housing. The bulldozer flattened the last of the original houses by 2012. Ironically, the Block is now associated more in the minds of most Australians with a popular reality TV show of the same name, where middle-class couples compete to renovate run-down inner-city real estate for profit.

heritage secret, they are now embracing it.

Visitors can learn something about this culture by visiting gallery and museum exhibitions and cultural centers, attending music and dance performances, shopping for indigenous art and artifacts, or joining tours to significant sites led by Aboriginal guides (see p. 133).

Aboriginal Sites

All the national parks around Sydney have significant Aboriginal sites that include carvings, paintings, and middens (campsites where people gathered to eat oysters, mussels, and other shellfish). Many of these sites are carefully protected, but there is still much to be seen.

At **Ku-ring-gai Chase National Park** (see pp. 174–175) north of the city, the Aboriginal heritage walk, part of the Resolute Trail from the Resolute picnic area, takes in the well-known ocher hand stencil paintings at Red Hands Cave, then some rock engravings and a cave shelter. A short way along the Basin Track, you'll find a significant site: here Dreamtime (see sidebar p. 39) figures, animals, people, weapons, and tools are carved into exposed rock. The Sphinx and Warrimoo Tracks near Bobbin Head have middens and rock engravings, and there are other cave shelters, engravings, and ax-grinding grooves in the West Head area.

One of the most accessible rock carving sites is in **Royal National Park** (see pp. 193–195), on Port Hacking Point near the tiny township of Bundeena. Take the ferry from Cronulla, then walk along Loftus Street and Jibbon Beach to the point. This is the start of the coast walk to the southern end of the park (see p. 195).

Rock engravings and other sites are dotted all around Sydney—at the **Bondi Golf Course,** for example, and if you do the popular **Bondi Beach to Tamarama cliff walk,** keep an eye out for an engraved whale in the rock shelf right next to the path. The **Manly Scenic Walkway** (see pp. 102–103) also passes several Aboriginal engravings, and the **Sydney Harbour National Park** contains numerous Aboriginal sites. The National Parks and Wildlife Service sometimes runs tours focusing on the park's cultural heritage. Check the website or its office in Cadman's Cottage at The Rocks (see p. 75).

Cultural Centers

The only solely Aborigine-operated center near Sydney is the **Muru Mittigar Aboriginal Cultural Centre** *(tel 4729 2377,* *www.murumittigar.com.au)*, highlighting the culture of the Darug people, the traditional inhabitants of the area. Located in Penrith, one hour west of Sydney via the M4 freeway, its museum showcases Aboriginal art, artifacts, and the stories of the Darug and other Aboriginal peoples.

The center has cultural talks, boomerang throwing and didgeridoo workshops, Dreamtime storytelling, dance performances, bush-food tastings, and painting workshops for groups. It also sells Aboriginal art. Muru Mittigar is open daily *(9 a.m.–4 p.m.)*; call ahead to check what's on, which depends on group visits. It may be best to visit on an arranged tour. Sydney Boutique Tours *(tel 9499 5444)* includes the center in its Blue Mountains tour.

The newly opened **Koomurri Aboriginal Centre** *(tel 4782 1979, www.koomurriaboriginalcentre.com.au)* at Katoomba in the Blue Mountains is a cultural center and commercial art gallery offering a good chance to see Aboriginal performances. Corroboree dance shows incorporating four or five different dances are staged throughout the day, as well as didgeridoo performances. The center is right near the Three Sisters lookout at Echo Point.

Major Museum Exhibits

All of Sydney's major museums have Aboriginal sections. Two in particular—the Art Gallery of New South Wales and the Australian Museum—have substantial collections that should not be missed.

Art Gallery of New South Wales: The Art Gallery of New South Wales's (see pp. 61–65) indigenous exhibition, Yiribana,

Where to Buy Aboriginal Art

Many galleries around the city specialize in Aboriginal art, with a broad spectrum of styles and prices. Most reputable dealers provide information on the artists and their cultural origins. If you are considering a major purchase, it is worth visiting the Art Gallery of New South Wales (see pp. 61–65) to get a good grounding in Aboriginal art beforehand. Shops here and at the Australian Museum (see pp. 66–67) have good selections of books on Aboriginal art.

The Artery *(Shop 2, The Westbury, Darlinghurst, tel 9380 8234, www.artery.com.au)* specializes in art from remote Aboriginal communities, such as the Utopia, Mount Leibig, and Pupunya communities in the Northern Territory, to mention a few. The gallery is small but well stocked, with prices to suit most budgets.

The **Boomalli Aboriginal Artists Cooperative** *(55–59 Flood St., Leichhardt, tel 9560 2541, www.boomalli.com.au)* is a long-running art gallery with constantly changing exhibition space. Most works tend to be contemporary, although many reflect Aboriginal culture.

Coo-ee Aboriginal Art Gallery *(31 Lamrock Ave., Bondi Beach, tel 9300 9233, www.cooeeart.com.au)* has a large collections of paintings, prints, and sculptures from all over Australia.

Kate Owen Gallery *(680 Darling St., Rozelle, tel 9555 5283, www.kateowengallery.com.au)* has an extensive Aboriginal painting collection from emerging and established artists such as the famous Clifford Possum. Traditional and contemporary art, including the work of Kudditji Kngwarreye, are represented.

Utopia Art Sydney *(2 Danks St., Waterloo, tel 9699 2900, www.utopiaartsydney.com.au)* specializes in artwork from the Utopia community of central Australia, but the gallery also represents nonindigenous artists.

Major auction houses conduct regular sales of Aboriginal art. Get details from **Christie's** *(www.christies.com)* and **Sotheby's** *(www.sothebysaustralia.com.au)*.

Yiribana Aboriginal and Torres Strait Islander Gallery, Art Gallery of New South Wales, Sydney

is one of Australia's most extensive collections of Aboriginal and Torres Strait Islander art and culture. It reflects the fundamental connection between Aboriginal art and the land and includes items collected in the 1930s and '40s. Contemporary works reflect the Aborigines' emerging sense of cultural pride, often mixed with a sense of humor. Notable are the works of Emily Kame Kngwarreye (circa 1916–1996), deeply personal expressions of central Australia, her homeland. Lin Onus (1948–1996) depicts the meeting of Aboriginal and European culture with gentle humor in his sculpture "Fruit Bats."

Australian Museum: In the Indigenous Australians gallery of the Australian Museum (see pp. 66–67), artifacts from the past illuminate spirituality and cultural heritage, while contemporary materials explain current social justice issues. A wide variety of tools and weapons from different tribal groups across the country are presented, as are types of shelters, bush foods, and cooking methods. The struggle of Aboriginal people for recognition of their very existence and for land rights is presented in picture and video.

Other Museums: Aboriginal canoes that are thousands of years old can be seen at the **Australian National Maritime Museum** (see pp. 138–140). The **Powerhouse Museum** (see pp. 124–126) mounts regular exhibitions on specific areas of art and culture. The **Museum of Sydney** (see p. 52) has an interesting section on Aboriginal culture and Aboriginal leaders at the time of the first settlement. The **Aboriginal Heritage Museum & Keeping Place** *(39/137–145 Sailors Bay Rd., Northbridge, tel 9949 9882, closed Sat.–Sun.)* has an interesting collection of Aboriginal tools, weapons, and everyday items, as well as detailing the impact of colonialism, at its small museum in northern Sydney.

Australian National Maritime Museum

The Australian National Maritime Museum is housed at the western end of Pyrmont Bridge in a distinctive building that resembles the spread of sail of a tall ship. Opened in 1991, its aim is to represent the relationship between Australians and the sea throughout the country's history. So, in one gallery you'll see dugout canoes built by Aborigines several thousand years ago, and in another, high-tech 18-footers constructed from space-age materials.

Museumgoers may board several wooden sailing boats and other vessels moored outside.

In between are many relics and treasures, including some of the earliest maps of Australia, navigational equipment, and presentations illustrating convict transportation and the arrival immigrants to Australian shores.

For those interested in 18-footers, there are two examples of the craft from very different eras. One is a cedar-built racer from the 1940s; the other is one of the ultimate racing machines from the 1970s (see pp. 156–157). One of the museum's greatest treasures, the Blaeu celestial globe hides in a darkened corner to protect it from deterioration. This priceless

INSIDER TIP:

A tour of the H.M.A.S. *Onslow,* an Oberon class submarine, is a must-do at the maritime museum.

—STEPHEN CAHOON
Acting deputy director, Maritime and Logistics Management, National Centre for Ports and Shipping, Australian Maritime College

1602 globe was one of the first to the show the Southern Cross and other constellations of the Southern Hemisphere.

On the lower level, you can see the slowly rotating steam engine that was originally used in one of the car ferries that serviced North Sydney before the Harbour Bridge was built. Here, too, is the U.S.A. Gallery, housing both permanent and visiting exhibitions. Funded by the United States, the gallery mounts exhibitions that explore the shared maritime and trade history between the two countries. The ties go back to the 18th century, when the first foreign vessel to visit the fledgling colony in Sydney was a U.S. trading ship, the brig *Philadelphia,* which arrived in November 1792.

Outdoor Exhibits

For many, the vessels moored on the wharf outside are the main highlight. Look for the *Krait,* a World War II commando boat that was used in daring raids in Southeast Asia; a racing cutter dating from 1888; and a Vietnamese fishing boat used by refugees fleeing to Australia after the Vietnam War (1975). Pearling luggers and Indonesian fishing boats are on display, and often visiting yachts are invited to moor here because they have features of interest to visitors.

The H.M.B. *Endeavour* is a stunningly accurate reproduction of the ship that James Cook captained on his voyage of discovery, circumnavigating the world 1768–1771. It usually takes pride of place on the dock, though it sails around the country a couple of months a year; then, other rigs take its place, such as the tall ship *James Craig* (see sidebar p. 140).

And, of course, there is the H.M.A.S. *Vampire,* one of the last big-gun destroyers (these days

Australian National Maritime Museum

- Map p. 123
- 2 Murray St., Darling Harbour
- 9298 3777
- $$ ($$$$ including entry to wharf vessels)
- Pyrmont Bay Station, bus 433 from Circular Quay, or City Sightseeing bus
- Pyrmont Bay

www.anmm.gov.au

Captain Cook & the Hubble Telescope

One of the maritime museum's most interesting exhibits is the reproduction of Capt. James Cook's ship *Endeavour.* In the eyes of many Australians, the vessel is almost a holy relic, and while the ship reflects the close ties Australia has with England, it also has an interesting connection with the United States. Two engravings from the *Endeavour* were taken aboard the space shuttle *Endeavour* when it flew a mission to repair the Hubble Telescope. The connection is even more appropriate because one of Cook's tasks during his world voyage was to observe the 1769 transit of Venus across the face of the sun—he traveled to Tahiti to do so—an astronomical activity akin to the Hubble's today.

James Craig

The pride of the Australian National Maritime Museum fleet, the magnificently restored tall ship *James Craig* was built in 1874 and hauled cargo around the world, passing Cape Horn 23 times, before settling on the trans-Tasman route between Australia and New Zealand. She remained in service until 1934, when she became beached and was abandoned in Tasmania; the long process of rehabilitation began in 1972. The *James Craig* relives the age of sail on cruises most weekends *(tel 9298 3888, www.shf.org.au, $$$$$).*

they're all guided missiles). Other vessels that may be on display include the H.M.A.S. *Onslow,* a submarine decommissioned in 1999.

On the water is the CLS4 lighthouse ship *Carpentaria* (once used in the Gulf of Carpentaria), and on the dock you can climb the relocated Cape Bowling Green Lighthouse.

Note that the area between the museum and the water is open to the public, which means that you can view the boats for free, though you will have to pay to board them.

If all this exposure to things maritime has you itching to take to the water, join the introductory sailing school that operates from the wharf area. And on weekends, several of the local boating societies run short voyages aboard steam vessels and tugboats.

A café in front of the museum overlooks the waterfront, and the museum shop is well stocked with nautical gifts and books. ■

The museum reveals the full breadth of Australia's maritime history.

Beach culture, elegant harborside living, artists' enclaves, the gay scene, and much more—all compressed between the city and the sea

Eastern Suburbs

Introduction & Map 142–143

Paddington & Woollahra 144–145

Experience: Watch a Rugby Match 145

Bohemian Sydney 146–147

Experience: Explore Gay Sydney 147

Feature: Mardi Gras 148

Eastern Sydney Beaches 149–151

Experience: A Day at the Beach 150

A Walk Around South Head 152–153

The Bays 154–158

Experience: Flightsee the Bays 155

Feature: Eighteen-Foot Sailing Skiffs 156–157

Experience: Learn to Sail 157

Hotels & Restaurants 247–251

A juggler performs outside Paddington Markets

Eastern Suburbs

Covering the area east of the city to the coast, the eastern suburbs represent suburban, cosmopolitan, and cultural diversity. They are an incredible mix of the salubrious and the salacious—wealth, poverty, hedonism, and the highbrow. This is the most desirable precinct of Sydney, containing within its borders just about every lifestyle imaginable and every amenity of modern life.

The village-like feel of working-class Surry Hills

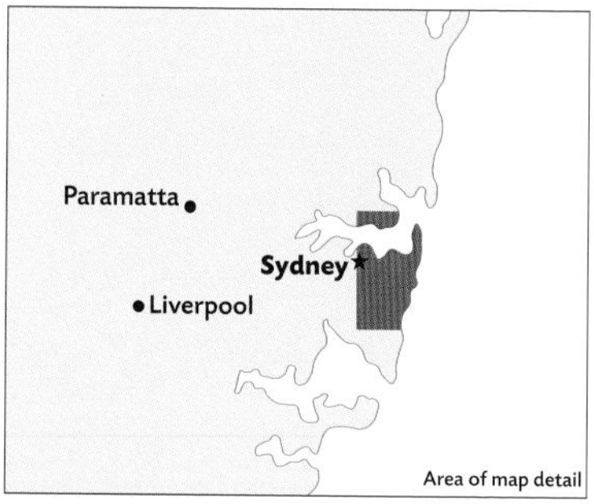

Here you'll find major art galleries and museums, more restaurants and cafés than you could ever hope to try in one visit, and some of the most seriously rich harborfront living available. If you've made it here, you've probably made it everywhere, as the list of overseas property owners can attest—movie stars, business people, royalty.

Some of the most significant early houses in the country are found here, too, including Elizabeth Bay House and Vaucluse House, both beautifully preserved.

The eastern suburbs are also the center of Sydney's gay community, which is concentrated on the city end of Oxford Street and the surrounding area. The annual Sydney Gay and Lesbian Mardi Gras festival culminates in the Mardi Gras parade—one of the biggest street parades in the world, with hundreds of spectacular floats watched by hundreds of thousands of people.

On the shores of the harbor, the various bays offer safe anchorage, restaurants, walks, and swimming. Beach life centers on Australia's most famous beach, Bondi. There can be no greater pleasure than a plunge into the Pacific Ocean breakers (always take care to swim between the flags), followed by an ice cream or fish-and-chips at one of the beach cafés. ■

NOT TO BE MISSED:

Browsing Paddington's market 144

The walk to Coogee around the cliffs from Bondi 151

Day-tripping to Watsons Bay and walking to South Head 152–153

Historic Elizabeth Bay House 154

Flightseeing from Rose Bay on a seaplane 155

Visiting Vaucluse House for a slice of colonial history 158

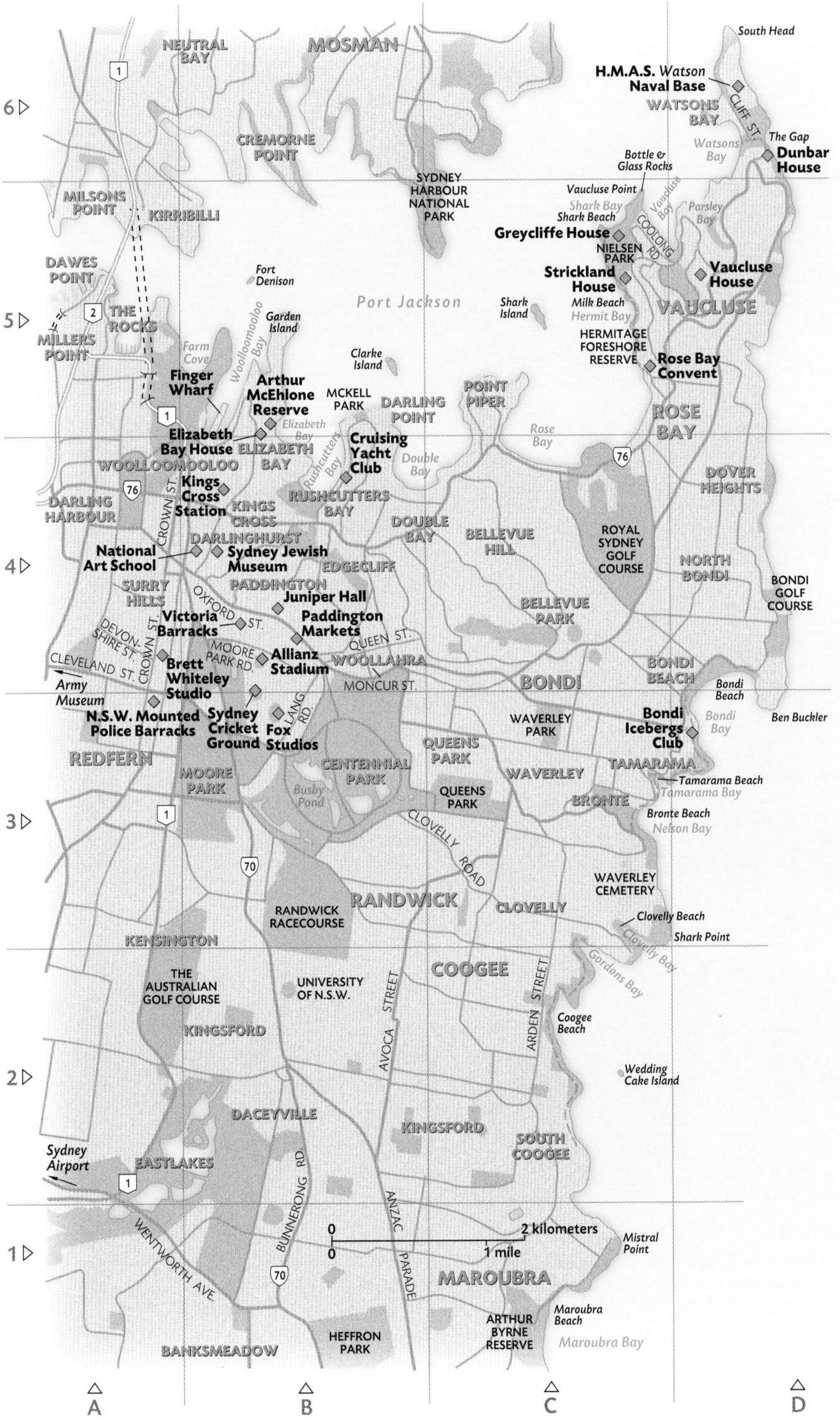
NEUTRAL BAY
MOSMAN
South Head
H.M.A.S. Watson Naval Base
WATSONS BAY
CLIFF ST.
The Gap
Dunbar House
Watsons Bay
CREMORNE POINT
Bottle & Glass Rocks
SYDNEY HARBOUR NATIONAL PARK
Vaucluse Point
Shark Bay
Vaucluse Bay
Parsley Bay
Shark Beach
MILSONS POINT
KIRRIBILLI
Greycliffe House
COOLONG RD.
NIELSEN PARK
DAWES POINT
Fort Denison
Strickland House
Vaucluse House
Port Jackson
Shark Island
Milk Beach
Hermit Bay
VAUCLUSE
THE ROCKS
Garden Island
Woolloomooloo Bay
MILLERS POINT
Farm Cove
HERMITAGE FORESHORE RESERVE
Clarke Island
Rose Bay Convent
Finger Wharf
Arthur McElhone Reserve
MCKELL PARK
DARLING POINT
POINT PIPER
ROSE BAY
Elizabeth Bay House
Elizabeth Bay
ELIZABETH BAY
Cruising Yacht Club
Rushcutters Bay
Rose Bay
Double Bay
WOOLLOOMOOLOO
Kings Cross Station
KINGS CROSS
DOVER HEIGHTS
DARLING HARBOUR
CROWN ST.
RUSHCUTTERS BAY
DOUBLE BAY
BELLEVUE HILL
ROYAL SYDNEY GOLF COURSE
DARLINGHURST
National Art School
Sydney Jewish Museum
EDGECLIFF
NORTH BONDI
BONDI GOLF COURSE
SURRY HILLS
PADDINGTON
OXFORD ST.
Juniper Hall
BELLEVUE PARK
Victoria Barracks
Paddington Markets
DEVONSHIRE ST.
QUEEN ST.
MOORE PARK RD.
Allianz Stadium
WOOLLAHRA
BONDI BEACH
CLEVELAND ST.
Brett Whiteley Studio
MONCUR ST.
BONDI
Bondi Beach
Army Museum
N.S.W. Mounted Police Barracks
Sydney Cricket Ground
LANG RD.
Fox Studios
WAVERLEY PARK
Bondi Icebergs Club
Bondi Bay
Ben Buckler
REDFERN
MOORE PARK
CENTENNIAL PARK
QUEENS PARK
WAVERLEY
TAMARAMA
Tamarama Beach
Tamarama Bay
Busby Pond
QUEENS PARK
BRONTE
Bronte Beach
Nelson Bay
CLOVELLY ROAD
WAVERLEY CEMETERY
RANDWICK RACECOURSE
RANDWICK
CLOVELLY
Clovelly Beach
Shark Point
KENSINGTON
Clovelly Bay
Gordons Bay
THE AUSTRALIAN GOLF COURSE
UNIVERSITY OF N.S.W.
COOGEE
AVOCA STREET
ARDEN STREET
Coogee Beach
KINGSFORD
Wedding Cake Island
DACEYVILLE
KINGSFORD
SOUTH COOGEE
Sydney Airport
EASTLAKES
BUNNERONG RD.
ANZAC PARADE
0 2 kilometers
0 1 mile
Mistral Point
WENTWORTH AVE.
MAROUBRA
ARTHUR BYRNE RESERVE
Maroubra Beach
Maroubra Bay
HEFFRON PARK
BANKSMEADOW
1
2
76
70
6
5
4
3
2
1
A
B
C
D

Paddington & Woollahra

Originally a down-at-heel, working-class district southeast of the city center, Paddington is now one of the most sought-after addresses in Sydney. Long gentrified by young professionals eager to live close to the center, whole streetscapes of Victorian terrace houses remain intact thanks to the area's heritage values. Elegant boutiques and eateries are dotted along the main thoroughfare, Oxford Street, which really comes alive on Saturdays when the market is held.

The Paddington Markets draw people from far and wide.

Paddington & Woollahra
143 B4

Victoria Barracks
Oxford St., Paddington
9339 3170
Museum & tour Thurs., museum only Sun.
Donation
Bus 333, 380, 392, & 396

To appreciate the true character of Paddington, from the shopping area in the middle section of Oxford Street, deviate into the many side streets. Here you'll see beautiful houses with wrought-iron lace balconies, railings, arched windows, and window boxes spilling flowers. Some of the most interesting shops and boutiques can be found down William Street.

Also on Oxford Street is **Victoria Barracks,** established in 1841, where Sydney's armed forces are stationed. The beautifully proportioned main building, which faces the parade ground, was built in the Georgian style by Lt. Col. George Barney of the Royal Engineers and 150 convicts, including many French Canadians, transported after a rebellion in 1837–1838. A changing-of-the-guard ceremony takes place at the barracks main gate on Thursdays at 10 a.m., followed by guided tours and band performances. You can also visit the **Army Museum** *(Thurs. & Sun. only),* housed in the original military prison. Opposite the barracks, designer boutiques line Oxford Street and Glenmore Road.

At 248 Oxford Street is **Juniper Hall.** Now owned by the National Trust, it is rented as a commercial property. It is the oldest building east of the city, built in 1824 by Robert Cooper (a gin distiller, hence the hall's name) in colonial style.

On Saturdays, you can browse the **Paddington Markets** on the grounds of the Paddington Uniting Church from 10 a.m. to 4 p.m. Clothes, trinkets, handicrafts, food, and more are for sale. *(Note that parking is very difficult on weekends.)*

Woollahra

Just before reaching the large intersection of Oxford Street and Moore Park Road, Queen Street branches off east toward the suburb of Woollahra. Queen Street's grand terraces soon give way to a string of fine art and antiques stores. Woollahra has long been one of the redoubts of old Sydney money. At the intersection with Moncur Street, you'll find one of the city's better known eateries, Bistro Moncur (see Travelwise p. 249).

If instead of turning off to Queen Street you continue to the intersection of Oxford and Moore Park, you'll find one of the entrances to **Centennial Park,** the city's premier recreational area. The park has ample parking and free barbecue facilities. An extensive lake system attracts plenty of birdlife and birders, while a fine café serves lunches *(tel 9380 9350, weekend reservations essential)* with an attached kiosk for light fare. You can rent horses or take lessons from the Equestrian Centre *(tel 9332 2809)*. Bicycles can be hired in the park *(tel 9398 5027)* near the Grand Drive–Hamilton Drive intersection, and an in-line skate rental shop *(122 Lang Rd., tel 9368 0945)* is nearby.

Across Lang Road is Moore Park and the **Entertainment Quarter.** Home to Fox Studios, where *The Matrix, Moulin Rouge,* and other movies were made, the quarter boasts entertainment venues, movie theaters, a bowling alley, restaurants, bars, and shops. A produce market is held here Wednesdays and Saturdays, while Sundays' market features clothing, jewelry, and housewares.

Next door you'll find the **Sydney Cricket Ground** (SCG), and the **Allianz Stadium,** two of the city's main sporting venues. The SCG has a sports museum, which can be visited on a tour *(tel 1300 724 737, $$$$$)* that takes in both venues. ■

EXPERIENCE: Watch a Rugby Match

For insight into the gladiatorial passion of this sports-crazed city, catch a game of rugby football, the "gentleman's game played by hooligans." Rugby union, founded at England's elite Rugby School, is the purist form of the game, and international matches attract big audiences, particularly when Australia plays New Zealand's All Blacks. However, rugby league—the tough, working-class, cut-down version of the game—is the most popular spectator sport in Sydney.

The two main venues to see a rugby league match are the Olympic Stadium at Homebush (see p. 167) and, closer to the city, the Allianz Stadium in Woollahra. Olympic Stadium, home ground of the Canterbury-Bankstown Bulldogs and the South Sydney Rabbitohs (owned by actor Russell Crowe), is an impressive venue, but it takes a big crowd to fill and you can be a long way from the action. The smaller Allianz *(Moore Park Rd., tel 9360 6601, www.scgt.nsw.gov.au)*, home to the Sydney Roosters, Wests Tigers, and rugby union's Waratahs, will get you closer to the play. Buy tickets at the grounds or through online agencies such as Ticketek *(premier .ticketek.com.au)* and Ticketmaster *(www .ticketmaster.com.au)*.

Bohemian Sydney

From the tip of Garden Island, south through Woolloomooloo and Kings Cross, Darlinghurst and Surry Hills, to Redfern, there is about as broad a cross section of life as you are likely to find anywhere. This is an area where artists, writers, and actors live and congregate, and where you'll find Sydney's gay community, educational establishments, and some great small museums.

The interior of the Sydney Jewish Museum, showing one of the points of its Star of David design

Woolloomooloo & Kings Cross
143 A4–B4

Darlinghurst
143 B4

Woolloomooloo & Kings Cross

Woolloomooloo was once disreputable and boisterous—full of sailors on shore leave, small-time criminals, prostitutes, and gangs. These days, it is a lot safer and more respectable. Renovated **Finger Wharf** is the site of the chic Blue Hotel (see Travelwise p. 247), upmarket restaurants, and exclusive apartments favored by Sydney A-listers such as Russell Crowe.

Up the hill is Macleay Street, the main thoroughfare of **Kings Cross.** In the 1960s, it became famous for its strip clubs and brawling bars around the El Alamein Fountain, catering to soldiers on R&R from Vietnam. Sleaze is slowly being cleaned up, and backpackers now flock here. Head to Victoria Street—a beautiful, wide, tree-lined street with cheap hostels on its grand terraces—for several good-quality but affordable cafés and restaurants.

Darlinghurst

Darlinghurst, primarily an area of apartments, restaurants, and small art galleries, begins on the south side of William Street. It boasts restaurant strips along Crown Street at its intersection with Stanley Street, Darlinghurst Road, Victoria Street, and Oxford Street.

The **Sydney Jewish Museum** sits on the corner of Burton Street and Darlinghurst Road. Many European Jews who escaped the Holocaust recorded their stories for the museum, and these now form part of a memorial to the history of Australian Jews reaching back to the First Fleet. Many of the museum's guides are Holocaust survivors, and the building is arranged around a Star of David.

INSIDER TIP:

Stop at historic Harry's Café de Wheels in Woolloomooloo *(Cowper Wharf & Brougham Rds., www.harryscafedewheels.com.au)* for one of their famous "pies and peas."

—CATHERINE PEARSON
National Geographic contributor

The old Darlinghurst jail, across from the museum, is now the **National Art School.** The buildings, designed by Francis Greenway, date back to the 1820s and house an interesting historical exhibit upstairs. A stroll through the grounds will bring you to Oxford Street and Taylor Square, the hub of the gay community.

EXPERIENCE: Explore Gay Sydney

Dive into Sydney's gay community beyond the streets of Darlinghurst and its neighboring suburbs by treating yourself to an evening tour inspired by the 1994 Oscar-winning (best costume design) movie *The Adventures of Priscilla, Queen of the Desert*, the tale of Sydney drag queens taking their show to the outback. Professional diva Portia Turbo, who appeared in the movie, leads the flamboyant city tours *(tel 9310 0200, www.toursbydiva.com.au, $$$$$)*, providing an entertaining running commentary. As you sip champagne, you'll take in the usual (Opera House, Harbour Bridge) and the bent (Oxford Strip gay haunts), with opportunities to don a wig and perform.

Surry Hills & East Redfern

South of Darlinghurst is Surry Hills, another former working-class suburb undergoing gentrification. It is quieter than nearby Darlinghurst, and the shops and restaurants along Crown Street have a village feel. Cleveland Street is known for its Middle Eastern restaurants. The **Brett Whiteley Studio,** a block east of Crown Street, is a museum devoted to one of Sydney's most famous painters.

Farther down Crown Street, just across Cleveland Street in East Redfern, is the **N.S.W. Mounted Police Barracks.** The mounted unit is the world's oldest. Group tours of the barracks and its small museum operate Tuesdays and Thursdays only *(tel 9319 2154, reservations essential).* ■

Sydney Jewish Museum
- Map: 143 B4
- Address: 148 Darlinghurst Rd., Darlinghurst
- Tel: 9360 7999
- Closed Sat.
- $$

www.sydneyjewishmuseum.com.au

National Art School
- Map: 143 A4
- Address: Forbes St., Darlinghurst
- Tel: 9339 8744

Surry Hills & East Redfern
- Map: 143 A3–A4

Brett Whiteley Studio
- Map: 143 A4
- Address: 2 Raper St., Surry Hills
- Tel: 9225 1744 (Art Gallery of N.S.W.)

Mardi Gras

Light shows, fireworks, thumping pop music, incredible costumes, colorful floats, thousands upon thousands of people: The sheer spectacle of the Gay and Lesbian Mardi Gras parade along Oxford and Flinders Streets in Darlinghurst, held every year in late February or early March, is one of the highlights of Sydney's annual calendar of events.

Evening wear, Mardi Gras style

The parade has its origins in a June 24, 1978, march commemorating the ninth anniversary of the Stonewall uprising in New York, which centered on gay and lesbian rights. When a parade began at Taylor Square, New South Wales police attempted to stop its progress. The marchers regrouped down the hill on William Street but were forced into Darlinghurst Road, where the police were waiting to set upon the marchers. Violence had been prevalent in the police force for years, but on this occasion TV cameras, photographers, and journalists were on hand.

The brutality gave credence to claims of intimidation that had been circulating for years. It also added to the increasing pressure for change, and the parade became both an annual event and a potent force on the political agenda. The parade has become a mainstream event, televised every year and attended by growing crowds, providing a clear insight into how far Sydney has come.

A Spectacle of Sequins

For many participants, there are only two dress options—bare flesh or sequins. For others, however, the parade is still closely linked to its origins, so among the razzle-dazzle, there are more subdued groups representing the different services and organizations found in all communities.

However, it is the showstopping element of the festival that draws the large crowds. Usually kicking off the proceedings every year are the Dykes on Bikes—bare-breasted lesbian women riding large motorcycles. One of the highlights of the parade is the Marching Boys, who perform elaborate routines along the mile-long (1.6 km) parade route. Other groups specialize in biting satirical comment.

There are a few tips worth noting for those intending to witness the parade spectacles.

- Be prepared for some sights you may not have seen before. Complete nudity isn't permitted, but many entrants get very close to it.
- Bring some refreshments. There are food and drink outlets, but you may lose a good viewing position while you are trying to buy something.
- Locate the portable toilet facilities and make sure you can get to and from them without getting lost.
- Try to bring something safe to stand on so that you can see over people's heads.

Afterward, be prepared for chaos on the roads and huge crowds trying to take public transportation. Most importantly, though, have a great time.

Details about the festival can be found online at *www.mardigras.org.au*.

Eastern Sydney Beaches

Sydney has some of the most beautiful beaches in the world right on its doorstep. An office worker in the city can finish for the day and be in the waves half an hour later. From famous Bondi Beach to stylish Tamarama and family-oriented Clovelly and Coogee Beaches, this coast offers something for everyone.

The sands of Bondi Beach are backed by some of the most sought-after real estate anywhere.

Bondi Beach

No beach in Australia is better known to overseas visitors by name than Bondi. To Australians, it is a symbol of the relaxed outdoor lifestyle they cherish.

The Bondi Surf Bathers' Life Saving Club, the first of its kind in the world, was formed here in 1907 (see sidebar p. 151). The Bondi Icebergs are a hardy bunch who swim throughout winter in baths at the southern end of the beach.

Bondi is the most accessible beach from the city, a mere 5 miles (8 km) away. Being surrounded by apartments on all but the ocean side, it has been described as "Venice with a swell."

If you choose to swim, do so between the pairs of flags placed at intervals along the beach and try to avoid taking any valuables to the beach. Note that there are protected swimming baths at both ends of the beach that are suitable for children.

Bondi Beach

143 D3–D4

Bus 380 from the city; train to Bondi Junction Station then bus 380 or 381; or City Sightseeing Bondi Explorer bus

Tamarama Beach
143 C3
Bus 381 from Bondi Junction Station

Bronte Beach
143 C3
Bus 378 from Bondi Junction Station

Clovelly Beach
143 C3
Bus 339 or L94 from the city

Coogee Beach
143 C2
Bus 372, 373 or 377 from the city.

Youth hostels abound here, and there are some good-quality hotels as well.

South of Bondi

The first beach south from Bondi is **Tamarama Beach,** one of the smallest along this stretch of coast. The sand is often littered with beautiful people. There is a kiosk/café, and the beach has a surf patrol.

Winding around the next headland, you descend to **Bronte Beach,** popular with surfers wanting to catch the strong current (a rip) out to the back breakers. The beach is patrolled, but tends to have fairly rough and unforgiving surf. There is a sheltered ocean pool, however, with plenty of picnic areas and cafés nearby.

Continue around the headland and through the Waverley Cemetery onto the paths and suburban streets leading to **Clovelly Beach.** Due to its sheltered position, this beach and its pool are ideal for families with children.

Farther on is **Gordons Bay.** This is just a small unpatrolled patch of sand, but the area is popular for snorkeling, and there is an underwater "marine walk" for diving enthusiasts.

Next is **Coogee Beach,** one of the perennial favorites with families, as it is usually fairly sheltered from the ocean waves. There are ocean-fed pools as well.

Offshore is **Wedding Cake Island,** a rock named for its shape and white "icing" of guano. Back from the water is a shopping strip.

EXPERIENCE: A Day at the Beach

Enjoy a quintessential Australian pastime: a day at the beach swimming, surfing, and socializing. Most beaches have a pavilion with changing rooms and kiosks selling light refreshments. Shops and other dining options are usually just across the road. While some rent sporting equipment (kayaks, windsurfers, boogie boards), bring your own beach chair, umbrella, and towel. Don't forget the sunscreen, and always swim between the red-and-yellow flags at patrolled surf beaches.

But which beach? There are dozens of superb options less than an hour from Sydney. The ocean surf beaches top most polls, but sheltered harbor beaches offer safe swimming, with many netted to keep out sharks. As you head southward from Sydney Harbour, you'll find **Bondi Beach** is crowded but great for people-watching, with plenty of nearby bars, cafés, and shops. Pretty **Tamarama Beach,** dubbed "Glamarama" for its beautiful people, has just one café; watch the savage rips here. **Bronte Beach** offers safe swimming in the rock pool, and **Coogee Beach** is a smaller version of Bondi. The farthest beach is **Cronulla Beach;** it has excellent surf beaches just a short stroll from the shopping center and train station.

North of Sydney Harbour, **Manly Beach,** worth it for the ferry ride alone, is hard to beat and has lots of nearby dining; small, protected **Shelly Beach** is a short walk away. North of Manly, **Freshwater Beach** has excellent surf, a rock pool, and no tourists.

Of the harbor beaches, popular **Balmoral Beach** has an art deco pavilion with restaurants and kayak rental. Hidden gem **Shark Beach** in Nielsen Park, Vaucluse, is netted and has a pavilion with a café.

Surf Lifesaving Clubs

Nothing evokes Sydney better than images of blue sky, golden sand, and the bronzed figures of its legendary surf lifesavers in their distinctive red-and-yellow caps. The world's first surf lifesaving club was formed at the Bondi Pavilion in 1907 in response to a rising number of drownings, as increasing numbers of people began to pursue the new craze of bodysurfing. Few knew anything about riptides or surf conditions then, because until around 1900, the authorities had outlawed daylight swimming as an affront to public decency.

Surf lifesaving clubs quickly sprang up all around Australia. There are now 305 of them, with 25,000 active members who rescue about 13,000 swimmers each year. Surf lifesaving has also become a sport in its own right, with colorful surf carnivals.

Bondi lifesavers, who guard Australia's busiest and most famous beach and have inspired their own reality TV show, *Bondi Rescue,* pluck more than 1,000 people out of the surf every year. To make sure you don't add to the tally, swim between the red-and-yellow flags. If you do get caught in a riptide, do not try to fight it. Raise your hand to attract attention and swim parallel to the beach to get out of the tide.

Maroubra Beach, 2.5 miles (4 km) farther south, is more suburban than the other beaches, but it offers an ocean pool and safe swimming as well as legendary surfing. You'll find a café at the northern headland, and showers and a kiosk on the beach.

You can explore the coast on foot via the 3.5-mile (6 km) **Bondi to Coogee walk** that starts from the southern end of Bondi Beach and ends at Coogee Beach. Bus routes to the beaches along the way make it possible to catch a ride back to the city. ■

Maroubra Beach

143 C1

Bus 376, 377, 396, or 397 from the city

When not on Bondi's famous beach, people crowd the town's outdoor cafés.

A Walk Around South Head

This pleasant walk from Watsons Bay combines harbor and ocean views, including a great view of the entrance to Sydney Harbour. There are also several sites that have historical connections with the First Fleet, shipwrecks, and 19th- and 20th-century defenses such as cannon and antisubmarine stations.

The *Dunbar's* anchor takes pride of place at the memorial lookout that honors the wrecked clipper.

Start from **Fishermans Wharf ❶** at Watsons Bay *(reached by ferry from Circular Quay, or bus routes 324 & 325)* and take the promenade past the Watsons Bay Hotel, with its beer garden and outdoor bistro area, and Doyles on the Beach seafood restaurant (see Travelwise p. 249), one of the city's institutions. Climb the stairs at the end of the promenade, then turn left and left again onto Pacific Street. At the end of Pacific Street, you will come to a small headland, **Laings Point ❷**. Here are the remains of World War II gun emplacements and the antitorpedo and antisubmarine boom that was stretched across the harbor during the war years.

Continue to the right, where there is a memorial to Governor Phillip. The small beach below is called **Camp Cove Beach ❸**; this is where Phillip first landed when he entered Sydney Harbour in January 1788 with the First Fleet and spent his first night on Australian soil. At the other side of the sandy stretch of beach, ascend the stairs and you will shortly pass a gun that dates from 1872, part of the defenses built as fortification against a threat of invasion by Russia.

A little farther on is **Lady Bay Beach ❹**,

NOT TO BE MISSED:

Laings Point • Camp Cove Beach • Hornby Lighthouse • Naval Chapel

currently the harbor's only designated nude bathing beach. The path passes discreetly above the beach, and just beyond the beach it breaks clear of the trees onto low headland heath, which Sydney Harbour National Park is regenerating to its original condition.

The Headland & The Gap

On the headland itself are two historic lighthouse keeper's cottages and the **Hornby Lighthouse ❺,** a little farther on. All were built in 1858 after two tragic disasters the year before: the wrecks of the *Dunbar* and the *Catherine Adamson* (see p. 100). You can also see World War II fortifications and gun emplacements on the headland.

Follow the path as it loops around the seaward side of the headland before rejoining the path from Lady Bay and heading south.

Next, turn onto Cliff Street. A little ways down, a small path cuts straight across national park land to the Tasman Sea coast and The Gap, where the *Dunbar* came to grief. There are several paths around the cliff tops here; one leads to the **Dunbar Memorial Lookout ❻.** From here, it's just a short stroll west along Military Road to the bus stop and the wharf on Watsons Bay.

- See also map p. 143 D6
- ➤ Watsons Bay wharf
- Allow 1.5–2 hours
- 2 miles (3 km)
- ➤ Watsons Bay wharf

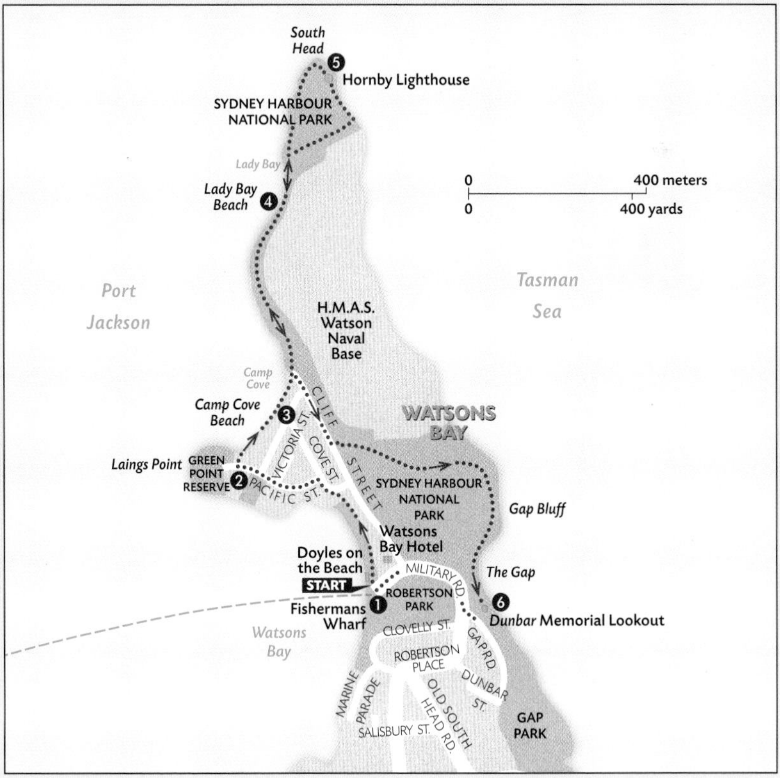

The Bays

One of the features of the eastern suburbs that gives the area much of its character is the succession of bays and headlands that stretches from Garden Island eastward along the harbor to South Head. The bays boast some of the most expensive real estate in the world, with lavish waterfront houses, delightful parks, and historic estates dating from the 19th century.

The town of Watsons Bay offers cliffside walks that overlook the Pacific Ocean.

Elizabeth Bay
143 B4–B5

Rushcutters Bay
143 B4

Elizabeth & Rushcutters

Heading east from the city, the first bay you reach is Elizabeth Bay, just down the hill from Kings Cross railway station. A pleasant place for a picnic, and a pocket of some of the city's most expensive real estate, one of its prime assets is **Elizabeth Bay House,** on Onslow Avenue. Completed in 1839 for the colonial secretary of New South Wales, Alexander Macleay, its showpiece is the oval main saloon with a cantilevered stone staircase and soaring, domed ceiling. The views from the upper windows across Sydney Harbour to the heads are alone worth the price of admission.

After your visit, cut through the tiny Arthur McElhone Reserve in front to Bilyard Avenue, turn right, then at the end turn left on Ithaca Road. This will bring you to **Beare Park,** once part of the Macleay estate, offering fine harbor views and an overview of Elizabeth Bay.

The next bay eastward is Rushcutters Bay, where the Cruising Yacht Club of Australia is based. The club, at the head of the bay, is responsible for the Sydney end of the Sydney to Hobart Yacht Race. In the days prior to the start of the race on December 26, the whole area takes on a carnival atmosphere as the boats begin to assemble. The very expensive piece of real estate that forms the next headland is **Darling Point,** where there is a delightful little picnic and scenic spot, **McKell Park,** the site of a former hospital.

INSIDER TIP:

The eastern suburbs are where the rich and famous live. In Rose Bay, treat yourself to lunch at Catalina (*catalinarosebay.com .au*), which has million-dollar harbor views.

—DEAN DEZIUS

Director of programming, National Geographic Channel Australia

Double, Rose, & Shark

On the other side of Darling Point is Double Bay. Two things are of particular note here: exclusive real estate and the elite of Sydney Harbour skiff racing (see pp. 156–157). Synonymous with old money, Double Bay boasts fine restaurants, expensive shops, and the Stamford Plaza Hotel, once the haunt of movie stars and presidents, though Double Bay is not the magnet for visiting elites it used to be.

Double Bay
143 B4–C4

Rose Bay
143 C4–C5

Shark Bay
143 C5

EXPERIENCE: Flightsee the Bays

Sydney Harbour sparkles and dazzles from any angle on any sunny day, but views from the air will take your breath away. In Rose Bay, you can board a seaplane: **Sydney Seaplanes** *(www.seaplanes.com.au)* and **Sydney by Seaplane** *(www.sydneybyseaplane.com)* both fly north along the Pacific coast to Palm Beach. **Sydney by Air** *(tel 9760 4066)* and **Australia by Air** *(www.australiabyair.com.au)* fly out of Bankstown airport and offer Sydney coast, Blue Mountains, Hunter Valley, and even outback scenic flights. **Bondi Helicopters** *(www.bondihelicopters.com.au)* takes in the eastern beaches and Sydney Harbour. Farther afield, ballooning is very popular north of Sydney in the Hunter Valley with **Cloud 9 Balloon Flights** *(www.cloud9balloons.com.au).*

Beyond the next exclusive headland, **Point Piper,** is Rose Bay. From here, you can take a seaplane ride (see sidebar this page), either on a joy ride or up to Pittwater (see pp. 176–178) and beyond. The impressive building on the hill is the Rose Bay Convent. You can walk around the headland to Watsons Bay (see p. 158) from Rose Bay, although you should allow about half a day to do this.

If you get off the bus *(route 324 or 325)* at Tivoli Avenue and

(continued on p. 158)

Elizabeth Bay House
143 B5
7 Onslow Ave., Elizabeth Bay
9356 3022
Closed Mon.
$$
Kings Cross Station, or bus 325 or L94

www.hht.nsw.gov.au

Eighteen-Foot Sailing Skiffs

Sydneysiders never, ever, do anything by halves, and this applies to the way they sail. As a recent world champion skiff sailor said of the 18-footers: "There used to be only two rules—the boat couldn't be more than 18 feet long; and you had to be at the start at 2:30 p.m." The width of the boat, the height of the mast, and the material used in the construction of the hull were entirely up to the crew.

Sydneysiders' love affair with the fast 18-foot skiff, aka the Aussie 18, dates back to the 1890s.

The ultimate 18-foot skiff is part of the collection of the Australian National Maritime Museum (see pp. 138–140). Called *Colorbond,* it is 27 feet (8 m) across—thanks to the two enormous "wings" that extend on either side of the hull to give the boat stability—and the mast is 45 feet (14 m) high. Made in 1985 of space-age carbon fiber, it cost in the region of U.S.$250,000. Since *Colorbond* was built, the rules have been changed to make the sport more affordable, although corporate sponsorship is still necessary to compete at the elite level.

Early Days

The modern skiffs developed from the open workboats of the 19th century. In the 1890s, the Sydney Flying Squadron (SFS) skiff club was formed, and the first regular races were held with boats built and crewed by workers from the waterfront. The races were followed by large spectator fleets of chartered ferries, and the Sydney penchant for gambling found an outlet that was relatively safe from surprise raids by the police.

In the old days, the boats used to sail one leg upwind and then one flying leg downwind. The huge sails made it very difficult to keep the boats upright on the upwind leg, which meant 16 or more "crew" were bundled aboard. These crews often consisted of beefy football (rugby league) players who were coerced into sailing during the off season and were seen wearing the "footy" sweaters that identified their club. On the return leg, however, this "ballast" was no longer needed, and in fact the excess weight stopped the boats from skimming before the breeze. So what did the skippers do? They threw most of the crew overboard at the top mark, leaving them to cling to a buoy and wait to be picked up by a following ferry. These days, the rules state that you must finish a race with the same number of crew that you start with. There is no mention of it being the same crew, however.

In recent years, there has been a nostalgic revival of the older-style boats, and crews wearing the sweaters of clubs from past eras can be seen sailing beautiful wooden boats.

Eighteen-foot skiff racing is a sailing class where the crew spend most of their time "overboard."

Watching the Races

The modern sailing 18-footers—which are some of the fastest monohulls to handle—are a spectacular sight as they scud across the water under their brightly colored sails. Either follow the boats from the shore, from a vantage point such as Bradleys Head (see sidebar p. 97), or board one of the charter ferries that convey passengers and gamblers around the harbor to watch the races.

During the racing season, September through April, the SFS *(tel 9955 8350, www.sydneyflyingsquadron.com.au)* conducts races from Milsons Point on Saturdays; the Australian 18 Footers League *(tel 9363 2995, www.18footers.com.au)* races from Double Bay on Sundays. Taking the ferry (see club websites for details) from these venues allows you to watch the boats and crews up close. The SFS has published a book, *Sydney's Flying Sailors,* which is available from the club.

EXPERIENCE: Learn to Sail

If you ever wanted to gybe, tack, and hoist a mainsail, Sydney Harbour is a great place to learn. Every second person has a yacht, it seems, and plenty of sailing schools offer everything from sail-and-see to longer courses designed to make you a competent crew member.

Sydney by Sail *(tel 9280 1110, www.sydneysail.com)* at the Australian National Maritime Museum, Darling Harbour, offers learn-to-sail courses through to advanced skippering. **Eastsail** *(tel 9327 1166, www.eastsail.com.au)*, **Pacific Sailing School** *(tel 8999 8446, pacificsailingschool.rtrk.com.au)*, and **Manly Sailing** *(tel 9977 4000, www.manlysailing.com)* are other well-established schools with a variety of courses. The classes run one day at a minimum, with most courses two days or longer, depending on skill level.

Vaucluse House

Vaucluse House *(map 143 D5, Wentworth Rd., Vaucluse, tel 9388 7922, www.hht.nsw.gov.au, closed Mon., $$)*, **located between Watsons Bay and Nielsen Park, was built in the 1830s for explorer and political figure William Charles Wentworth (1793–1872). Wentworth was one of the party that found a route across the Blue Mountains. The house, a well-preserved example of colonial architecture with grand halls and wide balconies, is lavishly furnished with period items. Formal gardens and parkland make up the grounds, which reach down to the harbor. The well-known tearooms serve refreshments.**

Vaucluse Bay
143 C5–D5

Parsley Bay
143 D5

Watsons Bay
143 D6

follow it down to the end of Bayview Hill Road, you reach the **Hermitage Foreshore Reserve.** A short walk through the reserve passes tiny Hermit Bay and Milk Beach (below Strickland House, a former convalescent hospital) and continues around to Shark Bay and Nielsen Park *(also accessible by bus 324 or 325)*. Just back from the water at Nielsen Park is **Greycliffe House**, built in 1852 and now an office for the National Parks and Wildlife Service. **Shark Beach** is netted and safe for swimming, and the Nielsen Park Restaurant & Café *(tel 9337 7333)* is popular.

Though nominally built in the Gothic Revival style, Vaucluse House is actually a mix of architectural styles.

Vaucluse, Parsley, & Watsons

Beyond Shark Bay is **Vaucluse Point** and the Bottle and Glass Rocks. This is a great spot to watch yachts sweeping down the harbor under spinnaker on a summer's afternoon.

Continue along Coolong Road to Vaucluse Bay and **Vaucluse House** (see sidebar this page). Cut across Boambillee Avenue and Fitzwilliam Road to the inlet of **Parsley Bay,** where a large grassy area attracts weekend picnickers in droves.

The major tourist mecca, however, is Watsons Bay, tucked into the western side of the peninsula as it narrows toward **South Head.** Formerly a military base and fishing village, the suburb has a small-town feel, and you'll find swimming pools, picnic spots, restaurants, and walks. On weekends, it is very popular (and often easier to visit by ferry or bus than by car). As you face the shore, note **Dunbar House,** an 1830s mansion, now a reception center. ■

Vast suburbs offering different aspects of the city—the Olympics site, interesting shopping, and a range of immigrant cultures

Western Suburbs

Introduction & Map 160–161

Inner West 162–165

Experience: Kayak Balmain 163

Sydney Olympic Park 166–169

More Places to Visit in the Western Suburbs 170

Hotels & Restaurants 251–252

In dog-friendly Newtown, "Guardian Dogs" act as gateways to the town's arts and entertainment district.

Western Suburbs

Considering Sydney's size (nearly 5,000 square miles/13,000 sq km), it is not surprising that it should have a number of "centers" beyond the main business district. Many localities are communities in their own right and attract large numbers of visitors. Don't miss the historic buildings of Parramatta, the gentrified workers' suburbs of Balmain and Glebe, and the ethnic diversity of Cabramatta and Campsie.

Balmain and Parramatta offer some of the oldest buildings in the city, along with picnicking, walking, and boating. Some precincts are just a cluster of shops, but contain particular gems—especially foods such as sausages, breads, or pastries—that attract people from miles around.

And then, of course, there is the main Olympic site at Homebush Bay, one of the main sporting precincts of the city, built for the 2000 Summer Games. Sports events are held here year-round, while the parks and recreational facilities draw many visitors in search of fresh air or exercise.

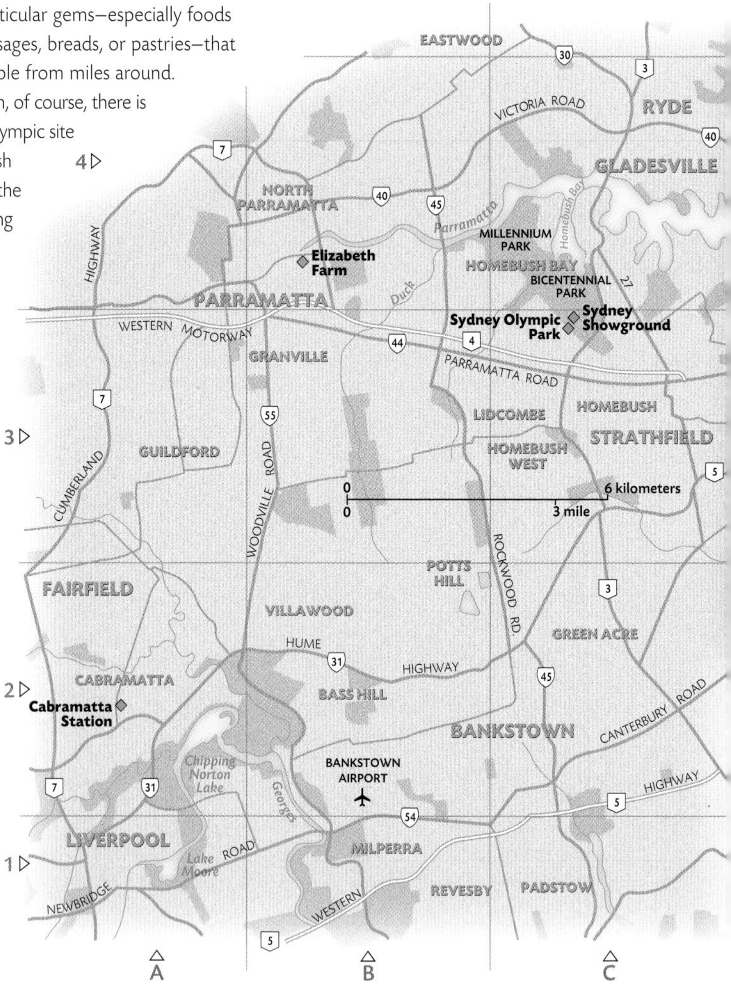

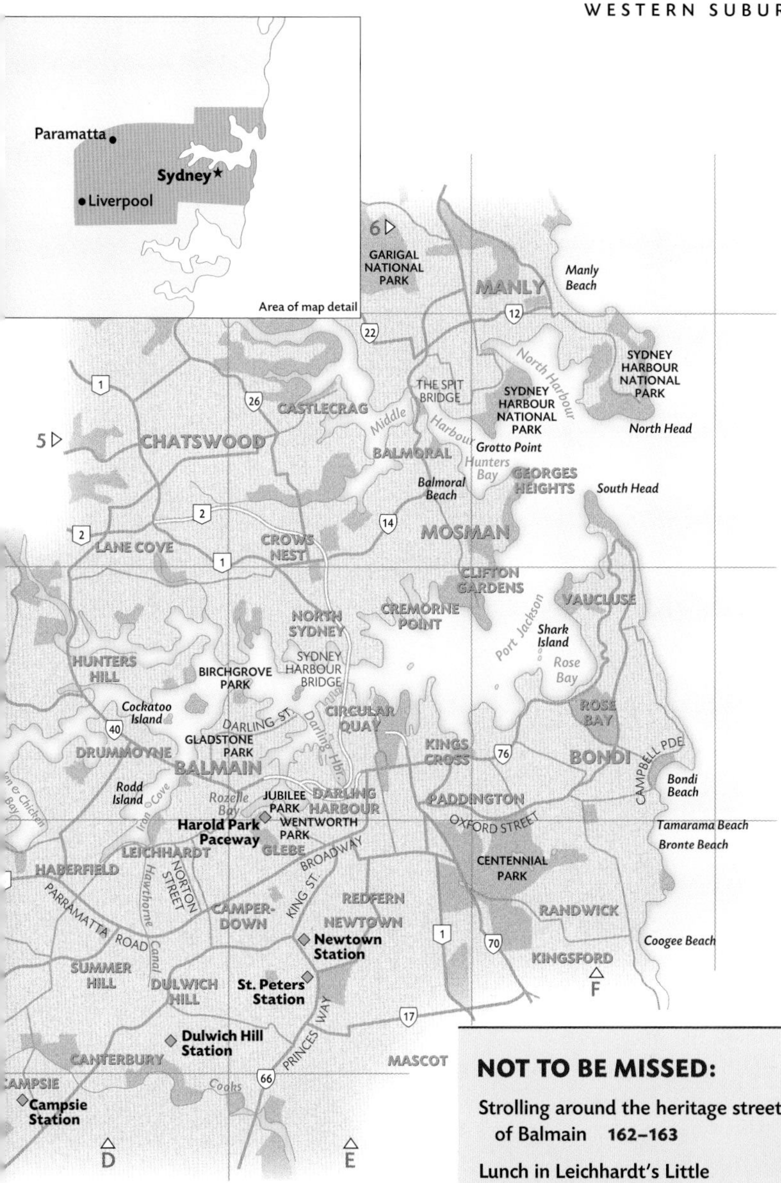

In a sense, this section is a kaleidoscope of places and things to see and do. Whether it is a tour of some of Australia's oldest and most historic buildings, a visit to a famous sporting venue, a stroll through an exclusive shopping precinct, or a relaxed coffee in a café full of Sydneysiders, there are many places where you can get a feel for the Sydney that the locals enjoy. ■

NOT TO BE MISSED:

Strolling around the heritage streets of Balmain 162–163

Lunch in Leichhardt's Little Italy 163

Browsing in the funky shops of King Street in Newtown 164

The sandstone architecture of the University of Sydney 164

Swimming in the Olympic pool or bird-watching at Homebush Bay Olympic site 166–169

Inner West

All across Sydney, there are several areas where the locals congregate in droves. Many are mentioned elsewhere in the book—Darlinghurst, Kings Cross, Manly, Bondi, Paddington, and others—but several more are worth visiting, too. The following districts lie west and south of the city center.

Balmain
161 D4–E4

Balmain

Another of the former working-class suburbs of Sydney, Balmain occupies the peninsula between Iron Cove and Darling Harbour. Its abundance of once affordable waterfront property has made this one of the most sought-after districts in the city. Today, most of the working-class cottages and row houses have been renovated, and the lifestyle here rivals that of the affluent eastern suburbs (see pp. 141–158).

This is a suburb of successful artists, actors, and businesspeople. Numerous boutique pubs are dotted around the peninsula, and lively cafés, bookshops, bakeries, and antiques shops line **Darling Street,** which runs the length of the peninsula.

Every Saturday, a market is held on the grounds of St. Andrew's Church, on the other side of Gladstone Park.

Down the hill from St. Andrew's Church, the **Balmain Watch House** at 179 Darling Street was once a police lockup; it dates from 1854 and was designed by Edmund Blacket. The simple, elegant building is now the headquarters of the Balmain Association, which aims to preserve local buildings. Other notable historic buildings on Darling Street include the **Court House** (1886) at No. 386 and the old **Town Hall** next door.

Two lovely parks for picnics can be reached by ferry from Circular Quay—**Birchgrove Park** and Balmain East's **Iloura**

A main thoroughfare with shops and restaurants, Darling Street runs through the heart of Balmain.

Reserve. A smaller park, Yurulbin Park, near Birchgrove Park at the end of Long Nose Point, is also accessible by ferry to Louisa Street Wharf, Birchgrove.

Apart from its physical heritage, the suburb of Balmain has also contributed major figures to the national and world stage. Dr. H. V. Evatt, one of the founders of the United Nations and president of the U.N. General Assembly (1948–1949), was the local member in the state and federal parliaments. A prime minister, Billy Hughes, had been a shopkeeper in Balmain, and Olympic gold medal swimmer Dawn Fraser is also identified as a local.

Access to Balmain is by bus route 433 or 435, or take a ferry from Circular Quay to Darling Street Wharf.

EXPERIENCE: Kayak Balmain

One of the most serene ways you can see Sydney Harbour is low to the water in a kayak. Natural Wanders *(tel 0427 225 072, www.kayaksydney.com.au, $$$$$)* runs weekend excursions along the Balmain coastline, starting from Lavender Bay, near the Harbour Bridge around from Luna Park. The 6-mile (10 km) paddle heads across Sydney Harbour at one of its narrowest points, past Goat Island to Balmain, where you'll get glimpses of its shipbuilding and coal-mining heritage, before heading to Mort Bay, home base for Sydney Ferries, and on to Birchgrove and scenic Snails Bay, passing exclusive real estate favored by local celebrities. On the return trip, you'll disembark at Berry Island, now joined to the mainland, for a walk through native bushland to see Aboriginal rock engravings.

Leichhardt

To get a sense of the multicultural flavor of Sydney, try Leichhardt, a precinct just south of Balmain. The area was named after a German explorer who disappeared in the northern regions of Australia in 1848 and was the inspiration for Nobel Prize–winning author Patrick White's book *Voss,* which is partly set in Sydney.

During the 19th century, Leichhardt was often visited by whalers, who used to row up Hawthorne Canal to the pubs here and in nearby Summer Hill.

Leichhardt is the so-called Little Italy of Sydney, with a string of Italian restaurants and cafés along the main restaurant strip, **Norton Street.** The **Italian Festa** street party in October is a lot of fun, and there is even an Italian-themed mall, the Italian Forum, with an outdoor piazza, Italian restaurants, shops, and a library.

Access to Leichhardt is by car or bus routes 436 and 438 from the city.

Glebe

Much of this suburb—more properly called The Glebe—north of the University of Sydney, was originally owned by the Anglican Church. By the 1820s, however, most of it had been sold, and handsome Victorian houses sprang up in the following years. Look for the deep verandas and detailed wrought-iron work.

Leichhardt
Map 161 D3

Glebe
Map 161 E3

Newtown
161 E3

Macleay Museum
Science Rd., University of Sydney
9351 2222

Set by the harbor just across the water from the Sydney Fish Market near Darling Harbour, the area features several pleasant waterside parks. It consists largely of workers' cottages dating from the last century, with a scattering of grand Victorian terraces.

Great Expectations

One of the graves in Newtown's Camperdown Cemetery is that of Eliza Donnithorne. Jilted by her fiancé on her wedding day in 1854, Eliza kept her table set for her wedding feast for the next 30 years, often wore her wedding dress, and sometimes left the front door of her house ajar in the hope that her beloved would return. Her story is thought to be a possible source for Miss Havisham in Charles Dickens's *Great Expectations.*

The suburb's main thoroughfare, **Glebe Point Road,** stretches from Broadway, one of the main routes into the city from the west, over to Jubilee Park at Rozelle Bay. For most of its length, Glebe Point Road is lined with cafés, gift shops, and bookstores. Gleebooks *(tel 9660 2333)* at No. 49 is one of the best bookstores in town. Readings by local and overseas writers are held here regularly.

Very popular markets take place at the Glebe Public School every Saturday, and you'll find a YHA hostel *(tel 9692 8418)* at No. 262. Elsewhere in the suburb is a dog track (Wentworth Park) and a harness racing track (Harold Park Paceway).

Glebe is a short taxi ride from the city, or bus routes 431 and 433 depart from the city.

Newtown

Newtown, below Glebe, revolves around **King Street,** one of the longest food and shopping streets in the city. It reaches from the University of Sydney to Newtown Station and then continues on to St. Peters Station. The precinct is an enclave for students and a kaleidoscope of alternative lifestyles, the prime activity being to sit in the cafés and watch the human menagerie pass by—punks, hippies, goths, students, musicians, artists. Funky boutiques, handicraft shops, and good Thai restaurants abound, but plenty of other cuisines are represented as well.

Northeast of Newtown is the **University of Sydney,** Australia's oldest university. It dates from the 1850s and has many fine neo-Gothic buildings designed by colonial architect Edmund Blacket. Don't miss the quadrangle, the beautiful Great Hall, and the clock tower *(tours weekdays, bookings essential, tel 9351 8746, $$).*

Also worth visiting at the university are the **Nicholson Museum** with its ancient antiquities, the small **University Art Gallery,** and the **Macleay Museum,** off Science Road on the Glebe side of the campus. Established by the Macleay family, who built **Elizabeth Bay House** (see p. 154), the museum's eclectic, if sometimes macabre, collection features zoological specimens, bark paintings, Aboriginal artifacts, and early photographs of Sydney.

Alexander Macleay, colonial secretary and father of the family, is buried in **Camperdown Cemetery,** surrounding St. Stephen's Church (1849) at 189 Church Street, in the heart of Newtown. The Macleay tomb stands at the back left-hand corner of the cemetery. As you face the grave, a short way along the wall to the left is the mass tomb containing all the unidentified bodies from the wrecks of the *Dunbar* and the *Catherine Adamson,* which between them took 142 lives in 1857 (see p. 100). More graves of *Dunbar* victims are back toward the church on this side, as is the grave of Napoleon Bonaparte's harpist, Robert Boscha.

Access is by rail to Newtown Station (as you leave the station, most of the action is along the street to the right). ■

INSIDER TIP:

Visit Jubilee Park at Glebe Point on Thursday nights to watch the weekly fire-twirling spectacle, then head to Newtown for dinner or a cocktail to round out the evening.

—BEN KEAR
National Geographic field researcher

Many Victorian- and Edwardian-style storefronts line King Street, Newtown.

Sydney Olympic Park

Sydney Olympic Park at Homebush Bay, the main venue of the 2000 Summer Olympics, is the sports and recreation hub of the city. As well as a host of stadiums, the Homebush Bay site includes Millennium Park—a vast recreation area and natural habitat for numerous birds and animals—hotels, restaurants and a nonstop program of concerts and sporting and cultural events.

The Sydney Olympic Park Aquatic Centre maximizes the use of natural light and ventilation.

Sydney Olympic Park

160 C3–C4

Visitor Information

Showground Rd. & Herb Elliott Ave., Homebush Bay

9714 7888

www.sydneyolympicpark.com.au

Millennium Park

At 1,086 acres (439 ha), Millennium Park is the largest park in Sydney and incorporates the 250-acre (100 ha) **Bicentennial Park,** opened in 1988.

Within the park are the wetlands and mangroves of Homebush Bay, the former quarry for the State Brickworks (which has since been identified as a breeding ground for the green and golden bell frog), and remnant eucalyptus forest and regenerated casuarina pine forests, both of which are breeding grounds for parrots and some of the 140 other species of birds found around the Homebush Bay site. On weekends, bird lovers can visit the displays at the **BirdLife Discovery Centre** *(tel 9647 1033)* in the north of park.

Easter Show

Each year, in the first two weeks of April, the **Sydney**

INSIDER TIP:

Get into the Aussie spirit and attend a rugby match at Olympic Stadium. But big SLR cameras are not allowed, so don't try to sneak one in.

—JILL SCHNEIDER
National Geographic photographer

Royal Easter Show *(tel 9704 1111)* is held at the Sydney Showground. Here you can enjoy rides in Sideshow Alley and see displays and exhibitions of New South Wales's best produce and livestock. The Sydney Royal Easter Show moved here in 1998 from its traditional home near the city to make way for Fox Studios and the Entertainment Quarter.

Olympic Stadium

Though it changes its name with the latest sponsor (currently it is the ANZ Stadium), the main Olympic Stadium is the focal point of the Homebush Bay Olympic site. Designed to seat 110,000 spectators, redevelopment has reduced this to 83,000, but it remains the city's premier sports stadium, hosting major football matches (Australian rules football, soccer, and both rugby league and rugby union) and other events such as major rock concerts. You can take one of two behind-the-scenes tours *(tel 8765 2300, $$$$$)* of the Olympic Stadium, both usually offered daily.

Olympic Stadium

✉ Olympic Blvd., Homebush Bay

☎ 8765 2000

www.anzstadium.com.au

Sydney 2000 Olympic Games

The games of the XXVII Olympiad provided a massive boost to the city leading up to and during the year 2000. A huge building program spurred local businesses and provided the ongoing legacy of Sydney Olympic Park and its extensive facilities at Homebush. Billions of dollars stimulated the economy, and tourism boomed. But most of all, the games gave Sydney an opportunity to showcase Australia to the world.

This was nowhere more evident than in the opening ceremony, a musical, dance, and light show spectacular paying homage to Australian culture. Tap-dancing construction workers, synchronized lawn mowing, stockmen riding horses, and Aboriginal women invoking protective spirits all contributed to the telling of the Australian story, aided by a host of well-known local performers. Outside the stadiums, an army of nearly 50,000 volunteers ensured a smooth and successful games that put Sydney in the world spotlight.

Inevitably, in the aftermath, the number crunchers set to work and the "most successful games ever," as they were touted in Australia, turned out to be financially less than stunning. Tourism quickly returned to its long-term average and has since fallen. The building industry stalled and, all in all, costs far outweighed returns, resulting in an overall loss of A$2.1 billion in private and public consumption.

But ask anyone in Sydney if they thought the games were worth it, and the answer will most likely be, "Too right," if only for the record number of medals this sports-mad nation garnered that year.

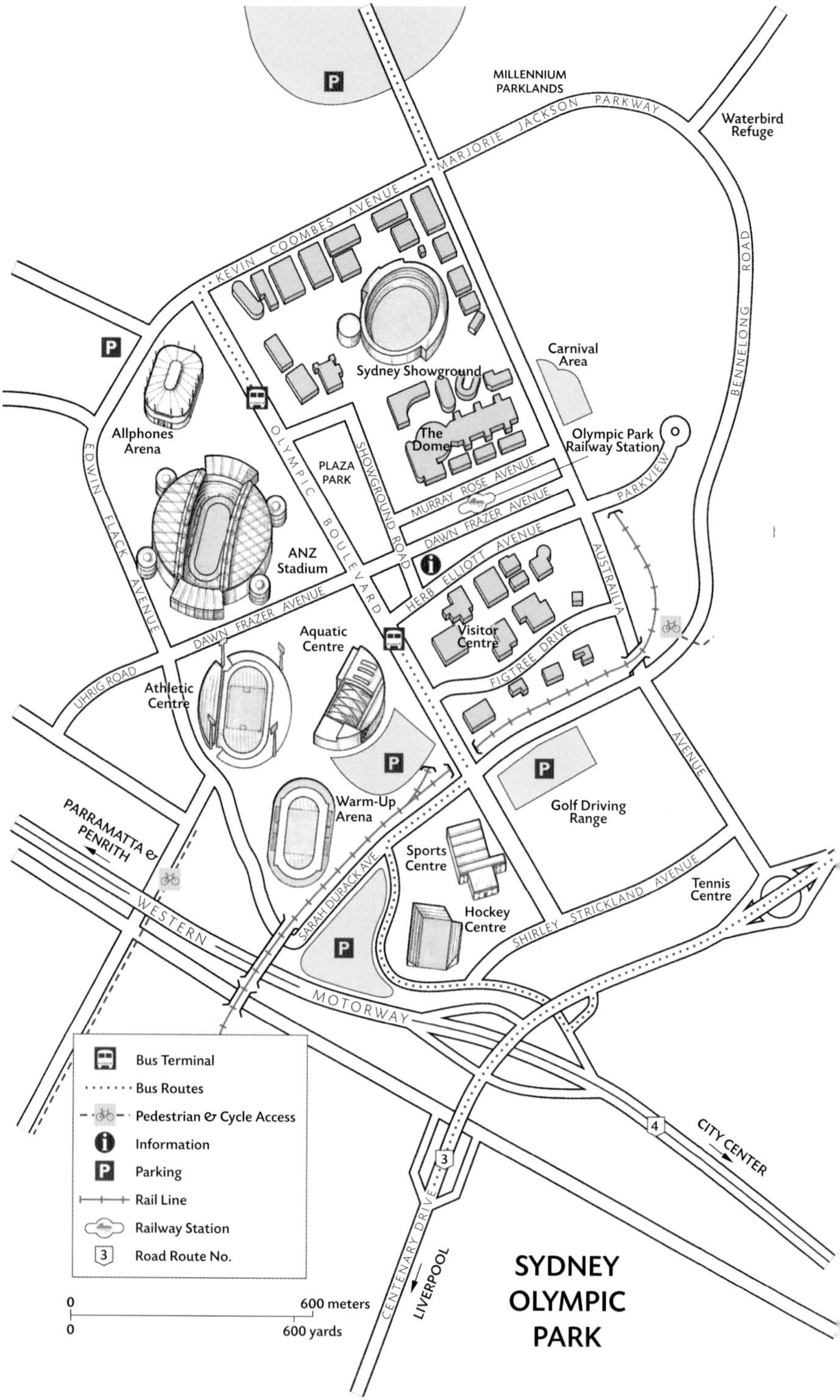
MILLENNIUM PARKLANDS
MARJORIE JACKSON PARKWAY
Waterbird Refuge
KEVIN COOMBES AVENUE
BENNELONG ROAD
Carnival Area
Allphones Arena
Sydney Showground
The Dome
Olympic Park Railway Station
PARKVIEW
EDWIN FLACK AVENUE
OLYMPIC BOULEVARD
PLAZA PARK
SHOWGROUND ROAD
MURRAY ROSE AVENUE
DAWN FRAZER AVENUE
ANZ Stadium
HERB ELLIOTT AVENUE
AUSTRALIA
Visitor Centre
FIGTREE DRIVE
Aquatic Centre
UHRIG ROAD
Athletic Centre
AVENUE
Golf Driving Range
Warm-Up Arena
PARRAMATTA & PENRITH
Sports Centre
SARAH DURACK AVE.
Hockey Centre
Tennis Centre
SHIRLEY STRICKLAND AVENUE
WESTERN MOTORWAY
4
CITY CENTER
3
CENTENARY DRIVE
LIVERPOOL
Bus Terminal
Bus Routes
Pedestrian & Cycle Access
Information
Parking
Rail Line
Railway Station
3 Road Route No.
0 600 meters
0 600 yards
SYDNEY OLYMPIC PARK

Aquatic Centre

Equally adaptable is the Sydney Olympic Park Aquatic Centre, built in 1994. Currently it seats about 10,000 people, but during the Olympics, the capacity was expanded to accommodate 17,000. Facilities include the international-competition-standard pool; leisure, training, and diving pools within a temperature-controlled building; and landscaped gardens. In addition, there is a gymnasium, a café, a swimwear shop, water slides, and fountains. The center is also the base for the swimmers of the New South Wales Institute of Sport.

Other Facilities

Other facilities in the Sydney Olympic Park include an archery site, a baseball field, a golf driving range, a hockey center, a tennis center, an athletics center and training facilities, and the indoor sports center.

Apart from the regular events (check the website), you can tour the park on a rented bike or Segway, hit out at the golf driving range, play tennis, swim or hit the gym at the magnificent Aquatic Centre, skateboard, or learn archery. When you first arrive, check in at the visitor center for a map and details of what's on.

Limited car parking means visitors are strongly encouraged to use public transportation, especially when a big event is on. The site is extremely well served, with a ferry stop on the Circular Quay–Parramatta RiverCat run and regular trains to the Olympic Park Station beside the Sydney Showground site (which is less than half a mile/1 km from the Olympic Stadium), plus bus services. ■

Sydney Olympic Park Aquatic Centre

✉ Olympic Blvd., Homebush Bay

☎ 9752 3666

$ $$

www.aquaticcentre.com.au

Spectators stream out of the 83,000-seat Olympic Stadium after watching a rugby match.

More Places to Visit in the Western Suburbs

A Vietnamese Australian examines the goods for sale at a fabric store in Cabramatta, in Sydney's west, though the town feels closer to Ho Chi Minh City.

Cabramatta

For a totally different experience, take the train out west to the suburb of Cabramatta. The area around the railway station is given over to Vietnamese shops, restaurants, and businesses, to the extent that it has been nicknamed "Vietnamatta." It's as if a piece of the exotic Far East has been transplanted in suburban Sydney. The food here is some of the best Vietnamese cuisine this side of Ho Chi Minh City.

160 A2 Train to Cabramatta Station

Campsie

A little closer to the city than Cabramatta, the same sort of cultural makeover has taken place at Campsie, except here the dominant culture is Korean, with an increasing Chinese influence. Australian and Korean cuisines have a great deal in common—they both have a strong emphasis on barbecuing. The center of the action is on Beamish Street.

161 D2 Train to Campsie Station

Dulwich Hill

If you happen to be passing 425 New Canterbury Road in Dulwich Hill, check out **Samir Abla Patisserie.** Behind the unassuming-looking storefront is a wonderful selection of Lebanese specialties. There are gigantic trays of baklava, *kounfa, mafroukeh,* Damascus rose, and date semolina slices on display, and an area where you can sit down with the locals to enjoy cake and coffee, Turkish Delight, or ice cream.

161 D3 Train to Dulwich Hill Station

National parks, pristine waterways, wildlife parks, and historic towns where you can take a picnic for a day, or stay for weeks

Day Trips

North 172–183

Introduction & Map 172–173

Ku-ring-gai Chase National Park 174–175

Pittwater 176–178

Experience: Dive Sydney's Waters 177

Experience: Get Out on Pittwater 178

Hawkesbury River 179–182

Experience: Houseboat on the Hawkesbury 182

More Places to Visit in the North 183

West & South 184–202

Introduction & Map 184–185

Parramatta 186–187

Botany Bay 188–189

Experience: Look for Whales 189

A Walk in Cronulla 190–191

Port Hacking & Georges River 192

Royal National Park 193–195

Experience: Ride a Vintage Tram Into Royal NP 194

The kookaburra, a bird well known for its "laughing" call

Feature: Wildlife of the Sydney Region 196–201

Experience: Bird-Watch & Bushwalk 197

More Places to Visit in the West & South 202

Hotels & Restaurants 252

North

Just an hour to the north of the city, a pocket of spectacular wilderness reaches in an almost unbroken chain inland from the coast to the Blue Mountains.

It includes a string of beaches, the boating paradises of the Hawkesbury River and Pittwater, and the largely unspoiled succession of national parks that includes Bouddi, Brisbane Water, Ku-ring-gai Chase, Marramarra, Dharug, and Wollemi. Within the northern suburbs are two smaller national parks, Lane Cove and Garigal.

NOT TO BE MISSED:

Exploring Aboriginal rock art sites in Ku-ring-gai Chase National Park **174**

A day trip past the northern beaches to exclusive Palm Beach **177**

Driving alongside or cruising the Hawkesbury River **179–182**

Not surprisingly, the emphasis in many of these areas is on recreation. Pittwater is especially popular for weekend getaways—it is only an hour from the city and can claim some of the best scenery and boating anywhere in the world. Farther west, the Hawkesbury is a beautiful river system with stunning scenery along its lower reaches and historic towns and lush farmlands around the upper reaches.

Throughout this area, you may find that the people tend to be relaxed and largely unstressed (even more than most other Sydneysiders). Perhaps it's hard to get tense about life when you can go for a swim in the sea in the early morning and wet a line after work in the afternoon. Or else it is true that "there is nothing half so much worth doing as simply messing around in boats." ■

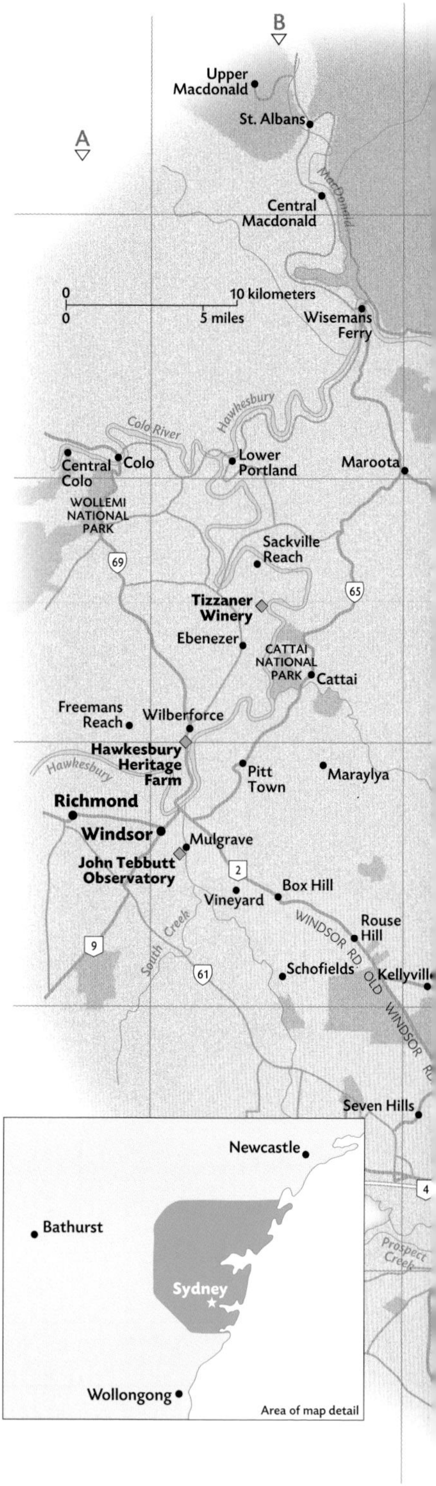

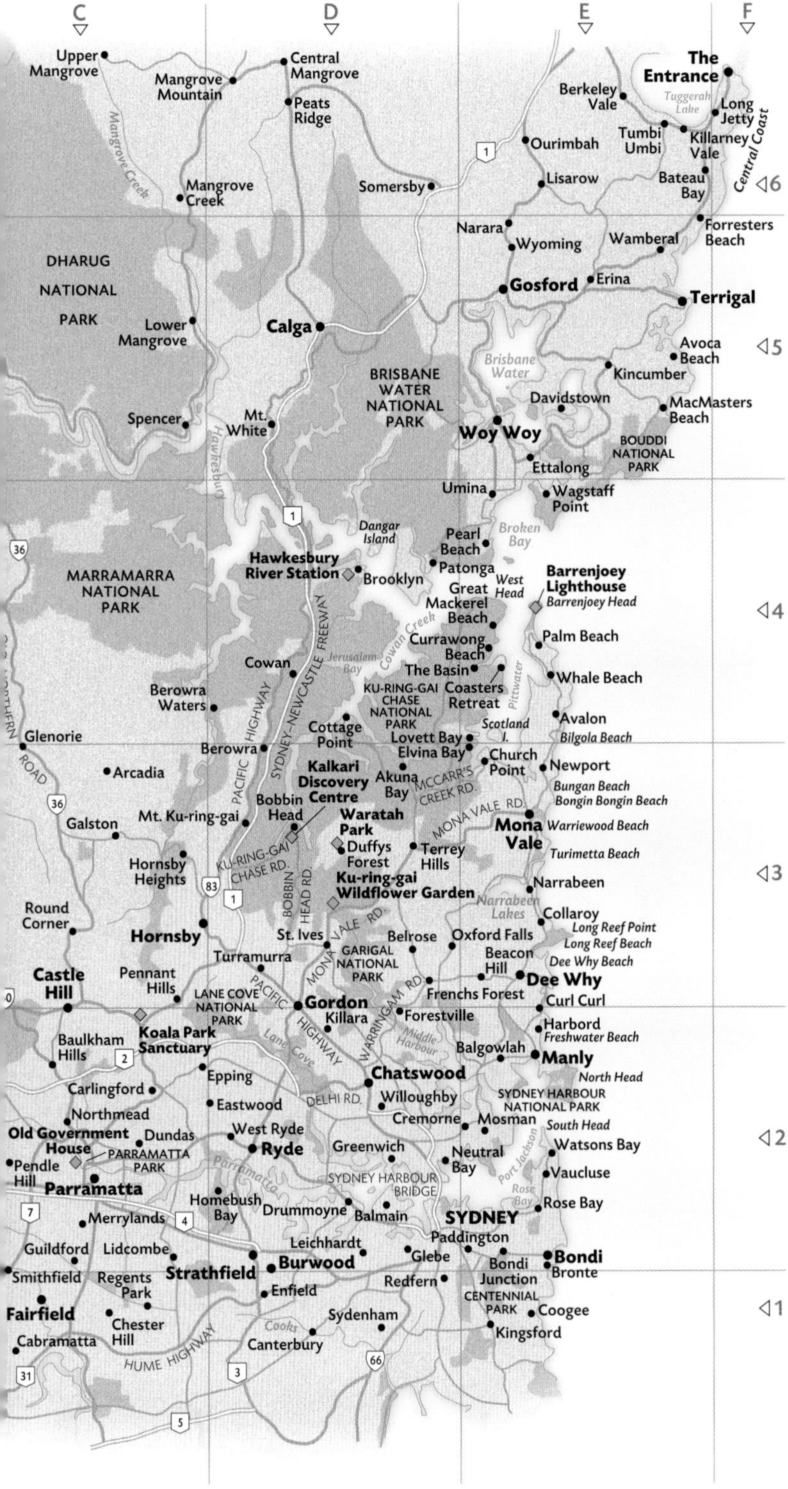
C
D
E
F
Upper Mangrove
Mangrove Mountain
Central Mangrove
Peats Ridge
Mangrove Creek
Somersby
Berkeley Vale
The Entrance
Tuggerah Lake
Long Jetty
Tumbi Umbi
Killarney Vale
Ourimbah
Lisarow
Bateau Bay
Central Coast
Narara
Wyoming
Wamberal
Forresters Beach
DHARUG NATIONAL PARK
Gosford
Erina
Terrigal
Lower Mangrove
Calga
Avoca Beach
Brisbane Water
BRISBANE WATER NATIONAL PARK
Kincumber
Davidstown
MacMasters Beach
Spencer
Mt. White
Hawkesbury
Woy Woy
BOUDDI NATIONAL PARK
Ettalong
Umina
Wagstaff Point
Dangar Island
Pearl Beach
Broken Bay
Hawkesbury River Station
Brooklyn
Patonga
MARRAMARRA NATIONAL PARK
Great Mackerel Beach
West Head
Barrenjoey Lighthouse
Barrenjoey Head
Currawong Beach
Cowan Creek
Palm Beach
Cowan
Jerusalem Bay
The Basin
Whale Beach
Berowra Waters
KU-RING-GAI CHASE NATIONAL PARK
Coasters Retreat
Pittwater
Avalon
Glenorie
Cottage Point
Scotland I.
Bilgola Beach
Berowra
Lovett Bay
Elvina Bay
Church Point
Newport
Arcadia
Kalkari Discovery Centre
Akuna Bay
McCARR'S CREEK RD.
Bungan Beach
Bongin Bongin Beach
Galston
Mt. Ku-ring-gai
Bobbin Head
Waratah Park
MONA VALE RD.
Mona Vale
Warriewood Beach
Duffys Forest
Terrey Hills
Turimetta Beach
Hornsby Heights
KU-RING-GAI CHASE RD.
BOBBIN HEAD RD.
Ku-ring-gai Wildflower Garden
Narrabeen
Round Corner
Narrabeen Lakes
Collaroy
Long Reef Point
Long Reef Beach
Hornsby
St. Ives
Belrose
Oxford Falls
Beacon Hill
Dee Why Beach
Turramurra
GARIGAL NATIONAL PARK
Castle Hill
Pennant Hills
LANE COVE NATIONAL PARK
PACIFIC HIGHWAY
Gordon
Dee Why
Frenchs Forest
Curl Curl
WARRINGAH RD.
Killara
Forestville
Harbord
Freshwater Beach
Baulkham Hills
Koala Park Sanctuary
Lane Cove
Middle Harbour
Balgowlah
Manly
Epping
Chatswood
North Head
Carlingford
Willoughby
SYDNEY HARBOUR NATIONAL PARK
Eastwood
DELHI RD.
Northmead
Cremorne
Mosman
South Head
Old Government House
Dundas
West Ryde
Ryde
Greenwich
Neutral Bay
Watsons Bay
Pendle Hill
PARRAMATTA PARK
Parramatta
Port Jackson
Vaucluse
Parramatta
SYDNEY HARBOUR BRIDGE
Rose Bay
Homebush Bay
Merrylands
Drummoyne
Balmain
SYDNEY
Paddington
Guildford
Lidcombe
Leichhardt
Glebe
Bondi
Smithfield
Regents Park
Strathfield
Burwood
Bondi Junction
Bronte
Enfield
Redfern
CENTENNIAL PARK
Fairfield
Chester Hill
Cooks
Sydenham
Coogee
Cabramatta
Canterbury
Kingsford
HUME HIGHWAY
SYDNEY-NEWCASTLE FREEWAY
NORTHERN ROAD
1
36
83
2
4
7
3
66
31
5
6
5
4
3
2
1

Ku-ring-gai Chase National Park

The sandstone bushland of Ku-ring-gai Chase is cut by deep gorges full of eucalyptus and ferns tumbling to the water's edge. Many of the gorges are partly inundated by seawater and extend several miles inland. Adjoining Pittwater, the Lower Hawkesbury River, and Cowan Creek, this 37,000-acre (15,000 ha) national park is the second oldest in Australia (established in 1894) and has a rich mixture of Aboriginal and European history.

Several lovely waterfalls dot the national park, including Upper Gledhill Falls on McCarrs Creek.

One of the great delights here is waking up on a boat moored in a small bay with the Australian bush tumbling down steep slopes on all sides. As parrots shriek in the trees and kookaburras give their distinctive laughing cry, remind yourself that you are only an hour from Sydney.

Among the highlights of the park is its Aboriginal rock engravings, many of which are accessible to the public (see p. 133). There are also numerous walking trails and several small towns, marinas, and boat-rental areas, plus plenty of picnic spots in scenic locations.

Accessible by road is **West Head.** Until 1951, this area was in the hands of the Australian Navy, and some of the fortifications from World War II are still visible. It is a favorite stopping point for visitors because of the spectacular views over Pittwater, Barrenjoey Head, Lion Island, and Broken Bay. From the road running out to West Head, several walking trails lead to secluded beaches and bays on the Pittwater and Cowan Creek sides.

Major visitor facilities can be found at **Akuna Bay** (marina and boat rental) and **Bobbin Head,** located between two drowned river gorges, a very sheltered spot well inland. Bobbin Head is home to the park information center, kiosks, picnic areas, boat rental, and ferry cruises *(Sat.–Sun. at 12 p.m.)*. Shorelink bus 577 from Turamurra train station will drop you at the park gates, 3 miles (4.5 km) away.

On the hill 1 mile (1.5 km) from Bobbin Head is the **Kalkari Discovery Centre.** Here you can watch videos about the park, Aboriginal heritage, or wildlife. Kangaroos and emus inhabit the enclosed 20 acres (8 ha) of the **Discovery Trail.** A program of guided walking tours is conducted from Kalkari. Guides to the park's many day walks are also available.

INSIDER TIP:

For those without a car, a great day walk in Ku-ring-gai Chase is the five-hour Mackerel Beach–West Head Loop. Catch a ferry or water taxi from Palm Beach to Mackeral Beach and back.

—PETER TURNER
National Geographic author

Cottage Point is one of the few waterside villages that can be reached by car as well as boat. Watch the vessels drift by while dining at the chic Cottage Point Inn or the Cottage Point Kiosk, which also rents boats and kayaks.

Camping *(tel 9974 1011)* in the park is permitted at The Basin, a sheltered bay on Pittwater accessible by boat or walking trail only. Reservations are required, especially during school vacations. A ferry service, Fantasea Palm Beach *(tel 9974 2411)*, is available from Palm Beach, as are water taxis *(tel 0415 408 831)*.

For well-prepared hikers without a car, several routes enter the park from train stations along the main northern line. From Mount Kuring-gai Station, a 4-mile (6 km) track leads to Bobbin Head; from Berowra, one leads to Waratah Bay; and from Cowan, another accesses Jerusalem Bay. These trails down to the water are quite steep. You can also walk from Mount Kuring-gai Station to Berowra Station, or from the Hawkesbury River Station in the town of Brooklyn along a section of the Great North Walk to Cowan Station.

Road access to the park is from Ku-ring-gai Chase Road and Bobbin Head Road, both of which access Bobbin Head. Mona Vale Road and McCarrs Creek Road provide access to Church Point, Akuna Bay, and West Head. ■

Waratah Park

On the way to Ku-ring-gai Chase, Waratah Park *(13 Namba Rd., Duffys Forest, tel 9450 2377)* was the home of Skippy, the bush kangaroo and star of an eponymous popular 1960s TV series. Unfortunately, the 30 acres (13 ha) of native bush was given over to developers and the native animals shipped out. After a public outcry, the Waratah Park Nature Reserve Foundation *(www.waratahpark.org.au)* was set up to lobby for restoration of the park, but as yet it remains closed.

Ku-ring-gai Chase National Park

Map 173 D3–E4

Visitor Information

Bobbin Head Road, Bobbin Head

9472 8949

www.environment.nsw.gov.au

Kalkari Discovery Centre

Map 173 D3

Ku-ring-gai Chase Rd.

9472 9300

Kalkari Visitor Centre

Ku-ring-gai Chase Rd.

9454 9853

Pittwater

If Sydney Harbour is the city's working port, Pittwater is its playground. Lying at the northern extremity of a long series of golden beaches, this huge waterway is protected by the mighty buttress of Barrenjoey Head. It hugs the shore of Ku-ring-gai Chase National Park and extends beyond Lion Island into Broken Bay.

The southern end of the golden sweep of Palm Beach, a very popular stretch of sand

Pittwater
173 E3–E4

The region comprises such a labyrinth of inlets, coves, and drowned river valleys that it took the first settlers a couple of years to discover the major river that enters it, the Hawkesbury.

Northern Beaches

Between Sydney Harbour and Pittwater is the region known as the northern beaches. Stretching north from Manly, these beaches include Harbord (also called Freshwater), Curl Curl, Dee Why, Long Reef—with the 3-mile (4 km) strand of Collaroy at one end and Narrabeen at the other (nearby **Narrabeen Lakes** is a sheltered waterway popular with dinghy sailors and sailboarders, and boat and kayak rentals are also available here)—and tiny Turimetta Beach.

Next come Warriewood, Mona Vale, Bongin Bongin, and Bungan Beaches. At this point, the southernmost reach of Pittwater forms a peninsula, with sheltered waters on one side and ocean on the other. Beaches facing the ocean, on the western side of the peninsula, include Newport, Bilgola, Avalon, Whale, and, finally, the idyllic **Palm Beach**—the sandy isthmus ending at the imposing **Barrenjoey Head.**

EXPERIENCE: Dive Sydney's Waters

Dive into the waters for a visual feast. You may not find Great Barrier Reef corals or the visibility of South Pacific atolls, but you will delight in the colorful sponges, abundant fish life, shipwrecks, and interesting underwater terrain. Dive shops in nearly every waterside town will rent you equipment and/or offer dive trips; many offer scuba certification courses for neophytes as well as advanced training if you want to improve your skills.

Several dive shops, including Dive Centre Bondi *(tel 9369 3855, www.divebondi.com.au)*, run boat dives to Pittwater, where you'll find the wrecks of the *Valiant* off Palm Beach and the S.S. *Dee Why* ferry on Long Reef. Other top dive sites are off Cronulla in Botany Bay and Camp Cove in Sydney Harbour, with many sites accessible from land. Another good dive shop is Dive Centre Manly *(tel 9977 4355, www.divesydney.com)*.

Palm Beach: The peninsula in particular has long been a vacation destination for wealthy Sydneysiders; today, only the very rich can afford houses here. It's hard to park on weekends when the restaurants here fill up.

The beach is a glorious sweep of sand and dunes that separates the Pacific from Pittwater. It comes to a dramatic stop at the headland topped by **Barrenjoey Lighthouse.** Pedestrian access is via the beach, then a path up to the lighthouse. The 360-degree views over Palm Beach, the ocean, Broken Bay to the north, West Head, and Pittwater are well worth the long uphill walk.

From atop Barrenjoey, you can sometimes see seaplanes taking off or landing on Pittwater. Golfers will notice the pocket golf course on one side of the isthmus.

Flightseeing tours leaving from Rose Bay in Sydney Harbour offer spectacular views of the city, coastline, and Pittwater (see sidebar p. 155).

Fantasea Palm Beach ferries *(tel 9974 2411)* from the wharf in town connects with the hamlets of **Great Mackerel Beach, Coasters Retreat, Currawong Beach,** and **The Basin** in Ku-ring-gai Chase National Park (none have road access). Northward, ferries go to Wagstaff and Ettalong Beach on the Central Coast peninsula. Palm Beach & Hawkesbury River Cruises *(tel 0414 466 635)* has daily cruises via Patonga and Bobbin Head at 11 a.m., and there are also water taxis *(tel 0415 408 831)*.

Palm Beach has upmarket accommodations, and houses for longer-term holiday rental. Ku-ring-gai Chase National Park has camping at The Basin (see p. 175).

Barrenjoey Beach is an absolute mecca for sailboarding. The gently shelving beach and prevailing northeasterly wind offer sheltered water and breezes for beginners, while farther out from shore, more experienced sailors can get into some serious wind.

Keep an eye out for wind gusts known to locals as "Barrenjoey bullets"—gusts that roar down off the headland and hit small patches of the water, where they can pick up boards and riders and toss them about like leaves.

LION ISLAND: Whether you're on Barrenjoey Head, West Head, or out on the water, you'll be curious to know what the "resting lion" crouched out in the middle of Broken Bay facing the ocean is called. It's Lion Island, which would be Sydney's nominee if they ever hold a world's most beautiful island competition. The uninhabited island is a wildlife reserve and has no public access.

Southern Pittwater: While the wind, the scenery, and the lure of the open sea are the attractions at the northern end of Pittwater, most boating activity is based at the southern end. There are several boat-rental operations in the vicinity, plus the Royal Prince Alfred Yacht Club, on Mitala Street in **Newport,** which is the main yachting center for the entire waterway. At most times of the year, berths can be arranged here, although in summer, when all of yachting Sydney descends in hordes, vacant dock space becomes extremely scarce *(tel 9997 1022 for details on affiliations, availability, and assistance finding crew places on boats for twilight or weekend races).*

Also in Newport is the major pub for the peninsula area, the **Newport Arms Hotel** *(Kalinya St., tel 9997 4900).* The hotel is a large venue by any standards, with several eating areas and a wonderful, huge outdoor area overlooking the water. Accommodations are available, or the Newport Mirage across the road is more salubrious.

Across the bay from Newport is **Church Point.** From here, ferries *(tel 9999 3492)* ply to Scotland Island, Lovett Bay, and Elvina Bay (no car access), all of which have several beautiful houses. There is a YHA hostel at Pittwater *(tel 9999 5748, ferry only from Church Point, reservations essential)* that is highly regarded and extremely popular.

From Church Point, McCarrs Creek Road winds around to Ku-ring-gai Chase park, where the inland waterways of Cowan Creek split into numerous steeply sided bush valleys. Although the road provides access to the bush landscape of West Head and the cafés and anchorages of Cottage Point and Akuna Bay, the ideal way to explore this area is by boat.

Access to Pittwater is by car (one hour) or bus. From the city, bus route L90 runs from Wynyard Station to Palm Beach. Another option is to take the ferry to Manly (see pp. 101–104), bus 155 or 169 to Brookvale, then the L90. ■

EXPERIENCE: Get Out on Pittwater

To really enjoy the Pittwater waterway, you need to get out on a boat. Vessels of every description, from canoes to cruisers, can be rented from a plethora of companies based from Newport to the Nepean (see sidebar p. 180). The major yacht rental companies include **Pittwater Yacht Charter** *(yachtcharter-australia.com),* and **Church Point Charter** *(www.churchpointcharter.com.au),* while **Clipper Cruiser Holidays, Akuna Bay** *(www.clippercruises.com.au)* and **Skipper a Clipper** *(www.skipperaclipper.com.au)* rent out cabin cruisers and motorboats. A good guide to rental boats can be found online at *www.charterguide.com.au.*

You do not normally need a special license to rent vessels, although for yachts, sailing experience is usually necessary (if it isn't, start worrying about the rental company). Several of the companies mentioned can also provide skippered yachts. Alternatively, if your time is limited, it can be just as much fun to rent a dinghy from a marina for an afternoon and try to snag a fish.

Hawkesbury River

A continuation of the spectacular waterway of Pittwater, the Hawkesbury River is an extensive river system that winds between rugged bushland and rich farmland from well north of Sydney, around to the city's west side, and then back down to the south. It is a scenic river that can be explored for much of its length by car, but the preferable way to see it is from the water.

Although roads now serve many communities along the Hawkesbury River, the scenic waterway still serves as a transportation route, even if much of the traffic is now recreational in nature.

The first settlers, thinking they had fully explored Pittwater and Broken Bay shortly after their arrival, were surprised to find the river a year later along what "was supposed to be a short creek." The first exploration party, led by Governor Phillip, got 20 miles (32 km) upstream before their supplies ran low and they turned back.

Once it was fully explored, the Hawkesbury River rapidly became an important means of transporting cargo from inland areas down to Broken Bay and a vital link in the spread of settlement north. Some of the earliest towns, buildings, and structures in Australia are found along its banks.

Starting at the lower reaches, one of the most pleasant towns is **Brooklyn.** It is named after the Brooklyn Bridge Company, which built the rail bridge across the Hawkesbury at the turn of

Hawkesbury River
172 A3–173 D4

Brooklyn
173 D4

Wisemans Ferry
172 B5

St. Albans
172 B6

Hawkesbury/ Nepean

When the early settlers first explored the area, they thought the upper and lower reaches of the Hawkesbury were two different waterways. As a result, they called the waters upstream from Richmond the Nepean, and those downstream the Hawkesbury.

the 19th century. Brooklyn can be reached by car via the F3, aka the Sydney–Newcastle Freeway (one of the great engineering feats of the 1960s, with gigantic cuttings and bridges), or by train from Central Station in under two hours (the station at Brooklyn is called Hawkesbury River).

The town provides full services to cruising people, and the waterfront area is popular for weekend fishing. Just offshore, in the center of the river, is **Dangar Island.** A ferry service runs out to the island from Brooklyn; there is a pleasant café alongside the wharf and also some nice walks and sandy beaches. Accommodations are available on the island, at Brooklyn, and on the small, isolated beaches and coves nearby.

One enjoyable way to see this part of the Hawkesbury is to ride with the riverboat postman *(tel 0400 600 111)*. Several communities can be accessed only by water, and a ferry runs the postal service. Tourism is the main business now, but it still delivers mail and other supplies. The service operates weekdays at 10 a.m., returning by 1:15 p.m. The 7:45 a.m. train from Central Station in the city arrives at Hawkesbury River Station in time for the morning ferry. Several other cruise companies have their offices at Brooklyn.

Wisemans Ferry & the Macdonald Valley

Although the ideal way to explore the river is by boat, there is quite a pleasant drive along the northern shores of the river. On the F3, cross the river and take the exit to Peats Ridge. Through Mangrove, follow signs to Spencer and Wisemans Ferry and you'll find yourself on a long, winding drive with the river on one side and national parks on the other. There are several camping spots along the way, and some walks, but only limited facilities.

INSIDER TIP:

Be prepared to leave your car behind if you visit Dangar Island—no cars are allowed. But the island is small, so you won't need one.

—JANE SUNDERLAND
National Geographic contributor

Wisemans Ferry is named after Solomon Wiseman, who set up the ferry service in 1827. The Wisemans Inn *(tel 4566 4301)* was originally his home. Accommodations, camping, and

Dharug National Park
172 B6–173 C5

www.environment.nsw.gov.au

St. Albans
172 B6

houseboat, boat, and kayak rentals are available in the township. At Wisemans Ferry, the Macdonald River joins the Hawkesbury, and two car punts service the north (Wisemans Ferry) and south banks (Webbs Creek Ferry).

If you are coming direct from the city (on the M2 and Old Northern Road), turn left on Settlers Road when you come off the main ferry, and within a mile (1.5 km) you will see signs to the Old Great North Road (no car access). The road, now part of **Dharug National Park,** was dug out of the sheer cliff face by convicts between 1826 and 1830. This section, open to walkers only, forms part of the **Great North Walk,** which extends from the city to the Hunter Valley (details from the Sydney Visitor Centre, see p. 75). At this point, the road features sandstone walls and buttresses, and handmade sandstone drains run beneath the road. The marks of the convict chisels can still be seen on nearly every piece of stone as you ascend the trail, taking in views of the Hawkesbury and the Macdonald Valley. You need walk for only 10–15 minutes along the road to find a pleasant spot for a quiet picnic.

Back at your vehicle, continue along the narrow, mostly unsurfaced Mogo Creek Road into the Macdonald Valley and the village of **St. Albans.** This rich farming area was settled soon after it was discovered (only a year after the First Fleet arrived), although amenities such as electricity weren't installed until the late 1960s. Just before the village is a cemetery where seven First Fleeters are buried, although the graves aren't marked.

St. Albans itself is the heart of a little community of artists and smallholders. At its center is the **Settlers Arms Inn** *(tel 4568 2111)*, which dates from 1836 and has rustic accommodations, plus information on several historic sites. The pub was originally built to service Cobb & Co. coaches traveling the Great North Road. These days, the area is usually rather sleepy, but the local folk festival brings visitors flocking in April. Return by the main, sealed St. Albans Road and the Webbs Creek Ferry

Brooklyn provides food, fuel, and more to river users.

Macquarie Towns

Back at the Hawkesbury River, you can explore numerous villages along its banks. Five were established by Lachlan Macquarie in 1810; they are still known as the Macquarie Towns and comprise **Richmond, Pitt**

Macquarie Towns
172 A3–B4

Cattai National Park
172 B4

Town, Wilberforce, Castlereagh (the only town that didn't survive), and **Windsor.**

Richmond and Windsor are the two major centers of the Upper Hawkesbury and can be accessed by rail as well as the M2 tollway from the city.

Many historic buildings can be seen in Windsor, including **St. Matthew's Church,** designed by Francis Greenway and built between 1817 and 1822, and the **Macquarie Arms** (1815), on George Street, the country's oldest pub and still operating. Of particular interest is the beautiful **John Tebbutt Observatory** (*tel 4577 7306*) on Palmer Street. The 19th-century astronomer John Tebbutt had a crater on the moon named after him and his observations, especially of comets, provided valuable data that is still being referred to today. There is a restaurant and function center, and night tours for groups can be arranged, usually run by a member of the Tebbutt family.

The Hawkesbury River paddle steamer and other boats cruise the river. The Hawkesbury Visitor Information Centre (*tel 4578 0233*) in Windsor has details and brochures on the area's history.

Highlights of some of the smaller towns in the area include the oldest church in Australia—the **Presbyterian Church** at Ebenezer, which dates from 1809—and the oldest wooden cottage in the country: **Rose Cottage,** on Rose Street in Wilberforce, built between 1811 and 1816, the oldest slab hut in the country. Near Ebenezer, the Tuscan-inspired 1887 **Tizzana Winery** (*tel 4579 1150*) makes a pleasant stop and has a small selection of wines and ports grown in a nearby vineyard.

Also on the river is **Cattai National Park** (*tel 4572 3100*), which occupies 1,048 acres (424 ha). Here you can see rain forest remnants and historic buildings, and there are picnic areas. Camping can be booked. ■

EXPERIENCE: Houseboat on the Hawkesbury

Long a favorite vacation break with Sydneysiders, cruising down the Hawkesbury on a fully equipped houseboat is an idyllic way to see the river. You don't need a license, and experts take you through the operation of the boat and navigation rules and onto the water first to make sure you are comfortable handling the boat. Bookings are heavy and prices soar during holiday periods, but they are reasonable at other times, particularly midweek. Prices start at around A$1,000 for two nights on a 2–4 berth houseboat, A$1,000 for an 8–10 berther. The bigger operators include the following:

Able Hawkesbury House Boats, River Rd., Wisemans Ferry, tel 4566 4308, www.hawkesburyhouseboats.com.au

Ripples Houseboat Holidays, 87 Brooklyn Rd., Brooklyn, tel 9985 5534, www.ripples.com.au

Luxury Afloat Houseboats, Kangaroo Point Cruise Terminal, Pacific Hwy., Brooklyn, tel 9985 7344, www.luxuryafloat.org

More Places to Visit in the North

Beautiful Lane Cove National Park features wet eucalyptus forests, grassy woodlands, and wetlands.

Garigal National Park

Just 7 miles (11 km) north of Sydney's city center, the 5,367-acre (2,172 ha) Garigal National Park is an impressive pocket of sandstone bushland north from the upper reaches of Middle Harbour. There are facilities at Davidson Park Picnic Area and a network of walking and horseback-riding trails. Details are available at the entrance.
www.environment.nsw.gov.au 173 D3
Warringah Rd., Forestville 9451 3479

Koala Park Sanctuary

Northwest of the city, the Koala Park Sanctuary was established in the 1920s on 10 acres (4 ha) of native bushland. Koalas roam free, and there are photo opportunities during feeding times *(10:20 a.m., 11:45 a.m., 2 p.m., & 3 p.m.)*. The park also has a long-established and successful breeding and study program. Other creatures to be seen—either wandering loose or in enclosures—are wallabies, wombats, kangaroos, and cockatoos.

A visit to the park could be combined with a trip to Windsor and the Hawkesbury River (see pp. 179–182), a detour off the M2 tollway. To get to the park, take a train to Pennant Hills Station, then Glenorie Bus routes 651 to 655.
www.koalaparksanctuary.com.au 173 C2
84 Castle Hill Rd., West Pennant Hills
9484 3141

Lane Cove National Park

The 916-acre (371 ha) Lane Cove National Park sits just 7 miles (11 km) northwest of Sydney's center, stretching along the Lane Cove River, which runs into Sydney Harbour. There are picnic areas, two kiosks, and a small visitor center with heritage displays.

Details of trails for bushwalkers are available at the upper and lower entrances. Boating is the preferred way to see the park, however, with rowboats and canoes available for rent. Swimming above the weir is discouraged due to submerged rocks and branches.

Access is from Lane Cove Road, Delhi Road, and Lady Game Drive. Bus 256 from Chatswood Station operates to the park.
www.environment.nsw.gov.au 173 D2–D3
9412 1811 Closed at sunset

West & South

Just west of the city, between Sydney Harbour and the Blue Mountains, lies the vast Sydney Basin, an area in which most of the population lives in suburb after suburb of red-tiled, brick houses on "quarter-acre blocks." This was the stuff of the Australian dream, the desire to have your own home and block of land, which many people realized in the years after World War II.

Before then, however, there was another dream: to find land that could be used to grow crops to sustain the first settlement. Find it they did, and as a consequence some of the buildings in the western area of Sydney are among the oldest and best preserved in the country.

In this spacious western area, wildlife parks, botanic gardens, and recreational amenities preserve, protect, and display some of Australia's rich natural heritage.

The southern region of Sydney may lack the grand scenery or idyllic beaches to be found in the Blue Mountains or the northern beaches, but there are several enjoyable excursions to be made.

Botany Bay was almost the cradle of the nation, for example, and several historic sites remain. Just south of the bay, the commercial and recreational center of Cronulla offers beaches, boating, easy walking, and some interesting history.

From Cronulla, a short ferry ride can take you to Royal National Park. The second oldest national park in the world, the 40,300-acre (16,300 ha) Royal offers first-class walking, bird- and wildlife-watching, and beautiful coastal scenery. ■

NOT TO BE MISSED:

Parramatta's Elizabeth Farm, the oldest house in the country 187

Following in Captain Cook's wake on a Botany Bay cruise 188–189

Catching at wave at one the fine beaches in Cronulla 190

The lovely scenery of Royal National Park, the country's oldest national park 193–195

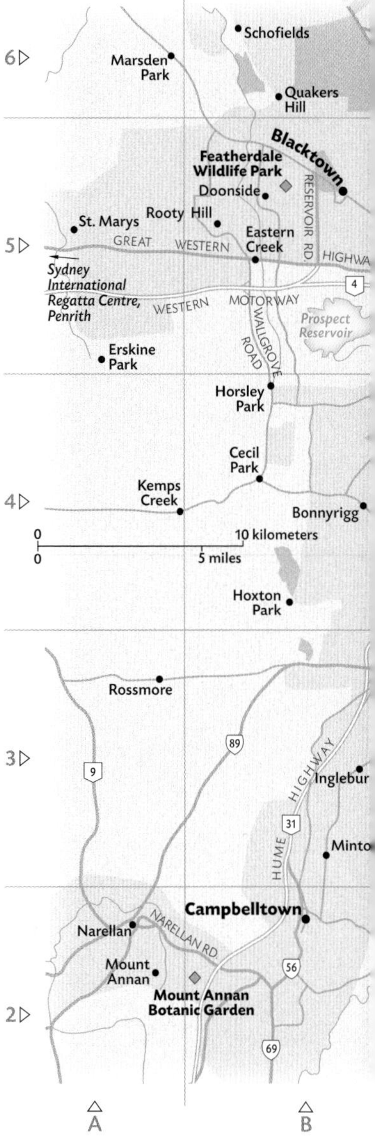

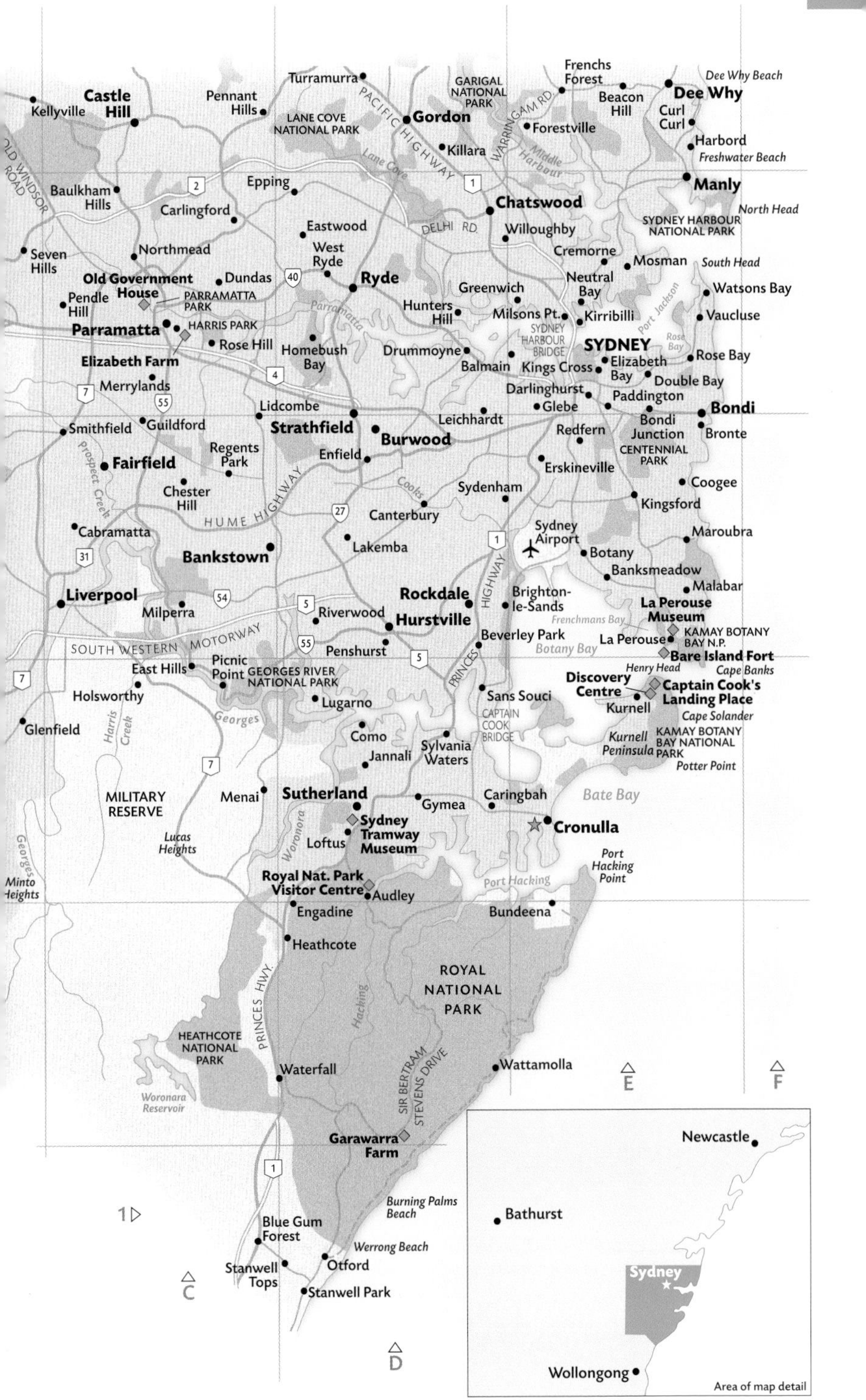
Castle Hill
Kellyville
Pennant Hills
Turramurra
Gordon
Killara
Lane Cove National Park
Garigal National Park
Frenchs Forest
Beacon Hill
Dee Why
Dee Why Beach
Curl Curl
Forestville
Harbord
Freshwater Beach
Manly
North Head
Sydney Harbour National Park
South Head
Watsons Bay
Vaucluse
Old Windsor Road
Baulkham Hills
Epping
Carlingford
Eastwood
Chatswood
Willoughby
Delhi Rd.
Pacific Highway
Warringah Rd.
Middle Harbour
Lane Cove
Cremorne
Mosman
Neutral Bay
Kirribilli
Port Jackson
Seven Hills
Northmead
West Ryde
Ryde
Dundas
Old Government House
Parramatta Park
Pendle Hill
Parramatta
Harris Park
Rose Hill
Elizabeth Farm
Homebush Bay
Hunters Hill
Greenwich
Milsons Pt.
Sydney Harbour Bridge
Sydney
Rose Bay
Drummoyne
Balmain
Kings Cross
Elizabeth Bay
Double Bay
Darlinghurst
Paddington
Bondi
Bondi Junction
Bronte
Centennial Park
Merrylands
Lidcombe
Strathfield
Burwood
Leichhardt
Glebe
Redfern
Smithfield
Guildford
Regents Park
Enfield
Erskineville
Fairfield
Prospect Creek
Chester Hill
Hume Highway
Cooks
Sydenham
Canterbury
Coogee
Kingsford
Cabramatta
Lakemba
Sydney Airport
Maroubra
Botany
Banksmeadow
Bankstown
Liverpool
Milperra
Rockdale
Highway
Brighton-le-Sands
Malabar
La Perouse Museum
Riverwood
Hurstville
Frenchmans Bay
Kamay Botany Bay N.P.
Beverley Park
Botany Bay
La Perouse
Bare Island Fort
South Western Motorway
Penshurst
Princes
Henry Head
Cape Banks
East Hills
Picnic Point
Georges River National Park
Discovery Centre
Captain Cook's Landing Place
Holsworthy
Lugarno
Sans Souci
Kurnell
Captain Cook Bridge
Cape Solander
Glenfield
Harris Creek
Georges
Como
Sylvania Waters
Jannali
Kurnell Peninsula
Kamay Botany Bay National Park
Potter Point
Military Reserve
Menai
Sutherland
Gymea
Caringbah
Bate Bay
Sydney Tramway Museum
Cronulla
Lucas Heights
Loftus
Woronora
Port Hacking Point
Georges
Minto Heights
Royal Nat. Park Visitor Centre
Audley
Port Hacking
Engadine
Bundeena
Heathcote
Royal National Park
Princes Hwy.
Hacking
Heathcote National Park
Waterfall
Sir Bertram Stevens Drive
Wattamolla
Woronara Reservoir
Garawarra Farm
Burning Palms Beach
Blue Gum Forest
Werrong Beach
Stanwell Tops
Otford
Stanwell Park
Newcastle
Bathurst
Sydney
Wollongong
Area of map detail

Parramatta

Parramatta was established in November 1788—less than a year after the arrival of the First Fleet—as the soils in the area were found to be better suited to farming than those at Sydney Cove. During the early years of the colony, while it was battling for survival, the population of Parramatta was larger than that of Sydney Cove, and a number of buildings from this period have survived.

Much of Parramatta Town Hall, in the town center, has been restored to its original 1883 grandeur.

Parramatta
185 C5
Visitor Information
346a Church St.
8839 3311

Parramatta Park
O'Connell St.
8833 5000
Closed Mon.

Many of the town's historic sites are now almost swamped by development, but they are still worth seeking out.

Parramatta Park

Parramatta Park, on O'Connell Street, contains several buildings that have survived from the early years of the colony in the 18th century. The most significant is **Old Government House,** built in 1799 by Governor Hunter and added to by Gov. Lachlan Macquarie in 1815. The building is now in the hands of the National Trust and has been fully restored and decorated with early 19th-century furniture. There is a gift shop and Lachlan's Restaurant & Café *(tel 1300 596 286).*

The oldest surviving headstone in Australia, dating from January 1791, is also located on O'Connell Street, in **St. John's Cemetery;** it belongs to Henry Dodd. There are numerous other graves of early settlers, too, including the "flogging parson," Samuel Marsden (see sidebar page opposite).

Parramatta Park was set aside for the public by Macquarie.

INSIDER TIP:

If you're going to Parramatta, take the scenic route—a ferry from Circular Quay (*www.sydneyferries.info*).

—DEAN DEZIUS
Director of programming, National Geographic Channel Australia

It occupies more than 618 acres (250 ha), and its other buildings include the Governor's Dairy, the Tudor gatehouse off O'Connell Street, rotundas, and a bathhouse built by Governor Brisbane in 1822.

Rose Hill & Harris Park

On the opposite side of the main shopping and business district are the small suburbs of Rose Hill and Harris Park, where two of the oldest buildings in the country can be found. Rose Hill was the original name given to Parramatta, but Governor Phillip changed the name of the township to the Aboriginal for "place where eels lie down" on June 4, 1791.

In the same year, **Experiment Farm Cottage** *(9 Ruse St., Parramatta, tel 9635 5655, closed Mon.)* was built on 30 acres (12 ha) of land granted to convict James Ruse, the first farmer in the colony to declare himself self-sufficient. The surviving cottage homestead—now restored and furnished in period style by the National Trust—was built on the land in 1834 by a surgeon, John Harris.

One of the most significant buildings in the Parramatta district is **Elizabeth Farm** *(70 Alice St., Rose Hill, tel 9635 9488)*, built by John and Elizabeth Macarthur (see p. 29), the oldest surviving house in the country. The attractive colonial-style house, part of which dates from 1793, is set in a pleasant garden that was first laid out in 1830. Many of the plants and trees, native and exotic, have significant historical and botanical interest.

Access to Parramatta from Sydney is by train or by car via the M4 tollway. Or, for a more scenic approach, the Sydney Ferries's Parramatta RiverCat travels through many attractive harborside suburbs, past the Homebush Bay Olympic site (see pp. 166–169) and on to the Charles Street Wharf at Parramatta.

Samuel Marsden

Samuel Marsden (1764–1838), a parson, was appointed as a magistrate in Sydney in 1795. He was a stern disciplinarian who gained a reputation for having convicts lashed severely for minor indiscretions. In 1800, he used torture to extract a confession, and did so again after the Vinegar Hill Rebellion in 1804 (see p. 30).

The Parramatta Visitor Information Centre, on the right-hand side of the second bridge up the river from the ferry wharf, has heritage exhibits and walking, driving, and architectural guides to the many historic sites in this precinct (some guides are also available at the wharf). ■

Botany Bay

Only 5 miles (8 km) south of the Central Business District, Sydney's second major waterway is famous as the intended site of the colony's original settlement. Botany Bay had been visited by Capt. James Cook in 1770, and the historic site where he landed is now part of Kamay Botany Bay National Park. Large parts of its shores have been given over to industry, but you will find a few gems tucked away, and the western shore is a cycling, walking, and boating haven.

Captain Cook described the isle off today's La Perouse as "a small bare island." The name stuck.

Botany Bay
185 E3–E4

Within **Kamay Botany Bay National Park** is the **La Perouse Museum,** devoted to French explorer Comte de la Pérouse, who arrived in Botany Bay shortly after the First Fleet. He and his vessels disappeared not long after his visit, and he was mourned as much by the English, whose respect he had earned, as he was by the French. Also in the museum building—a former cable station—rotating exhibits highlight the Aboriginal, environmental, and local history of the area. The tower near the museum was completed in 1822 to watch for smugglers landing in the bay.

Nearby in La Perouse rises

the **Bare Island Fort,** built in 1881–1885 to upgrade the bay's defense system. It is accessed by footbridge. You can rent a boat at Frenchmans Bay, below the museum, and there are small beaches at Congwong Bay and Little Congwong.

Take a stroll or do some bird-watching along the Henry Head Walk, where there are a number of places to picnic, fish, and scuba dive. Access is by car along Anzac Parade or bus routes 391 and L94 from the city.

INSIDER TIP:

Laddie Timbery from the Bidjigal clan in the Eora Nation conducts boomerang-throwing and clap stick demonstrations at La Perouse Museum on Sundays.

—PETER TURNER
National Geographic author

On the western side of Botany Bay, from the Cooks River down to the Georges River, is an almost continuous stretch of calm-water beachfront with walking and biking trails, picnic areas, boat ramps, and netted pools. The bike trails reach around to **Cronulla** (see pp. 190–191) and (with a few nasty traffic spots) the Olympic venues at Homebush Bay (see pp. 166–169). A bike path to the city along the Alexandra Canal is planned. Meanwhile, cyclists will find plenty of cafés at Brighton-le-Sands, facing Botany Bay.

The Southern Headland

The main section of the 1,074-acre (435 ha) Kamay Botany Bay National Park covers the southern headland of the bay, the site of several significant relics of the Captain Cook landing. The **Kurnell Visitor Centre** has historical and Aboriginal exhibitions, while scattered about the park you'll find monuments to Cook and Joseph Banks, **Captain Cook's Landing Place,** and the grave of one of Cook's crew, Forby Sutherland, who was buried here after his death in 1770.

As with the north side of the national park, the south side has several picnic areas and quite a few walking trails, plus fishing, swimming, and bird-watching opportunities. ■

EXPERIENCE:

Look for Whales

Humpback whales migrate up the Pacific coast annually in June and July, then return south from September to November, often coming close to shore. You can get up close to these magnificent beasts—and sometimes southern right, blue, and sperm whales, too—on whale-watching cruises.

Whale Watching Sydney *(tel 9583 1199, www.whalewatchingsydney.net, $$$$$)* is the major operator, offering a number of cruises departing from Darling Harbour and Circular Quay as well as from Sans Souci in Botany Bay. Its two-hour Adventure Tour combines thrills with whale-watching in a high-speed rescue boat. **Vagabond** *(tel 1300 862 784, www.vagabond.com.au, $$$$$)* also has tours departing from Sydney Harbour.

Kamay Botany Bay National Park

Map 185 E3–E4

Visitor Information

Kurnell Visitor Centre, Cape Solander Dr., Kurnell

Tel 9668 2000

www.environment.nsw.gov.au

La Perouse Museum

Map 185 E4

Cable Station, Anzac Parade, La Perouse

Tel 9311 3379

Closed Mon.–Sat.

A Walk in Cronulla

The beachside suburb of Cronulla, a precinct of Sydney near the southern section of Kamay Botany Bay National Park and adjacent to the northern section of Royal National Park, offers a wealth of recreational opportunities—beaches, inshore waterways, less pressured leisure activity. This route includes headland walking trails, several beaches, and Gunnamatta Bay, with mostly level walking.

From Cronulla Station, cross at the traffic lights and walk down the left-hand side of Munro Park. Follow the pedestrian walkway to **South Cronulla Beach ❶,** where you might be tempted to take your first dive into the Pacific.

If you can resist, turn right and follow the track around Cronulla Point to tiny **Blackwoods Beach ❷.** This beach is unpatrolled and rather rocky, but it has a popular surfing spot at the end of a rock shelf half a mile (1 km) offshore. The heights above the beach make a superb vantage point.

Continue on to **Shelly Beach ❸,** another small beach, which has toilets and changing facilities and a large ocean pool with wheelchair access all the way into the water. Onshore is a large picnic area with plenty of shady trees. Farther on still, at **Oak Park,** you'll find another surf break, a small beach, and another pool on Glaisher Point.

At the southern end of the promontory is the **Bass and Flinders Memorial ❹,** a monument to George Bass and Matthew Flinders, who first explored Port Hacking in March 1796 in nothing more than a tiny rowboat, named *Tom Thumb*. Bass Strait, the treacherous stretch of wild water between Victoria and Tasmania, is also named after George Bass, who discovered it in January 1798, thereby reducing the traveling time from London to the colony in New South Wales.

From Bass and Flinders Point, enjoy the view across Port Hacking to the township of Bundeena, Jibbon Beach, and Royal National Park's northern edge. All of these are accessible by ferry, which departs from a wharf at the end of this walk.

NOT TO BE MISSED:

Shelly Beach • Bass and Flinders Memorial • Gunnamatta Park

Cronulla Riots

Sydney's reputation as a tolerant, multicultural melting pot was severely tested in 2005 when 5,000 mostly Anglo-Australians flocked to Cronulla to "reclaim the beach." Whipped up by radio shock jocks after two lifesavers were allegedly assaulted by Middle Eastern men, the flag-draped, alcohol-fueled mob set upon anyone who looked Lebanese, a reference to long-simmering problems with Lebanese gangs in western Sydney. Police were unable to control the riot, and counter-riots continued in pockets around Sydney for two days before calm was restored.

Heading Inland

From the memorial, turn your back on the ocean and start to head inland. Just down the slope you'll notice that the terrain and the vegetation change. Instead of the Norfolk pines of cultivated gardens, eucalyptuses and figs of the Australian bush predominate.

In **Salmon Haul Reserve ❺,** just down the hill, notice the fig tree with its trunk growing sideways due to the strong southerly winds.

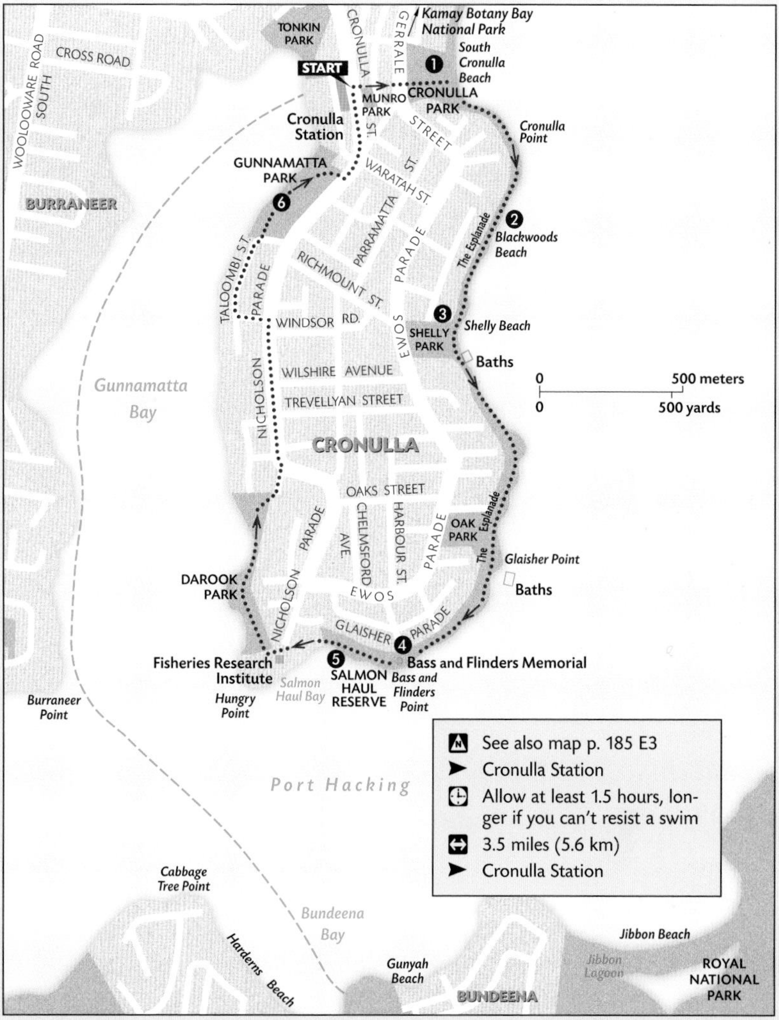

At the end of Salmon Haul Reserve, take the stairs on the far side of the large white house and walk through to Nicholson Parade, past the entrance of the Fisheries Research Centre, and continue along the path to **Darook Park.** As you follow the path to the right, notice the holes in the trees that accommodate a variety of parrots, including eastern rosellas and cockatoos.

From here, either make your way down to the water, where at low tide the sand flats in front of the houses and seawall make for fairly easy walking, or continue to the far side of Darook Park and climb up to Nicholson Parade and follow it to Leumeah Street.

Turn left, then right at Taloombi Street to **Gunnamatta Park 6.** Here there is a mesh-enclosed swimming area, a large pavilion, and a vast picnic area. Go through the park to reach the ferry wharf, just below the railway station, where this walk began.

For more on the ferries to Bundeena and Port Hacking cruises, see page 192.

Port Hacking & Georges River

The Georges River and Port Hacking, two of Sydney's lesser-known waterways, are both worth exploring for their scenery. They offer quiet reaches of native bushland and mangrove wetlands, and Towra Point Reserve, in Botany Bay, is renowned for waterbirds such as stilts, spoonbills, and pelicans.

The *Tom Thumb III*, moored at the Port Hacking marina

Port Hacking
185 D3–E3

Georges River
185 C4–D3

The ferry wharf and marina below the Cronulla Station at Tonkin Street is the base for **Cronulla and National Park Ferry Cruises** *(tel 9523 2990, www.cronullaferries.com.au)*, which operates an hourly service to and from Bundeena and Royal National Park (see pp. 193–195). Their cruises around Port Hacking and up the Hacking River are conducted aboard two quaint wooden ferries, the M.V. *Curranulla* and M.V. *Tom Thumb III* *(daily at 10:30 a.m, except Thurs. & Sat. during winter; reservations recommended)*. Breakfast and dinner cruises on a modern two-deck vessel are also offered.

The *Tom Thumb III* is named after the vessel used by explorers George Bass and Matthew Flinders (see p. 190). Cruises take three hours and tour both the national park side of the port and river, with its cliffs and slopes of native bush and mangroves, and the opposite bank, where numerous opulent houses nestle in the bays or make bold statements on the hillsides. Light refreshments are served on board.

Bass and Flinders Cruises *(tel 9583 1199, bassflinders.com.au)* operates cruises from Sans Souci Wharf, on the western side of Captain Cook Bridge. Sunday sightseeing cruises *(12:30 p.m., with optional lunch)* explore the Georges River, which threads between suburbia, golf courses, riverside parks, and mangroves; there are also Friday and Saturday dinner cruises. It also operates popular Coastal Explorer Cruises from Darling Harbour, taking in Sydney Harbour, Bondi Beach, Botany Bay, and Port Hacking. To reach Sans Souci, take bus 476 or 477 from the city.

Towra Point opposite Sans Souci is one of the most significant coastal wetlands regions and is vital for migratory birds from as far away as China and Siberia. It is accessible by road via Cronulla. ■

Royal National Park

Diverse flora and fauna grace the 40,300 acres (16,300 ha) of coastal heath, littoral rain forest, and bushland that comprise Royal National Park. Visit rock engravings and hand stencils left by the Dharawal people, or enjoy the beaches and rivers, many of which have enticing swimming pools. A real attraction is the lack of vehicular roads; you can spend an afternoon at an almost deserted beach or "go native" for days, exploring inland and coastal walks.

Located 20 miles (32 km) south of Sydney, Royal National Park was established in 1879. It boasts some 12 miles (19 km) of coastline, an inland river—the Hacking—many streams, a network of walking trails, camping areas, scenic drives, and several stunning coastal lookouts.

You'll find here a wide variety of animal and bird life. Most of the park's 43 mammal species inhabit the tall, moist eucalyptus forests and rain forests of the Hacking River Valley. The short-nosed echidna populates the heathlands, while the shy swamp wallaby is found along the coast. More than 140 bird species are resident, nest, or occur regularly in the park, with another 100 or so sighted. Look for the sulphur-crested cockatoo in the eucalyptus forests and the fantail cuckoo along the coast.

Royal National Park

185 D1–D3

Visitor Information

Audley Visitor Information Centre, Audley Rd., Audley

9542 0648

www.environment.nsw.gov.au

Rugged sandstone cliffs punctuate the coastline of Royal National Park.

Getting to the Park

Access to the park is by car and train or the ferry from Cronulla to the township of **Bundeena** (an enclave surrounded by the park on the south side of Port Hacking). Several roads prove ideal for cycling.

Walking trails enter the park from Loftus, Engadine, Heathcote, Waterfall, or Otford railway stations. Roads enter from the Princes Highway on the western side and at Otford in the south. For a particularly scenic drive, enter the park at Audley and follow **Sir Bertram Stevens Drive** to the southern side of the park where, at Otford Lookout and Stanwell Tops, hang gliders launch off the hilltop and soar out over the Pacific Ocean, which beats against the rocks far below. The view from here extends south well down the coast to the city of **Wollongong.** Or drive east to the settlements of **Maianbar** and **Bundeen,** noted for artist studios.

INSIDER TIP:

Relatively flat, the park's 6-mile-long (10 km) Lady Carrington Drive—an old carriage-way closed to cars—is a popular walking and moutain-biking track for families with small children.

—JANE SUNDERLAND
National Geographic contributor

Touring by Car

Visitors arriving by car usually start at **Audley,** at the crossing of the Hacking River. Here you'll find a visitor center, displays on the park, a shop, and information on walks within the park. Nearby are wide expanses of picnic areas, safe swimming areas, and rowboat, canoe and bike rental. There is road access to a number of beaches within the park, several of which are

EXPERIENCE: Ride a Vintage Tram Into Royal NP

Arrive at Royal National Park the old-fashioned way—by rail. Passengers first arrived at the park via rail in 1886; after regular train service was discontinued in 1991, the **Sydney Tramway Museum** *(map 185 D3, Rawson Ave. & Princes Hwy., Loftus, tel 9542 3646, www.sydneytramwaymuseum.com.au, open Wed., Sun., & public holidays, $$$)* began running a vintage tram along the 1.2-mile (2 km) track into the park. Hop aboard the tram at the Loftus railway station, next to the museum, and with the clang of a bell, you're off. The trip is short—seven minutes—but novel, and it ends just a short walk from the park's visitor center and Bungoona Lookout.

A combination ticket allows you entry to the museum itself, which features relics from the days when Sydney had a comprehensive tramway system. These include the R-class Commodore and the oldest electric tram in the Southern Hemisphere, a C-class dating from 1894. The local expression "he was off like a Bondi tram" refers to the way the trams flew down the hill to the beach. Vehicles from several other Australian cities, as well as from overseas, are also on display.

patrolled, including **Garie, Era,** and **Burning Palms.** With only a few basic facilities, they make quite a contrast to the city beaches with their busy shopping and food strips. Smaller picnic areas with road access are tucked away all over the park.

Car camping is permitted only at **Bonnie Vale,** facing Port Hacking. Nude bathing is permitted at **Werrong Beach,** on the southern edge of the park, a mile (1.5 km) from Otford Lookout.

The premier walk in the park is the two-day, 16-mile (26 km) **Coast Track** that starts from the ferry at Bundeena and follows the headlands and beaches south to the railway station at Otford. The views of beaches, rugged headlands, heath, and rain forest are superb. Along the way, you'll find camping sites that comply with the park requirement that sites must be at least half a mile (1 km) from roads and picnic grounds. If you're very energetic, it is possible to do this route in a day, but two days will give you time to swim and enjoy the sights. Some sections of the track are also quite steep. Note, too, that camping permits are required and should be reserved in advance *(tel 9542 0683)*. For noncampers, the park is open during daylight hours. ■

A scenic lookout in Royal National Park provides panoramic views over the forest to the Tasman Sea.

Walking Trails

The park offers walking trails to suit every level of fitness and desire for adventure. One of the shortest trails, the **Bungoona Path** to the Bungoona Lookout, is less than a mile. Some walks follow streams or escarpments through the park's inland areas.

Wildlife of the Sydney Region

Whether you have penetrated into the wilds of one of the national parks or are wandering through Hyde Park in the middle of the city, the rich diversity of wildlife in the Sydney area is never far away. You'll be able to check off many of the creatures on these pages even during the briefest of stays.

The Australian pelican has the largest bill of all bird species in the world.

Visitors seeking a longer list than is presented here could consider *Burnum Burnum's Wild Things,* a pocket guide that has many more of the birds and animals of the Sydney region. A large part of this volume also covers the wide variety of native plants. For bird-watchers, there are several excellent field guides available from bookstores in the city.

Birds

Australian Pelican *(Pelecanus conspicillatus):* Ungainly on the ground, with short legs, large body, and long bill on a long neck, these birds are superb flyers. Sexes are similar. Growing to 64 inches (1.6 m), they are found all over Australia in shallow marine and inland waters. They can rise to great heights on thermals and glide huge distances to reach food. They tend to forage rather than plunge-dive. There is often a flotilla of them loitering around the docks at the Sydney Fish Market.

Black Swan *(Cygnus atratus):* A graceful bird, common on inland waters, the black swan can often be found on the lakes at Centennial Park and the Royal Botanic Gardens' ponds. It grows to 50 inches (1.3 m) and has a black, or sometimes brownish, plumage and a red bill with a white tip. Males have slightly thicker necks than females and hold them straighter when they swim. They make a honk or bugle sound and hiss when they are protecting their territory. It is best to keep clear of them when they have young.

Eastern Rosella ***(Platycercus eximius):*** This is one of many beautiful parrots found around Sydney. Common. At 11–12 inches (28–30.5 cm), it is slightly larger than a budgerigar and quite a lot more colorful. Sexes are alike. They are frequently seen in open country and the parks and gardens of the city. They are great flyers and quite quick, so you may hear their shrill screech and only catch a flash of color as they pass. Also commonly seen around Sydney is the crimson rosella, which has a red head and body with blue cheeks and wings.

Kookaburra ***(Dacelo novaguineae):*** Famous for its laugh, the kookaburra is commonly seen around bushland areas. It grows to 18 inches (45.5 cm), and both sexes are similar. The most distinguishing feature of this rather handsome bird is its laughing call, which sounds like it has just heard the best joke ever told. Kookaburras are predatory birds, hunting small reptiles and mammals, and can often be seen in a conspicuous position on the edges of forest clearings watching the ground for a prospective meal.

Little Penguin ***(Eudyptula minor):*** The only species of penguin found in Australian mainland waters, the little penguin (also called the fairy penguin in Australia) can be found as far north as subtropical Queensland. They are slate blue in color, with a white chest. Sexes are similar, though the male has a heavier bill. They grow to 16 inches (40 cm). There is a colony near Manly, and they can be seen around Manly Cove and the heads. They may also be seen on Gordon's Bay, near Coogee in the eastern suburbs.

Rainbow Lorikeet ***(Trichoglossus heamatodus):*** This striking parrot commonly found in Sydney can grow to 10–12 inches (25.5–30.5 cm). It is the only lorikeet with a blue head. Sexes are alike. The lorikeet is a noisy bird that can usually be seen in flocks and heard chattering when feeding. These birds tend to be arboreal and feed on flowering trees and shrubs. Like cockatoos and parrots, they have a hooked beak, but

EXPERIENCE: Bird-Watch & Bushwalk

Get to know some of the more than 350 species of birds in the Sydney region by visiting the study centers in several national parks and wetland areas or going on outings offered by birding clubs, including the NSW Field Ornithologists Club, aka Birding NSW ***(www.birdingnsw.org.au),*** **and BirdLife Australia** ***(www.birdlife.org.au),*** **which runs the BirdLife Discovery Centre at Olympic Park (see p. 166). Both clubs have information on numerous bird sanctuaries in and around Sydney; contact the clubs for details on participating in outings.**

Bushwalking (hiking) offers great birding opportunities, too. Several clubs organize walks almost every weekend that you can join ***(www.bushwalking.org.au*** **lists clubs*),* or consider a longer walking experience offered by companies such as Red Roo Adventures** ***(www.redrooadventures.com.au),*** **Aus Walk** ***(www.auswalk.com.au),*** **and Oz Trek Adventure Tours** ***(www.oztrek.com.au).***

they also have an adapted brushlike tongue that helps them feed on nectar.

Silvereye *(Zosterops lateralis)*: This very attractive small bird is common on coastal heaths and in the coastal forest understory from South Australia to Queensland. It grows to 4 inches (10 cm); males and females are similar. Interestingly, there are mainland Australian silvereyes and Tasmanian silvereyes, and while the mainland birds are nonmigratory, the Tasmanians are sometimes seen on the mainland, although they do not breed while visiting. The silvereye's diet consists of insects, fruit, and nectar.

Sulphur-crested Cockatoo *(Cacatua galerita)*: Big and raucous, with a deafening scraping screech, the sulphur-crested cockatoo is common, particularly in riverside areas and timbered countryside, such as Centennial Park. Growing to 20 inches (51 cm), it has a distinctive yellow crest that it lifts in an impressive display, resembling somewhat the sails of the Sydney Opera House. Sexes are similar. A sulphur-crested holds the record for the oldest known bird: It was 80 years old when it died at London Zoo in 1982.

White-bellied Sea Eagle *(Haliaeetus leucogaster)*: A glorious predatory bird found patrolling seas, lakes, and rivers, this eagle is white breasted with gray to dark-gray wings and back. The males grow to 30 inches (76 cm), females to 34 inches (86 cm). They can be seen on the Hawkesbury waterways, often perched on dead tree branches. The sea eagle—one of 24 raptors that inhabit Australia—is so superbly adapted to hunting that it spends only a few minutes each day seeking its food.

INSIDER TIP:
Walk through the Royal Botanic Gardens in Sydney at sunset to see the flying foxes fly from the trees, where they roost during the day.

—JILL SCHNEIDER
National Geographic photographer

Mammals

Eastern Gray Kangaroo *(Macropus giganteus)*: This is the most common species of kangaroo in the Sydney region. They are often seen in the national parks and are a standard item in all wildlife parks, where you can feed them, pet them, and have your photo taken with them. Kangaroos are marsupials, which means that the young are born highly underdeveloped and are then suckled in the mother's pouch until they are able to survive. Of 19 marsupial families, 16 are found in Australia.

The Koala: A Species Under Threat?

Australia's koala population is estimated at around 80,000, but numbers are dropping due to loss of habitat, dog attacks, and disease, including chlamydia (which has lowered fertility rates). Though the koala is not endangered, in 2012 the Australian government moved to list the species as threatened in parts of the country. Protected since the 1920s after the export fur trade was banned, koalas are listed as rare and vulnerable in the Sydney region. However, isolated colonies still thrive in forested areas, particularly in Victoria and parts of Queensland—and in some areas, overpopulation has resulted in relocation. Even in high-density areas, koalas are hard to spot, preferring leafy treetops, but you may hear them. Many a camper has been scared witless in the night by the shy marsupials' loud, throaty mating growls.

Kin to the gray-headed flying fox, the black flying fox is extending its range into the Sydney region.

Gray-headed Flying Fox *(Pteropus poliocephalus):* A huge bat. Look closer and you'll see that they have quite foxlike faces. Most Sydneysiders love them and think they're cute. These guys are harmless and live on fruit and nectar. To see them, just look up at night or listen for their raucous chatter in the Moreton Bay fig trees and flowering eucalyptuses in all the city parks. There is a colony just behind the kiosk/café in the Royal Botanic Gardens right next to the Central Business District.

Koala *(Phascolarctos cinereus):* Generally nocturnal, these arboreal marsupials tend to sleep very high in the trees, which means they are far easier to find in wildlife parks than in the wild. Sometimes referred to as "koala bears," they are not bears, and naturalists will be quick to correct you if you call them so. Eating a diet of eucalyptus leaves, these creatures are 2 to 3 feet (61–91 cm) tall fully grown, but have an intestinal pouch (appendix) up to 23 feet (7 m) long to help their digestion.

Platypus *(Ornithorhynchus anatinus):* The platypus is a strange-looking creature: It has a duck's bill, a rabbit's body, webbed feet, and a short but thick, beaverlike tail—and as a monotreme, it also lays eggs. The first specimen sent to England was denounced as a hoax. They are difficult to find in the wild, where they are highly susceptible to any disturbance to their environment, but Taronga Zoo has several. The platypus's bill finds invertebrate prey by sensing electrical fields. Note: The small spurs on the ankles of adult males are poisonous.

Ringtail Possum *(Pseudocheirus peregrinus):* This is the most common of several possums found around Sydney. They take their name from American opossums, which they resemble, but when he named them

A blue-tongue lizard reveals its namesake.

in 1770, Capt. James Cook omitted the "o." Possums are nocturnal creatures and enjoy insects, blossoms and pollen, and fruit left out by Sydneysiders who encourage them around their houses. There are several of them in Hyde Park, which you can sometimes see hopping about the grass.

Short-beaked Echidna *(Tachyglossus aculeatus):* An egg-laying mammal that lives on termites, the echidna is shy and difficult to find, but there is a good exhibit at Taronga Zoo. With the long-beaked echidna (a native of New Guinea, to the north of Australia) and the one species of platypus, the short-beaked echidna is one of only three living monotremes (egg-laying mammals) on the planet. Echidnas live on ants and termites caught by means of a long, sticky tongue.

Swamp Wallaby *(Wallabia bicolor):* The swamp wallaby prefers forest areas, where it browses on foliage. It is elusive, but can be spotted on walks away from built-up areas. There are swamp wallabies in the Discovery enclosure at the Kalkari Visitor Centre in Ku-ring-gai Chase National Park, but even there they are shy. Wallabies, kangaroos, and rat-kangaroos belong to the marsupial family Macropodidae (meaning "large-footed") and are characterized by large, powerful hind legs that are used for hopping. An adult swamp wallaby is 5.5 feet tall (1.7 m) when fully grown.

Reptiles

Blue-tongue Lizard *(Tiliqua scincoides):* You only get to see this lizard's tongue, which is a remarkably vivid blue, if it pokes it out to ward off predators. For the blue-tongue lizard, running away certainly isn't an option; like quite a few members of the skink family (190 Australian species can be found from the tropics to deserts to subalpine zones), blue-tongues have heavy bodies and short legs and virtually drag themselves along the ground. They are quite common in suburban gardens around bushland areas.

Lace Monitor *(Varanus varius):* A species of goanna (a corruption of iguana), lace monitors can grow to over 6 feet (2 m) long. They climb trees and feed on birds and eggs, mammals, and insects. They are often seen scavenging around picnic areas in the bush. Though not dangerous and usually quite timid, a lizard this big isn't something you'd want to annoy. If they do bite, the wound tends to become infected and can often require dozens of stitches. The largest goanna is the perentie *(Varanus giganteus),* found in central Australia.

Red-bellied Black Snake *(Pseudechis porphyriacus):* This snake is venomous, but not particularly aggressive, and can usually be found near water. It grows to 5 feet (1.5 m) in length. Australia has the world's most venomous land snakes and is the only continent where venomous snakes outnumber nonvenomous ones. For comparison, there are 18 Australian snakes more dangerous than rattlesnakes. Most fatalities in Australia occur when a person attempts to kill the snake—so live and let live.

Marine Life

Blue-ring Octopus *(Hapalochleana maculosa):* This octopus frequents ocean and harbor rock pools, but it is very difficult to find. The blue-ring octopus is small (its body is only up to 3 inches/6 cm long), but it is venomous and its bite has been fatal. (Bites have only been inflicted when the creature was being handled.) Normally a plain brown camouflaged color, they display the blue rings and spots when disturbed. Victims usually recover if artificial respiration is given for approximately 12 hours.

Bottlenose Dolphin *(Tursiops truncatus):* Dolphins are increasingly common around Sydney as efforts to clean up waterways produce results. They are starting to venture into the harbor and may be glimpsed around the heads. The bottlenose is one of 13 dolphin species found in Australian waters. They usually travel in small groups in coastal waters. The most famous colony of bottlenose dolphins is a group in Western Australia, at Monkey Mia, which have been hand-fed since 1964.

Humpback Whale *(Megaptera novaeangliae):* Hundreds of whales migrate north up the coast annually in June and July, then south from September to November, sometimes very close to shore. Other species can also be seen, such as right, blue, and sperm whales. Radio stations often broadcast details of their presence, so tune in if you are keen to observe them. Whaling stations once dotted the Australian coast, but since 1980, whaling in Australia has been banned and the whales' numbers are recovering.

Humpback whales make a unique curving of their backs when they dive—thus their common name.

More Places to Visit in the West & South

Featherdale Wildlife Park

Featherdale contains one of the largest private collections of native fauna in Australia, with particular emphasis on birdlife. It has more than 200 species of native birds, including a wide variety of stunningly plumaged parrots. The park also boasts one of the largest koala colonies in New South Wales. The park is small, but its admission is half the price of Taronga Zoo.

The big attraction here is getting up close and personal with the animals, including petting the koalas and feeding the kangaroos (the encounters are all free with the price of admission). Some of the other animals include little penguins, saltwater crocodiles, common wombats, possums, and Tasmanian devils. Educational talks and tours cover koalas, dingoes, wombats, crocodiles, reptiles, and more. There is also a restaurant and a picnic area.

Featherdale is between Blacktown and Doonside railway stations and could be combined with a trip to the Blue Mountains (see pp. 215–220) or Parramatta (see pp. 186–187).

Access is from the M4 motorway via the Blacktown exit. Bus 725 from Blacktown Station stops at the park.

www.featherdale.com.au 184 B5 217 Kildare Rd., Doonside 9622 1644 $$$$

Mount Annan Botanic Garden

Opened in 1988, the Mount Annan Botanic Garden is a branch of the Royal Botanic Gardens (see pp. 54–56). Its main role is to accommodate the bulk of the Royal Botanic Gardens' collection of native plants. Originally occupied by a group of dairy farms settled by Scottish immigrants, the site is named after the Scottish town of Annan.

The 1,025-acre (416 ha) garden features walking trails, ornamental lakes, and, of course, one of the world's finest collections of Australian native plants—bottlebrushes, wattles (more than 300 species), banksias, and eucalyptuses. There are wetland areas, beds of annuals, and the **Terrace Garden,** which features 2,500 species of plants. The ultimate aim of the garden is to display most of the 25,000 species of plants known to exist throughout Australia.

Facilities include picnic areas, free gas barbecues, a café, a visitor information center, and an education center. Because of its size, you can drive through the gardens, and there are mountain bike trails (see sidebar this page).

Access is from Narellan Road, via the M5 southwestern freeway (Hume Highway). Buses 891 to 896 leave from Campbelltown Station.

www.rbgsyd.nsw.gov.au/annan 184 B2 Mount Annan Dr., Mount Annan 4634 7900

Mount Annan Mountain Bike Trail

The ideal way to get around the expansive Mount Annan Botanical Garden is by bicycle. Among the Australian plants, lakes, and fine views of the gardens, Mount Annan has a purpose-built 6-mile (10 km) mountain biking track—the Enduro Trail—for competent and intermediate mountain bikers, with an advanced trail planned for the future. The trail starts opposite the Big Idea Garden, which focuses on sustainability, and wends its way north through bushland and open terrain.

You can drive to the garden, park, and ride your bike, or catch the train to Campbellfield railway station and cycle the 5 miles (8 km) to the garden. Bicycles can be rented in central Sydney for a day out. Try Bonza Tours *(30 Harrington St., tel 9247 8800, www.bonzabiketours.com),* located in The Rocks; it rents bikes and also offers a host of bike tours around Sydney.

Mountain scenery, pristine waterways, and some excellent wines—all within a few hours of the city

Excursions

Introduction & Map 204–205

Hunter Valley & Newcastle 206–212

Experience: A Hunter Valley Working Holiday 207

A Drive to the Hunter Valley Wineries 208–209

Feature: Australian Wine 210–211

Central Coast 213–214

Blue Mountains 215–220

Experience: Walk the Six Foot Track 216

South Coast 221–222

Experience: Go Game Fishing 222

Southern Highlands 223–224

Canberra 225–228

Experience: Remembering Anzac Day 228

Hotels & Restaurants 253–257

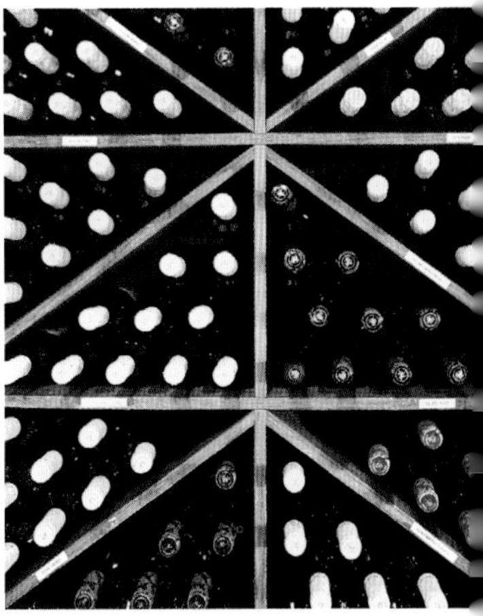

A selection of Hunter Valley wines

Excursions

When you need a respite from the delights of Sydney, the options are boundless. Within three hours' drive of the city, there is a world of waterways, beaches, and mountain scenery to be discovered. Visit a world-renowned wine region, or swim, surf, sail, hike, or ride in an idyllic setting.

The Central Coast offers numerous beaches and seaside villages where the most you'll have to worry about is deciding what strength sunscreen to use. Then there are the wineries of the Hunter Valley, just a little over two hours away and one of the premier districts in a country where winemaking has come of age. Nondrinkers can still enjoy the lovely scenery of rolling hills covered in vines, lunch in superb garden settings, join a cycle tour, or go ballooning.

To the west of the city, the rugged Blue Mountains present spectacular scenery, mountain villages, and cooler-climate flora and fauna. To the southwest, the Southern Highlands are less rugged but no less attractive, and the tulip festival is a highlight every year.

The coast south of Sydney and Wollongong is possibly even quieter than that to the north, and there are some delightful unspoiled bays and beaches to discover. And, of course, there are the wonderful cheeses from the thriving dairy industry.

The capital of Australia, the ornamental city of Canberra, is nearly four hours to the southwest. It features one of the country's finest art galleries, and as the seat of national government, it also features major institutions housed in stunning architecture. ■

NOT TO BE MISSED:

Sampling the fine wines of the Hunter Valley **206–211**

A beach holiday at a Central Coast resort **213–214**

The cool air and panoramas of the Blue Mountains **215–220**

Visiting Jenolan Caves **220**

The dazzling white-sand beaches at Jervis Bay **222**

Relaxing in the lush Southern Highlands **223–224**

Tour the nation's capital, Canberra **225–228**

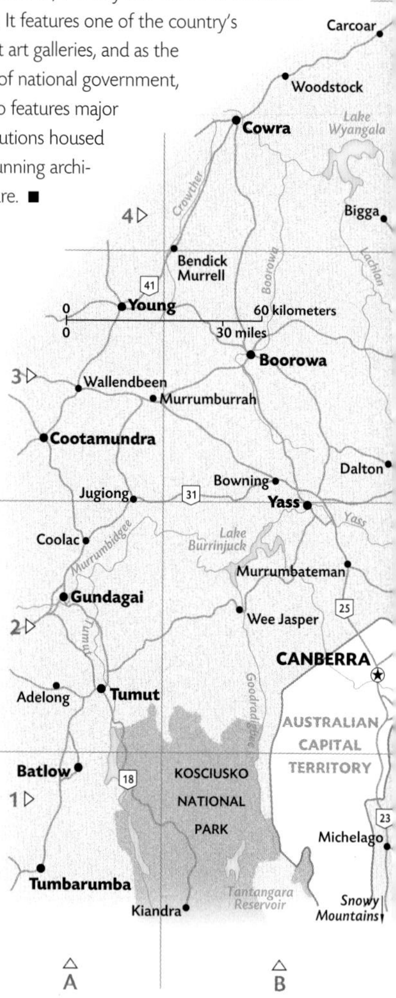

Gulgong
Bylong
Denman
Dungog
East Gresford
Mudgee
Jerry Plains
Singleton
Hunter Valley
Lue
Bulga
Branxton
Lake Windamere
Rylstone
Kandos
Hargraves
Howes Valley
Hungerford Hill
Maitland
Raymond Terrace
Kurri Kurri
Cessnock
Newcastle
Hill End
Ilford
Bogee
WOLLEMI NATIONAL PARK
YENGO NATIONAL PARK
Lake Macquarie
Belmont
Sofala
Capertee
Glen Davis
Morisset
Swansea
DHARUG N. P.
Australian Rainforest Sanctuary
Budgewai
Wyong
Tuggerah Lake
The Entrance
Portland
Australian Reptile Park & Wildlife Sanctuary
Wisemans Ferry
Gosford
Bathurst
Wallerawang
Mount Wilson
Terrigal
Avoca
Bell
GREAT WESTERN HIGHWAY
BELL'S LINE OF ROAD
Lithgow
Grovetts Leap
BRISBANE WATER N. P.
Pearl Beach
Brisbane Water
BOUDDI NATIONAL PARK
Blayney
Hydro Majestic Hotel
Mt. Victoria
Perrys Lookdown
Broken Bay
Windsor
Palm Beach
Blackheath
Evans Lookout
Cowan
Pittwater
Richmond
Explorers Marked Tree
Medlow Bath
Springwood
Mona Vale
Oberon
Rockley
Leura
Hornsby
Katoomba
Echo Point
Glenbrook
Penrith
PACIFIC WAY
Black Springs
Jenolan Caves
Blue Mts
Three Sisters
Wentworth Falls
Manly
Trunkey Creek
Parramatta
Port Jackson
Jamison Valley
SYDNEY
KANANGRA BOYD NATIONAL PARK
Lake Burragorang
Liverpool
BLUE MOUNTAINS NATIONAL PARK
Botany Bay
Tuena
Camden
Sutherland
Abercrombie
Campbelltown
Audley
ROYAL NATIONAL PARK
Picton
Tahmoor
Stanwell Park
Bargo
PRINCES HIGHWAY
Bulli
Laggan
Taralga
ILLAWARRA HWY.
Unanderra
Wollongong
Berrima
Crookwell
TARLO RIVER NATIONAL PARK
Wollondilly
Southern Highlands
Mittagong
Moss Vale
Bowral
Dapto
Port Kembla
Grabben Gullen
Fitzroy Falls
Shellharbour
Exeter
Minnamurra Rainforest
Bundanoon
Jamberoo
Kiama
Marulan
Kangeroo Valley
Gerringong
Gerroa
Gunning
Goulburn
Berry
Seven Mile Beach
Bomaderry
Bungonia
Nowra
Collector
MORTON NATIONAL PARK
Lake Bathurst
Huskisson
Tarago
Jervis Bay
Sutton
Lake George
Charleyong
Bungendore
BUDAWANG NATIONAL PARK
Milton
Ulladulla
Queanbeyan
Braidwood
Shoalhaven
Clyde
Googong Reservoir
Termeil
TINDERRY NATIONAL RESERVE
Captains Flat
Nelligen
Batemans Bay
DEUA NATIONAL PARK
Moruya
15
1
86
32
31
23
6
5
C
D
E
F
QUEENSLAND
SOUTH AUSTRALIA
NEW SOUTH WALES
Sydney
Canberra
A.C.T.
VICTORIA
Area of map detail

Hunter Valley & Newcastle

Two hours north of Sydney is a broad and fertile valley—perhaps the closest thing Australia has to the land of milk and honey. It extends more than 100 miles (160 km) inland; near the coast, a wide alluvial plain gives way to rolling hills, to farms and vineyards. Its edges are defined by the steeply wooded slopes of the Great Dividing Range. Coal mining is also a major industry in the region, as the entire area sits on a gigantic seam of coal.

Many of the Hunter Valley's most prestigious wineries are found in the valley's lower half.

Hunter Valley
205 E6
Visitor Information
Vintage Hunter Wine & Visitors Centre, 455 Wine Country Dr., Pokolbin
4990 0900
www.winecountry.com.au

Since the latter half of the 20th century, the Hunter Valley's main attraction for tourists has been as one of the premier wine-growing districts of the world. Grapes have been grown in the area since 1824, when James Busby, among the fathers of Australian viticulture, took up a grant of 2,000 acres (810 ha) on the Hunter River between Branxton and Singleton. These days, wineries are found in the lower and upper Hunter Valley, primarily growing Semillon and Shiraz, although the locally popular Chardonnay is increasingly prevalent.

The gateway to the region is the town of **Cessnock,** where the vineyards reach right to the edge of town, though the heart of the winemaking area is **Pokolbin,** 6 miles (10 km) north, where the Vintage Hunter Wine & Visitors Centre has details about all the wineries, accommodations, and activities in the area. A full calendar of events throughout the year includes concerts in the vineyards and food festivals. Highlights include **Hunter Valley Wine and Food Month** (June), **Jazz in the Vines,** and **Opera in the Vineyards** (both in October).

INSIDER TIP:

The Hunter Valley Gardens *(www.hvg.com.au)* in Pokolbin are really lovely. The Storybook Garden makes you feel like you've stumbled into *Alice in Wonderland.*

—DANIEL WALKINGTON
Promo producer, National Geographic Channel Australia

Because of its proximity to Sydney, numerous day and weekend tours are conducted to the Hunter Valley from the city (*Sydney Visitor Centre, tel 9240 8788*).

The hospitality at the wineries is what you would expect from Australians—friendly and very helpful. Tastings at most venues are free, and there is no pressure to buy (at least not that you would notice). The main guideline is that most wineries prefer groups to reserve visits in advance, so they don't get overwhelmed by six tour buses at once. Most wineries can organize shipment to any location on the planet, and some can even set up a regular delivery service of their latest vintages, which means you can "revisit" the Hunter year after year.

Apart from the wineries, the valley offers pleasant scenery and is dotted with restaurants, intimate cottage accommodations, and hotels. You can also follow pursuits such as ballooning, horseback riding, skydiving, golf, and cycling.

(continued on p. 212)

EXPERIENCE: A Hunter Valley Working Holiday

Throw yourself into the winemaking world by participating in the Hunter Valley's annual grape harvest. If you're traveling on a working holiday visa (subject to age—18 to 30—and time restrictions and limited to certain nationalities, including citizens of Canada, the United Kingdom, and the United States; check *www.immi.gov.au* for full details), you may undertake short-term work in Australia. Harvest season fruit-picking is a popular and simple way to help finance your travels. Grape-picking work in the wine area of the Hunter Valley is hot but plentiful during the months of February and March.

Good sources of information on finding harvest work are **Harvest Trail** *(jobsearch.gov.au/harvesttrail)*, detailing harvest locations and times, and **Workabout Australia** *(www.workaboutaustralia.com.au)*. But know that the work can be hard and your room and board are usually your own responsibility. Some farms provide accommodation and cooking facilities, but many do not. Check around.

A Drive to the Hunter Valley Wineries

The following lower Hunter wineries, just a short drive from Cessnock, include some of the major players in the region and are located in very scenic areas. Around McDonalds Road, between Broke and Marrowbone Roads, you'll find more than a dozen wineries large and small. Don't hesitate to make detours. With another 40 or so wineries in the Hunter Valley, you'll likely run out of time before you run out of places to visit.

Leave Cessnock and drive north on Allandale Road to reach Broke Road, just after the Hunter Valley Wine Country information center, where you can stock up maps and get details of wineries and accommodations.

Peterson House ❶ *(tel 4998 7881)*, on Broke Road, is a beautiful building with a good selection of sparkling wines, a fine restaurant, and an oyster bar on the deck. Semillon-Pinot and Pinot Noir–Chardonnay are their signature sparkling wines, much of it produced at their winery on Mount View Road, west of Cessnock.

Farther along Broke Road, turn off to **Pepper Tree Wines** ❷ *(Halls Rd., tel 4998 7539)*. This highly regarded boutique winery is set in beautiful gardens, next to **Peppers Convent.** This former nunnery was transported to the site from the New South Wales country town of Coonamble and is now a fine hotel (see Travelwise p. 256).

Back toward Broke Road, **Tower Estate** *(Halls & Broke Rds., tel 4998 7989)* produces wines ranging from Hunter Valley Semillon to Pinot Noir sourced from Tasmanian grapes. It is also home to **Roberts,** an iconic Hunter Valley restaurant, and the luxury **Tower Lodge,** with its intimate Nine Restaurant and superbly appointed rooms, the valley's most expensive.

At McDonalds Road, turn right then left onto Gillards Road, which leads to **Scarborough Wines** ❸ *(tel 4998 7563)*. Ian Scarborough certainly knows how to make Chardonnay, and the winery enjoys one of the prettiest locations in the area.

NOT TO BE MISSED:

Hunter Valley Cheese Company • View from picnic area between Tamburlaine Wines and Lindemans Winery

---

Return once again to Broke Road. Turn to reach **Tyrrell's Vineyards** ❹ *(tel 4998 7000)*. The Tyrrell family is one of the major forces in Australian wines, with a tradition going back to 1858. This winery is a must, as is the daily tour *($, no reservations)* at 10:30 a.m.

Return along Broke Road to its intersection with McDonalds Road, where you'll find **McGuigan Cellars** *(tel 4998 7402)* and the **Hunter Valley Cheese Company** *(tel 4998 7744)*, which share the same premises. The cheese company is one of the largest cheese producers in the valley, and its great selection of strongly flavored cheeses is a superb complement to the local wines.

Next door to McGuigan, on McDonalds Road, is **Brokenwood Wines** ❺ *(tel 4998 7559)*. Brokenwood has a reputation for producing great Semillon and Chardonnay wines from grapes grown in the valley and other districts. The prices are a notch higher, but it's hard to argue with quality like this.

Across McDonalds Road is the **Small Winemakers Centre** *(tel 4998 7668)*, which represents seven of the valley's boutique wineries that are either set in remote locations or without their own cellar doors.

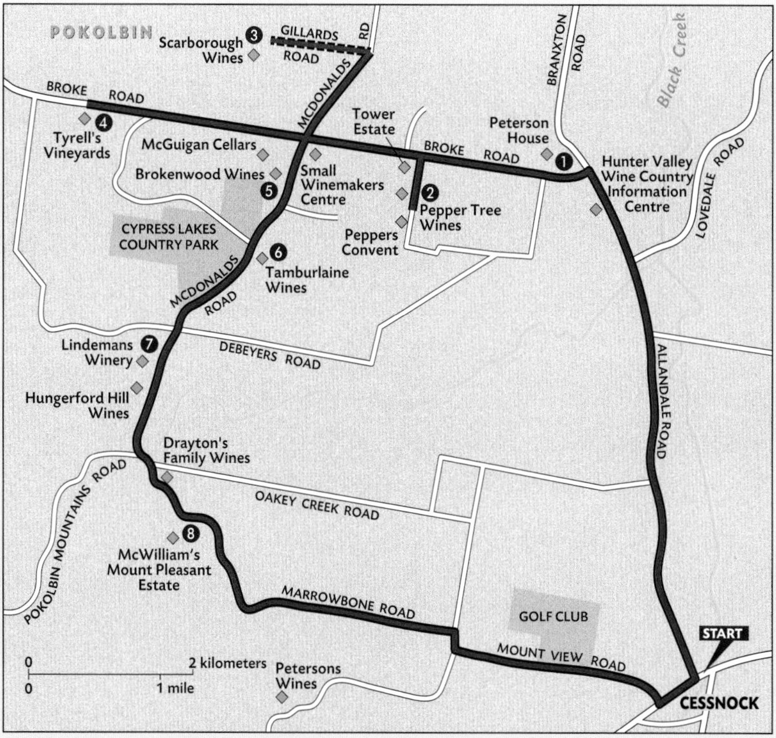

Heading Away From Broke Road

Turn south onto McDonalds Road and head for **Tamburlaine Wines** ❻ *(tel 4998 7570).* The staff here are passionate about their organic wines and spend time passing on their interest to visitors.

A short drive beyond Tamburlaine takes you to the best picnic spot in the Hunter, atop a small hill with a scattering of gazebos and a parking area. You may even have live music for your picnic if there is an outdoor function at **Lindemans Winery** ❼ *(tel 4998 7684)* just below. Lindemans is one of the stalwarts of the region, established in 1843.

Next door, in a quaint former church, is **Hungerford Hill Wines** *(tel 4990 0715)*, one of the innovative players in Australian winemaking with a range of wines made from grapes from a number of New South Wales regions such as Cowra and Tumbarumba.

- See also map p. 205 E6
- Cessnock
- Allow 4–6 hours
- 20 miles (30 km)
- Cessnock

Turn left at the end of McDonalds Road onto Oakey Creek Road to reach **Drayton's Family Wines** *(tel 4998 7513)*. Established in 1853, the sixth generation still shows great skill in its winemaking, and the winery has a fine new cellar door and café.

Just off nearby Marrowbone Road is **McWilliam's Mount Pleasant Estate** ❽ *(tel 4998 7505)*, established in 1921 in an idyllic setting. The company has an enviable reputation as a large winemaker with skills in equal measure. To return to Cessnock, continue along Marrowbone Road, turn right at Oakey Creek Road, then left onto Mount View Road.

Australian Wine

In the last three decades, Australia's long but isolated tradition of great winemaking has blossomed, and the country has emerged as one of the great winemaking nations, using innovative techniques to produce bold wines and setting the benchmark in varietals such as Chardonnay and Shiraz. The world has reaped the benefits, and Australia is now the world's fourth largest wine exporter.

A number of wineries in the Hunter Valley open their doors to tourists for wine tastings and tours.

The history of Australian wine reaches all the way back to Governor Phillip and the First Fleet. Shortly after his arrival in 1788, Phillip became the country's first vigneron when he had vine cuttings and grape seeds that had been brought with the fleet from England planted in the garden of Government House.

The site of Phillip's vineyard is thought to be where the Hotel InterContinental, in the Treasury Building on Macquarie Street, stands (see p. 69).

Start of the Industry

In fact, the vines first planted in Sydney, attacked by fungal disease in the humid climate, did poorly, whereas the vineyards in Parramatta and farther west flourished and gradually began to produce wines that were noticed in Europe. A fortified red from a vineyard at Eastwood, in northwest Sydney, won a silver medal in London in 1823, for example. The vineyard was owned by Gregory Blaxland, one of the explorers who had pioneered the

The Hunter Valley's Iron Gate Estate winery produces a number of fine wines.

route over the Blue Mountains. William Macarthur also established a commercial vineyard on the banks of the Nepean.

James Busby's vineyard on his 2,000-acre (810 ha) land grant was the first in the Hunter Valley, and Busby also established an agricultural institute that taught viticulture and winemaking in Liverpool, in Sydney's southwest. During the wine industry's early development, immigrants from Europe brought with them winemaking skills and new grape varieties.

INSIDER TIP:

Don't miss traveling to the Hunter Valley, one of the oldest wine regions in Australia, and tasting the famous Hunter Semillon wines.

—CHRIS STEEL

Professor, National Wine and Grape Industry Centre, School of Agricultural & Wine Sciences, Charles Sturt University

Today's Market

In last two decades, there has been an explosion in the number of vineyards in Australia as the quality of the local product has gained acceptance here and overseas, especially in Great Britain, the United States, and Canada. The growth of the industry has meant that the latest methods and technologies have been installed in the new wineries, and Australian wines are now in demand in many foreign countries.

In New South Wales, the main wine-growing region is the Hunter Valley (see pp. 206–209). Other regions include Mudgee, Cowra, and the Southern Highlands areas around Canberra and Tumbarumba.

In Victoria, Rutherglen is highly regarded for its fortified wines, the Yarra Valley attracts the likes of Domaine Chandon with its Chardonnay, and the Mornington Peninsula is great Sauvignon Blanc country, as are the Pyrenees and western Victoria.

Neighboring South Australia is also blessed with some great wine-growing areas and is the biggest producer of wine in the country, accounting for 45 percent of all production. The main regions are Coonawarra (Cabernet Sauvignon), the Clare Valley (Cabernet and Shiraz), and the mighty Barossa Valley (Cabernet and Shiraz, including Penfold's Grange and Henschke's Hill of Grace) that are comparable with Bordeaux in France.

Over in the far west, vineyards prosper in the Margaret River region, with Rieslings, Chardonnays, and reds that are on a par with wines from the eastern state winemakers.

Newcastle
205 F5
Visitor Information
Newcastle Visitor Centre, 3 Honeysuckle Dr.
4929 2588

Newcastle

The Hunter Valley isn't all wineries, however. At the mouth of the Hunter is Newcastle, the second largest city in New South Wales after Sydney. Traditionally a coal and steel town, it has undergone something of a renaissance since the giant B.H.P. steel mills closed in 1999. The port still thrives (it is the world's biggest coal port), but Newcastle has taken on a cleaner, greener air, with imposing heritage buildings, thriving arts and food scenes, and wonderful beaches.

A chain of sparkling beaches stretches north and south of the city, and Newcastle's historic central precinct has been extensively refurbished. The waterfront area features restaurants and pedestrian walkways, and just east of the center, **Fort Scratchley** *(Fort Dr., tel 4974 5000, www.fortscratchley.org.au, closed Tues.)* is worth a visit for the coastal views alone. Tour the barracks and battlements with a free map, or guided tours *($$$)* include the tunnels. From the fort, take a fine walk along **Nobbys Beach** past the lighthouse to the spit.

Escaped convicts were the first to reach the area, in 1791, where they found coal protruding from the riverbanks. The Hunter was named Coal River in 1796 and a penal station established in 1801. The settlement was named Newcastle in 1804. Interesting historic buildings in the area include **Newcastle East Public School** (1908), **East Newcastle Gaol** (1817–1818), the hospital (1817), **Christ Church Anglican Cathedral** (1883), and the **Courthouse** (1822).

Newcastle Visitor Centre has information on everything that this pleasant, breezy city and the surrounding district have to offer. Access is by rail, road, or tours from Sydney *(details from Sydney Visitor Centre, tel 9240 8788).* ■

Biters & Stingers

Australia lacks dangerous mammals, but it has its share of other creatures to keep a keen eye out for.

Common varieties of snakes include the tiger snake (named for its stripes), brown snake, and red-bellied black snake. Deadlier but less common are the taipan and the suitably named death adder. The only deadly spiders are the funnel web, found along Australia's eastern coast, and the red-back, widespread though only occasionally fatal. Saltwater crocodiles, the world's largest reptiles, are found in far north Australia.

With all that coastline, Australia has many species of shark. Great white, tiger, bull, and whaler sharks all feed on large sea mammals. From November to March, look out in northern tropical waters for the box jellyfish, which can deliver potentially fatal stings from its trailing tentacles. Other dangers include the poisonous-spined stonefish and the pretty, but potentially fatal, blue-ring octopus.

You are much more likely to be in a car accident than face any of these threats. Snakes are rarely sighted, and antivenins are widely available. Sharks strike only a handful of people annually—usually surfers and others in deep water.

Central Coast

From the north side of Broken Bay, the Central Coast extends to Newcastle and the Hunter Valley in a succession of beachside towns and resorts. Here you can sunbathe and surf on clean, sandy beaches, try to catch a fish, or navigate the many sheltered waterways.

The coastal sandstone formations at Terrigal, below the Skillion headland

Across the north shore of the Hawkesbury River and Broken Bay, several national parks offer superb scenery, quiet tracks and beaches, and Aboriginal carvings. These include **Brisbane Water National Park** and **Bouddi National Park** *(visitor information for both parks, 207 Albany St. N., Ste. 36–38, Gosford, tel 4320 4200, www.environment.nsw.gov.au).*

Between these two parks is exclusive **Pearl Beach.** There are views across to Lion Island (see p. 177), the entrance to Brisbane Water, and the town of **Gosford** *(visitor information, 200 Mann St., tel 4343 4444)*, where boats can be rented.

A few miles inland west of Gosford are two attractions that are fun for the whole family. The specialty at **Australian Reptile Park and Wildlife Sanctuary** is reptiles, especially snakes and crocodiles, but you'll find koalas, kangaroos, and other animals, too. You can handle some of the nonvenomous snakes and watch venomous varieties being milked of their poison. This is part of the park's research programs to improve antidotes.

Central Coast

Map: 205 E4–E5

Australian Reptile Park and Wildlife Sanctuary

Map: 205 E5

Address: Pacific Hwy., Somersby

Tel: 4340 1022

Price: $$$$

www.reptilepark.com.au

Australian Rainforest Sanctuary

- 205 E5
- Ourimbah Creek Rd., Ourimbah
- 4362 1855
- Closed Mon.–Tues.

INSIDER TIP:

In Avoca, follow the beachfront road north up to the Captain Cook Lookout on the First Point headland; it offers stellar views north and south.

—JANE SUNDERLAND
National Geographic contributor

The nearby **Australian Rainforest Sanctuary** is a natural rain forest laced with walkways. There are more than 120 species of birds, plus wallabies and other native animals.

Back on the coast, just east of Gosford, the beachside towns of **Avoca** *(visitor information, 69 Avoca Dr., tel 4382 1667)* and **Terrigal** *(visitor information, 112 Terrigal Esplanade, tel 4385 9564)* offer two different paces of life, Avoca being quieter than the larger Terrigal. The Avoca Beach Picture Theatre has screenings at reasonable prices. Behind the beach, a small lake with boat and windsurfer rentals is popular with families.

Terrigal's increasingly sophisticated resort caters to all needs, with swimming pools, a sheltered lagoon, spas, water sports facilities, boat rental, health clubs, cafés, and boutiques.

For superb coastal views, walk to the **Skillion** headland. Farther north is **The Entrance** *(visitor information, Marine Parade, tel 4334 4213)*, the mouth of Tuggerah Lake, another safe boating area with surf and sand and a booming resort town. Pelicans are fed daily at 3:30 p.m. in the Memorial Park.

Farther north along the coast lies Australia's largest saltwater lake, **Lake Macquarie;** it is the major lake of the region. Large areas of it are navigable, although sand flats exist in some areas. It is ideal for houseboats, which can be rented from Lake Macquarie Luxury Houseboats *(tel 4956 6266)* or Newcastle Holiday Houseboats *(tel 4952 2343)*. Plenty of waterside accommodations are available, and there are some relaxed resorts. On the eastern side of the lake, the beaches are never far away. ■

Central Coast Attractions

For most visitors to the Central Coast, sun, sea, and sand are the main attractions, and the coast has plenty of water-based activities and tours.

Go game fishing with **Central Coast Reef & Game Fishing** *(tel 0427 665 544, Terrigal, www.reefandgamefishing.com)*, learn to surf with **Central Coast Surf School** *(tel 0417 673 277, Avoca, Terrigal, & Umina Beaches, www.centralcoastsurfschool.com.au)*, scuba dive with **Gosford Dive Services** *(tel 4342 1855, gosfordive.com.au)*, go kayaking with **Ocean Planet Kayak Tours** *(tel 4342 2222, www.kayaktours.com.au)*, or cruise Brisbane Water with **Starship Cruises** *(tel 4323 1655, www.starshipcruises.com.au)*, to mention but a few outfitters that can help make your stay enjoyable.

For accommodations and other visitor information, contact **Central Coast Tourism** *(tel 4343 4400)*.

Blue Mountains

The Blue Mountains once formed an impenetrable barrier between Sydney and the interior of New South Wales. When seen from the heights of the city, the mountains are unmistakably blue, possibly due to the fine mist of eucalyptus oil exuded by the eucalyptus forests. These days, the region is a haven for visitors, offering incredible scenery, clear mountain air, and attractive English-style gardens.

The Three Sisters stand guard over the eucalyptus-clad Jamison Valley.

The mountains form part of **Blue Mountains National Park,** one of Australia's principal and most accessible national parks. The park is characterized by extensive areas of 1,000-foot-high (300 m) sheer cliffs with lookouts that offer sweeping panoramas and views into shadowy precipitous gorges with dramatic waterfalls.

The varied mountain environments range from windswept outcrops of rock and poor sandy soil to sheltered, well-watered valleys with rich volcanic soil; the range of microclimates supports an incredibly diverse range of plant species.

Numerous well-marked walking trails of varying lengths fan out from the mountain towns. Use

Blue Mountains

205 D4

Visitor Information

Hamment Pl., Glenbrook

1300 653 408

Katoomba
205 D4
Visitor Information
Echo Point Visitor Centre, Echo Point Rd., Katoomba
1300 653 408

extreme caution near the edge of cliffs, however, as the local sandstone is notorious for breaking away without warning.

Around Katoomba

One of the premier attractions of the park is the upper mountains area around the town of Katoomba. Here the highlights include **Echo Point,** a stunning viewpoint overlooking the **Three Sisters** and **Jamison Valley.**

INSIDER TIP:

The entire Katoomba community gets involved in the annual Winter Magic Festival held on the third weekend of June. Its main street closed to traffic, the town brims with music, art, and dance.

—JEANINE BARONE
National Geographic writer

EXPERIENCE: Walk the Six Foot Track

If you're up to the challenge, there's nothing more demanding or rewarding than walking the classic, three-day Six Foot Track all the way from Katoomba to Jenolan Caves. Originally cleared as a bridle path in 1884, the track begins at the Explorers Tree on the highway just outside Katoomba (the Katoomba visitor center has walk maps) and stretches 28 miles (45 km). Along the track, you'll take in lush forest, river valleys, and mountain ridges. There are two campsites and a hikers' lodge en route. If you'd like company, guided walks are available courtesy of the outfitter **Life's an Adventure** *(www.lifesanadventure.com.au)*. Spring and autumn are the peak times for the walk, avoiding the winter cold and the heat of summer. In March, the Six Foot Track Marathon footrace is held. A good reference for walk details and maps is online at *www.wildwalks.com.*

The Three Sisters are three enormous sandstone pillars that tower above the precipices that drop 1,000 feet (300 m) into the valley below. This is one of the must-see destinations for tours of every description; at night, the Sisters are floodlit until 11 p.m.

Just before the lookout, you can see dances at the **Koomurri Aboriginal Centre** (see p. 136).

The **Prince Henry Cliff Walk** goes from Leura, past Leura Cascades and Echo Point, along a spectacular trail (allow at least two hours) that ends near the Scenic Railway in Katoomba.

You can descend to the valley from Echo Point by way of the **Giant Stairway,** a steep 860-step staircase cut into the rock. A walk of about 1.25 miles (2 km) then takes you to the **Scenic Railway,** which you can ride to the cliff top west of Echo Point. Formerly used to transport coal miners from the valley below. The railway has one unique feature—it runs up the cliff on rails that are nearly vertical, making it the steepest tourist railway in the world. The railway is part of **Scenic World** *(Violet St. & Cliff Dr., tel 4780 0200),* which also includes Scenic Skyway, traversing a spur above the Jamison Valley; Scenic Cableway, a cable car running into the valley; a Scenic

A popular Blue Mountains attraction, the Scenic Skyway provides stunning views of the valley.

Walkway; and even Scenic Cinema, with a 30-minute feature on the Blue Mountains if you can't get enough of the scenery or the weather is bad.

Cliff Drive, a 5-mile (8 km) road with view points, connects Katoomba with the small mountain town of **Leura.** Its main street with old-fashioned shops has a relaxed atmosphere. In the first week in October, many of the houses open for the **Leura Gardens Festival.** The colder climate makes for some attractive English-style gardens. For details of this and other mountain events, call the Blue Mountains information center (see p. 215).

East of Katoomba, just a short distance from the town of **Wentworth Falls,** are the waterfalls of the same name that plunge into the Jamison Valley. One of the most enjoyable ways of reaching the falls is along **Darwins Walk,** named after English naturalist Charles Darwin (1809–1882), who visited the area during an excursion ashore from H.M.S. *Beagle* in 1836. The track starts from a small park just down the hill from the railway station and is about an hour of easy walking each way, following the stream down to the falls along fern- and tea-tree-filled gullies.

West of Katoomba

A mile (1.5 km) past Katoomba on the Great Western Highway, heading toward Blackheath, is the **Explorers Marked Tree.** The tree, now just a stump protected by a small shelter, had a blaze cut into it by explorers Gregory Blaxland, William Wentworth, and William Lawson in 1813 as they passed by on the first successful crossing of the mountains.

A little farther on in Medlow Bath is the **Hydro Majestic Hotel,** which has long been a mountain institution. Because the eucalyptus-laden air was believed to have therapeutic powers, hoteliers hoped guests would come to take the waters as well, and contemplate the superb views of the Megalong Valley. Extensive renovations promise to return it to its heyday glory.

Blackheath, farther west, is another peaceful mountain village. It has access to breathtaking scenery at Govetts Leap, Evans Lookout, Pulpit Rock, Perry's Lookdown, and Anvil Rock. The National Parks and Wildlife Service's **Blackheath Heritage Centre** *(Govetts Leap Rd., tel 4787 8877)* provides a wealth of information on the flora, fauna, and indigenous culture of the mountains, and from here the **Fairfax Heritage Track** leads to Govetts Leap Lookout. The center is the main source of information on the national park, with displays, walking track guides, maps, and books on the mountains.

The most westerly and highest of the mountain villages is delightful **Mount Victoria,** listed as an urban conservation area and classified by the National Trust. It features typical mountain houses—wooden chalets with shady verandas that both catch the sun and block the wind. Shortly after passing through the village, the highway starts its descent to the western plains. At Mount Victoria, you can turn off to Bell and then take **Bell's Line of Road,** an alternative route back to the city through the mountains via the towns of Richmond and Windsor (see pp. 181–182).

Christmas in July

Numerous resorts and hotels in the Blue Mountains participate in Yulefest *(www.yulefest.com)*, an alternative Christmas festival in the mountains during the Australian winter, given that Christmas falls in the middle of Sydney's summer. Dinner with all the trimmings, log fires, and even Santa impersonators are included. Snow does sometimes fall in the Blue Mountains, but frost is a more likely white Christmas accompaniment.

Along Bell's Line of Road

The first place you will come to along the Bell's Line of Road is **Mount Wilson** *(turn off 5 miles/8 km E of Bell)*. The mountains have long been a popular destination for Sydneysiders seeking great scenery and a milder climate, and during the last century Mount Wilson became an enclave of the well-to-do, who created mini-estates among the bushland setting and a rare patch of fertile land.

Mount Wilson's **Cathedral of Ferns,** just under a mile (1 km) from the village center, is a natural rain forest area that displays yet another facet of the diverse flora and fauna of the mountains. You explore it via a 20-minute walk.

One of the best gardens in the Mount Wilson area is **Yengo Sculpture Garden** *(tel 4756 2002, closed Mon.–Fri. & June–Sept. & Dec.–March)* on Queens Avenue, designed between 1877 and 1880 by Charles Moore, the first director of the Royal Botanic Gardens. It is a walled garden featuring azaleas and rhododendrons, with Catalan wrought-iron grills and bronze statues (for sale). Another fine garden in the area is **Nooroo** *(tel 4756 2018)*, which was featured on Australian stamps and is more than a century old.

The major garden on the Bell's Line of Road is **Mount Tomah Botanic Garden** *(tel 4567 2154)*, the cool-climate garden annex of the Royal Botanic Gardens (see pp. 54–56). The gardens are beautifully landscaped with ponds and waterfalls and have the bonus of sumptuous views to the north over the Grose Valley. There are also a visitor center with a shop, a good restaurant, and a popular picnic area with barbecue grills. The access from Bell's Line of Road involves a pleasant drive through apple and soft-fruit orchards, then through native bush and rocky escarpments from Richmond up to Mount Victoria.

Between the towns of Bell and Lithgow, you'll find the **Zig Zag Railway** *(tel 6355 2955, $$$$$)*. Built in the 1860s to transport coal from the rich deposits of Lithgow, the railway has a system of tunnels, viaducts, and cuttings to negotiate the Blue Mountains. The 10-mile (16 km) ride is quite memorable. The train is usually hauled by steam locomotive, sometimes by vintage diesel rail motor. Call to check the daily timetable, which often varies to accommodate groups.

The Bell's Line of Road takes longer than the highway, but is very scenic and has some great views of the Grose Valley. Along

A creek makes a precipitous drop off the plateau, falling into Jamison Valley in a dramatic cascade.

Jenolan Caves
205 D4
Jenolan Caves Rd.
6359 3911
$$$$$
www.jenolancaves.org.au

the way is the town of **Bilpin,** center of a major apple-growing area with many roadside stalls.

Jenolan Caves

About 34 miles (55 km) southwest of Mount Victoria, one hour by car, are the Jenolan Caves *(turn off Great Western Hwy. just past the historic village of Hartley)*. Discovered in 1838 by the bushranger James McKeown, an escaped convict, the caves are located at the end of a scenic if slightly nerve-racking road that runs through a stunning gorge, a grand cavern, and a tunnel.

INSIDER TIP:

The final stretch of road from Katoomba into the Jenolan Valley is one-way (inbound) 11:45 a.m.–1:15 p.m. There are alternate routes out of the valley, but plan ahead.

—ROFF SMITH
National Geographic author

Only a dozen of the area's hundreds of caves are open to the public, with limestone chandeliers and columns, and underground lakes and river systems. Ladders and well-constructed paths provide access to guided tours. Access is by guided tour only—the group sizes are limited for participant comfort and safety—but this includes a self-guided option for two other caves. Tours average 1.5 hours and operate daily. Cave adventure tours—involving caving gear, lamps, crawling, and climbing—are also available.

About 5,970 acres (2,416 ha) of nature reserve surround the caves, with several walking tracks that, given the steeply sloping terrain, can be quite strenuous.

Accommodations are plentiful here, including Jenolan Caves House *(tel 6359 3911)*, the area's grande, if faded, dame with cabins and a lodge in addition to the main building.

In the lower mountains, the **Glenbrook** area is dotted with picnic areas, swimming holes, walking tracks, and lookouts. The Blue Mountains information center is based here. Car camping is available at Euroka Clearing *(tel 4588 2400, or 4739 2950 on weekends)*.

Getting to the Blue Mountains

Access to the Blue Mountains is by car from the city (a journey of about two hours) along the M4 motorway. A frequent rail service stops at all the mountain towns mentioned, except Mount Wilson, Jenolan Caves, and localities on the Bell's Line of Road. Popular bus tours and ecotours depart Sydney daily for the main Blue Mountains sites. Transfers can be arranged from most city hotels, or local operators pick up in the Blue Mountains. Information on accommodations and tours is available from the Sydney Visitor Centre *(tel 9240 8788)*, the Echo Point Visitor Centre, and the Blue Mountains information center. ■

South Coast

Stretching south from Sydney to the border with the state of Victoria, the New South Wales South Coast has a milder climate than that of the North Coast, and a distinctly different character. One of the major industries here is dairying, and numerous cheese companies can be found along the southbound Princes Highway.

Fog and mist add to the drama of the Illawarra region's rain forest.

A good two-day trip is to take in the South Coast sights down to Jervis Bay (see p. 222) on day one, then either stay overnight in Huskisson or continue up to the resorts of the Southern Highlands (see pp. 223–224), just 50 miles (80 km) away. From there, you can take in the sights en route back to Sydney. In the summer months, be sure to reserve ahead.

Wollongong & Around

Within close range of Sydney, Wollongong is a once heavily industrialized port looking to reinvent itself as a tourist destination. It has a pleasant harbor area, good cafés (try along Keira Street), and great beaches. As an alternative to the freeway, drive through **Royal National Park** (see pp. 193–195) via Audley, then along a spectacular,

Wollongong
205 E3
Visitor Information
93 Crown St.
4267 5910

snaking, coastal cliff road. Eventually the cliffs give way to the **Illawarra** region, a scenic coastal plain that starts just south of the national park and continues south beyond Wollongong.

EXPERIENCE: Go Game Fishing

Reel in a trophy-size catch: The harbor and coastal waters around Sydney teem with game fish. Numerous fishing charter companies offer day and live-aboard outings, providing all necessary equipment. You just need to know what you want to catch to decide when to visit. From December to May, there's excellent fishing for blue, black, and striped marlin as well as mahimahi, wahoo, and kingfish, while from June to November, yellowfin tuna, bonito, and shark (mako, blue, tiger) abound. Sportfishing is also well catered for, with big snapper, leatherjacket, sweep, trevally, flathead, and plenty of reef species. The Sydney Visitor Centre *(tel 9240 8788)* has fishing charter lists, or try online at *www.charterguide.com*.

Kiama
205 E3
Visitor Information
Blowhole Point, Rd.
4232 3322

Minnamurra Rainforest
205 D3
4236 0469

Jervis Bay
205 D2

Just south of Wollongong *(via Jamberoo on the Princes Hwy., past the turnoff to the Illawarra Hwy.)* is the **Minnamurra Rainforest,** a small pocket of subtropical rain forest with a national park visitor center. From an elevated boardwalk, you can study the ferns and orchids in the rain forest canopy and watch the birds feeding.

Kiama to Jervis Bay

Farther down the coast is **Kiama,** a popular stop famous for its blowhole that sends up large geysers of water from an ocean cavern.

From Kiama, the route winds south through rugged headlands and dairy country, via the prettily located headland town of **Gerroa,** to **Seven Mile Beach.** Here there are camping grounds and expanses of empty sand, ideal for beachcombing and being alone with nature.

Inland lies the picture-postcard town of **Berry** and the turnoff to **Kangaroo Valley** (see p. 224).

Continue down the Princes Highway to **Nowra** (information from Shoalhaven Tourist Centre). As well as dairy products, the area is noted for its oysters, freshly shucked at Crookhaven Oyster Farmers, at the end of Green Point Road in Greenwell Point, 10 miles (15 km) east of Nowra.

Vacation resorts can be found at the southern end of Seven Mile Beach and at **Jervis Bay,** 15 miles (24 km) south of town. The bay is one of the most beautiful pieces of protected waterway on the South Coast and a deservedly popular destination. Guarded by the striking precipice of Point Perpendicular, its crystal clear waters are ideal for boating, fishing, scuba diving, and snorkeling. The sands of the beaches are reputed to be among the cleanest and whitest anywhere in the world, and there are waterside villages and camping areas.

The main center of the bay is **Huskisson,** a former boatbuilding and fishing town. Here you'll find Dolphin Watch Cruises *(tel 4441 6311)*, which also take in penguins, and the **Lady Denman Heritage Complex** *(tel 4441 5675)*, with a museum, walks, and fish feedings. ■

Southern Highlands

Located to the southwest of Sydney, two hours by road, the highlands differ from the Blue Mountains in having a gentler terrain of rolling hills, more suited to farming. The area reminded Lachlan Macquarie of England when he visited it in 1820.

Since then, the Southern Highlands have been gentrified by wealthy businessmen from the city who fancy themselves as lords of the manor and weekend farmers. There are several English-style gardens with flowering annuals, rhododendrons, and azaleas.

The principal towns are Mittagong, Bowral, Moss Vale, and Berrima, while villages such as Bundanoon and Exeter are worth exploring for their fruit stalls and antiques shops.

A network of country roads laces through the area, making a pleasant alternative to the main highways and providing cyclists with options for short rides from town to town.

Visitors will find antiques shops, many with agriculture-related goods, throughout the Southern Highlands.

Bowral

One of the main attractions of Bowral is the annual **Tulip Time Festival** *(tel 4871 2888, www.southern-highlands.com.au/tulip-time)*, staged over two weekends and a week in late September and early October. During this time, numerous parks and gardens around the town become a riot of floral color, music, foods, and country wares. Flower festivals and garden open days also take place in the town in summer and fall.

The **Bradman Museum** *(Glebe Park, St. Jude St., tel 4862 1247)* honors Australian cricket's greatest batsman and Bowral's most famous son, Sir Donald Bradman (1908–2001; see sidebar p. 224). There are photos, films, memorabilia, tearooms, and a view over the Bradman Oval, where commemorative and gala matches are sometimes played. Follow the Bradman Walk from the museum past Bradman's nearby former home and other haunts.

Berrima

Several of the buildings in the historic town of Berrima date from the 1830s. One not to miss seeing is the Georgian-style **Courthouse**

Southern Highlands

205 D3

Visitor Information

Mittagong Visitor Information Centre, 62–70 Main St., Mittagong

4871 2888

www.southern-highlands.com.au

(1836–1838; *Wilshire & Argyle Sts., tel 4877 1505*), designed by colonial architect Mortimer Lewis, now a museum focusing on Berrima's history. **Berrima House** is where Ben Hall (1837–1865), a farmer who became a notorious bushranger in the region after persecution by the law, is reputed to have stayed. Visit the low-security **Berrima Gaol; Harpers Mansion** *(tel 4877 1508, closed Mon.–Fri.)*, a National Trust building; and the **Surveyor-General Inn** *(tel 4877 1226)*, first opened in 1835.

Around the Highlands

Getting to the Southern Highlands can be an adventure in itself. If driving direct from the city via Liverpool, a diversion to Camden takes you past the **Mount Annan Botanic Garden** (see p. 202). From there, the road climbs to Picton, where there is a boutique brewery, **Scharer's Little Brewery,** in the George IV Hotel *(180 Argyle St.)*.

A tour of the South Coast (see pp. 221–222) could be combined with a drive through the scenic **Kangaroo Valley,** visiting the 250-foot (76 m) **Fitzroy Falls** near Moss Vale, then continuing to the Southern Highlands and back to Sydney. The falls, a short walk from the parking lot, can be disappointing after a long dry spell, but are well worth a visit after heavy rain.

The **Cockatoo Run** steam train travels the scenic 37 miles (59 km) from Port Kembla on the coast to Robertson and Moss Vale in the highlands—three hours each way. The train departs at 9:30 a.m. Saturday through Tuesday *(tel 9699 2737, www.3801limited.com.au, $$$$$)*.

You could also combine the sights of the Southern Highlands with a visit to the nation's capital, **Canberra** (see pp. 225–228). ■

Sir Donald Bradman: Cricketer Extraordinaire

When polls are run to nominate the greatest Australians of all time, cricketer Sir Donald Bradman (1908–2001) regularly tops the list. The batting hero was not only the preeminent cricketer of his time—Australians regard him as the greatest sportsman ever. Raised in Bowral (see p. 223), where he showed prodigious talent from an early age, the young Bradman first represented Australia against England in 1928 and quickly set about amassing record batting scores. By the time he toured England as captain for the last time in 1948, he had cemented his place as the greatest batter the game had seen. In his final test match, needing just four runs to give him a freakish career batting average of 100, he was out second ball without scoring. His average of 99.94 fell just short of the magic number, but remains almost double that of any cricketer before or since.

"The Don" retired to Adelaide, where he became a statesman of the game, giving audiences to young cricketers and politicians alike, his name often used to invoke the nationalist cause. The word Bradmanesque has entered the Australian lexicon and means succeeding far above all others.

Canberra

As a city whose main industry is government, Canberra is extremely tidy and well manicured. Neat gardens, streets, and buildings present an attractive facade, but you may find that after spending time in Sydney, Canberra lacks the lively hustle and bustle of a major city. Still, there are several must-sees here—art galleries, museums, and scenic lookouts in particular.

Bert Flugelman's "Cones" (1976–1982), Sculpture Garden, National Gallery of Australia

Australia's capital city is situated 175 miles (280 km) southwest of Sydney, between the Southern Highlands and the Snowy Mountains, Australia's highest mountain range.

In 1909, after much bickering between Sydney and Melbourne as to which of the two cities should be the capital, it was decided to create an entirely new city, on what was at the time a prosperous sheep farm. It was named Canberra, the local Aboriginal word for "meeting place." Perhaps a word meaning "compromise" might have been a better choice. Nevertheless, the city designed in 1913 by Chicago landscape architect Walter Burley Griffin (1876–1937) has become one of the most picturesque in the country, with a population of 350,000. The

Canberra

204 B2

Visitor Information

330 Northbourne Ave., Dickson

1300 554 114

www.visitcanberra.com.au

city plan includes an extensive system of bike paths., especially surrounding **Lake Burley Griffin** (see p. 228).

Aside from the major public buildings associated with Australia's government, national institutions include the National Library, the National Gallery of Australia, and the Australian War Memorial, all of them found within the Parliamentary Triangle, formed by Commonwealth, Kings, and Constitution Avenues.

Parliamentary Triangle

The **National Gallery of Australia** *(Parkes Pl., tel 6340 6502, nga.gov.au)* has 120,000 works in its collection, encompassing traditional forms, textiles, costumes, and much more. Aboriginal and Australian art is well represented, and there are fine examples of Impressionist and contemporary European and American art as well. Major touring exhibitions—works from the Russian Hermitage or Turner paintings, for example—bring together significant works from all over the world. Outside the gallery, the Sculpture Garden presents works by Auguste Rodin, Henry Moore, and others among eucalyptuses and ponds. The gallery has coffee shops and an excellent restaurant.

Next door to the gallery, on King Edward Terrace, is the **High Court of Australia** *(tel 6270 6811)*, the country's top court. Inside, large murals depict the founding of Australia and its constitution. The court is open for inspection most days, and court sittings can be attended by the public.

The interactive exhibits and demonstrations at Questacon make learning about science fun.

Also on King Edward Terrace is **Questacon** *(tel 6270 2800, www.questacon.edu.au, $$$$),* the National Science and Technology Centre. Questacon is oriented toward children and features many interactive demonstrations of scientific principles. Don't miss Brain and Senses (sight, hearing, and touch); the Force Gallery, complete with an earthquake machine; or the musical instruments. Constantly changing shows and demonstrations take place, too.

A short walk away is the imposing **National Library of Australia** *(Parkes Pl., tel 6262 1111, www.nla.gov.au).* It has one of the largest collections of books and manuscripts in the country. It frequently mounts exhibitions illuminating both local and national events and people.

Parliament House: The Commonwealth of Australia's Parliament House *(tel 6277 5399)* sits back from Lake Burley Griffin on Capital Hill. The hill was excavated to hold the bulk of the building, which lies partly submerged in the landscape and is partly roofed with grass. The understated design is then contradicted by a four-legged, 260-foot (80 m) flagpole that straddles the entire structure.

Parliament House contains both houses of the federal government, the House of Representatives and the Senate; the Great Hall; and the offices of the politicians and their staffs. It is open to the public every day, and you can watch the affairs of state from the public galleries whenever the houses are sitting.

INSIDER TIP:

Walk or ride a bike around Lake Burley Griffin. The 3.75-mile (6 km) route around the lake offers lots of fantastic photo ops.

—HOLLY SHALDERS
National Geographic contributor

The building looks down on the Old Parliament House, which was used from 1927. Now the **Museum of Australian Democracy** *(King George Terr., tel 6720 8222),* it is well worth a visit. The old chambers and prime minister's office, all leather and wood paneling, are just as the politicians left them in 1988.

Australian War Memorial: The building at the end of the grand boulevard of Anzac Avenue is the Australian War Memorial *(www.awm.gov.au).* This is one of the most visited attractions in the country, a testimony to the loss of life throughout Australia due to war. There are numerous exhibits that use film, sound, and interactive displays to depict the many conflicts Australia has participated in, usually as an ally of England or its post–World War II security partner, the United States. One of the midget submarines that attacked Sydney Harbour in 1942 (see p. 34) can also be seen here. However, the main function of the memorial is as a monument to the fallen, and its courtyard and shrine of remembrance bear quiet witness to their sacrifice. Try to visit on Anzac Day (see sidebar this page).

Canberra's Green Spaces

Black Mountain, topped by a large communications tower with a viewing platform and the revolving Black Mountain Tower Restaurant *(tel 6247 5518),* is the major scenic viewpoint of the city. The view over the city to the distant mountain ranges provides a magnificent panorama that extends for more than 50 miles (80 km).

Lake Burley Griffin, ringed by bike paths and parks, provides a focus for the recreational activities of Canberrans. The major parks in the city include **Black Mountain Reserve,** with barbecue facilities and picnic areas, and **Weston Park,** which has similar facilities, plus a kiosk and model-train rides. The extensive **Australian National Botanic Gardens** at the foot of Black Mountain hold more than 6,000 species of Australian flora.

Opposite the Parliamentary Triangle, **Commonwealth Park** is the closest park to the Central Business District. A restaurant and café overlook the water and the Captain Cook memorial water jet. The park is also the venue for Canberra's annual spring flower festival, Floriade *(tel 6205 0044).* This spectacular event, held from mid-September to mid-October, consists of massed plantings throughout the park, with marquee restaurants and food outlets, music, and entertainment. ■

EXPERIENCE: Remembering Anzac Day

If you are in Canberra on April 25, attend the Anzac Day events to get a sense of Australian pride. Anzac Day is the nation's most solemn day on the holiday calendar, remembering the war dead in moving ceremonies across the country. Originally it honored those who died in World War I, and it is synonymous with the ill-fated campaign of Gallipoli in Turkey, where more than 8,000 men of the Australian and New Zealand Army Corps (ANZAC) died, but the fallen from all wars through to Afghanistan are remembered.

In Canberra, the day begins with a poignant dawn service at the **Australian War Memorial** (see pp. 227–228); the grounds open at 4:30 a.m. (bring a flashlight and dress warmly). Veterans and invited dignitaries stand in the Commemorative Courtyard, while thousands more gather on the parade ground. After the half-hour ceremony, the public may enter the Hall of Memory, where you can lay a poppy on the Tomb of the Unknown Soldier. Later in the morning, line up with other spectators on Anzac Parade to watch the march, which features returned servicemen and -women and military bands.

Similar events take place in Sydney, with a dawn service at the **Cenotaph** (see p. 53) and a march down George and Bathurst Streets to the Anzac Memorial in Hyde Park. Other gathering points and routes are printed in newspapers countrywide, and the **Returned Services League** *(www.rsl.org.au)* is instrumental in organizing marches.

Travelwise

Planning Your Trip 230–232

How to Get to Sydney 232

Getting Around 232–234

Practical Advice 234–237

Emergencies 237

Health 237

Hotels & Restaurants 238–257

Shopping 258–261

Entertainment & Activities 262–265

Yachting on Sydney Harbour

TRAVELWISE

PLANNING YOUR TRIP

When to Go

Climate

Sydney has a warm, temperate climate virtually year-round. The city is usually free of extremes of heat or cold. Close to the coast, frosts and heat waves are rare, and some restaurants have outdoor dining at night even in winter. Farther inland, frosts may occur and temperatures can climb above 100°F (37°C). In the Blue Mountains, the winters are colder, with temperatures falling to around 45°F (7°C) and occasional snow. The summers tend to be milder, but century temperatures are not unheard of.

Average temperatures for Sydney:
Spring (Sept.–Nov.): 63°F (17°C)
Summer (Dec.–Feb.): 72°F (22°C)
Fall (March–May): 64°F (18°C)
Winter (June–Aug.): 55°F (13°C)

Rainfall is moderate (approximately 45 inches/116 cm a year), with most rain falling in the first half of the year and the least falling in spring.

Events & Festivals

January

Sydney Festival, tel 8248 6500, www.sydneyfestival.org.au. International, monthlong festival held in midsummer, including theater, dance, music, and visual arts. There are numerous free events, including major outdoor performances in the Domain (opera, classical, jazz).

Apia International Sydney, tel 9024 7700, www.apiainternational.com.au. Major international tennis stars feature in this event, held at Sydney Olympic Park Tennis Centre, Homebush Bay in mid-month. The tournament is a lead-up to the Australian Open grand slam event, held in Melbourne.

Chinese New Year. Fireworks, dragon dances, and processions.

February

Sydney Gay & Lesbian Mardi Gras, tel 9557 4332, www.mardigras.org.au. The parade, usually at the end of February, is the culmination of the monthlong Mardi Gras festival (see p. 148).

March

Archibald, Wynne, and Sulman Prizes. Announced mid-March, the Archibald (portraiture), Wynne (landscape), and Sulman (subject painting or mural) Prizes attract plenty of local attention. The winners and top contenders are displayed at the Art Gallery of New South Wales (see pp. 61–65) until mid-April, and there is an opportunity to register your personal tastes for a People's Choice award.

April

Sydney Royal Easter Show, tel 9704 1111. Held during the first two weeks of April at Homebush Bay, the Easter Show is a display of New South Wales agricultural excellence, plus sideshows and a diverse range of exhibits and performances.

June

Sydney Film Festival, tel 9660 3844, www.sff.org.au. Held in early June, this two-week film fest features local and international movies shown in Australia for the first time. It is also a great opportunity to get into the spectacular State Theatre (see pp. 111–113) and admire the interior.

Manly Food & Wine Festival, tel 9977 1088. Usually held on the first weekend of June, this gastronomic festival turns the Manly Corso into one long food stall, with music and entertainment to boot.

Vivid Sydney, tel 8114 2400, www.vividsydney.com. A festival of music, light, and ideas with a strong music program thanks to high-profile curators such as Lou Reed and Brain Eno, but the light installations steal the show. Iconic buildings such as the Sydney Opera House and Customs House become canvases for stunning lighting effects.

August

City2Surf, www.city2surf.com.au. More than 60,000 competitors from all over the world run, walk, and wheelchair this 8.7-mile (14 km) race from Hyde Park to Bondi Beach.

September

Festival of the Winds, Bondi Beach, tel 8362 3400. In mid-month, all manner of kites take to the skies over the beach, with kite shops and workshops held among food stalls and wandering entertainers.

September–October

Floriade, Canberra, tel 6205 0776, www.floriadeaustralia.com. From mid-September to mid-October, a stunning floral display of tulips and annuals can be seen in the national capital's Commonwealth Gardens.

Bowral Tulip Time Festival, tel 4871 2888, www.southern-highlands.com.au/tulip-time. One of the oldest garden festivals sees many gardens open throughout the Bowral area of the Southern Highlands, displaying masses of tulips.

October

Manly Jazz Festival, tel 9976 1500. During the first week of October, thousands flock to hear jazz, from big band to contemporary, at stages set up around Manly.

Opera in the Vineyards, Hunter Valley, tel 1800 675 875, www.operainthevineyards.com.au. In mid-October, great performers attend this popular event, which is considerably more than an excuse to visit the vineyards. But if you need one . . .

Jazz in the Vines, Hunter Valley, tel 4930 9190, www.jazzinthevines.com.au. Held in late October, for those who don't go in for opera (see above).

October–November

Crave Sydney Food & Wine Festival, tel 9931 1111. All the best chefs and winemakers demonstrate their skills in a series of dinners, seminars, and workshops. An Asian hawker-style market sets up in Hyde Park, and Breakfast on Bondi attracts thousands.

December

Carols by Candlelight, www.carolsinthedomain.com. Held outdoors in the Domain, usually two weeks prior to Christmas, this annual event is extremely popular with families.

Sydney to Hobart Yacht Race, rolexsydneyhobart.com. For more than 60 years, the spectacular start to Australia's leading ocean race on Boxing Day (Dec. 26) has drawn huge crowds of spectators onto the water and the headlands around the city. The Sydney to Hobart Yacht Race is one of the world's blue-water sailing classics, and the start of the race sees Sydney at its most colorful, with giant maxi yachts and pocket racers being followed by a gigantic spectator fleet. A number of boats take passengers onto the water for the start (check online at *www.sailaustralia.com.au* for a list of participating boats).

What to Take

Sydney's temperate climate and natural setting mean that you should be prepared for weather that is mild to warm. Among the must-brings are comfortable walking shoes, a hat to keep the sun off (a baseball cap may not be adequate if you have sensitive skin), and a swimsuit. It is possible to get sunburned even in the middle of winter, so sunscreen with a protection factor of 15+ is recommended. Insect repellent is also needed, especially in the evening. Hats, sunscreen, and bug repellent are available from all drugstores (known in Australia as chemists).

In late spring, summer, and early fall, lightweight clothing is all you'll need during the day, with a light sweater for the rare cool evening. In the winter months in the city, you may need a jacket, although the temperature rarely gets below 46°F (8°C). However, if you are visiting the Blue Mountains, be prepared for temperatures that can go below freezing.

For evening wear, neat, casual attire is acceptable in most venues. For men, a jacket and tie may be required for theater and top-class restaurants; for women, semiformal clothing is appropriate. In cosmopolitan venues, black is practically a uniform.

Just before you head for the airport, check you have your passport, visa or ETA, driver's license, airline ticket, traveler's checks, and insurance papers.

Travel Insurance

Before your visit, you should arrange sufficient medical and travel insurance. Ensure the policy is adequate to cover costs for ambulance or helicopter rescue, emergency surgery, or transportation home.

If renting a car, compulsory third-party insurance is included in the rental. Additional insurance should be considered if you are planning to drive on country roads, especially to reduce your costs in the event of windshield damage.

Should you need to make a claim for property theft, report the matter to the police, obtain a copy of the report, and refer the matter to the insurer via the emergency phone number provided with your policy.

Entry Formalities

Visas

Many travelers not holding an Australian or New Zealand passport can obtain authority to enter Australia through the Electronic Travel Authority (ETA) system, which replaces the need for an Australian visa. The A$20 ETA is valid for multiple entries into Australia (each entry to a maximum of three months) over a period of one year for tourism or business. The similar eVisitor is free for passport holders of the European Union and some other

European countries. You can apply online *(www.eta.immi.gov.au)* at least two weeks prior to your trip, or ETAs can be obtained from your travel agent.

Visitors not eligible for an ETA and those wishing to stay for longer than three months, or to work, must obtain a visa to enter. Further advice and application forms may be obtained from your travel agent or from the Australian embassy, high commission, or consular office.

Customs
Customs controls at all Australian ports of entry are tight, particularly with regard to food, plant material, and animal products, and you should expect to have your personal luggage searched. Visitors over the age of 18 are restricted to a duty-free limit of 2.25 liters of liquor and 250 cigarettes, plus other goods such as perfume and jewelry to the value of A$900 (about U.S.$900). Travelers under 18 may bring gifts to the value of A$450 without paying duty.

Currency Restrictions
There is no limit to the amount of Australian or foreign currency you can bring in or take out for personal use, though sums in excess of A$10,000 (about U.S.$10,000), or its equivalent, should be declared on the appropriate customs forms.

Quarantine
Australia is free from many pests and diseases that could cause irreparable damage to the country's agriculture or environment. To prevent their entry, the importation of fresh or packaged food, fruit, eggs and egg products, vegetables, seeds, cultures, animals, plants, and plant products is strictly controlled. Declare any of these products upon entry.

Drugs & Narcotics
Searches for a range of prohibited substances are frequently made by customs, often with sniffer dogs. Penalties for drug importation are severe. You should clearly label medicines for personal use and obtain a statement from your doctor if you are importing a large number of pharmaceuticals, or if they are of a restricted type.

HOW TO GET TO SYDNEY
Airlines
Sydney is the main destination for inbound flights to Australia, with connections to and from most countries in Asia, Europe, and North and South America. Australia's major carrier is Qantas, with connections to all continents. From the United States, other carriers with direct flights include United Airlines, Air New Zealand, Virgin Australia, and Hawaiian Airlines. The flight time from Los Angeles is 14 hours. From the United Kingdom, British Airways, Singapore Airlines, Cathay Pacific, and many others have regular flights.

Useful numbers in Sydney:
Air New Zealand, tel 13 2476
British Airways, tel 1300 767 177
Cathay Pacific, tel 13 1747
Qantas, tel 13 1313
Singapore Airlines, tel 13 1011
United Airlines, tel 13 1777

Airports
Almost all arrivals to Sydney are via the international Kingsford Smith Airport, the only major airport. It is 7 miles (11 km) from the city and is serviced by bus, rail, and taxi. The airport has two main terminal complexes 2 miles (4 km) apart: the international terminal and the domestic terminal. Less-than-reliable shuttle buses or better rail services connect the two. Starting in 2014, the domestic terminal will handle all Qantas and Jetstar flights, and all other airlines will use the international terminal.

The rail service is the fastest and most convenient public transportation to central Sydney. Trains run every 10 minutes and take just 13 minutes to Central Station (A$16), then go via the City Circle to Museum, St. James, Circular Quay, Wynyard, and Town Hall stations. Change at Central Station for services to the suburbs.

Sydney Buses route 400 goes to Bondi Junction from the airport, otherwise shuttle buses will take you to your hotel. **KST Sydney Airporter** *(tel 9666 9988, www.kst.com.au)* runs fairly regularly from bus stops outside the terminals. It will drop off and pick up (minimum three hours' notice) at hotels in central Sydney. Tickets cost A$18/32 one-way/round-trip. Numerous other operators run shuttle and charter services. Inquire at the visitor information booths in the terminals.

The taxi trip to the city takes 30 minutes or less and costs about A$40–$50, including airport tax and road tolls. In rush hour, delays from and to the airport should be anticipated. Taxi rank queues can be long, particularly weekday evenings.

GETTING AROUND
Traveling In & Around Sydney
By Car
Visitors can drive in New South Wales on a valid driver's license

from their country of origin for the same class of vehicle. The license and the driver's passport must be carried when driving. If the license is not in English, a translation must also be carried. Traffic can be trying, especially at peak hours, and parking difficult, even on weekends at prime tourist spots.

Renting a Car

Vehicle rental daily rates start from as low as A$40 (U.S.$40) for a good-quality, small vehicle. Basic insurance is included, but it will normally cost extra to reduce heavy deductibles, though your travel insurance may cover it. Rental companies require drivers be at least 21 years of age, with higher premiums for people under 25 years of age.

The major international companies are represented, and all have desks at the airport. There are also several budget-rental companies in the city and Kings Cross area.

Reservations

Avis, tel 13 6333
Budget, tel 13 2727
Europcar, tel 1300 13 1390
Hertz, tel 13 3090
Thrifty, tel 1300 367 227

Campers and motor homes are available from **Britz** *(tel 1800 331 454)* and **Maui** *(tel 1800 670 232)*, and the major companies rent 4WD vehicles.

Sydney has plenty of toll roads, most notably the Harbour Bridge and Tunnel. Most rental car operators have e-Tags that automatically bill the tolls, but check details when you pick up the car or you may get a nasty bill shock later.

Driving information

In Australia, traffic drives on the left-hand side of the road. Details of regulations and road signs are available from **Roads & Traffic Authority** *(tel 13 2213, www.rta.nsw.gov.au)*. The **National Roads and Motorists Association** (NRMA; *tel 13 2132*) can also provide information from its office at 74–76 King Street, Sydney, and regional offices throughout Sydney and New South Wales.

Breakdown Assistance

The NRMA has reciprocal arrangements with most international motoring associations and provides a 24-hour emergency breakdown service *(tel 13 2132)*. It is also a good source for touring maps.

Drunk Driving

It is an offense to drive while under the influence of alcohol or other prohibited substances. A blood alcohol level above 0.05 percent can result in loss of license, fines of A$1,100 or more, or jail. Random breath testing (drivers can be pulled over without the police being required to have reasonable suspicion) is widespread, at all hours of the day and night. If you have an accident while under the influence of alcohol, it is likely to invalidate your car's insurance. As a guide, if you have more than two full-strength beers, or two glasses of wine, or a nip of spirits, don't drive. Don't drive the following morning after heavy drinking if you suspect you may still have too much alcohol in your system.

Fuel

Gasoline (petrol) comes in unleaded (regular and premium) grades and is sold by the liter (approximately one-quarter of a gallon) and costs between A$1.30 and A$1.70 a liter (about U.S.$4.90–$6.40 per U.S. gallon). Diesel and LPG are also available.

Maps

Road atlases for the Sydney area are available from bookshops and most service stations and are well worthwhile if you are planning to do a lot of local driving. Rental car companies also rent GPS units.

Seat Belts

The wearing of seat belts is compulsory, in both the front and back seats. Children must also be suitably restrained.

Speed Limits

Speed limits are posted in kilometers: usually 50 kph (28 mph) in urban areas (40 kph/22 mph in the vicinity of schools during school hours), 60 kph (33 mph) or more on main roads, 100 kph (55 mph) in the country, and 110 kph (61 mph) on certain freeways.

By Public Transportation

Sydney's public transportation system extends into nearly all the areas described in this travel guide.

Timetable Information

Details for government-run buses, trains, and ferries are available 24/7 *(tel 13 1500, www.131500.com.au)*. Brochures and timetables are available from information counters at Circular Quay.

Bus

Private and government buses cover the entire city area. Government-run **Sydney Buses** *(www.sydneybuses.info)* has service between the city and the suburbs.

Most buses to the North Shore depart from outside Wynyard Station; to the south, east, and inner west, from Circular Quay. Route numbers prefixed with "X" are express services and "L" buses are limited-stop services operating longer routes. Most buses are prepaid from 7 a.m. to 7 p.m., some all day, meaning you cannot buy a ticket on the bus. Buy your ticket before boarding from ticket outlets such as convenience stores and newsdealers.

Tourist bus services include **City Sightseeing Sydney** *(tel 9567 8400, www.citysightseeing.com.au)*, with a hop-on, hop-off city loop covering the main attractions in central Sydney, plus a loop through the eastern suburbs to Bondi. City buses run every 15–20 minutes, every 30–40 minutes on the Bondi run. A full-fare 24-hour adult ticket costs A$40, a 48-hour ticket A$60.

Ferry

Traveling by ferry is the most convenient, inexpensive, and pleasurable way to take in the harbor sights. Ferry services operate to the uppermost reaches of nearly every waterway and all depart from the Circular Quay Ferry Terminal. See the website of **Sydney Ferries** *(www.sydneyferries.info)* for full information.

Rail

CityRail trains *(www.sydneyrail.info)* serve much of the Central Business District as well as the outer suburbs. Services run from around 5 a.m. to midnight. Interurban trains run to the South Coast, Newcastle, and the Blue Mountains.

The **Metro Light Rail** runs from Central Station past the casino and fish market to Lilyfield in the inner west. The **Monorail** loops around the city center to Darling Harbour and acts primarily as a sightseeing trip for visitors, but not for long—the government plans to tear it down (see sidebar p. 126). More information on both the Metro Light Rail and Monorail can be found online at *www.metrotransport.com.au.*

For a map of the rail network, see the inside back cover.

Ticket Information

The most expensive ticket option is usually a single-ride ticket. Numerous other tickets are available at discount rates, such as the MyBus10 allowing 10 bus trips in peak or off-peak hours, or similar MyTrain10 and MyFerry10 tickets.

You can buy train and ferry tickets at stations and wharves, either from counters or ticket machines, but many buses now require you to buy your ticket before you board. Bus tickets (as well as ferry and rail tickets) can be bought from convenience stores, post offices, and newsdealers—look for the purple PrePay flag—or bus TransitShops at Circular Quay, Wynyard Station, and other locales. These outlets also sell combined MyMulti tickets covering all transportation.

The MyMulti Day Pass (A$21) covers all buses, trains, and ferries for a day; weekly tickets (from A$43 for inner-city travel to A$60 for the whole of Sydney) are an even better value if you plan on using a lot of public transportation. Best of all, Family Funday Sunday tickets cost just A$2.50 for unlimited Sunday travel.

On the rail system, off-peak tickets, purchased after 9 a.m. and on weekends, are substantially less expensive than peak-hour tickets.

By Taxi

Meter-operated taxicabs travel across the Sydney metropolitan area and in the various regions described in this guide. Taxi stands can be found at airports, most train stations, and major ferry stops such as Circular Quay and Manly. Taxis can also be hailed from the street, or you can call the following major companies for reservations or immediate pickup:

Taxis Combined, tel 13 3300
Legion Cabs, tel 13 1451
Premier Cabs, tel 13 1017
RSL Cabs, tel 9581 1111

Water taxis operate on the harbor: Yellow Water Taxis, tel 9299 0199.

Taxis that cater to those with disabilities are also available. Taxi drivers do not expect to be tipped but will accept gratuities offered.

PRACTICAL ADVICE

Communications

Post Offices

Sydney's General Post Office (G.P.O.), or rather the small post shop that once comprised the whole grand building, is at 1 Martin Place, near Pitt Street. It is open from 8:15 a.m. to 5:30 p.m. weekdays, 10 a.m. to 2 p.m. on Saturday. Several other post offices are at key locations around the city. Services at some offices include fax and e-mail. Sydney G.P.O.'s poste restante address is c/o G.P.O., 1 Martin Place, Sydney, N.S.W. 2000, Australia. For postal inquiries, call 13 1317.

Telephones

Public phones take either coins, credit cards, or phonecards (A$5, A$10, A$20, and A$50 denominations) available from newsstands, post offices, and service stations. Local calls cost 50 cents for unlimited conversation. Calls outside the local area are timed and require further coins to continue. International calls are very expensive, but prepaid calling cards sold at convenience stores have cheaper international rates via a local number.

Telstra and Optus operate the two main cell (mobile) networks, while Vodaphone and Three have smaller networks. Check with your supplier to ensure your mobile roaming coverage. Prepaid SIM cards can readily be bought at supermarkets, newsdealers, electronics stores, and other outlets (bring ID). Local call rates are around 80 cents a minute, while international calls cost around A$1 per minute to the United States and United Kingdom. 3G data SIMs for internet access are also available (Telstra is fastest, Virgin better value) and work out much cheaper than most hotel Internet rates.

Using the Telephone

Most Australian telephone numbers comprise eight digits and there are only four area codes covering the entire country. To call Sydney from overseas: Dial 61 for the country and 2 for Sydney and New South Wales. When calling Sydney (or elsewhere within New South Wales) from other parts of Australia, dial 02. If you are in the 02 area, you do not need to dial the code.

To make an international call from Sydney, dial 0011, then the country code (1 for the United States and Canada, 44 for the United Kingdom), then the area code (without the leading zero), followed by the number. Calls to six-digit telephone numbers beginning with 13 are charged at the local rate from anywhere within the country. Numbers prefixed with 1800 are toll free.

Useful Telephone Numbers

Emergency, 000
Directory assistance, 1223
Operator, 1234

Conversions

Australia uses the metric system of weights and measures.

Speed and distances are in kilometers:
1 mile = 1.6 km

Weights are in kilograms and tonnes:
1 kg = 2.2 lbs
1 tonne = 0.91 ton

Volumes are in liters:
1 liter = 2.11 pints

Temperatures are in Celsius:
0°C = 32°F

Electricity

Australian electricity operates at 240 volts, 50 Hertz, and a three-pin adapter is needed for most non-Australian appliances. U.S. appliances require a voltage transformer. Many hotels provide 110-volt shaver sockets.

Holidays

On public holidays, banks, post offices, and government and private offices generally close, as do many shops. Public transportation operates on a Sunday schedule, but many restaurants, bars, shopping malls, and tourist attractions remain open. Nearly everything shuts down for Good Friday and Christmas Day. The following are public holidays in Sydney and New South Wales:

January 1 (New Year's Day)
Fourth Monday in January (Australia Day)
Late March/Early April (Good Friday, Easter Saturday, Easter Monday)
April 25 (Anzac Day, varies slightly from year to year)
Second Monday in June (Queen Elizabeth II's official birthday)
First Monday in August (Bank Holiday, banks only; not a statewide closure)
First Monday in October (Labor Day)
December 25 (Christmas Day)
December 26 (Boxing Day)

Liquor Laws

It is against the law for anyone under the age of 18 to buy alcohol or consume alcohol in public. Service hours for public bars are generally Monday to Saturday 10 a.m. to 10 p.m.; Sunday hours vary. Restaurants, clubs, and hotel lounges have more flexible hours. Alcohol is sold at hotels, liquor stores, and other licensed premises. Many restaurants are also licensed to sell alcohol. Some venues are able to sell alcohol only with a meal; others are B.Y.O. (bring your own). Some licensed restaurants allow you to B.Y.O., but may apply corkage fees for opening the bottle and serving it.

Media

Newspapers

Sydney is served by three major metropolitan dailies (Monday to Saturday). There are two quality broadsheet newspapers: the *Sydney Morning Herald* and the *Australian.* Both are heavily weighted to local news, but the latter is oriented a bit more toward national interests. Both have daily international news sections and some international sports results (English soccer, American football, baseball, and basketball, for example). The third metropolitan newspaper is the tabloid *Daily Telegraph,* the most sensationalist of the three, although it is fairly restrained compared to some of the newspapers published in Britain or the United States. There are two Sunday papers: the *Sunday Telegraph* and the *Sun-Herald.*

Television

Sydney has five main broadcast television stations. There are three commercial networks (Seven, Nine, and Ten), the government-owned but substantially independent Australian Broadcasting Corporation (ABC, channel 2), and the similarly established multicultural broadcaster SBS. With the introduction of digital television, all five networks broadcast extra channels with expanded programming. The cable provider, Foxtel, features sports channels, movie channels, and news channels such as CNN.

Radio

There are numerous radio stations on the AM and FM bands with specializations such as news and talkback (2GB and 2BL), popular music (2WS, 2DAY-FM, and MMM), youth (JJJ), and classical (ABC-FM and 2MBS).

Money Matters

Australian currency is decimal based, with the dollar as the basic unit of currency. There are 100 cents to the dollar. Notes, which are plastic and have a clear window and a hologram (quite a good souvenir in themselves), come in $100, $50, $20, $10, and $5 denominations. Coins come in 5c, 10c, 20c, 50c, $1, and $2. Transactions involving cents are rounded up or down to the nearest multiple of 5 cents.

There are currency exchanges at the international airport, Pitt Street Mall, Circular Quay, and numerous locations around the city (usually 9 a.m.–5 p.m.). Major banks and hotels also provide exchange facilities in all major currencies. As a general rule, bank and money-changer rates are poor. All major traveler's checks are accepted, but often incur additional exchange fees.

Automatic teller machines (ATMs) may also be used if your card has international access, and they are generally the best way to access cash. Contact your bank at home for details of availability and charges.

MasterCard and Visa are the most widely accepted credit cards, followed by American Express, then Diners Club. Some outlets may add a credit card surcharge, especially for American Express and Diners Club.

Opening Times

Thursday nights are late-night shopping nights until 9 p.m. Some stores close on Saturday afternoons and Sundays; however, major department stores and shopping malls are open daily until 6 p.m., or 4 p.m. on weekends.

Banks are generally open from 9:30 a.m. to 4 p.m. Monday to Thursday, until 5 p.m. on Fridays.

Religion

Christianity is the most widespread faith; however, there are also Jewish and Muslim congregations. Your hotel should be able to provide details of the nearest places of worship. Here are a few of note:

Anglican: St. Andrews Cathedral, Town Hall; St. James, Queens Square, Macquarie St.

Baptist: Central Baptist Church, 619 George St.

Jewish: Great Synagogue, 189 Elizabeth St.

Muslim: Islamic Council of N.S.W., tel 9742 5752

Presbyterian: Scots Church, 44 Margaret St.

Roman Catholic: St. Mary's Cathedral, College St.

Time Differences

The time differential from Greenwich mean time (GMT) is +11 hours in summer, +10 hours during the rest of the year. From Los Angeles, the difference is +19 (summer) and +18 hours (winter). Daylight saving in N.S.W. operates from the first Sunday in October until the last Sunday in March. Other states observe different arrangements, and some don't have daylight saving at all.

Travelers With Disabilities

Australia is very aware of the need for facilities for the disabled and is a signatory to international treaties ensuring equality of access. Most airlines, hotels, and transportation offices can arrange assistance when given advance notice and details of your needs. Restaurants and cinemas are often well equipped to assist with your requirements, and most modern buildings provide wheelchair access.

Visitor Information

Information on the city's many attractions, current events, and activities can be obtained from a range of sources, including the **Sydney Visitor Centre** *(tel 9240 8788)* at The Rocks *(Argyle & Playfair Sts.)* and at Darling Harbour *(bet. Cockle Bay Wharf & Harbourside).*

Daily newspapers also have the latest about what's going on around the city. The *Sydney Morning Herald* has a daily entertainment section detailing performances and cinema screenings; the newspaper's Friday supplement gives comprehensive details of just about everything that is happening over the weekend and ensuing week. Other sources include the *Daily Telegraph.*

Tourist Offices

Tourism Australia operates tourist information offices in North America and Europe.

United States: 6100 Center Dr., Los Angeles, CA 90045, tel 310 /695 3200, fax 310/695 3201

United Kingdom: Australia House, 6th Fl., The Strand, London WC2B 4LA, tel 20 7438 4601, fax 20 7240 6690

Internet Information

Tourism Australia and Destination New South Wales give travel and reservations advice at the following Web addresses:
www.australian.com
www.visitnsw.com
www.sydney.com

EMERGENCIES

Embassies in Sydney

Most embassies are located in the national capital, Canberra, but many countries also have consular offices in Sydney:

U.S. Consulate, Level 10, 19–29 Martin Pl., tel 9373 9200

U.K. Consulate, Level 16, Gateway Bldg., 1 Macquarie Pl., tel 9247 7521

Canadian Consulate, Level 5, 111 Harrington St., tel 9364 3000

Emergency Phone Numbers

Ambulance, fire, or police, tel 000
Emergency Prescription Service, tel 9235 0333
Lifeline, tel 13 1114
Prince of Wales Hospital Emergency, High St., Randwick, tel 9382 2222
St. Vincents Hospital Emergency, Victoria St., Darlinghurst, tel 8382 1111
Sydney Hospital Emergency, Macquarie St., tel 9382 7111

Report lost or stolen traveler's checks or credit cards to the issuer:

American Express: Cards, tel 9271 8664; Checks, tel 1800 688 022
Bank of America, tel 9931 4200
MasterCard, tel 1800 120 113
Thomas Cook, tel 1800 127 495
Visa, tel 1800 450 346

What to Do in Case of a Car Accident

The police must be called if someone is injured, if the other driver fails to stop or swap details, or if a vehicle needs to be towed. You should exchange details with the other driver if another vehicle is involved—name, address, telephone number, registration number of the vehicle. Note that the driver's details are contained on his/her license, which also has his/her photo on it. You should also seek the details of any independent witnesses. Inform your insurance company as quickly as possible.

HEALTH

Visitors are permitted to bring reasonable quantities of prescribed (non-narcotic) medication into the country (see p. 232). Australian pharmacies (called chemists) can fill most prescriptions, but they must be written by an Australian-registered doctor.

Vaccinations are not required if you are traveling direct to Australia, unless you have come from or visited a yellow fever–infected country or zone within six days prior to arrival. You do not need a health certificate to enter Australia.

Most overseas travelers are not covered by the government Medicare service, tel 13 2011. Emergency medical treatment is available under the local Medicare system for visitors from the U.K., New Zealand, Sweden, the Netherlands, and a few other countries. There is no coverage for U.S. visitors: Take out a health insurance policy prior to your visit to cover the period of your stay (see p. 231).

Health risks are no greater in Australia than in any other advanced Western country. Sydney's water is considered safe to drink.

Hotels & Restaurants

In Sydney, it is possible to spend a small fortune and be treated like royalty—several Sydney hotels have pampered princesses and presidents—but very comfortable lodgings can be found that have equally comfortable tariffs. However, even budget travelers should consider saving up for a big night at one of the hotels that has a sweeping harbor view. You haven't lived until you've seen the sun go down or rise over one of the world's great waterways.

HOTELS

Most hotels are to be found in the central city area, The Rocks, Kings Cross, and Darlinghurst. If you're keen on the beach, a few hotels from Bondi to Coogee have been included. There are many motels in suburban areas, but these are not usually frequented by overseas travelers.

Farther afield, areas such as the Hunter Valley and the Blue Mountains tend toward boutique-style accommodations, which are very popular with Sydneysiders, especially on weekends. Savvy travelers visit these areas during the week, when tariffs are lower, or book well in advance if they are planning a weekend break.

Online booking sites often have the best rates, but not always. You may do better on the hotel website. *Wotif.com* is the biggest local booking site with the largest selection of Sydney hotels.

RESTAURANTS

When it comes to restaurants, Sydney has a quite dazzling range of cuisines and settings to choose from. Prices compare favorably with other cities. Here, though, you'll find many eateries that can provide an outstanding meal for a handful of coins. An emphasis on fresh produce and palate-cleansing flavors reflects the warm year-round climate and the preference for lighter meals. Just as refreshing, it is usually fairly easy to get a table at Sydney restaurants. Only a handful are booked up months ahead.

ARRANGEMENT & ABBREVIATIONS

Hotels and restaurants are listed separately, first by price, then in alphabetical order.

The following abbreviations are used in these listings:

L = Lunch
D = Dinner
B.Y.O. = Bring your own (wine)
AE = American Express
DC = Diners Club
MC = MasterCard
V = Visa

CIRCULAR QUAY & EAST

HOTELS

FOUR SEASONS SYDNEY
$$$$
199 GEORGE ST.
TEL 9250 3100
FAX 9251 2851
www.fourseasons.com/sydney

Great location right on Circular Quay, next door to The Rocks. This large hotel has understated opulence and excellent service. Luxurious rooms are spacious, and bathrooms have Italian marble. Its restaurant, **Kable's** (see p. 239), is excellent.

531 P 110 All major cards

INTERCONTINENTAL
$$$$
117 MACQUARIE ST.
TEL 9230 0200
FAX 9240 1240
www.intercontinental.com

Located minutes from the Central Business District, the Opera House, Sydney Harbour, and the Botanic Gardens. A modern tower is linked to the preserved 1850s Treasury Building (see p. 69) via the Cortile—a dramatic glass-domed sandstone courtyard that serves as the hotel's central meeting place. Rooms and suites are classically elegant, and many have harbor views. **Cafe Opera** in the grand Treasury Building serves sumptuous buffets or à la carte selections.

509 P 131 All major cards

MARRIOTT
$$$$
36 COLLEGE ST.
TEL 9361 8400
FAX 9361 8599
www.marriott.com.au

Luxury hotel on the eastern side of Hyde Park. Elegant contemporary decor. Rooms have microwaves, wet bars, computer data ports, voice mail, fax lines, and work desks. The restaurant overlooking the park features Australian and international cuisine.

241 P 150 All major cards

SHERATON ON THE PARK
$$$$
161 ELIZABETH ST.
TEL 9286 6000
FAX 9286 6686
www.starwoodhotels.com

One of the city's finest hotels, with a wonderful location

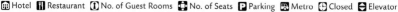

PRICES

HOTELS

An indication of the cost of a double room in the high season is given by **$** signs.

$$$$$	Over $280
$$$$	$200–$280
$$$	$120–$200
$$	$80–$120
$	Under $80

RESTAURANTS

An indication of the cost of a three-course meal without drinks is given by **$** signs.

$$$$$	Over $90
$$$$	$70–$90
$$$	$50–$70
$$	$30–$50
$	Under $30

facing Hyde Park and close to all city attractions. Rooms are stylish and contemporary; of the 49 suites, 23 have balconies that overlook the park. The **Botanica Brasserie** offers à la carte dining and a famed seafood buffet, while the **Gallery Tea Lounge** does a superb high tea.

557 P 200 All major cards

SOFITEL WENTWORTH

$$$$

61–101 PHILLIP ST.
TEL 9230 0700
FAX 9227 9133
www.sofitelsydney.com.au

A highly regarded hotel in the city—and one of the more affordable for the standards on offer—with a high level of elegance and service.

436 P 175 All major cards

OAKS HYDE PARK PLAZA

$$$

38 COLLEGE ST.
TEL 9331 6933
FAX 9331 6022
www.oakshotelsresorts.com/hydeparkplaza

Apartment-style suites are available in this well-appointed hotel on the eastern side of Hyde Park, close to the city, the Australian Museum, Oxford Street, and transportation. Some rooms are tired, but discounted rates make this hotel a good value in expensive Sydney.

182 P 50 All major cards

SYDNEY HARBOUR MARRIOTT

$$$

30 PITT ST.
TEL 9372 2233
FAX 9251 1122
www.marriott.com.au

Luxury hotel just behind Circular Quay. The rooms, recently remodeled, show clean modern lines, and it's worth paying extra for the Harbour Bridge or Opera House view rooms. A 150-year-old pub on the site has been retained and recently renovated.

531 P 40 All major cards

RESTAURANTS

GUILLAUME AT BENNELONG

$$$$$

SYDNEY OPERA HOUSE
BENNELONG POINT
TEL 9250 7548
guillaumeatbennelong.com.au

This premier restaurant under the Opera House's small sails is split-level. One area is fine French dining, enjoying fabulous views and a consistent reputation as one of the city's best restaurants under the guidance of chef Guillaume Brahimi. The upper level is a bar (reservations not required) for cocktails or a wine from the impressive wine list.

140 P 3,000 Train: Circular Quay Closed Sun.–Mon. & L Tues.–Wed. & Sat. All major cards

BOTANIC GARDENS

$$$$

ROYAL BOTANIC GARDENS
MRS MACQUARIES RD.
TEL 9241 2419
www.trippaswhitegroup.com.au

A splendid setting amid the gardens with indoor and outdoor areas serving modern Australian cuisine with fusion influences.

142 Train: Martin Place, Circular Quay Closed D All major cards

KABLE'S

$$$$

FOUR SEASONS SYDNEY
199 GEORGE ST.
TEL 9255 0226
www.fourseasons.com/sydney

The signature restaurant at the Four Seasons Sydney (see p. 238) with a reputation for varied and innovative cuisine and modern takes on old classics. The brasserie-style cuisine features a range of gourmet appetizers, pasta, risotto, meat, fresh seafood, and desserts.

120 P 200 Train: Circular Quay All major cards

SYDNEY COVE OYSTER BAR

$$$–$$$$

1 CIRCULAR QUAY E.
SYDNEY COVE
TEL 9247 2937
www.sydneycoveoysterbar.com

Delightful harborside stopping point on the concourse between Circular Quay ferries and the Opera House. Alfresco, informal dining and local seafood.

140 Train: Circular Quay All major cards

OPERA KITCHEN

$$

LOWER CONCOURSE LEVEL
SYDNEY OPERA HOUSE
TEL 0450 099 888
www.operakitchen.com.au

What a winning formula, combining outlets from some of Sydney's best known gastronomic brands to form the fanciest food court in town. The harbor views are simply stunning, even if the wagyu burgers are a tad expensive. Highlights include the sushi bar at Kenji, the plank-roasted king salmon at Cloudy Bay Fish Co., and tiger prawn and green mango rice-paper rolls at Misschu. This is a quieter complement to the always buzzing outdoor Opera Bar next door.

150 All major cards

THE ROCKS

HOTELS

OBSERVATORY

$$$$$

89–113 KENT ST.
TEL 9256 2222
FAX 8248 5205
www.observatoryhotel.com.au

Old-world opulence set in the heart of The Rocks, this hotel re-creates the atmosphere of a grand Australian home, to luxury standard, with views of the entrance to Darling Harbour.

100 20 All major cards

SOMETHING SPECIAL

PARK HYATT SYDNEY

$$$$$

7 HICKSON RD.
TEL 9241 1234
FAX 9256 1555
www.sydney.park.hyatt.com

The ultimate. Absolute luxury in an absolutely prime position on the harbor. Recently reopened after extensive renovations, this hotel is Sydney's most expensive, catering to a large corporate clientele. Modern-style rooms are suitably opulent, and floor-to-ceiling glass doors open onto private balconies with exclusive harbor views. A team of butlers is on hand, and the upscale restaurant has the Opera House for a backdrop.

155 55 All major cards

QUAY WEST SYDNEY

$$$$$

98 GLOUCESTER ST.
TEL 9240 6000
FAX 9240 6060
www.mirvachotels.com/quay-west-suites-sydney

Luxury apartment/hotel complex with prime-position views of the main harbor and Opera House. All units have a spacious living room, separate bedroom, marble bathrooms, fully equipped kitchen, and laundry. **Harrington's** restaurant is on the mezzanine level, and the 24th floor boasts a Roman-style heated swimming pool, spa, sauna, gym, and sweeping views.

110 40 All major cards

SOMETHING SPECIAL

SHANGRI-LA SYDNEY

$$$$$

176 CUMBERLAND ST.
TEL 9250 6000
FAX 9250 6250
www.shangri-la.com/Sydney

Great harbor views from every room at this luxury hotel. Refurbished rooms feature triple glazing for restful nights and specially designed window seats to take in the million-dollar views. On level 36 is the **Altitude Restaurant** and **Blu Bar,** and the hotel also has a spa and well-equipped business center.

563 120 All major cards

HARBOUR ROCKS

$$$$

34–52 HARRINGTON ST.
TEL 8220 9999
FAX 8220 9998
www.harbourrocks.com.au

Renovated 150-year-old boutique hotel in the heart of The Rocks. It is charming and comfortable with shopping at hand.

59 All major cards

HOLIDAY INN OLD SYDNEY

$$$$

55 GEORGE ST.
TEL 9252 0524
FAX 9251 2093
www.holidayinn.com

This lovely hotel in the middle of The Rocks has views from the rooftop pool and spa that will take your breath away.

174 50 All major cards

SEBEL PIER ONE

$$$$

11 HICKSON RD.
THE ROCKS
TEL 8298 9999
FAX 8298 9777
www.sebelpierone.com.au

Under the shadow of Harbour Bridge in an old shipping wharf, this hotel is in the quiet arts precinct, but close to the bustle of The Rocks. Right on the harbor (literally—you can see the water below you in the glass-floored lobby),

elegant harbor-view rooms bring a premium, but all are high quality. The hotel has a waterfront restaurant, a bar, and a pontoon for catching water taxis into town.
160 Valet All major cards

LORD NELSON BREWERY HOTEL
$$$
19 KENT ST.
TEL 9251 4044
FAX 9251 1532
www.lordnelsonbrewery.com
Break free from the chain hotels and stay at this 1841 pub. Lots of character, in a good location, and offering mostly big rooms, some with shared bathrooms. The lively pub bar is a good place to mingle.
8 All major cards

RESTAURANTS

QUAY
$$$$$
UPPER LEVEL, OVERSEAS PASSENGER TERMINAL
CIRCULAR QUAY W.
TEL 9251 5600
www.quay.com.au
Stupendous views of the Opera House and modern Australian cuisine combine to make this an excellent dining experience. Rated by some as Australia's finest restaurant, the cuisine is delicate and inspired: Try the jasmine-tea-poached chicken, pink snapper with ginger-scented milk curd and shaved abalone, or desserts such as the famous snow egg.
85 16 Train: Circular Quay Closed L Sat.–Sun. All major cards

BEL MONDO
$$$$
LEVEL 3, ARGYLE STORES
12–24 ARGYLE ST.
TEL 9241 3700
www.belmondo.com.au
On the third floor of Sydney's original Metcalf Bond Store in the historic Rocks precinct. A dramatic space with cathedral ceilings, a kitchen on a stage, and views of the Harbour Bridge and the Opera House. High-quality, Italian-inspired cuisine and a romantic atmosphere.
160 Train: Circular Quay Closed L Sat.–Thurs., D Sun., & Mon. All major cards

ROCKPOOL
$$$$
107 GEORGE ST.
TEL 9252 1888
www.rockpool.com
What, no harbor view? Superlative chef Neil Perry, a restaurant and catering emperor, doesn't need one for his multiaward-winning, jewel-in-the-crown, 20-year-old Rockpool restaurant. The menu has a strong emphasis on seafood. Try the slow-cooked abalone with braised goose and XO sauce, or the wagyu beef short rib with black sesame, celeriac, enoki, and pear. Perry cultivates a close relationship with Australian winemakers and offers an extensive menu of premium Australian and imported wines. Not to be confused with sister restaurant Rockpool Bar & Grill, where meat rules, on Hunter Street.
100 Train: Circular Quay Closed Sun.–Mon. & L Tues.–Thurs. All major cards

WHARF RESTAURANT
$$$–$$$$
PIER 4, HICKSON RD.
WALSH BAY
TEL 9250 1761
www.wharfrestaurant.com.au
A tribute to the days of sail, this converted pier, with its soaring tree trunks supporting the roof, straddles the water; its walls of glass and balconies overlook the inner harbor. Lots of arty activity here; the Sydney Theatre Company foyer is the restaurant's bar area. The Wharf has a small kitchen and a short menu of brasserie-style food with a Mediterranean influence and always three or four seafood items.
100 Train: Circular Quay Closed Sun. All major cards

SOMETHING SPECIAL

SAILOR'S THAI
$$–$$$
106 GEORGE ST.
TEL 9251 2466
www.sailorsthai.com.au
The most interesting Thai food in Sydney. Housed in the sandstone old Sailor's Home (1864), modern Thai food is served with style at the restaurant downstairs, or squeeze in at long tables in the cheaper canteen upstairs. Oysters, sugar banana blossom, wagyu beef, and pork hock are just some of the less usual Thai ingredients given a unique, unusual makeover.
80 All major cards

MCA CAFÉ
$$
MUSEUM OF CONTEMPORARY ART
140 GEORGE ST.
TEL 9250 8443
www.mca.com.au
Contemporary art meets indoor and outdoor dining with a view across Sydney Cove for a well-earned break from sightseeing. Shared plates, gourmet sandwiches, and burgers feature on the affordable menu. The café—and a fine-dining restaurant opening soon—has had a complete makeover since the museum added a contempo-

rary new wing to match the art deco classic.
150 Train: Circular Quay Closed D All major cards

SYDNEY HARBOUR

HOTELS

SOMETHING SPECIAL

COCKATOO ISLAND HISTORIC HOUSES & APARTMENTS
$$$$$
COCKATOO ISLAND
TEL 8898 9774
www.cockatooisland.gov.au
For something completely different, get water views from the middle of the harbor on Cockatoo Island. The trust that runs the island has completely renovated the heritage houses once home to senior shipyard staff. Stylish, fully self-contained one- and two-bedroom apartments and four-bedroom houses are ideal for families or groups. Camping and its upscale cousin "glamping" are also offered. The island has a canteen open in the day, plus the happening Island Bar in summer, but be prepared to bring everything with you. Hourly ferries run to the island until 11:30 p.m. Monday through Saturday, and until 7 p.m. on Sunday.
6 Ferry: Cockatoo Island All major cards

NOVOTEL MANLY PACIFIC
$$$$
55 N. STEYNE
MANLY
TEL 9977 7666
FAX 9977 7822
manlypacificsydney.com.au
Popular hotel overlooking Manly Beach and the Pacific Ocean. Half the rooms face east over the beach, the other half have westerly views over Manly. All rooms have balconies. Lobby bar and cocktail bar with open deck look at the Pacific; there's also a restaurant.
213 80 All major cards

SEBEL MANLY BEACH
$$$$
8–13 S. STEYNE
MANLY
TEL 9977 8866
FAX 9977 8209
www.mirvachotels.com/sebel-manly-beach
Intimate boutique hotel at the southern end of Manly Beach. Every room has a balcony, and those in the north tower have ocean views. The location is hard to beat: at the quieter end of Manly opposite the surf beach, but just two blocks from the Corso.
83 50 All major cards

NORTH SYDNEY HARBOURVIEW
$$$
17 BLUE ST.
TEL 9955 0499
FAX 9922 3689
www.viewhotels.com.au
Older high-rise, affordable hotel on the north side of the harbor, with views over the water and city. Try to get a corner room. Transportation to the city takes a matter of minutes on the train, one stop away.
210 60 All major cards

RYDGES NORTH SYDNEY
$$$
54 MCLAREN ST.
TEL 9922 1311
FAX 9922 4939
www.rydges.com/north sydney
Great views from this recently refurbished hotel set in the heart of the North Sydney business district.
167 45 All major cards

PRICES

HOTELS
An indication of the cost of a double room in the high season is given by **$** signs.

$$$$$	Over $280
$$$$	$200–$280
$$$	$120–$200
$$	$80–$120
$	Under $80

RESTAURANTS
An indication of the cost of a three-course meal without drinks is given by **$** signs.

$$$$$	Over $90
$$$$	$70–$90
$$$	$50–$70
$$	$30–$50
$	Under $30

RESTAURANTS

SOMETHING SPECIAL

BATHERS PAVILION
$$$$$
THE ESPLANADE
BALMORAL
TEL 9969 5050
www.batherspavilion.com.au
Delightful site at water's edge in a Spanish mission-style heritage building. Perfect for a sunny stroll; in winter, warmed by open fires. The chef is the renowned Serge Dansereau, who has trained many of the best chefs in Sydney since the 1970s. Known for his close

rapport with small producers, he combines a mature and modern approach to food with traditional techniques such as slow cooking in wood-fired ovens and grilling on vine leaves. Fixed-price and à la carte menus, and a cheaper cafe next door.

250 in all venues Water taxi, or ferry to Mosman Wharf then bus 233 All major cards

---

M.V. *SYDNEY 2000* DINNER CRUISE

$$$$$

CAPTAIN COOK CRUISES
NO. 6 JETTY
CIRCULAR QUAY
TEL 9206 1111
www.captaincook.com.au

The chicken, beef, fish, or vegetarian dishes cooked with modern flourishes are surprisingly good, but the harbor cruise experience is what this restaurant is all about, and that is exceptional. Price varies depending on the deck level and food options. For other waterborne lunch and dinner cruises, check the tour operators around Circular Quay and Darling Harbour.

700 Train: Circular Quay Closed L All major cards

CITY CENTER & SOUTH

HOTELS

SYDNEY HILTON

$$$$

488 GEORGE ST.
TEL 9266 2000
FAX 9265 6065
www.hiltonsydney.com.au

One of the older but still one of the best international hotels, right in the center of the city with cinemas and shopping close by. Celebrity chef Luke Mangan is in charge of the fine-dining **Glass Brasserie** and bars, including the **Zeta Bar,** with its rooftop terrace, and the 106-year-old **Marble Bar,** a glorious relic of an earlier hotel. Specials can make this hotel a good buy.

585 1,000 All major cards

SEBEL SURRY HILLS

$$$–$$$$

28 ALBION ST.
SURRY HILLS
TEL 9281 0333
FAX 9281 0222
www.mirvachotels.com/Sebel

One of a number of Sebel Hotels in Sydney, this one is in a quiet area slightly away from the action but close to Chinatown and trendy Surry Hills, and only a five-minute walk to Central Station. Though no longer the celeb hotel it was in the 1970s, online discounts can make it a good deal.

271 200 All major cards

METRO HOTEL ON PITT

$$$

300 PITT ST.
TEL 9283 8088
FAX 9283 2825
www.metrohotels.com.au

Art deco hotel with a modernized interior in the heart of the city. This good midrange option offers value for a top location. Budget rooms are very small, though; it's worth paying a little extra for standard rooms. Its sister Metro Hotel Sydney Central farther down Pitt Street is slightly cheaper, but a notch down in quality and position.

115 All major cards

PARK8 HOTEL

$$$

185 CASTLEREAGH ST.
TEL 9283 5000
FAX 9283 2710
www.8hotels.com

Small boutique hotel with studio and loft apartments close to tourist attractions, transportation, the Central Business District, and shopping. A good midrange hotel with a recent modern makeover.

36 All major cards

GLASGOW ARMS

$$–$$$

527 HARRIS ST.
ULTIMO
TEL 9211 2354
FAX 9211 7670

Small, budget, country-style pub opposite the Powerhouse Museum within walking distance of Darling Harbour, restaurants, and entertainment. The few single rooms are among the cheapest in the city, but most are double, some with balcony. The bar and a Chinese restaurant are on the ground floor.

12 All major cards

RESTAURANTS

BECASSE

$$$$$

LEVEL 5, WESTFIELD SYDNEY
PITT STREET MALL
TEL 9283 3440
www.becasse.com.au

Exclusive, intimate dining in sumptuous, almost baroque surrounds, yet this restaurant is in a shopping mall in the middle of the city. Quirky, indeed—as is the food, with artistry and technical muscle equally evident on the plate. One of the city's most acclaimed restaurants, with prices to match, dining here is an event. The ultimate event is the chef's table dining experience inside the kitchen, watching the team at work as your own waiter attends you.

25 Closed Sun. All major cards

SOMETHING SPECIAL

TETSUYA'S

$$$$$

529 KENT ST.

TEL 9267 2900

www.tetsuyas.com

The danger with recommending this restaurant is that someone will try to lure Tetsuya Wakuda away from Sydney. Don't do it, he's ours. You'll need to reserve well ahead if you want to discover the genius of his French-Japanese fixed-price eating experience—a ten-course degustation delight.

90 Closed L, D Sun., & Mon. All major cards

PENDOLINO

$$$$

SHOP 100, LEVEL 2

STRAND ARCADE

412–414 GEORGE ST.

TEL 9231 6117

www.pendolino.com.au

Superior Italian food in the glorious Victorian-era Strand Arcade. This dark, intimate restaurant specializes in regionally inspired Italian cuisine, homemade pasta, and the finest olive oils, which it sells at its store. Try the crispy *porchetta* (suckling pig) or truffled chicken liver and mushroom lasagna.

140 Closed Sun. All major cards

BODHI

$$

COOK AND PHILLIP PARK

2 COLLEGE ST.

TEL 9360 2523

www.bodhi.id.au

Chinese vegetarian eatery next to an aquatic center on the eastern edge of Hyde Park with a gorgeous outdoor terrace under spreading fig trees. The *yum cha* (11 a.m.–4 p.m. daily) is mouthwateringly good and perfect for the budget traveler or adventurous diner. Dinner also features pan-Asian dishes such as Malay curry, and the vegetarian Peking "duck" is a regular favorite.

300 Train: St. James Closed Mon. All major cards

DIETHNES

$$

336 PITT ST.

TEL 9267 8956

www.diethnes.com.au

Often called "the Greeks," this restaurant is wonderfully noisy, chaotic, and fun. Traditional Greek fare: cabbage rolls, moussaka, stuffed vine leaves, salads with feta cheese, and olives. Big servings, great value. A Sydney institution for over 35 years.

200 Train: Museum Closed Sun. All major cards

GOLDEN CENTURY

$$

393–399 SUSSEX ST.

TEL 9212 3901

www.goldencentury.com.au

One of the innumerable good-quality Cantonese restaurants in Chinatown, all encompassing *yum cha* during the day and an impressive range of dishes, specializing in seafood, at night.

600 P Train: Town Hall, Central, & Light Rail to Haymarket All major cards

MIRO

$$

76 LIVERPOOL ST.

TEL 9267 3126

www.mirotapasbar.com.au

Hidden downstairs, and well worth seeking out, this establishment is one of the Spanish Quarter's better tapas restaurants. Paella, seafood, and other specialties feature on the menu, and the paintings of Joan Miró adorn the walls.

200 Train: Town Hall All major cards

CAFECITO

$

SHOP 25, TOWN HALL SQUARE

473 KENT ST.

TEL 9267 5575

www.cafecitosydney.com.au

A lunch and breakfast spot where "Brazilians meet and eat." An easily missed café in the shopping arcade on the corner of Bathhurst Street, try the *picanha* steak with rice, black beans, rice and fries, or the *bife a role* (beef stuffed with chorizo). Wonderful Brazilian home cooking.

50 Train: Town Hall Closed Sat.–Sun. Cash only

CHAT THAI

$

20 CAMPBELL ST.

HAYMARKET

TEL 9211 1808

www.chatthai.com.au

Very busy, very popular restaurant open until 2 a.m. opposite the Capitol Theatre in "Thai Town" near the Chinatown district. A line of frantic wok chefs turns out a big array of authentic Thai food at reasonable prices. It has branches on Level 6 of Westfield Sydney on Pitt Street and at the Galeries Food Court, 600 George Street, as well as at Manly and Randwick.

80 Train: Central & Light Rail to Capitol Square MC, V

MAMAK

$

15 GOULBURN ST.

HAYMARKET

TEL 9211 1668

www.mamak.com.au

Malaysian chefs twirl and stretch dough into giant, paper-thin sails, then slap them onto the griddle to make flaky roti bread, perfect for dipping in rich coconut curries. Satay, *nasi lemak*, and other Malay specialties feature at this Chinatown favorite.

90 Train: Town Hall & Sydney Light Rail to Haymarket All major cards

MISO JAPANESE RESTAURANT
$
SHOP 20, WORLD SQUARE
680 GEORGE ST.
TEL 9283 9686

Tucked away in the bustling World Square Shopping Centre on the corner of Liverpool Street, this small, bright, no-frills restaurant has excellent Japanese set meals, noodles, curries, and bento boxes at affordable prices. Tonkatsu-crumbed pork is a winner. B.Y.O.

50 Train: Town Hall Closed Sat. L & Sun. All major cards

SUPERBOWL
$
41 DIXON ST.
TEL 9281 2462
www.superbowlchinese restaurant.com.au

The specialty here is congee (rice porridge) in all its savory forms—king prawn, fish head, frog, beef, and more. Open from breakfast to late-night supper.

70 Train: Town Hall & Light Rail to Haymarket AE, MC, V

DARLING HARBOUR

HOTELS

THE DARLING AT THE STAR
$$$$$
80 PYRMONT ST.
PYRMONT
TEL 9777 9000
FAX 9657 8680
www.thedarling.com.au

With this much luxury on offer, staying at Sydney's only legal casino isn't a gamble, but shop online for the best deal. Serious harbor views, restaurants, and entertainment are contained in the one vast facility (see p. 130). Not to be confused with the other hotel complex here: the Astral Residences, which has one-, two-, and three-bedroom apartments.

171 P 2,500 All major cards

THE GRACE
$$$$
77 YORK ST.
TEL 9272 6888
FAX 9299 8189
www.gracehotel.com.au

This beautifully restored commercial Gothic hotel was modeled on the Chicago Tribune Building. Features such as stairwells, elevators, pressed-metal ceilings, marble flooring, and decorative ironwork have been retained. Rooms come with voice mail, computer data ports, and interactive TV.

382 P 60 All major cards

NOVOTEL SYDNEY ON DARLING HARBOUR
$$$$
100 MURRAY ST.
PYRMONT
TEL 9934 0000
FAX 9288 7189
www.novoteldarlingharbour .com.au

Superior accommodations with all facilities, including a tennis court, right in the middle of the Darling Harbour entertainment precinct.

525 P 60 All major cards

FOUR POINTS BY SHERATON DARLING HARBOUR
$$$–$$$$
161 SUSSEX ST.
TEL 9290 4000
FAX 9290 4040
www.starwoodhotels.com

Built in 1991, this very large luxury hotel was designed to echo the feel of a 1920s ocean liner. The foyer has marble floors and wood paneling; furnishings in rooms and suites echo the art deco, nautical feel. The site includes two heritage-listed buildings dating from the 1850s: the Corn Exchange and the Dundee Arms pub. The informal **Corn Exchange** restaurant specializes in buffets. Some good deals on the city view rooms, but hard to resist the harbor views.

630 P 30 All major cards

HOLIDAY INN DARLING HARBOUR
$$$–$$$$
68 HARBOUR ST.
TEL 9281 0400
FAX 9281 1212
www.holidayinn.com

One of four Holiday Inns in Sydney, this one sits across from the Entertainment Centre, occupying an 1890s wool warehouse, with a modern wing extension. It features a restaurant, a bar, and a health club with gym, sauna, steam room, and spa.

266 P Valet All major cards

PARKROYAL AT DARLING HARBOUR
$$$–$$$$
150 DAY ST.
TEL 9261 1188
FAX 9261 8766
www.parkroyalhotels.com

Fully appointed hotel with views over the water. Great location, with good service

and value.
345 Valet
All major cards

CITIGATE CENTRAL SYDNEY
$$$
169–179 THOMAS ST.
TEL 9281 6888
FAX 9281 6688
www.mirvachotels.com/Citigate
Large rooms and some Darling Harbour views from this well-appointed hotel in the Chinatown entertainment district.
252 600
All major cards

IBIS DARLING HARBOUR
$$$
70 MURRAY ST.
PYRMONT
TEL 9563 0888
FAX 9563 0899
www.hotelibisdarlingharbour.com.au
Affordable hotel accommodations with great city views and Darling Harbour entertainment at the door. Modern, with basic facilities and compact rooms. It has a bar and restaurant.
256 100
All major cards

MENZIES SYDNEY
$$$
14 CARRINGTON ST.
TEL 9299 1000
FAX 9290 3819
www.parkroyalhotels.com
Centrally located in the city, facing Wynyard Park with transportation literally at the door. The lobby is in rich maroons with crystal chandeliers and black granite floors. The well-appointed rooms are a little dated, but this classy midscale hotel has high standards at discount rates. There is a restaurant, a bar showing sports on satellite TV, and a brasserie and wine bar.
446
All major cards

RENDEZVOUS STUDIO HOTEL SYDNEY CENTRAL
$$$
GEORGE & QUAY STS.
TEL 9212 2544
FAX 9281 3794
www.rendezvoushotels.com
Affordable hotel with good facilities close to Central Station, Chinatown, and Darling Harbour. Pleasant contemporary rooms with a recent makeover are good value.
116 40 50%
All major cards

TRAVELODGE WYNYARD
$$$
7–9 YORK ST.
TEL 9274 1222
FAX 9274 1274
www.travelodge.com.au
Well-located hotel with train and bus at the door, a short walk to the northern end of Darling Harbour and the city center. The decor features natural colors, contemporary styling, and lots of glass. Rooms are quite large; some family rooms, suites, apartments, and balcony rooms. **Citrus Grove Restaurant & Bar** serves modern Australian cuisine. Very good hotel for the price.
277 40
All major cards

WALDORF APARTMENT HOTEL
$$$
57 LIVERPOOL ST.
TEL 9261 5355
FAX 9261 3753
www.waldorf-apartments-hotel-sydney.com.au
Terrific location in the Spanish Quarter, a few minutes' walk to Darling Harbour and Chinatown. Big one- and two-bedroom apartments have kitchens and balconies. The decor is tired and maintenance is sometimes needed, but this is great three-star value in expensive Sydney. Free parking is a rare bonus, but spaces are limited.
160 35
All major cards

PRICES

HOTELS
An indication of the cost of a double room in the high season is given by **$** signs.

$$$$$	Over $280
$$$$	$200–$280
$$$	$120–$200
$$	$80–$120
$	Under $80

RESTAURANTS
An indication of the cost of a three-course meal without drinks is given by **$** signs.

$$$$$	Over $90
$$$$	$70–$90
$$$	$50–$70
$$	$30–$50
$	Under $30

RESTAURANTS

THE MALAYA
$$$
39 LIME ST.
TEL 9279 1170
www.themalaya.com.au
In the upscale King Street Wharf precinct at the northern end of Darling Harbour, this Malaysian restaurant has indoor and outdoor dining with fine service, top-class food, and wonderful views across Darling Harbour. The

kapitan king prawns are a knockout.
300 Ferry or train to Wynyard All major cards

RIPPLES AT SYDNEY WHARF
$$$
56 PIRRAMA RD.
PYRMONT
TEL 9571 1999
www.ripplescafe.com.au
Near the Australian National Maritime Museum, fabulous water and city views complement modern dishes with an emphasis on local produce and seafood. Dining is indoors or out on the deck. A sister restaurant is at Milsons Point underneath the bridge on the north shore.
80 Closed D Sun. All major cards

ZAAFFRAN
$$$
LEVEL 2, 345 HARBOURSIDE
TEL 9211 8900
www.zaaffran.com
Excellent Indian food featuring all the usual korma, vindaloo, and tandoori favorites, but surprises include slow-cooked whole lamb shanks and lobster meat with mustard seed and coconut. You can find cheaper Indian restaurants in Sydney, but none have this aspect overlooking the water with the city skyline behind.
200 Light Rail to Harbourside All major cards

DOYLES AT THE FISH MARKET
$$
SYDNEY FISH MARKET
BLACKWATTLE BAY
PYRMONT
TEL 9552 4339
www.doyles.com.au
No prizes for guessing the cuisine here. The fish is served with typical Doyles skill. Indoor and outdoor dining; often very busy. Lunch only.
120 P 500 Light Rail to Fish Market Closed D DC, MC, V

EASTERN SUBURBS

HOTELS

ADINA APARTMENT HOTEL
$$$$
359 CROWN ST.
SURRY HILLS
TEL 9356 5061
FAX 9356 1070
www.medina.com.au
Located in the pleasant village atmosphere of Surry Hills, these one- and two-bedroom apartments are spacious with facilities of a high standard. Plenty of good restaurants are close at hand.
84 P 60 All major cards

SOMETHING SPECIAL

BLUE
$$$$
6 COWPER WHARF RD.
WOOLLOOMOOLOO
TEL 9331 9000
FAX 9331 9031
www.tajhotels.com/sydney
Historic wharf building converted to chic hotel. The facade and internal touches of the former wool and freight stores remain, and yes, it is blue, as is the water on a sunny day. Modern-decor rooms and lofts have a view of Sydney Harbour or Woolloomooloo behind. The wharf has a selection of upscale drinking and dining spots. Neighbors include Russell Crowe in the celebrity-favored apartments next door.
100 P 200 All major cards

SOMETHING SPECIAL

CROWNE PLAZE COOGEE BEACH
$$$$
242 ARDEN ST.
COOGEE
TEL 9315 7600
FAX 9315 9100
www.crowneplaza.com
Have a beach holiday in the city. This hotel has seven floors of well-appointed accommodations right opposite Coogee Beach. Over half the rooms have balconies and panoramic ocean views, as do the pool terrace and the **Bluesalt Restaurant,** which specializes in seafood. Wine list emphasizes New South Wales wineries.
207 P 200 All major cards

MEDUSA
$$$$
267 DARLINGHURST RD.
DARLINGHURST
TEL 9331 1000
FAX 9380 6901
www.medusa.com.au
Contemporary boutique hotel with plenty of urban chic and a courtyard with an elegant reflecting pool. Quiet location, yet close to all transportation. A great small hotel alternative.
17 All major cards

RAVESI'S ON BONDI BEACH
$$$$
CAMPBELL PARADE & HALL ST.
BONDI BEACH
TEL 9365 4422
FAX 9365 1481
www.ravesis.com.au
Small boutique hotel right on the esplanade of Australia's most famous beach. It was developed by gutting an old hotel. Arched doors open out

onto balconies overlooking the water. Its large, eponymous first-floor restaurant (see p. 250) has a relaxed atmosphere.

12 All major cards

BAYVIEW BOULEVARD
$$$

90 WILLIAM ST.
TEL 9383 7222
FAX 9356 3786
www.bayviewhotels.com/boulevard

Between the city and Kings Cross, with sweeping views of the Domain, the Opera House, and the harbor. Modern-decor rooms are well appointed and good value.

272 P 25 All major cards

COOGEE BAY HOTEL
$$$

9 VICAR ST.
COOGEE
TEL 9665 0001
FAX 9664 2103
www.coogeebayhotel.com.au

Art deco–style accommodations away from the bustle of the city, with the usually sheltered waters of Coogee Beach nearby. The pub-style rooms above the bar are overpriced, but the boutique rooms in the block behind are much better, and some have kitchen facilities.

83 P 100 All major cards

KIRKETON
$$$

229 DARLINGHURST RD.
DARLINGHURST
TEL 9332 2011
FAX 9332 2499
www.8hotels.com

Similar to its sister hotel Altamont (both run by 8hotels), this contemporary hotel was remodeled by Sydney's leading designer, Ian Halliday. Casual atmosphere and reasonable prices. Also home to **Eau de Vie,** one of Sydney's coolest cocktail bars, so the higher up your room, the better.

40 P 10 All major cards

SAVOY DOUBLE BAY
$$$

41–45 KNOX ST.
DOUBLE BAY
TEL 9362 4455
FAX 9362 4744
www.savoyhotel.com.au

Behind the main street of classy Double Bay, this small hotel offers comfortable, good-value rooms away from the city bustle, but with exclusive shopping, a thriving café scene, and the ferry nearby.

38 All major cards

SWISS GRAND RESORT BONDI BEACH
$$$

CAMPBELL PARADE & BEACH RD.
BONDI BEACH
TEL 9365 5666
FAX 9365 5330
www.swissgrand.com.au

Old-fashioned architecture in a newish hotel facing Bondi Beach. All suites, most with balconies overlooking the water. Grand lobby with a high atrium. This hotel is all about the position, and it doesn't get much better. A day spa is attached.

203 P 200 All major cards

ALTAMONT HOTEL
$$–$$$

207 DARLINGHURST RD.
DARLINGHURST
TEL 9360 6000
FAX 9360 7096
www.8hotels.com

This 1830 Georgian mansion was a nightclub in the 1970s before its recent incarnation as a modern budget hotel. There are good deals to be had at this small funky hotel featuring a rooftop garden. Lots of restaurants nearby. It's away from the heart of seedy Kings Cross, yet still close to the city.

14 All major cards

BAYSWATER SYDNEY
$$

17 BAYSWATER RD.
KINGS CROSS
TEL 9361 0911
FAX 9361 4972
www.sydneylodges.com

Just to one side of the hustle and bustle of the center of Kings Cross, this new hotel offers small, high-standard budget rooms and is just a short walk to Kings Cross train station.

51 All major cards

DE VERE
$

44–46 MACLEAY ST.
POTTS POINT
TEL 9358 1211
FAX 9358 4685
www.devere.com.au

Good, affordable accommodations in the middle of the lively Kings Cross entertainment and restaurant scene. Rooms are a little tired, but good value for Sydney.

100 All major cards

MACLEAY LODGE
$

71 MACLEAY ST.
POTTS POINT
TEL 9368 0660
www.sydneylodges.com

A five-minute walk to Kings Cross, but in a quieter, more salubrious area, this new hotel has student-style budget rooms. Rooms are small with shared bathrooms, but have kitchenettes. They don't come much cheaper in Sydney. Its similar sister hotel the Maisonette is just around the corner.

30 All major cards

RESTAURANTS

BISTRO MONCUR

$$$$

WOOLLAHRA HOTEL
116 QUEEN ST.
WOOLLAHRA
TEL 9327 9713
woollahrahotel.com.au

An institution in fashionable Woollahra, Damien Pignolet's French bistro is the place where celebrities and well-heeled locals like to dine. From French onion soufflé to salmon with scampi or duck breast with foie gras, the food is consistently excellent. The only drawback? The restaurant doesn't accept reservations.

100 Bus: 333 & 389 Closed L Mon. All major cards

DOYLES ON THE BEACH

$$$$

11 MARINE PARADE
WATSONS BAY
TEL 9337 2007
www.doyles.com.au

The Doyle family has been feeding Sydneysiders great fish for decades. They have restaurants all over the harbor, but it all started here. Dining is under the veranda, right next to the beach, and the ferry ride (last ferry 7 p.m.) to Watsons Bay is all part of the experience. For cheaper casual fish-and-chips, Doyles on the Wharf is at the ferry dock.

450 P 15 Bus: 324 & 325; Ferry: from Circular Quay; water taxi DC, MC, V

SOMETHING SPECIAL

GASTRO PARK

$$$$

5–9 ROSLYN ST.
KINGS CROSS
TEL 8068 1017
www.gastropark.com.au

The clean lines of the ship-styled dining room belie the innovative, intricately styled food, which is anything but casual. Grant King, former executive chef at the seafood-inspired Pier restaurant (see below), produces stunning food transformations such as snapper fillet topped with crispy fried fish scales (yes, fish scales), with a black prawn cracker resembling dredged pumice on the side. Fun, inventive, and technically outstanding food.

60 Train: Kings Cross Closed Sun.–Mon. & L Tues.–Thurs. All major cards

ICEBERGS DINING ROOM & BAR

$$$$

1 NOTTS AVE.
BONDI BEACH
TEL 9365 9000
www.idrb.com

Sydney has no shortage of waterfront dining, but it is worth the trip to Bondi for ocean views and Italian-inspired cuisine at this consistently excellent restaurant perched above the famed swimming club at the end of the beach.

120 Bus: 380 & L82 Closed Mon. All major cards

PIER

$$$$

594 NEW SOUTH HEAD RD.
ROSE BAY
TEL 9327 6561
www.pierrestaurant.com.au

In a city brimming with great harbor view and seafood restaurants, it's hard to pick the best, but this might be it. Chef Greg Doyle has been a leading light of the Sydney restaurant scene for 20 years, and his boathouse restaurant perched on the harbor has won numerous awards. Dishes might include roasted lobster with oyster sauce, kaffir lime, chili, and Thai basil; or seared yellowfin tuna with kombu and ginger-braised scallop, calamari, and prawn.

40 Ferry to Rose Bay then bus 324 All major cards

FISH FACE

$$$

132 DARLINGHURST RD.
DARLINGHURST
TEL 9332 4803
fishfaceaustralia.com.au

Upscale fish and seafood restaurant that creates a seaside fish shop atmosphere, but the quality of the produce would have them lining up out to sea. Menu depends on market availability, but might include pan-fried cuttlefish, scallops served in the shell, tempura prawns with sweet soy pepper, or trevalla with ponzu sauce.

40 Train: Kings Cross Closed L Mon.–Sat. MC, V

LA PESA TRATTORIA

$$$

174 LIVERPOOL ST.
EAST SYDNEY
TEL 9331 4358
www.lapesa.com.au

Milan meets Sydney in this converted house with a maze of dining rooms in an area that abounds in Italian restaurants. Specialties of the house include osso buco, handmade pastas, and Milanese meatballs through to tiramisu and *semifreddo* for dessert.

70 Train: Museum Closed Sat. L & Sun. All major cards

MACLEAY STREET BISTRO

$$$

73 MACLEAY ST.
POTTS POINT
TEL 9358 4891
www.macleaystbistro.com.au

A longish, narrow space, with

simple but charming decor and a couple of spots out front on the street. This restaurant always manages to reinvent itself and come up with exciting new ideas. Modern Australian cuisine with French touches—dishes might include ballotine of chicken with spinach, goat cheese, and toasted almonds on braised lentils. Make sure to check the blackboard specials before ordering.
65 Train: Kings Cross
Closed L Mon.–Thurs.
All major cards

RAVESI'S ON BONDI BEACH
$$$
CAMPBELL PARADE & HALL ST.
BONDI BEACH
TEL 9365 4422
www.ravesis.com.au
Modern Australian cuisine (think wagyu beef, fresh seafood, and the latest fads) with a seafood emphasis. Well, it would have to be, given its location overlooking Bondi Beach. There's a log fire in winter.
110 Bus: 380 & L82
All major cards

TOKO
$$$
490 CROWN ST.
SURRY HILLS
TEL 9357 6100
www.toko.com.au
Japanese informal *izakaya*-style bar dining comes to Sydney in this stylish buzzing restaurant with a decor reminiscent of London or Rome as much as Tokyo. Beautifully presented small plates with grill and sushi selections. Plenty of sake and other cocktails here and at the attached bar.
110 Train: Central
Closed L Sat.–Mon. & D Sun. All major cards

CENTENNIAL PARKLANDS DINING
$$–$$$
GRAND & PARKES DRS.
CENTENNIAL PARK
TEL 9380 9350
www.trippaswhitegroup.com.au
With a wonderful parkland setting, this revamped restaurant is a breakfast and lunchtime oasis in the city. Dishes might include shredded pork with red onion jam, wagyu brisket with green tomato chutney, and raspberry mousse. Indoor and outdoor dining where you can watch joggers, horseback riders, and cyclists sweep by.
150 Bus: 339, 373, & 396 Closed D All major cards

ONDE
$$–$$$
346 LIVERPOOL ST.
DARLINGHURST
TEL 9331 8749
www.onderestaurant.com
Popular French bistro in a busy restaurant district. Quality provincial French–influenced cuisine is varied and reasonably priced.
36 Train: Kings Cross
Closed L All major cards

BILL'S
$$
433 LIVERPOOL ST.
DARLINGHURST
TEL 9360 9631
www.bills.com.au
Upscale café, small, light, sunny, and busy, with an eclectic menu and all-day breakfasts. Try the prawn and chili linguine or slow-braised lamb shoulder. Also Bill's 2 *(359 Crown St., Surry Hills, tel 9360 4762 & 118 Queen Street, Woollahra, tel 9328 7997)*; B.Y.O.
40 Bus: 389 Closed Sun. & D All major cards

PRICES

HOTELS
An indication of the cost of a double room in the high season is given by **$** signs.

$$$$$	Over $280
$$$$	$200–$280
$$$	$120–$200
$$	$80–$120
$	Under $80

RESTAURANTS
An indication of the cost of a three-course meal without drinks is given by **$** signs.

$$$$$	Over $90
$$$$	$70–$90
$$$	$50–$70
$$	$30–$50
$	Under $30

RAW BAR
$$
WAIROA & WARNERS AVES.
BONDI BEACH
TEL 9365 7200
With its name, it would have to be Japanese, and it is, with views to North Bondi Beach. This busy little place does sushi, tempura, and ramen, including vegetarian options.
60 Bus: 378, 380, & L82
All major cards

BAR COLUZZI
$
322 VICTORIA ST.
DARLINGHURST
TEL 9380 5420
Open from 5 a.m. until around 7 p.m., this little café with a big reputation serves very good coffee. Opened in 1957 by Italian boxer Luigi Coluzzi, decades of upscale custom have made it a Sydney institution. Tables spilling onto the street are always busy.

40 Train: Kings Cross
Closed D Cash only

FORBES & BURTON

$

FORBES & BURTON STS.
EAST SYDNEY
TEL 9360 9594
www.forbesandburton.com.au

Stylish café serving a modern Australian menu in a renovated sandstone building. Popular with the chic set. Good breakfasts. Try the green eggs and ham (scrambled eggs with pesto and smoked ham on sourdough).

50 Train: Kings Cross
Closed Sun. & D MC, V

HARRY'S CAFÉ DE WHEELS

$

COWPER WHARF ROADWAY
WOOLLOOMOOLOO
TEL 9357 3074
www.harryscafedewheels.com.au

Food trucks are the latest buzz, with city-sanctioned trucks filling late-night dining black spots such as Circular Quay and Pitt Street Mall. The granddaddy of all food trucks since 1945, Harry's Café de Wheels serves meat pies smothered in peas and gravy, a unique local dish, until 3 or 4 a.m. This Sydney institution frequented by celebrities is opposite upscale Woolloomooloo Finger Wharf.

Take out only Cash only

WESTERN SUBURBS

RESTAURANTS

BOATHOUSE ON BLACKWATTLE BAY

$$$$

END OF FERRY RD.
GLEBE
TEL 9518 9011
www.boathouse.net.au

Seafood is the dominant influence in the modern Australian cuisine served at this superbly located restaurant overlooking Blackwattle Bay and the Sydney Fish Market.

100 P 40 Bus: 431; Light Rail to Wentworth Park
Closed Mon. & L Tues.–Wed. All major cards

BAU TRUONG

$$

308 ILLAWARRA RD.
MARRICKVILLE
TEL 9559 5078
www.bautruong.com.au

There are many Vietnamese restaurants in this area offering good budget Viet dining, but new kid Bau Truong is one of the best. Smart decor and service push for a more upmarket experience. The menu delivers old favorites and new twists such as stir-fried pumpkin with shrimp paste and sweet basil.

60 Bus: 423 & 426
Closed L All major cards

EFENDY

$$

79 ELLIOTT ST.
BALMAIN
TEL 9810 5466
www.efendy.com.au

Converted Victorian mansion with a number of dining rooms where restrained white-tablecloth elegance meets Turkish artwork. Owner Somer Sivrioglu pushes regional Turkish dishes in a new direction while making the most of local produce: almond-and-sumac-crusted coral trout, beef spareribs marinated in pomegranate jus, interesting mezes, and barbecue grill specials.

120 Bus: 506 & 518
Closed D Mon.
All major cards

LOVE.FISH

$$

580 DARLING ST.
ROZELLE
TEL 9818 7777
lovefish.com.au

Seafood restaurant that offers great value and superb standards. Small and busy, especially on weekends, it has minimalist decor in front of the open kitchen. A big selection of perfectly cooked fish and interesting starters such as the salmon sebago hash cakes or the kingfish carpaccio with pink grapefruit. Sustainability and green credentials extend to the wine list: There is none. B.Y.O. from the pub across the road for even more value.

36 P 8 Bus: 500
Closed L All major cards

THAI POTHONG

$$

294 KING ST.
NEWTOWN
TEL 9550 6277
www.thaipothong.com.au

Contender for best Thai restaurant on King Street (and in Sydney), the Pothong is lively and popular, yet affordably elegant. Extensive menu covers all tastes, with vegetarian, seafood, curry, stir fry, and Thai salad dishes. Comprehensive wine list; also B.Y.O. Gift shop and a branch restaurant at 322 Victoria Road, Marrickville. Note: Reservations are vital on Friday and Saturday nights.

280 Train: Newtown
All major cards

BAR ITALIA

$–$$

171 NORTON ST.
LEICHHARDT
TEL 9560 9981

One of the signature cafés of this Italian Quarter, where you can get industrial-strength coffee, focaccia, gelato, and

more while watching the beautiful people parade in the evenings. Straightforward, value Italian dining.
250 Bus: 438, 436, & 440 Cash only

ELIZABETH FARM TEA ROOM
$
70 ALICE ST.
ROSEHILL
TEL 9635 9488
www.hht.net.au
A pleasant setting for indoor or outdoor dining, with good-value meals. This is the ideal lunch stop if you are sightseeing around Parramatta.
90 Train: Parramatta or Harris Park; Ferry: from Circular Quay then Parramatta Explorer bus Closed L Mon.–Thurs. & D MC, V

GUZMAN Y GOMEZ
$
175 KING ST.
NEWTOWN
TEL 9517 1533
www.guzmanygomez.com
This is Sydney's favorite taqueria. A fun, casual place to grab a quick bite, and it does enormous trade on weekend nights, much of it to go. A bit more zing than your usual Sydney Tex-Mex. Now turning into a franchise with outlets cropping up all around Sydney.
40 Train: Newtown All major cards

NEWTOWN THAI
$
177 KING ST.
NEWTOWN
TEL 9557 2425
Always busy, the small hole-in-the-wall restaurant with a few tables in front swarms with locals on a street with plenty of Thai restaurants. Good-quality Thai food at rock-bottom prices, particularly the lunch specials.
30 Train: Newtown Closed L Mon. MC, V

DAY TRIPS

HAWKESBURY RIVER

WISEMANS FERRY COUNTRY RETREAT
$$$
OLD NORTHERN RD.
WISEMANS FERRY
TEL 4566 4422
FAX 4566 4613
www.wisemans.com.au
Motel-style accommodations in a beautiful setting on the banks of the Hawkesbury River. A nine-hole golf course, tennis courts, pool, and the good **Riverbend Restaurant** are pluses.
54 P 100+ All major cards

PITTWATER

ILUKA RESORT APARTMENTS
$$$$$
1097–1101 BARRENJOEY RD.
PALM BEACH
TEL 9974 3733
FAX 9974 3744
www.iluka-palmbeach.com.au
On the main street of exclusive Palm Beach, close to all amenities and the beach, spacious well-appointed one- and two-bedrooms apartments have full kitchens, balconies or courtyards, and Jacuzzis.
20 P 20 All major cards

JONAH'S RESTAURANT & ACCOMMODATION
$$$$$
69 BYNYA RD.
PALM BEACH
TEL 9974 5599
FAX 9974 1212
www.jonahs.com.au
Exclusive, luxury boutique retreat in Sydney's northern beaches region, an hour or so by car from the Central Business District. Peerless cliff-top site overlooking Whale Beach. The restaurant serves Mediterranean-infuenced food with an emphasis on seafood, and tapas at the Terrace bar.
11 P 40 All major cards

COTTAGE POINT INN
$$$$$
2 ANDERSON PL.
COTTAGE POINT
TEL 9456 1011
www.cottagepointinn.com.au
A slice of waterside heaven, this renovated boat shed overlooks the tranquil beauty of Cowan Waters and Coal and Candle Creeks in the Ku-ring-gai Chase National Park. Try the barramundi with mussels, caramelized fennel, and saffron broth, or the duck confit with balsamic red onion tart, Riesling-poached pear, and calvados jus.
95 Ferry: from Palm Beach; Seaplane: from Rose Bay Closed D Mon.–Thurs. All major cards

NEWPORT ARMS
$$
KALINYA ST.
NEWPORT
TEL 9997 4900
www.newportarms.com.au
Bistro, restaurant, or café—take your pick. There is plenty of seafood available to suit every budget, with pleasant views on huge terrace areas across the southern reaches of Pittwater.
1,000 P 200 Bus: L87, L88, & L90 All major cards

EXCURSIONS

BLUE MOUNTAINS

HOTELS

ECHOES
$$$$$
3 LILIANFELS AVE.
ECHO POINT
KATOOMBA
TEL 4782 1966
FAX 4782 3707
www.echoeshotel.com.au
This modern guesthouse was built to capitalize on splendid views of the Jamison Valley. The foyer has cathedral ceilings, while the upstairs restaurant and lounge have sofas and open fires in winter overlooking the valley. Upstairs rooms have balconies; downstairs they open onto verandas and the lawn. The restaurant serves lunch with stunning views from the terrace overhanging the valley, weather permitting, and a formal dinner with white-glove service and modern Australian fare.
14 P 14 All major cards

LILIANFELS BLUE MOUNTAINS
$$$$$
LILIANFELS AVE.
ECHO POINT
KATOOMBA
TEL 4780 1200
FAX 4780 1300
www.lilianfels.com.au
Multiaward-winning hotel with superb views of the Jamison Valley. The original National Trust–protected grand colonial house and gardens contain function rooms and a restaurant. The airy, spacious rooms are in a newer redbrick wing that echoes the Victorian opulence of the main building. There is also a huge lounge with floor-to-ceiling windows, piano, and open fire in winter. For the energetic, horseback riding, golf, bush walks, and mountain bike rides are all nearby. **Darley's,** with ornate fireplaces and crystal chandeliers, is one of the area's most awarded restaurants. With an emphasis on fresh local produce, set-course and degustation menus are offered, with a wine list showcasing both imported and Australian wines.
85 P 50 All major cards

SOMETHING SPECIAL

MILTON PARK
$$$$$
HORDERNS RD.
BOWRAL
TEL 4861 8100
FAX 4861 7962
www.milton-park.com.au
A grand old country-house hotel set on more than 300 acres (120 ha). The original house has a lounge with open fires in winter, and a restaurant with vaulted ceilings, rich tapestries, and warm colors. Guest rooms, in a newer wing, display period furniture and original paintings. **Horden's Restaurant,** a grand antique-style dining room, focuses on game and local produce. The hotel also has a day spa.
40 P 100 All major cards

SOMETHING SPECIAL

WOLGAN VALLEY RESORT & SPA
$$$$$
2600 WOLGAN RD.
WOLGAN VALLEY
TEL 6350 1800
FAX 6350 1801
www.wolganvalley.com
A world-class resort in the secluded Wolgan Valley with spectacular sandstone escarpments as backdrop. Freestanding luxury suites have their own terrace and swimming pool. Outdoor activities are organized and included in packages that also include all meals in the fine-dining restaurant. One of Australia's finest lodges.
40 P At gates, shuttle to hotel All major cards

FAIRMONT RESORT
$$$$
1 SUBLIME POINT RD.
LEURA
TEL 4785 0000
FAX 4785 0001
www.fairmontresort.com.au
Large, imposing resort hotel, built high on a ridgetop overlooking the rugged Jamison Valley. Spacious rooms, family accommodations, and suites overlook the valley, grounds, or nearby Leura golf course. The restaurant offers a Saturday buffet and formal dining several nights a week.
210 P 200 All major cards

JEMBY-RINJAH LODGE
$$$
336 EVANS LOOKOUT RD.
BLACKHEATH
TEL 4787 7622
FAX 4787 6230
www.jembyrinjahlodge.com.au
Situated on the road to Evans Lookout, this resort operates to stringent environmental principles and offers a beautiful bushland setting. Restaurant operates on weekends and some weeknights. Walking trails at the door. Cabins sleep two to six people.
10 P 10 All major cards

MOUNTAIN HERITAGE HOTEL
$$$
APEX & LOVEL STS.

KATOOMBA
TEL 4782 2155
FAX 4782 5323
www.mountainheritage.com.au
Grand turn-of-the-20th-century guesthouse in a secluded spot, but close to Katoomba's pubs and antique and gift shops. Set on a hill with wonderful views, its light and spacious rooms and suites have heritage decor. All have private bathrooms, some with spas and open fires. Lounge and dining room have open fires in winter and valley views.
41 P 50 All major cards

WALDORF LEURA GARDENS RESORT
$$$
44 FITZROY ST.
LEURA
TEL 4784 4000
FAX 4 784 4004
www.leuragardensresort.com.au
First-class motel amid 4 acres (2 ha) of award-winning landscaped gardens. Rooms feature country-style furnishings. Good value.
78 P 80 All major cards

BLACKHEATH MOTOR INN
$$
281 GREAT WESTERN HWY.
BLACKHEATH
TEL 4787 8788
FAX 4787 8929
www.blackheathmotorinn.com
Swiss chalet–style motel rooms and lush gardens. Good budget option for exploring the Blackheath area and trails.
9 P 9 All major cards

RESTAURANTS

VULCANS
$$$$
33 GOVETTS LEAP RD.
BLACKHEATH
TEL 4787 8456
Renowned chef Phillip Searle has turned this unprepossessing former bakery into one of the Blue Mountains' most awarded restaurant. Pride of place goes to the old baker's oven on the back wall of the restaurant, where culinary creations from bread to slow-cooked meats and vegetarian creations are born. Tastefully decorated with a selection of artworks, the dining room is warm and the service is impeccable. Leave room for the restaurant's famous chequerboard (licorice and pineapple) ice cream.
38 Train: Blackheath
Closed D & L Mon.–Thurs.
MC, V

AVALON
$$$
8–18 KATOOMBA ST.
KATOOMBA
TEL 4782 5532
www.avalonkatoomba.com
This restaurant is located upstairs in the old Savoy picture theater on the main street and is run by artists Glen Puster and Gail Pollard with an individual dash. Buzzing on weekends, quieter midweek with wonderful views across the valley and art deco ambience accompanied by antiques and artwork. Eclectic menu, daily specials. Try the Atlantic salmon fillet coated in black wattleseed, or desserts such as the shortbread sandwich filled with white and dark chocolate truffles, strawberries, and ice cream on crème anglaise.
80 Train: Katoomba
Closed L Mon.–Wed.
MC, V

PRICES

HOTELS

An indication of the cost of a double room in the high season is given by **$** signs.

$$$$$	Over $280
$$$$	$200–$280
$$$	$120–$200
$$	$80–$120
$	Under $80

RESTAURANTS

An indication of the cost of a three-course meal without drinks is given by **$** signs.

$$$$$	Over $90
$$$$	$70–$90
$$$	$50–$70
$$	$30–$50
$	Under $30

APPLE BAR
$$–$$$
2488 BELL'S LINE OF RD.
BILPIN
TEL 4567 0335
www.applebar.com.au
Dine outside on the veranda in summer, or inside near the oven for warmth in winter. Deservedly busy on weekends, fare includes gourmet pizzas and an eclectic mix from pea and ham soup to a bowl of mussels or angus beef steak, all done with flair.
100 P 25 Closed Tues.–Wed. AE, MC, V

RESTAURANT TOMAH
$$
BELL'S LINE OF RD.
MOUNT TOMAH, VIA BILPIN
TEL 4567 2060
www.restauranttomah.com.au
Indoor and outdoor dining at the Mount Tomah Botanic Garden and views that extend forever. Classic dishes

done well with flair, such as *chermoula*-crusted barramundi fillet with hand-cut fat chips, or the lamb and rosemary pie.
140 P 450 Closed D
MC, V

ARJUNA
$
16 VALLEY RD.
KATOOMBA
TEL 4782 4662
Classic north Indian and tandoori cuisine comes with spectacular Megalong and Jamison Valleys views. Spicy menu with ample vegetarian options. B.Y.O.
80 P 10 Train: Katoomba Closed Tues.–Wed. & L AE, MC, V

CANBERRA

HOTELS

CROWNE PLAZA CANBERRA
$$$$
1 BINARA ST.
CANBERRA CITY
TEL 6247 8999
FAX 6257 4903
www.crowneplazacanberra.com.au
This hotel offers top-notch accommodations in the business district. Rooms are larger than usual, and most overlook the green lawns of a park. Public areas are light and spacious with an atrium roof. Recently upgraded. The Canberra casino is nearby.
295 P 202
All major cards

HYATT CANBERRA
$$$$
COMMONWEALTH AVE.
YARRALUMLA
TEL 6270 1234
FAX 6281 5998
canberra.park.hyatt.com
Art deco–style building that was formerly (and to an extent still is) the favored watering hole of the city's power brokers. Accommodations are elegant and stylish. Canberra's best.
249 P 270
All major cards

ARIA HOTEL
$$$
45 DOORING ST.
DICKSON
TEL 6279 7000
FAX 6279 7299
www.ariahotel.com.au
New kid in town without the full facilities of the big hotels, but with some of the best equipped rooms, stylish one- or two-bedroom apartments, and spa suites.
128 P 80
All major cards

RESTAURANTS

WATER'S EDGE
$$$–$$$$
40 PARKES PL.
PARKES
TEL 6273 5066
watersedgecanberra.com.au
Fine-dining delight with modern inspirations in a wonderful lakeside locale. Lots of foam, jus, and innovative tastes in a technically stunning menu. Chef James Mussillon competes with himself for Canberra's best dining award with sister restaurant Courgette.
76 Closed D Mon. & L Mon.–Tues. All major cards

THE CHAIRMAN & YIP
$$$
108 BUNDA ST.
CANBERRA CITY
TEL 6248 7109
chairmangroup.com.au
Innovative Chinese food is fused with Western influences in this stylish restaurant. Try the beef and scallop ground-pepper hot pot, or sesame-crusted ocean trout with cinnamon-infused soy.
150 Closed Sun. & L Sat.–Mon. MC, V

TU DO
$
7 SARGOOD ST.
O'CONNOR
TEL 6248 6030
Belying its suburban premises, this Vietnamese restaurant sets a high standard with the food. Try the paper rolls with pork, prawns, and herbs; lemongrass and chili chicken; or satay king prawns.
50 All major cards

CENTRAL COAST

MERCURE LAKE MACQUARIE RAFFERTYS RESORT
$$$
7 RAFFERTYS RD.
CAMS WHARF
TEL 4972 5555
FAX 4972 5253
www.raffertysresort.com.au
Very comfortable detached and duplex cottage accommodations on the shores of Lake Macquarie, 70 miles (112 km) north of Sydney. The units have verandas, and each comes equipped with a stove, dishwasher, TV and VCR, washer and dryer, and air-conditioning. Set amid 35 acres (14 ha) of native flora, the resort has four swimming pools (one heated), barbecue facilities, tennis courts, canoes and dinghies, and a boat ramp. The resort also has Italian and Thai restaurants.
110 P 100
AE, MC, V

OAKS WATERFRONT RESORT
$$$
89 THE ENTRANCE RD.
THE ENTRANCE

TEL 4334 8000
FAX 4334 6094
www.oakshotelsresorts.com
Studio and one- and two-bedroom apartments (higher rooms have water views) are in a good central position opposite the beach with plenty of restaurants nearby. Facilities include large heated pool, gym, and spa.
145 90 All major cards

TIARRI TERRIGAL BEACH
$$$
16 TIARRI CRESCENT
TERRIGAL
TEL 4384 1423
FAX 4385 6325
www.tiarriterrigal.com.au
This upmarket motel with tropical gardens caters to couples. Spa suites are available as well as outdoor heated spa and barbecue. Close to the cliff tops, the motel is around half a mile (1 km) from the beach and main street shops and restaurants.
8 8 All major cards

HUNTER VALLEY

HOTELS

SOMETHING SPECIAL

TOWER LODGE
$$$$$
6 HALLS RD.
POKOLBIN
TEL 4998 7022
FAX 4998 7164
www.towerlodge.com.au
Exclusive luxury lodge at the Tower Estate Winery with individually styled rooms furnished with antiques. Some rooms have balconies, others courtyards with fountains, and one a private plunge pool. There is a library, golf course, heated pool, sauna, gym, massage treatment, and the fine dining **Nine** restaurant in the cellar with seating for just 12 people and a nine-course degustation menu for a special night out.
12 200 All major cards

PEPPERS CONVENT
$$$$
HALLS RD.
POKOLBIN
TEL 4998 4999
FAX 4998 7323
www.peppers.com.au/convent
The convent, built in 1909 in the New South Wales town of Coonamble, was saved from demolition and moved 375 miles (600 km) to the Hunter Valley. The spacious rooms have high ceilings, most opening out onto a balcony or veranda. The decor is romantic, with rich fabrics, gilt, and white cane furniture. A formal drawing room is furnished with antiques. Swimming pool, tennis court, and mountain bikes for rent.
17 20 All major cards

SEBEL KIRKTON PARK
$$$
336 OAKEY CREEK RD.
POKOLBIN
TEL 4998 7680
FAX 4998 7775
www.sebelhuntervalley.com.au
Colonial-style hotel on 75 acres (30 ha) with a big range of facilities from pool, sauna, and spa to tennis courts, gym, and billiard room. Close to many wineries. The rooms, like the hotel, are antique style and good value.
71 150 All major cards

RESTAURANTS

ESCA BIMBADGEN
$$$$
790 MCDONALDS RD.
POKOLBIN
TEL 4998 4666
www.bimbadgen.com.au
Popular and highly acclaimed restaurant at the Bimbadgen Estate with an emphasis on local produce and modern Australian cuisine. The contemporary-style restaurant features large glass windows and an open balcony.
110 60 Closed D Sun.–Tues. All major cards

RESTAURANT BOTANICA
$$$$
555 HERMITAGE RD.
POKOLBIN
TEL 1300 192 868
spicersgroup.com.au
At the Vineyards Estate, overlooking the grapevines, the quietly elegant dining room is matched by fine dining with Mediterranean influences showing great attention to detail. Two- or three-course options may include charred *chermoula*-drenched lamb or cardomom-and-pepper-crusted duck with smoked eggplant, Moroccan dates, and preserved lemon salad.
50 60 Closed D Mon.–Tues. & L Sun.–Wed. All major cards

ROBERTS
$$$$
HALLS RD.
POKOLBIN
TEL 4998 7330
This iconic restaurant of the Hunter Valley is in a cathedral-ceilinged homestead at the Tower Estate. Chef Robert Molines produces dishes such as quail with borlotti bean puree and caramelized onion

tarte, and desserts such as dark chocolate pudding with poached quince and hazelnut ice cream. Seafood often features prominently, and the wine list showcases Hunter Valley vineyards.

100 P All major cards

LEAVES & FISHES

$$$

737 LOVEDALE RD.
LOVEDALE
TEL 4930 7400
www.leavesandfishes.com

Yes, it's leafy and the restaurant is built out over a fish pond in a delightful setting. Dishes are meant to be shared and might include tempura of soft-shell crab, crispy skinned duck, or lamb ribs with pear, feta, and chive salad.

80 Closed Mon.–Tues. & D Wed.–Thurs., Sun. All major cards

SOUTH COAST

DRAWING ROOMS OF BERRY

$$$$

21 WATTAMOLLA RD.
WOODHILL
TEL 4464 3360
FAX 4464 1246
www.drawingrooms.com.au

Named after the impressive rock formations in this secluded valley outside the pretty town of Berry, this bed-and-breakfast has beautifully appointed rooms in the main guesthouse, separate lodges, or the exclusive villa with private decks and Jacuzzi.

10 P 10 All major cards

AT OUTRIGGERS MOLLYMOOK

$$$

13 SHEPHERD ST.
MOLLYMOOK
TEL 0400 331 037
www.atoutriggersmollymook.com.au

Luxury new one- to three-bedroom apartments provide some of the best accommodations on the coast. Close to a handsome beach.

4 P 4 MC, V

BEACH HOUSE MOLLYMOOK

$$$

3 GOLF AVE.
MOLLYMOOK
TEL 44551966
FAX 4455 3841
www.beachhousemollymook.com

Comfortable and affordable bed-and-breakfast motel-style accommodations in a beachfront location overlooking the Pacific Ocean and with a golf course at the door. Guest lounge and kitchen.

19 P 15 MC, V

SOUTHERN HIGHLANDS

PEPPERS MANOR HOUSE MOUNT BROUGHTON

$$$

KATER RD.
SUTTON FOREST
TEL 4860 3111
FAX 4868 3257
www.peppers.com.au/manor-house

First-class hotel in an idyllic rural setting, next to a golf course, with all facilities and considerable old-style opulence and charm. **Katers Restaurant** focuses on fresh seasonal produce such as fried barramundi with Moreton Bay bug cannelloni and squid ink crumbs, or Angus beef fillet served with red cabbage puree, corn cake, and Cabernet jus. A five-course degustation menu comes with or without matched wines.

43 P 45 All major cards

BERIDA MANOR COUNTRY HOTEL

$$

6 DAVID ST.
BOWRAL
TEL 4861 1177
FAX 4861 1219
www.beridamanor.com.au

Old-style guesthouse with full facilities in a parklike setting adjacent to the Royal Bowral Golf Course.

55 P 60 All major cards

Shopping

Names, names, names. A walk through Sydney's main shopping strips can sometimes be little different from a shopping trip in New York, Tokyo, or Paris. All the big names in fashion and jewelry are represented, but there are local items that are definitely worth seeking out.

Jewelry is the obvious first stop—with exquisite South Pacific pearls, dazzling opals, diamonds, and gold sourced from around the country and its seas. Aboriginal art and artifacts are extremely popular, and the best items are highly prized on the international market. Australian wines make great gifts, as well as a welcome addition to a harborside picnic. Finally, you can outfit yourself in genuine outback clothing so you not only look the part but can handle the worst the climate might throw at you.

Specialty shops are usually open 9 a.m. to 5 or 6 p.m. (to noon or later Saturdays, closed on Sundays), but in popular tourist areas such as The Rocks you'll find shops are considerably more flexible—often open all day and into the night seven days a week. Shopping malls are open seven days.

Antiques & Auction Houses

Christie's
287 New South Head Rd., Edgecliff, tel 9326 1422
International auction house specializing in Australian, European, and Southeast Asian paintings, plus Aboriginal art, jewelry, antiques, decorative arts, books, and memorabilia.

Lawsons Fine Art Auctions
1A The Crescent, Annandale, tel 9566 2377
Regular auctions of decorative art, fine jewelry, books, maps and prints, antique and modern silver, tribal art, and fine wines.

Sotheby's
Level 1, 118–122 Queen St., Woollahra, tel 9362 1000
International auction house specializing in Australian and European paintings and sculpture, Aboriginal and Oceanic art, jewelry, antiques, and decorative and Asian works of art.

Sydney Antique Centre
531 S. Dowling St., Surry Hills, tel 9361 3244
A collection of antiques stores all under one roof. Extensive stock ranging from small collectibles to large pieces, historically significant furniture, and vintage clothing.

Australian Crafts & Goods

Australian Craftworks
127 George St., The Rocks, tel 9247 7156
Housed in the city's historic Old Police Station. A retail and exhibition gallery representing 300 Australian craftspeople: ceramics, glass, hand-turned wood, textiles, jewelry, leather, prints, Aboriginal art.

Craft NSW
104 George St., The Rocks, tel 9241 5825
Outlet of the Society of Arts and Crafts of New South Wales. Gold, silver, and opal jewelry; ceramics; weaving; fabric collage; glass; hand-knitted goods; porcelain and silk painting; printmaking; and more.

Object
417 Bourke St., Surry Hills, tel 9361 4511
Nonprofit center for contemporary design, showcasing Australian crafts. Exhibition spaces, and a retail shop with Aboriginal and other crafts.

Books & Prints

Books Kinokuniya
The Galleries, Level 2, 500 George St., tel 9262 7996
Opposite the Queen Victoria Building, this bookstore is the city's biggest, with a wide range of subjects, guides, general titles, fiction, and a good magazine section. Also a big Japanese section.

Dymocks Booksellers
424–430 George St., tel 9235 0155
The second largest of Sydney's bookstores, with a great range of stationery, guides, specialty and general titles, and local and international fiction.

Ken Done Gallery
1–5 Hickson Rd., The Rocks, tel 8274 4599
A large selection of original oils on paper and canvas, both framed and unframed; limited-edition screen prints; and a small gallery shop selling posters, cards, and other Done merchandise.

Ken Duncan Gallery
73 George St., The Rocks, tel 9241 3460
Limited-edition panoramic Australian landscape photographs by Ken Duncan; also a range of books, posters, postcards, and more featuring his work.

Cameras

Paxton's Camera & Video
285 George St., tel 9299 2999

Still, digital, and video cameras and accessories.

Ted's Camera Store
317 Pitt St., tel 9264 1687
SLR, digital, and video cameras and accessories, professional cameras and accessories, darkroom equipment, a secondhand section, and processing services.

Clothing & Accessories

100 Squared
Level 1, Westfield Sydney, Pitt St. Mall, tel 9267 3887
One central outlet showcasing the talents of 12 emerging local designers, for stylish swimwear, bondage leather bags, cool summer frocks, and boho jewelry.

Akira Boutique
Strand Arcade, Level 2, 412–414 George St., tel 9232 1078
One of Australia's most celebrated designers, Akira Isogawa draws on Japanese themes, but is contemporary and unique. Gowns and dresses are standout works of art and have been exhibited at the city's leading galleries.

Alfred Dunhill
DFS Galleria, 155 George St., The Rocks, tel 8243 8666
Leather goods from international stockist of quality accessories.

Bally
Level 3, DFS Galleria, 155 George St., The Rocks, tel 9267 3887
Women's and men's fashions and accessories.

Chanel
Westfield Sydney, Pitt St. Mall, tel 8236 9200
Clothes, jewelry, watches, fragrances, cosmetics, leather goods, and sunglasses.

Country Road
Queen Victoria Building, 142–144 Pitt St., tel 9394 1818
Australian-designed men's and women's clothing labels. The emphasis is on quality and understated style. There are houseware lines as well.

Crumpler
Shop 26, Strand Arcade, 412–414 George St., tel 9222 1300
Australian manufacturer of stylish, hipster backpacks, laptop bags, camera cases, and travel bags made from high-tech fabrics.

Giorgio Armani
4 Martin Pl., tel 9231 3655
Jeans, T-shirts, casual wear, and evening wear from the international design house. Also at DFS Galleria in The Rocks.

Grandma Takes a Trip
263 Crown St., Surry Hills., tel 9356 3322
A well-stocked two-story flashback to the 1950s, '60s, and '70s for vintage fashion, in the heart of Sydney's vintage strip.

Gucci
Westfield Sydney, Castlereagh St., tel 9221 8999
Sydney flagship store selling handbags, leather goods, fashion, jewelry, sunglasses, and watches.

Hermès Paris
135 Elizabeth St., tel 9287 3200
Men's and women's clothing, bags, scarves, shoes, and leather goods.

Rip Curl
82 Campbell Pde., Bondi Beach, tel 9130 2660
Surfboard and clothing manufacturers such as Rip Curl, Quicksilver, and Billabong have made Australian surfwear famous. Plenty of other surf shops are located on Campbell Parade.

R. M. Williams Bushman's Outfitters
389 George St., tel 9262 2228; Chifley Plaza, Hunter & Phillip Sts., tel 9223 5608; and Level 3, Westfield Sydney, 188 Pitt St., tel 8246 9136
Finest quality Australiana for outback cow cockies and Pitt Street farmers: men's and women's elastic-sided riding boots, dress boots, moleskin skirts and trousers, oilskins, women's jodhpurs, men's dress trousers, and more.

Sass & Bide
132 Oxford St., Paddington, tel 9360 3900
Local designers who made it when celebrities started wearing their jeans, jackets, and minidresses.

Scanlan & Theodore
122 Oxford St., Paddington, tel 9380 9388
Top Australian designers since 1987, producing elegant, sleek outfits for around town and evening wear.

Department Stores

David Jones
Elizabeth & Market Sts., tel 9266 5544
Synonymous with sophisticated shopping in Sydney. Two buildings with local and international clothing, cosmetics, appliances, housewares, and a stunning food hall with several outlets for oysters, coffee, tea, and more.

Myer
436 George St., tel 9238 9111
Major city department store with a large range of local and international clothing, appliances, cosmetics, and more.

Food & Wine

Airport Fine Foods
Departure Level, International

Terminal, Sydney Airport, tel 9317 5874
Retail outlet selling Australian beef, pork, kangaroo, turkey, live lobsters, crabs, abalone, scallops, salmon, tuna, wines, cheeses, and canned and bottled foods.

Australian Wine Centre
1 Alfred St., Circular Quay, tel 9247 2755
Upscale bottle shop with a thousand different Australian wines in stock. They conduct tastings, deliver to most places worldwide, and have a wine bar next door for those who would like to try a glass.

Sydney Fish Market
Blackwattle Bay, Pyrmont, tel 9660 1611
Everything edible from under the sea (not to mention rivers and estuaries). Retail and wholesale vendors operate from the early hours. Numerous restaurants are also on the premises. Look for sashimi tuna and salmon, fresh oysters, and Atlantic salmon.

Gifts

Cartier
43 Castlereagh St., tel 9235 1322
Watches, jewelry, leather bags, wallets, pens, lighters, and scarves.

Clocktower Square
Argyle & Harrington Sts., The Rocks, tel 9247 6134
Jewelry, clothing, art, and souvenirs aimed at Sydney's international visitors.

DFS Australia
155 George St., The Rocks, tel 9258 7657
Duty-free and tax-free goods, including alcohol, watches, leather goods, ready-to-wear clothing, cosmetics, opals, food items, and souvenirs. The big international brands are represented here.

Orson & Blake
483 Riley St., Surry Hills, tel 8399 2525
Stylish housewares emporium with everything for the kitchen and bathroom, dinnerware and ceramics, and an increasing fine furniture range from local sources.

Puppet Shop at The Rocks
77 George St., The Rocks, tel 9247 9137
Hidden downstairs in a sandstone building, all manner of marionettes, toys, and masks from around the world line the wall and hang from the ceiling waiting to spring to life.

Jewelry & Gems

Angus & Coote
Westfield Sydney, Pitt Street Mall & Market St., tel 9232 6235
Watches in all price ranges, gold and silver jewelry, a range of opals, diamonds, cultured pearls, and some crystal glassware.

Flame Opals
119 George St., The Rocks, tel 9247 3446
Extensive range of solid stones set in 18-carat gold or sterling silver.

Makers Mark
Chifley Plaza, Phillip & Hunter Sts., Chifley Sq., tel 9231 6800
Exciting designs from Australia's leading studio jewelers, silversmiths, and craftspeople. Timeless classics and outrageous fashion statements, from silver coffee pots to distinctively Australian jewelry featuring everything from industrial offcuts to pink Argyle diamonds and exquisite South Sea pearls.

Opal Fields
155 George St., The Rocks, tel 9247 6800
Australian opal stones and jewelry, featuring the collections of seven designers, mostly set in white and yellow gold and platinum, but also many in silver. See, too, their museum of opal fossils and specimens.

Paspaley Pearls
2 Martin Pl., tel 9232 7633
Outlet for Australia's leading supplier of South Sea pearls to the world—among the finest to be found anywhere.

Percy Marks
60–70 Elizabeth St.
Local jeweler specializing in the finest Australian opals, diamonds, and South Sea pearls.

Rox Gems & Jewelry
Strand Arcade, 412–414 George St., tel 9232 7828
Rox has in-house designers who specialize in custom-made designs and distinctive contemporary pieces, often featuring platinum, diamonds, pearls, and unusual gemstones.

Tiffany & Co.
28 Castlereagh St., tel 1800 731 131
Flagship Australian store for the famed American company. Fine jewelry, watches, and gifts.

Markets

Balmain Markets
St. Andrews Church, Darling St. & Curtis Rd., Balmain, tel 0418 765 736
Typical range of clothing, jewelry, and art, much of it secondhand, but with the occasional gem among the trinkets.

Glebe Markets
Glebe Public School, Glebe Point Rd., Glebe, tel 4237 7499
One of the city's large and bustling weekend markets with

a leaning toward the more bohemian end of the clothing and jewelry spectrum.

Paddington Markets
Uniting Church, Oxford & Newcombe Sts., Paddington, tel 9331 2646
Extraordinary range of clothing, jewelry, and art stalls, plus food, massage, cosmetics, and some electrical goods. Very popular with locals. Many young designers start here and then gravitate to boutiques on Oxford Street.

Paddy's Markets
9 Hay St., Haymarket, tel 1300 361 589, www.paddysmarkets.com.au
Bustling market with everything from clothing to electrical goods to seafood, fruit, and vegetables. The Market City shopping center upstairs has cheap clothes and food courts.

The Rocks Markets
Upper George St., The Rocks, tel 9240 8717
A boost to the local outlets on the weekends—all manner of souvenirs, clothing, jewelry, and art are available. The Foodies Market is held on Fridays.

Suburban Shopping Precincts

Bondi Junction
Oxford St.
Easily accessed by train, Westfield Bondi Junction mall has more than 450 stores with most everything on offer. Not to be confused with Bondi Beach, 2 miles (3 km) east.

Newtown
King St.
One of the most bohemian and stylish of the city's shopping areas. Antiques shops, bookshops, and clothing and handicraft stores stretch among the restaurants for over a mile.

Paddington
Oxford & Queen Sts.
Food, clothing, housewares, and jewelry stores among the numerous cafés, pubs, and restaurants, catering to a chic eastern suburbs clientele.

Surry Hills
Crown St.
Happening suburb just southeast of the city center, with a thriving café and bar scene. Crown Street has lots of vintage clothing shops for retro fashionistas.

Sydney Arcades & Malls

Chifley Plaza
Chifley Sq., Hunter & Philip Sts., tel 9221 4500
Upscale arcade area with the emphasis on international clothing and jewelry names.

Harbourside Shopping Complex
Darling Harbour, tel 8204 1888
Excellent gift-oriented shopping, jewelry, and beachwear in a
popular tourist precinct.
Eateries and bars also abound.
Open to
9 p.m. every day.

MLC Centre
King & Castlereagh Sts., tel 9224 8333
Upscale arcade area with the emphasis on international clothing and jewelry names.

Pitt St. Mall
Pitt St.
Boutiques, music stores, and bookshops. Many Victorian facades. As the entrance to Strand Arcade, Skygarden Arcade, the Myer department store, and Westfield Sydney mall, Pitt Street forms the biggest repository of shops in the city.

Queen Victoria Building
455 George St., tel 9264 1955
Elegant, multilevel shopping gallery specializing in local and international designer wear and jewelers, plus giftwares and stylish cafés (see p. 113).

Skygarden Arcade
77 Castlereagh St., tel 9231 1811
Arcade with stores selling local and international clothing labels and jewelry.

Strand Arcade
412–414 George St., tel 9232 4199
Step back in time in this graceful Victorian arcade. Four levels of trendy Australian designer-label clothing, jewelry, accessories, cafés, unique gift shops, and chocolates. The Strand Hatters (where you can pick up a genuine Australian fur-felt Akubra or the finest quality Ecuadorian panama) has been there since the arcade opened in 1892.

Westfield Sydney
Pitt St., tel 8236 9200
Though not the biggest mall in Sydney, this is the largest in the city center, comprising three adjoining complexes under the shadow of the Sydney Tower. All manner of fashion, food, and goods can be found. Undergoing major redevelopment that will see it include 300 stores when finished.

Entertainment & Activities

It may be on the opposite side of the world from just about everywhere, but Sydney can dazzle most visitors with the range and quality of its arts and entertainment. The Sydney Opera House is the obvious focus for the arts—plays, opera, classical music, pop concerts, and more. There is certain to be something to see during even the shortest visit to Sydney.

Farther afield, there are theaters, cinemas, and performance spaces in the suburbs, with sports arenas and racetracks dotted around the greater metropolitan area. All through January, the city is in entertainment mode with the Sydney Festival (see p. 230) comprising performances of every type, many of them free. Every Friday, the *Sydney Morning Herald* newspaper has details of what's happening in the city over the weekend and following week.

There are two major ticketing agencies for theater and sports events with outlets throughout the city:

Ticketek, premier.ticketek .com.au
Ticketmaster, www.ticket master.com.au

ENTERTAINMENT

Ballet & Opera

Australian Ballet, Sydney Opera House, tel 9223 1088, www.australianballet.com.au
The best of contemporary and classical works from Australia's national ballet company.

Sydney Dance Company, Wharf Theatre, Pier 4, Hickson Rd., Walsh Bay; and Sydney Opera House, tel 9221 4811, www.sydneydancecompany .com Australia's leading contemporary dance company. It has toured overseas to considerable acclaim.

Opera Australia, Sydney Opera House, tel 9699 1099, www .opera-australia.org.au
One of the world's busiest opera companies. Its repertoire spans from Handel and Monteverdi to Britten, Janacek, and Berg.

Cinema

Chauvel Cinema, Oxford St. & Oately Rd., Paddington, tel 9361 5398
Venue for mostly foreign-language and nonmainstream films. The theater is the ballroom of the historic former Paddington Town Hall.

Dendy Cinemas, 261 King St., Newtown, tel 9550 5699; and Opera Quays, 2 East Circular Quay, tel 9247 3800
Cinemas screening an eclectic range of nonmainstream and art-theater films from Australia and around the world. The Opera Quay location is its luxury brand and serves beer and wine in the cinema.

Event Cinemas, 505–525 George St., tel 9273 7300
Major cinema showing mostly mainstream films, including Australian films. The city's biggest venue, it has 17 screens, cafés, and fast-food outlets.

Hadyn Orpheum, 380 Military Rd., Cremorne, tel 9908 4344
Gorgeous 1935 art deco cinema showing mainstream and art-house movies. "Movie luncheon Wednesdays" include a movie, light lunch, and recital on the original Wurlitzer organ.

Hoyts Cinemas, Lang Rd., Entertainment Quarter, Moore Park, tel 9332 1300
All the latest blockbusters are shown in this cineplex with over a dozen screens, including a big IMAX screen and La Premiere with sofas and table service.

Verona Cinema, 17 Oxford St., Paddington, tel 9360 6099
Venue for mainly art-theater films. Very popular designer bar/café on the second floor.

Entertainment Centers

State Theatre, 49 Market St., tel 9373 6655, www.state theatre.com.au
This venue is as interesting as the performances (see pp. 111–112). The wide variety of events includes the Sydney Film Festival in June (see p. 230).

Sydney Entertainment Centre, Harbour St., Darling Harbour, tel 9320 4200, www.sydentcent .com.au
Venue for everything from basketball games to pop concerts, all indoors and with audiences up to 12,000.

Sydney Opera House, Bennelong Point, tel 9250 7777, www.sydneyoperahouse.com
Not just for opera, the Opera House is the premier venue in the city for music, drama, dance, and more (see pp. 46–49).

Sydney Symphony Orchestra, Sydney Opera House, tel 8215 4600, www.sydney symphony.com

The principal orchestra of the city, performing everything from the great classics to contemporary music. The orchestra performs free in the Domain as part of the Sydney Festival (see p. 230) in January.

Sydney Town Hall, 483 George St., tel 9265 9007, www.sydneytownhall.com.au
The emphasis on performance may have shifted to the Sydney Opera House, but quite a lot still goes on here (see pp. 114–115). Occasional dance nights, especially during the Sydney Festival (see p. 230), and free lunchtime organ recitals.

Nightlife

Annandale Hotel, 17–19 Parramatta Rd., Annandale, tel 9550 1078
Long-running pub-band venue and spiritual home of the S ydney rock scene.

The Argyle, 18 Argyle St., The Rocks, tel 9247 5500
Big, cool, and crowded late, this is the epicenter of nightlife in The Rocks, where tourists and locals mingle. DJs pump out the music. There's a courtyard beer garden and a variety of bars.

ARQ, 16 Flinders St., Darlinghurst, tel 9380 8700
Big two-level gay club with a jumping, shirts-off dance floor. Thursday night amateur drag shows are a hoot.

The Basement, 29 Reiby Place, Circular Quay, tel 9251 2797
One of the city's leading jazz venues, with top local and international acts. Dinner and show packages, or show only with limited seating.

Chinese Laundry, Slip Inn, 111 Sussex St., tel 8295 9999
Popular large club with three rooms of house, electro, and tech; big sound system; and outdoor garden nights in summer.

The Colombian, Oxford & Crown Sts., Surry Hills, tel 9360 2151.
Welcome to the jungle in this Central American–styled dance club, one of the most popular in the Oxford Street gay scene.

Comedy Store, Entertainment Quarter, Bldg. 207, 122 Lang Rd., Moore Park, tel 9357 1419
The city's premier laugh venue with top local acts, and overseas comics when the Sydney Comedy Festival is on (April–May).

Empire Hotel, 103A Parramatta Road, Annandale, tel 9557 1701
The home of blues and roots, with an occasional side of rock, funk, or punk. Bands every Friday and Saturday.

Enmore Theatre, 130 Enmore Rd., Enmore, tel 9550 3666
Popular performance space a short distance from the city, with big-name indie artists and rock stars from yesteryear.

Island Bar, Cockatoo Island, tel 8969 2100
Quirky, popular afternoon/sunset bar (closes at 8:30 p.m.) in the middle of the harbor. Catch a ferry, grab a deck chair, and sip cocktails in the sun with Italian snacks. Closed in winter.

Ivy, 330 George St., tel 9254 8100
Sophisticated bar/restaurant complex with a host of venues, including the Ivy Bar and the rooftop pool club. Come early or join the long queues on weekends to get in.

Marble Bar, Sydney Hilton Hotel basement, 259 Pitt St., tel 9266 2000
Ornate and stylized rococo bar—a bit like the interior of the State Theatre on a small scale. A popular watering hole well worth a visit, with live music on offer Wednesday through Saturday nights.

Metro Theatre, 624 George St., tel 9550 3666
Ideally sized independent rock music venue that hosts a range of high-profile local and international acts in an intimate atmosphere.

Opera Bar, Sydney Opera House, Lower Concourse Level, tel 9247 1666
Outdoor bar with multimillion-dollar harbor views. Join the corporate crowd after work for a drink, linger for a bite to eat, or stay for the cool live music.

Oxford Art Factory, 38 Oxford St., Darlinghurst, tel 9322 3711
Super-stylish club attracting cool young things. Indie bands play in two rooms.

Oxford Hotel, 134 Oxford St., Darlinghurst, tel 9331 3467
A long-established gay bar in this section of Oxford Street with upstairs cocktail lounges.

The Star, 80 Pyrmont St., Pyrmont, tel 9777 9000
The city's only legal casino, with restaurants, bars, theaters, accommodations, and, of course, hundreds of gaming tables and machines.

The Vanguard, 42 King St. Newtown, tel 9557 7992
Intimate live-music venue and restaurant with 1920s decor, hosting some top-name acts. Jazz, blues, folk, and cabaret all

feature. Dinner and show, or standing-room show.

Venue 505, 280 Cleveland St., Surry Hills, venue505.com
Intimate live-music space featuring indie jazz, roots, reggae, and more every night. Tickets at the door only. Closed Mon.

Theater

Bell Shakespeare Company, tel 8298 9000, www.bellshakespeare.com.au
As the name suggests, the main work of this company is that of the Bard. When the company is not on tour, it usually performs at the Sydney Opera House. Several plays are staged each year.

Belvoir Street Theatre, 25 Belvoir St., Surry Hills, tel 9699 3444, www.belvoir.com.au
Highly regarded small theater complex—the base for Company B, which puts on international and Australian plays, modern works, and classics.

Capitol Theatre, 13 Campbell St., Haymarket, tel 8240 2290, www.capitoltheatre.com.au
Venue for a range of theatrical events, usually long-running musicals with special performances filling the gaps.

Ensemble Theatre, 78 McDougall St., Kirribilli, tel 9929 0644, ensemble.com.au
An intimate theater beside the harbor on Sydney's Lower North Shore. Mostly new works, but also classics performed by some of Australia's leading actors. Dine in the waterside restaurant.

SBW Stables Theatre, 10 Nimrod St., Darlinghurst, tel 9361 3817, www.griffintheatre.com.au
The birthplace of modern Australian theater in Sydney, the SBW Stables Theatre is home to the Griffin Theatre Company, the major outlet for new writing.

Sydney Theatre, 22 Hickson Rd. (Opposite Pier 6/7), Walsh Bay, tel 9250 1999, www.sydneytheatre.org.au
Biggest venue at the wharf complex for a variety of theater, dance, and other performances, including part of the Sydney Theatre Company's and Sydney Dance Company's seasons.

Theatre Royal, MLC Centre, King St., tel 9224 8444, www.theatreroyal.net.au
Venue for a range of events, including plays and musicals, with special performances.

ACTIVITIES

Active Sports

Diving

Good diving can be found in Sydney Harbour and along the nearby ocean coast. Dive shops of note include Pro Dive in Cronulla *(tel 9544 2200)*, Dive Centre Manly *(tel 9977 4355)*, and Dive Centre Bondi *(tel 9369 3855)*.

Golf

Bondi Golf Links, Military Rd., North Bondi, tel 9130 1981
Small nine-hole golf course on the headland of Bondi Beach.

Leura Golf Club, Sublime Point Rd., Leura, tel 4782 5011
Pleasant 18-hole course set among the Blue Mountains.

Moore Park Golf Club, Anzac Parade & Cleveland St., Moore Park, tel 9663 1064
Large golf course—the closest to the city—and a driving range open until 10 p.m.

Kayaking

Sydney Kayak Centre, The Spit Bridge, Mosman, tel 9960 4389
Single and double kayaks for rent in a sheltered area of Middle Harbour.

Sailing

There are a host of yacht and cruiser charter companies that serve Sydney Harbour; see pages 88–89 for a listing of companies and what they offer. There are also many places around the harbor where you can learn how to sail. In addition to the sailing school listed below, see the sidebar on page 157 for other sailing schools.

Northside Sailing School, The Spit, Mosman, tel 9969 3972
Middle Harbour-based sailboat and sailboard rental.

For sailing and cruising on Pittwater, see the sidebar on page 178 for a listing of some companies; some offer cruises, others boat rentals.

Squash

Hiscoes Fitness Club, 525 Crown St., Surry Hills, tel 9699 9222
Accessible venue with squash courts and a gym close to the city.

Surfing

If you do not know how to surf but would like to learn, there are plenty of surfing schools to teach you. Inquire at the local tourist information offices or at surf and dive shops. One of the best known beaches is Bondi, but Manly and Sydney's other northern beaches offer good surf, too. South of Sydney, probably the best is at Cronulla. See also page 105.

Swimming

Andrew (Boy) Charlton Pool, Mrs. Macquaries Rd., tel 9358 6686
Olympic-size harborside pool in the Domain. Lap swimming areas, speed lanes, and open swimming areas.

Ian Thorpe Aquatic Centre, 456 Harris St., Ultimo, tel 9518 7220
Impressive modern complex with heated pool, spa, sauna, and gym, next to the Powerhouse Museum at Darling Harbour.

North Sydney Olympic Pool, Alfred St. S., Milsons Point, tel 9955 2309
Harborside pool. Very popular at lunchtime and during the week; less busy on weekends. Covered and heated in winter.

Tennis

Palms Tennis Centre, Quarry Rd., Paddington, tel 9363 4955
A medium-size, well-presented tennis center in the eastern suburbs with great views.

Parklands Sports Centre, Lang Rd. & Anzac Parade, Moore Park, tel 9662 7033
A large tennis complex next to Centennial Park.

Spectator Sports

Basketball

Sydney Kings (men) at the Sydney Entertainment Centre *(Darling Harbour, tel 9320 4200)* and **Sydney Flames** (women) at the Sydney University Sports & Aquatic Centre *(Darlington, tel 9351 4978)* are the city's premier basketball teams, competing in the Australian national league.

Cricket

Sydney Cricket Ground, Driver Ave., Moore Park, tel 9360 6601
Usually the venue for at least one test cricket match each year, as well as international one-day and 20-20 games, and state cricket matches.

Football

Australian Rules Football, Sydney Cricket Ground, Moore Park, tel 9360 6601
The Sydney Swans' home ground is the Cricket Ground in the national competition of this Australian game.

Rugby League, tel 9339 8500; and **Rugby Union**
Two of the major spectator sports in the country. Sydney stages games at the club, state, and international levels. See also sidebar page 145.

Soccer, tel 8314 5100
The world game takes a back seat to other codes in Australia, but Sydney has club, state, and international games at a range of venues.

Greyhound Racing

Wentworth Park, Wentworth Park Rd., Glebe, tel 9552 1799
There are meets every Friday and Saturday night throughout the year. Major events in the fall.

Harness Racing

Menangle Park Paceway, Racecourse Rd., Menangle Park, tel 4645 2200
Meetings held Monday, Tuesday, and Saturday throughout the year. Carnival in the fall.

Horse Racing

Canterbury Park, King St., Canterbury, tel 9930 4000
Seven miles (11 km) south of the city. Bimonthly Wednesday day meetings, with some night meetings. Air-conditioned betting area. The whole track is visible to the naked eye.

Rosehill Gardens Racecourse, Grand Ave., Rosehill, tel 1300 729 668
Fourteen miles (23 km) west of the city. Modern stands, bars, and restaurants; betting ring under cover. Spring and fall carnivals and regular Saturday meetings.

Royal Randwick Racecourse, Alison Rd., Randwick, tel 9663 8400
A sweeping turf course and a blend of charming old structures and modern stands; excellent dining and bars. Classic races such as the Doncaster, the AJC Derby, and St. Leger Stakes (the oldest race in Australia). Frequent Saturday and midweek meets.

Warwick Farm Racecourse, Hume Hwy. & Gov. Macquarie Dr., tel 9602 6199
Rural atmosphere, tree-lined grounds; popular with family picnickers as well as regular racegoers. Mainly midweek.

INDEX

Bold page numbers indicate illustrations.
CAPS indicates thematic categories.

A
Aboriginal culture
  Aboriginal sites 133, **133,** 135
  art **13, 38,** 38–41, 136–137, **137**
  Bennelong (Eora elder) 28
  the Block, Redfern **135**
  buying Aboriginal art 136
  cultural centers 135–136
  Dreamtime 39
  experiences 133, **133**
  indigenous Sydney 134–137
  museum exhibits 66–67, 136–137, **137**
  World Youth Day **134**
Aboriginal Heritage Museum & Keeping Place 137
Activities & entertainment 130, 214, 262–265
Air travel 155, 232
Anzac Day 33, **34, 68,** 228
Anzac War Memorial 58
Aquariums
  Oceanworld 104
  Sydney Aquarium **12, 121,** 127, **127,** 128, **131,** 131–132
Architecture **82,** 82–83
Art Gallery of New South Wales **61,** 61–62, **63,** 65, **65,** 136–137, **137**
Arts
  Aboriginal art **13, 38,** 38–41, 136–137, **137**
  artists' views of Sydney Harbour 64, **64**
  introduction 36–42, **37, 38, 40**
  literature 42
  urban art 51
  see also MUSEUMS
ATMs (Automatic teller machines) 236
Australian English 16
Australian Museum **66,** 66–67, 137
Australian National Maritime Museum 128–129, 137, **138,** 138–140, **140**
Australian pelican 196, **196**
Australian Rainforest Sanctuary 214
Australian Reptile Park and Wildlife Sanctuary 213
Australian War Memorial, Canberra 227–228
Automatic teller machines (ATMs) 236
Avoca 214

B
Ballet **37,** 262
Balmain **162,** 162–163, 251, 260
Balmoral 106, **106,** 242–243
Banks 236
Barrenjoey Beach 177
Basketball 265
Bats 199, **199**
Bays, Eastern Suburbs **154,** 154–155, 158, **158**
Beaches
  Eastern Suburbs **149,** 149–151, **151**
  Manly **101,** 101–104
  northern beaches **176,** 176–178
  Palm Beach **176,** 177, 252
  safety 20, 21, 212
  surf lifesaving clubs 151
Bell's Line of Road 218–220
Belmore Park 116
Bennelong (Eora elder) 28
Berrima 223–224
Biking 202
Birds **171, 196,** 196–198
Black Mountain, Canberra 228
Black swan 196–197
Blackheath 218
Blue Mountains 133, **215,** 215–220, **217, 219,** 253–255
Blue-ring octopus 20, 201
Blue-tongue lizard 200, **200**
Boat trips
  ferries 88, **88,** 99, 234
  houseboat on the Hawkesbury 182
  Pittwater waterway 178
  Port Hacking 192, **192**
  Sydney Harbour cruises **88,** 88–89, 243
  see also Kayaking; Sailing
Bohemian Sydney **146,** 146–147
Bondi Beach **149,** 149–150
  Christmas **14–15**
  hotels & restaurants **151,** 247–248, 249, 250
  lifesavers 151
  shopping 120, 259
  surfing 105
Botanical gardens *see* GARDENS
Botany Bay **188,** 188–189
Bottlenose dolphins 201
Bowral 223, 253, 257
Box jellyfish 212
Bradleys Head 97
Bradman, Sir Donald 224
Bradman Museum, Bowral 223
Brokenwood Wines 208
Bronte Beach 150
Brooklyn 179–180, **181**
Bushwalking *see* Hiking; WALKS

C
Cabramatta 170, **170**
Cadman's Cottage 75
Campbells Cove 75
Camperdown Cemetery 164, 165
Campsie 170
Canberra **225,** 225–228, **226,** 255
Capitol Theatre 116
Car rental & driving information 233, 237
Cattai National Park 182
Caves 220
Centennial Park, Woollahra 145
Central Coast **213,** 213–214, 255–256
Chinatown **108, 117,** 117–120, **118**
Chinese Garden of Friendship **108, 118,** 119, 120, 128
CHURCHES
  Garrison Church 77
  Presbyterian Church, Ebenezer 182
  St. Andrew's Cathedral 115
  St. Mary's Cathedral 59–60
Cinema 42, 111–113, 130, 262
Circular Quay **44,** 50
  dinner cruise 243
  entertainment 264
  restaurants & bars **22**
  Rocks walk **76,** 76–79, **79**
  shopping 260
  walk from Hyde Park **58,** 58–60
Circular Quay & East 43–70
  Art Gallery of New South Wales **61,** 61–62, **63,** 65, **65,** 136–137, **137**
  Australian Museum **66,** 66–67, 137
  Circular Quay **22, 44,** 50, **76,** 76–79, **79,** 243, 260, 264
  Customs House **50,** 50–52
  Domain **56,** 56–57
  Great Synagogue 60
  hotels & restaurants **22,** 238–240
  Hyde Park Barracks 69
  Hyde Park to Circular Quay walk **58,** 58–60
  Justice & Police Museum 51–52
  Macquarie Place 52–53
  Macquarie Street **68,** 68–70, **70**
  maps 45, 59
  Martin Place 53
  Museum of Sydney 52, **52,** 137
  Royal Botanic Gardens **43, 54,** 54–56, 57, 133, 239
  Rum Hospital 70, **70**
  shopping 260
  State Library of New South Wales 69–70
  State Parliament House 70
  Sydney Opera House **37, 46,** 46–48, **48–49, 49,** 239, 262–263
City Center & South 107–120
  Chinatown **108, 117,** 117–120, **118**
  Chinese Garden of Friendship **108, 118,** 119, 120, 128
  City South 116
  hotels & restaurants 243–245
  itinerary 9–10
  maps 109, 119
  Market Street area **110,** 110–113, **113**
  National Opal Collection 112
  Queen Victoria Building **107,** 113, **113,** 259, 261
  shopping 111, 120
  St. Andrew's Cathedral 115
  State Theatre 111–113
  Sydney Monorail 126
  Sydney Tower **110,** 110–111
  Sydney Town Hall **114,** 114–115, 263
  walk to the Chinese Garden of Friendship **118,** 118–119
City South 116
Climate 10, 230
Clothing
  recommended 231
  shopping for 259
Cockatoo Island 99
Cockatoo Run steam train 224
Communications 234–235
Conversions (measurements) 235
Coogee Beach 150
Cook, James **26–27,** 27, 139
Cooking classes 78

Credit cards 236
Cricket 224, 265
Cronulla 105, 190–191
Cronulla Riots (2005) 190
Cruises **88,** 88–89, 243
see also Boat trips; Sailing
Currency 232, 236
Customs (border control) 232
Customs House **50,** 50–52

D

Dangar Island 180
Darling Harbour 121–140
Australian National Maritime Museum 128–129, 137, **138,** 138–140, **140**
entertainment 130, 262
hotels & restaurants **11,** 245–247
itinerary 9
maps 123, 129
Powerhouse Museum **124,** 124–126, **126,** 137
shopping 261
Sydney Aquarium **12, 121,** 127, **127,** 128, **131,** 131–132
Sydney Monorail 126
walk to Sydney Fish Market **128,** 128–129
Wild Life Sydney 128, 132
Darlinghurst 147, 148, **148**
entertainment 263, 264
hotels & restaurants 247, 248, 249, 250–251
Day Trips *see* Excursions; North Day Trips; West & South Day Trips
Dharug National Park 181
Dickens, Charles 164
Disabilities, travelers with 236
Diving 177, 264
Dolphins 201
Domain **56,** 56–57
Donnithorne, Eliza 164
Double Bay 155, 158, 248
Drayton's Family Wines 209
Dreamtime 39
DRIVES
car accidents 237
car rental & driving information 233
Hunter Valley wineries 208–209
Drugs & narcotics 232
Dulwich Hill 170
Dunbar (ship) 32

E

East Redfern 147
Easter Show 166–167, 230
Eastern gray kangaroo **8,** 198
Eastern rosella 197
Eastern Suburbs 141–158
bays **154,** 154–155, 158, **158**
beaches **149,** 149–151, **151**
Bohemian Sydney **146,** 146–147
Bondi Beach **14–15,** 105, 120, **149,** 149–150, 151, **151,** 247–248, 249, 250, 259
Darlinghurst 147, 148, **148,** 247, 248, 249, 250–251, 263, 264
Double Bay 155, 158, 248
East Redfern 147
Elizabeth Bay 154–155
hotels & restaurants 247–251
itinerary 10–11
Kings Cross 146, 248, 249
maps 143, 153
Mardi Gras 148, **148,** 230
Paddington 120, **141,** 144, **144,** 259, 261, 262, 265
Parsley Bay 158
Rose Bay 155, 158, 249
Rushcutters Bay 154–155
Shark Bay 155, 158
Surry Hills **142,** 147, 243, 247, 250, 258, 259, 260, 261, 263, 264
Vaucluse Bay 158
Vaucluse House 158, **158**
walk around South Head **152,** 152–153
Watsons Bay **100, 154,** 158, 249
Woollahra 145, 249, 258
Woolloomooloo 146, 247, 251
Echidna 200
Electricity 235
Elizabeth Bay 154–155
Elizabeth Farm, Rose Hill 187
Embassies & consulates 237
Emergency phone numbers 237
Endeavour (ship) 139
Entertainment & activities 130, 214, 262–265
Entertainment Quarter, Woollahra 145
"Eternity" (metal casting) 115
Events & festivals
calendar 230–231
Easter Show 166–167, 230
Mardi Gras 148, **148,** 230
New Year's Eve 57, **85**
Sydney Festival 47, 230
Tulip Time Festival, Bowral 223, 231
Yulefest 218
Excursions 203–228
Blue Mountains 133, **215,** 215–220, **217, 219,** 253–255
Canberra **225,** 225–228, **226,** 255
Central Coast **213,** 213–214, 255–256
drive to the Hunter Valley wineries 208–209
hotels & restaurants 253–257
Hunter Valley & Newcastle **203, 206,** 206–212, **210, 211,** 256–257
itinerary 11
maps 204–205, 209
South Coast **221,** 221–222
Southern Highlands **223,** 223–224
see also North Day Trips; West & South Day Trips
EXPERIENCES
Aboriginal culture 133, **133**
Anzac Day commemoration 228
architectural education 83
beaches 150
bird-watch & bushwalk 197
cooking Aussie style 78
diving 177
flightsee the bays 155
game fishing 222
gay Sydney 147
houseboat on the Hawkesbury 182
Hunter Valley working holiday 207
kayak Balmain 163
learn to sail 157
New Year's Eve in Royal Botanic Gardens 57
pick the perfect opal 112
Pittwater waterway 178
ride a vintage tram into Royal NP 194
Scale the Harbour Bridge 91
Sydney's markets 120
urban art 51
Vegemite 24
walk out to Bradleys Head 97
walk the Six Foot Track 216
watch a rugby game 145
whale watching 189
Experiment Farm Cottage, Parramatta 187

F

Fairy penguin 197
Featherdale Wildlife Park 202
Festivals *see* Events & festivals
Film 42, 111–113, 130, 262
Fishing 222
Flightseeing 155
FOOD & DRINK
Australian wine **210,** 210–211, **211**
cooking classes 78
introduction **22,** 22–25, **23, 25**
liquor laws 235
shopping for 259–260
Vegemite 24
Football 265
Foreshore **71, 74,** 74–75
Fort Denison 98–99
Fort Scratchley 212
Free attractions 62

G

Game fishing 222
Garden Island 99
GARDENS
Chinese Garden of Friendship **108, 118,** 119, 120, 128
Mount Annan Botanic Garden 202
Mount Tomah Botanic Garden 219
Royal Botanic Gardens **43, 54,** 54–56, 57, 133, 239
Sandringham Memorial Garden 58
Yengo Sculpture Garden 219
Garigal National Park 183
Garrison Church 77
Gay community 147, 148, **148**
George Street 78–79, **107**
Georges River 192, **192**
Glebe 120, 163–164, 251, 260–261, 265
Gloucester Walk 79
Goat Island 99
Golf 264
Gordons Bay 150
Government House 55–56, **82**
Gray-headed flying fox 199, **199**
Great Expectations (Dickens) 164
Great North Walk 181
Great Synagogue 60
Greyhound racing 265

H

Harbor islands **98,** 98–99

Harbour *see* Sydney Harbour
Harbour Bridge **2–3, 79, 85, 90,** 90–93, **92–93**
climbing 91
construction 93, **93**
vital statistics 91
walk **94,** 94–95
Harness racing 265
Harris Park 187
Hawkesbury River **179,** 179–182, 252
Health & medicine 20–21, 89, 231, 237
High Court of Australia, Canberra 226
Hiking 21, 195, 197, 216
History & culture 13–42
arts 36–42
food & drink 22–25
history of Sydney 26–35
Sydney today 14–21
Holidays 235
Horse racing 265
Hotel Inter-Continental 69
HOTELS & RESTAURANTS
Circular Quay & East **22,** 238–240
City Center & South 243–245
Darling Harbour **11,** 245–247
Day Trips 252
Eastern Suburbs 247–251
excursions 253–257
North Day Trips 178, 252
overview 238
the Rocks 77, 240–242
Sydney Harbour 242–243
Western Suburbs 251–252
Houseboats 182
Hubble Telescope 139
Humpback whales 189, 201, **201**
Hungerford Hill Wines 209
Hunter Valley Cheese Company 208
Hunter Valley & Newcastle 206–212
hotels & restaurants 256–257
map 209
Newcastle 212
winemaking experience 207
wineries **203, 206, 210,** 210–211, **211**
wineries drive 208–209
Hyde Park Barracks 69
Hyde Park to Circular Quay walk **58,** 58–60

I

IMAX Theatre 130
Inner West Suburbs **162,** 162–165, **165**
Insurance 231
Itineraries, suggested 8–11

J

James Craig (tall ship) 140
Jenolan Caves 220
John Tebbutt Observatory, Windsor 182
Justice & Police Museum 51–52

K

Kalkari Discovery Centre 175
Kamay Botany Bay National Park 188
Kangaroos **8,** 198
Katoomba 216–217, 253–254, 255
Kayaking 163, 264
Kings Cross 146, 248, 249
Koala Park Sanctuary 183
Koalas 183, 198, 199
Kookaburra **171,** 197
Koomurri Aboriginal Centre 136
Ku-ring-gai Chase National Park 135, **174,** 174–175

L

La Perouse Museum, Botany Bay 188
Lace monitor 200
Lane Cove National Park 183, **183**
Language 16
Leichhardt 163, 251–252
Leura 217
Lindemans Winery 209
Lion Island 177
Liquor laws 235
Literature 42
Little penguin 197
Lizards 200
Lord Nelson Brewery Hotel 77
Luna Park **94,** 95

M

Macarthur, John 29–30
Macdonald Valley 180–181
Macleay Museum 164–165
Macquarie, Lachlan 30–31
Macquarie, Lake 214
Macquarie Place 52–53
Macquarie Street **68,** 68–70, **70**
Macquarie Towns 181–182
Madame Tussauds 130
Mammals 198–200, **199**
Manly 101, **101,** 102–103, 104, 105, 242
Maps
Circular Quay & East 45, 59
City Center & South 109, 119
Cronulla 191
Darling Harbour 123, 129
Eastern Suburbs 143, 153
excursions 204–205, 209
Hunter Valley wineries 209
Hyde Park to Circular Quay walk 59
North Day Trips 172–173
the Rocks 73, 77
Sydney Harbour 86–87, 94–95, 102
Sydney Olympic Park 168
West & South Day Trips 184–185, 191
Western Suburbs 160–161
Mardi Gras 148, **148,** 230
Marine life 189, 201, **201**
Market Street area **110,** 110–113, **113**
Maroubra Beach 105, 151
Marsden, Samuel 187
Martin Place 53
Mary MacKillop Place 106
McWilliam's Mount Pleasant Estate 209
Media 235–236
Millennium Park 166
Minnamurra Rainforest 222
Money matters 236
Mosman 106
Mount Annan Botanic Garden 202
Mount Annan Mountain Bike Trail 202
Mount Tomah Botanic Garden 219
Mount Wilson 218–219
Mountain biking 202
Movies 42, 111–113, 130, 262
Muru Mittigar Aboriginal Cultural Centre 135–136
Museum of Australian Democracy, Canberra 227
Museum of Contemporary Art **74,** 74–75, 241–242
Museum of Sydney 52, **52,** 137
MUSEUMS
Art Gallery of New South Wales **61,** 61–62, **63,** 65, **65,** 136–137, **137**
Australian Museum **66,** 66–67, 137
Australian National Maritime Museum 128–129, 137, **138,** 138–140, **140**
Bradman Museum, Bowral 223
Hyde Park Barracks 69
Justice & Police Museum 51–52
La Perouse Museum, Botany Bay 188
Macleay Museum 164–165
Madame Tussauds 130
Mary MacKillop Place 106
Muru Mittigar Aboriginal Cultural Centre 135–136
Museum of Australian Democracy, Canberra 227
Museum of Contemporary Art **74,** 74–75, 241–242
Museum of Sydney 52, **52,** 137
National Gallery of Australia, Canberra 226
Powerhouse Museum **124,** 124–126, **126,** 137
Questacon, Canberra **226,** 227
S. H. Ervin Gallery 84
Sydney Jewish Museum, Darlinghurst **146,** 147
Sydney Tramway Museum 194

N

National Gallery of Australia, Canberra 226
National Library of Australia, Canberra 227
National Opal Collection 112
National Trust Centre 81, 84, **84**
Nepean River 180
New Year's Eve 57, **85**
Newcastle 212
Newport 178, 252
Newspapers 235–236
Newtown **159,** 164–165, **165,** 251, 252, 261, 263–264
Nightlife 263–264
North Day Trips 172–183
Garigal National Park 183
Hawkesbury River **179,** 179–182, 252
hotels & restaurants 178, 252
itinerary 11
Koala Park Sanctuary 183
Ku-ring-gai Chase National Park 135, **174,** 174–175
Lane Cove National Park 183, **183**
Macquarie Towns 181–182
map 172–173
northern beaches **176,** 176–178
Pittwater 176–178, 252
Waratah Park 175
Wisemans Ferry & the Macdonald Valley 180–181
see also Excursions
North Sydney Olympic Pool 94–95
Nutcote 106

O
Observatory Hill **80,** 80–81, 84, **84**
Oceanworld 104
Old Government House, Parramatta 186
Olympic Games (2000) 167
Olympic Park **166,** 166–169, **168, 169**
Olympic Stadium 167, **169**
Opals 112
Opening times 236
Opera House **37, 46,** 46–48, **48–49, 49,** 239, 262–263

P
Packing tips 231
Paddington 120, **141,** 144, **144,** 259, 261, 262, 265
Paddington Markets 120, **141,** 144, **144,** 261
Paddy's Markets **25,** 118, 120, 261
Palm Beach **176,** 177, 252
PARKS
Aboriginal culture 133, **133,** 135
Australian Rainforest Sanctuary 214
Australian Reptile Park and Wildlife Sanctuary 213
Belmore Park 116
Blue Mountains National Park 133, **215,** 215–220, **217, 219**
Canberra 228
Cattai National Park 182
Centennial Park, Woollahra 145
Dharug National Park 181
Domain **56,** 56–57
Featherdale Wildlife Park 202
Garigal National Park 183
Hyde Park **58,** 58–60
Kamay Botany Bay National Park 188
Koala Park Sanctuary 183
Ku-ring-gai Chase National Park 135, **174,** 174–175
Lane Cove National Park 183, **183**
Millennium Park 166
Pirrama Park 129
Royal National Park 133, **133,** 135, **193,** 193–195, **195**
Sydney Harbour National Park 98–99, 135
Waratah Park 175
Parliament House, Canberra 227
Parramatta **186,** 186–187
Parrots 197–198
Parsley Bay 158
Pelicans 196
Penguins 197
Pepper Tree Wines 208
Peterson House 208
Phillip, Arthur 28–29, **29**
Phones 235
Pirrama Park 129
Pittwater 176–178, 252
Platypus 199
Port Hacking 192, **192**
Possums 199–200
Post offices 234
Powerhouse Museum **124,** 124–126, **126,** 137
Presbyterian Church, Ebenezer 182
Pylon Lookout 94
Pyrmont Bridge 128

Q
Quarantine 232
Quarantine Station 104
Queen Victoria Building **107,** 113, **113,** 259, 261
Questacon, Canberra **226,** 227

R
Radio 236
Rainbow lorikeet 197–198
Red-bellied black snake 200–201
Religion 236
Reptiles 20, **200,** 200–201, 213
Restaurants *see* FOOD & DRINK; HOTELS & RESTAURANTS
Ringtail possum 199–200
The Rocks 71–84
entertainment 263
foreshore **71, 74,** 74–75
Gloucester Walk 79
hotels & restaurants 77, 240–242
itinerary 9
maps 73, 77
Museum of Contemporary Art **74,** 74–75, 241–242
National Trust Centre 81, 84, **84**
Observatory Hill **80,** 80–81, 84, **84**
S. H. Ervin Gallery 84
shopping 78, 120, 258, 259, 260, 261
Sydney Observatory **80,** 81
walk **76,** 76–79, **79**
Rose Bay 155, 158, 249
Rose Hill 187, 252, 265
Royal Botanic Gardens **43, 54,** 54–56, 57, 133, 239
Royal National Park 133, **133,** 135, **193,** 193–195, **195**
Rugby 145, 265
Rum Hospital 70, **70**
Rushcutters Bay 154–155

S
S. H. Ervin Gallery 84
Sailing 264
eighteen-foot skiffs **156,** 156–157, **157**
lessons 157
Pittwater waterway 178
Sydney Harbour 89, **229**
Salon des Refusés 84
Sandringham Memorial Garden 58
Scarborough Wines 208
Scuba diving 177, 264
Sea horses 53
Shark Bay 155, 158
Sharks 20, 212
Shipwrecks 32, 100, 165, 177
Shopping 258–261
Aboriginal art 136
downtown 111
markets 78, 120, 260–261
Short-beaked echidna 200
Silvereye 198
Six Foot Track 216
Slip, Slop, Slap (health campaign) 89
Small Winemakers Centre 208
Snakes 20, 200–201, 212
Soccer 265
South Coast **221,** 221–222
South Day Trips *see* West & South Day Trips
South Head **152,** 152–153, 158
South Sydney 116
Southern Highlands **223,** 223–224
Spiders 20
The Spit 102–103
Sports, spectator 145, 265
Squash 264
St. Albans 181
St. Andrew's Cathedral 115
St. Mary's Cathedral 59–60
Stace, Arthur 115
Star (casino) 130
State Library of New South Wales 69–70
State Parliament House 70
State Theatre 111–113
Strine (Australian English) 16
Sulphur-crested cockatoo 198
Surf lifesaving clubs 151
Surfing 105, **105,** 264–265
Surry Hills **142,** 147
entertainment 263, 264
hotels & restaurants 243, 247, 250
shopping 258, 259, 260, 261
Swamp wallaby 200
Swimming 21, 94–95, **166,** 169, 265
Sydney Aquarium **12, 121,** 127, **127,** 128, **131,** 131–132
Sydney Entertainment Centre 118–119
Sydney Festival 47, 230
Sydney Fish Market **128,** 128–129, 260
Sydney Harbour 85–106
artists' views 64, **64**
Balmoral 106, **106,** 242–243
cruises **88,** 88–89, 243
Garden Island 99
harbor islands **98,** 98–99
Harbour Bridge **2–3, 79, 85, 90,** 90–93, **92–93**
Harbour Bridge walk **94,** 94–95
hotels & restaurants 242–243
Manly 101, **101,** 104, 105, 242
maps 86–87, 94–95, 102
Mary MacKillop Place 106
Mosman 106
Nutcote 106
Oceanworld 104
Quarantine Station 104
shipwrecks 100
surfing 105, **105**
Taronga Zoo **96,** 96–97, 133
walk from the Spit to Manly 102–103
walk out to Bradleys Head 97
Sydney Harbour National Park 98–99, 135
Sydney Hospital 60, 70, **70**
Sydney Jewish Museum, Darlinghurst **146,** 147
Sydney Monorail 126
Sydney Observatory **80,** 81
Sydney Olympic Park **166,** 166–169, **168, 169**
Sydney Opera House **37, 46,** 46–48, **48–49, 49,** 239, 262–263
Sydney Royal Easter Show 166–167, 230

Sydney Tower **110,** 110–111
Sydney Town Hall **114,** 114–115, 263
Sydney Tramway Museum 194
Synagogues 60

T

Tamarama Beach 105, 150
Tamburlaine Wines 209
Taronga Zoo **96,** 96–97, 133
Taxis 234
Telephones 235
Television 236
Terrigal 214
Theater 264
Time ball 81
Time differences 236
Tipping 10, 234
Tourism information 9, 18, 236–237
Tower Estate 208
Town Hall **114,** 114–115, 263
Tram rides 194
Transportation 8, 126, 232–234
Travel insurance 231
Tulip Time Festival, Bowral 223, 231
TV 236
Tyrrell's Vineyards 208

U

University of Sydney 164–165

V

Vaucluse Bay 158
Vaucluse House 158, **158**
Vegemite 24
Victoria Barracks 144
Visas and passports 231–232
Visitor information 9, 18, 236–237
Vocabulary 16

W

WALKS
architectural 83
around South Head **152,** 152–153
to Bradleys Head 97
to the Chinese Garden of Friendship **118,** 118–119
Cronulla 190–191
Gloucester Walk 79
Hyde Park to Circular Quay **58,** 58–60
the Rocks **76,** 76–79, **79**
the Spit to Manly 102–103
to Sydney Fish Market **128,** 128–129
Wallabies 200
Waratah Park 175
Watsons Bay **100, 154,** 158, 249
Weather 10, 230
Wentworth Falls 217
West Head 174
West & South Day Trips 184–202
Botany Bay **188,** 188–189
Cronulla 105, 190–191
Featherdale Wildlife Park 202
hotels & restaurants 252
maps 184–185, 191
Mount Annan Botanic Garden 202
Mount Annan Mountain Bike Trail 202
Parramatta **186,** 186–187
Port Hacking & Georges River 192, **192**
Rose Hill & Harris Park 187, 252, 265
Royal National Park 133, **133,** 135, **193,** 193–195, **195**
see also Excursions
Western Suburbs 159–170
Balmain **162,** 162–163, 251, 260
Cabramatta 170, **170**
Campsie 170
Dulwich Hill 170
Glebe 120, 163–164, 251, 260–261, 265
hotels & restaurants 251–252
Inner West **162,** 162–165, **165**
itinerary 11
Leichhardt 163, 251–252
map 160–161
Millennium Park 166
Newtown **159,** 164–165, **165,** 251, 252, 261, 263–264
Sydney Olympic Park **166,** 166–169, **168, 169**
Whales 189, 201, **201**
White-bellied sea eagle 198
Wild Life Sydney 128, 132
Wildlife 196–201
birds **171, 196,** 196–198
dangerous 20–21, 212
mammals 198–200, **199**
marine life 189, 201, **201**
reptiles **200,** 200–201, 204, 213
sanctuaries 183, 202, 213
sea horses 53
Windsor 182
Wine
Australian wine **210,** 210–211, **211**
Hunter Valley wineries **203, 206,** 207–211, **210, 211**
introduction 25
shopping for 259–260
winemaking experience 207
Wisemans Ferry 180–181
Wollemi pine 55
Wollongong 221–222
Woollahra 145, 249, 258
Woolloomooloo 146, 247, 251

Y

Yachting *see* Sailing
Yengo Sculpture Garden 219
Yulefest 218

Z

Zig Zag Railway 219
Zoos
Featherdale Wildlife Park 202
Taronga Zoo **96,** 96–97, 133
Wild Life Sydney 128, 132
see also Aquariums; Wildlife

ILLUSTRATIONS CREDITS

All photographs by Jill Schneider unless otherwise noted:

2-3, Chad Ehlers/Stock Connection/Aurora Photos; 8, Eric Isselée/Shutterstock; 12, Guido Cozzi/SIME; 14-5, Annie Griffiths/National Geographic Stock; 19, AP Images/Rob Griffith; 20, Lars Schneider/Aurora Photos; 23, Susan Seubert/National Geographic Stock; 26-7, Landing of Captain Cook at Botany Bay in 1770, 1902 (oil on canvas), Fox, Emmanuel Phillips (1865-1915)/National Gallery of Victoria, Melbourne, Australia/Gilbee Bequest/The Bridgeman Art Library; 29, Captain Arthur Phillip (1738-1814) (engraving) (b/w photo), English School, (19th century)/Private Collection/The Bridgeman Art Library; 30-1, The City of Sydney, bird's-eye view by M.S. Hill, pub. 1888 (litho)/© National Library of Australia, Canberra, Australia/The Bridgeman Art Library; 34, Greg Wood/AFP/Getty Images; 37, Craig Greenhill/Newspix via Getty Images; 40, Ian Waldie/Getty Images; 56, Iconsinternational.Com/Alamy; 64, National Gallery of Victoria, Melbourne/Presented by the National Gallery Society of Victoria, 1967/© Estate of late Grace Cossington Smith; 65, Photograph by Jenni Carter/Sol LeWitt's Wall drawing #1091:arcs, circles and bands (room) 2003 (detail)/(c) Estate of Sol LeWitt/ARS Licensed by Viscopy, Sydney/Art Gallery of New South Wales, Sydney; 68, Daniel Hewlett/Alamy; 71, iofoto/123RF; 85, Beth Morley/Shutterstock; 100, Ron Ryan/Coo-ee Picture Library; 126, Powerhouse Museum; 133, Rob Reichenfeld/Dorling Kindersley Collection/Getty Images; 134, Robert Harding Picture Library Ltd/Alamy; 137, Bosiljka Zutich/Alamy; 156, Andrew Woodley/Alamy; 157, Kos Picture Source Ltd/Alamy; 171, Vladimir Wrangel/Shutterstock; 174, Yury Prokopenko/Flickr/Getty Images; 179, Craigsteck123/Dreamstime.com; 183, Deep diver/Bigstock.com; 193, Rovenko Design/Shutterstock; 196, Durden Images/Shutterstock; 199, EcoPrint/Shutterstock; 200, Peter Waters/Shutterstock; 201, Jan Kratochvila/Shutterstock; 215, Jan Rihak/iStockphoto; 223, David Hancock/Alamy; 229, Christophe Launay/Aurora Photos.

National Geographic
TRAVELER
Sydney

CELEBRATING 125 YEARS

Published by the National Geographic Society
John M. Fahey, *Chairman of the Board and Chief Executive Officer*
Timothy T. Kelly, *President*
Declan Moore, *Executive Vice President; President, Publishing and Digital Media*
Melina Gerosa Bellows, *Executive Vice President; Chief Creative Officer, Books, Kids, and Family*
Lynn Cutter, *Executive Vice President, Travel*
Keith Bellows, *Senior Vice President and Editor in Chief, National Geographic Travel Media*

Prepared by the Book Division
Hector Sierra, *Senior Vice President and General Manager*
Jonathan Halling, *Design Director, Books and Children's Publishing*
Marianne R. Koszorus, *Design Director, Books*
Barbara A. Noe, *Senior Editor, National Geographic Travel Books*
R. Gary Colbert, *Production Director*
Jennifer A. Thornton, *Director of Managing Editorial*
Susan S. Blair, *Director of Photography*
Meredith C. Wilcox, *Director, Administration and Rights Clearance*

Staff for This Book
Matt Propert, *Illustrations Editor*
Carl Mehler, *Director of Maps*
Michael McNey and Mapping Specialists, *Map Production*
Marshall Kiker, Michael O'Connor, *Associate Managing Editors*
Galen Young, *Rights Clearance Specialist*
Katie Olsen, *Production Design Assistant*
Sarah Alban, *Contributor*

Manufacturing and Quality Management
Phillip L. Schlosser, *Senior Vice President*
Chris Brown, *Vice President, NG Book Manufacturing*
George Bounelis, *Vice President, Production Services*
Nicole Elliott, *Manager*
Rachel Faulise, *Manager*
Robert L. Barr, *Manager*

KKComm, LLC
Kay Kobor Hankins, *Project Manager/Art Director*
Jane Sunderland, *Project Editor*
Jack Brostrom, *Contributor*

First edition: Edited and designed by AA Publishing (a trading name of Automobile Association Developments Limited, whose registered office is Norfolk House, Priestley Road, Basingstoke, Hampshire, England RG24 9NY. Registered number: 1878835).

Cutaway illustrations drawn by Maltings Partnership, Derby, England

Printed in China
12/TS/1

The National Geographic Society is one of the world's largest nonprofit scientific and educational organizations. Founded in 1888 to "increase and diffuse geographic knowledge," the Society's mission is to inspire people to care about the planet. It reaches more than 400 million people worldwide each month through its official journal, *National Geographic,* and other magazines; National Geographic Channel; television documentaries; music; radio; films; books; DVDs; maps; exhibitions; live events; school publishing programs; interactive media; and merchandise. National Geographic has funded more than 10,000 scientific research, conservation and exploration projects and supports an education program promoting geographic literacy. For more information, visit www.nationalgeographic.com.

For more information, please call 1-800-NGS LINE (647-5463) or write to the following address:
National Geographic Society
1145 17th Street N.W.
Washington, D.C. 20036-4688 U.S.A.

For information about special discounts for bulk purchases, please contact National Geographic Books Special Sales: ngspecsales@ngs.org

For rights or permissions inquiries, please contact National Geographic Books Subsidiary Rights: ngbookrights@ngs.org

National Geographic Traveler: Sydney (Second Edition)
ISBN: 978-1-4262-1025-9

The Library of Congress has cataloged the first edition as follows:
McHugh, Evan.
The National Geographic Traveler. Sydney / Evan McHugh.
p. cm.
Includes index.
ISBN 0-7922-7435-0
1. Sydney (N.S.W.)—Guidebooks. I. Title. II. Title: Sydney.
DU178.M39 1999
919.44'10466–dc21 99-40370
CIP